THE
ANNALS
of the American Academy of
Political and Social Science

VOLUME 685 | SEPTEMBER 2019

New Policies, New Politics? Policy Feedback, Power-Building, and American Governance

SPECIAL EDITORS:

Jacob S. Hacker
Yale University

Paul Pierson
University of California, Berkeley

Los Angeles | London | New Delhi
Singapore | Washington DC | Melbourne

The American Academy of Political and Social Science

202 S. 36th Street, Annenberg School for Communication, University of Pennsylvania,
Philadelphia, PA 19104-3806; (215) 746-6500; (215) 573-2667 (fax); www.aapss.org

Origin and Purpose. The Academy was organized December 14, 1889, to promote the progress of political and social science, especially through publications and meetings. The Academy does not take sides in controverted questions, but seeks to gather and present reliable information to assist the public in forming an intelligent and accurate judgment.

Meetings. The Academy occasionally holds a meeting in the spring extending over two days.

Publications. THE ANNALS of The American Academy of Political and Social Science is the bimonthly publication of the Academy. Each issue contains articles on some prominent social or political problem, written at the invitation of the editors. These volumes constitute important reference works on the topics with which they deal, and they are extensively cited by authorities throughout the United States and abroad.

Subscriptions. THE ANNALS of The American Academy of Political and Social Science (ISSN 0002-7162) (J295) is published bimonthly—in January, March, May, July, September, and November—by SAGE Publishing, 2455 Teller Road, Thousand Oaks, CA 91320. Periodicals postage paid at Thousand Oaks, California, and at additional mailing offices. POSTMASTER: Send address changes to The Annals of The American Academy of Political and Social Science, c/o SAGE Publishing, 2455 Teller Road, Thousand Oaks, CA 91320. Institutions may subscribe to THE ANNALS at the annual rate: $1257 (clothbound, $1419). Individuals may subscribe to the ANNALS at the annual rate: $134 (clothbound, $197). Single issues of THE ANNALS may be obtained by individuals for $41 each (clothbound, $58). Single issues of THE ANNALS have proven to be excellent supplementary texts for classroom use. Direct inquiries regarding adoptions to THE ANNALS c/o SAGE Publishing (address below).

All correspondence concerning membership in the Academy, dues renewals, inquiries about membership status, and/or purchase of single issues of THE ANNALS should be sent to THE ANNALS c/o SAGE Publishing, 2455 Teller Road, Thousand Oaks, CA 91320. Telephone: (800) 818-SAGE (7243) and (805) 499-0721; Fax/Order line: (805) 375-1700; e-mail: journals@sagepub.com. *Please note that orders under $30 must be prepaid.* For all customers outside the Americas, please visit http://www.sagepub.co.uk/customerCare.nav for information.

THE ANNALS

© 2019 by The American Academy of Political and Social Science

Editorial Office: 202 S. 36th Street, Philadelphia, PA 19104-3806
For information about individual and institutional subscriptions address:
SAGE Publishing
2455 Teller Road
Thousand Oaks, CA 91320

For SAGE Publishing: Peter Geraghty (Production) and Mimi Nguyen (Marketing)

From India and South Asia,
write to:
SAGE PUBLICATIONS INDIA Pvt Ltd
B-42 Panchsheel Enclave, P.O. Box 4109
New Delhi 110 017
INDIA

From Europe, the Middle East,
and Africa, write to:
SAGE PUBLICATIONS LTD
1 Oliver's Yard, 55 City Road
London EC1Y 1SP
UNITED KINGDOM

International Standard Serial Number ISSN 0002-7162
ISBN 978-1-5443-9836-5 (Vol. 685, 2019) paper
ISBN 978-1-5443-9837-2 (Vol. 685, 2019) cloth
First printing, September 2019

Information about membership rates, institutional subscriptions, and back issue prices may be found on the facing page.

Advertising. Current rates and specifications may be obtained by writing to The Annals Advertising and Promotion Manager at the Thousand Oaks office (address above). Acceptance of advertising in this journal in no way implies endorsement of the advertised product or service by SAGE or the journal's affiliated society(ies) or the journal editor(s). No endorsement is intended or implied. SAGE reserves the right to reject any advertising it deems as inappropriate for this journal.

Claims. Claims for undelivered copies must be made no later than six months following month of publication. The publisher will supply replacement issues when losses have been sustained in transit and when the reserve stock will permit.

Change of Address. Six weeks' advance notice must be given when notifying of change of address. Please send the old address label along with the new address to the SAGE office address above to ensure proper identification. Please specify the name of the journal.

THE ANNALS
of the American Academy of Political and Social Science

VOLUME 685 | SEPTEMBER 2019

IN THIS ISSUE:

New Policies, New Politics? Policy Feedback,
Power-Building, and American Governance

Special Editors: JACOB S. HACKER and PAUL PIERSON

Introduction

Policy Feedback in an Age of Polarization . . . .*Jacob S. Hacker*   8
and Paul Pierson

General Lessons

Making What Government Does Apparent to Citizens: Policy
Feedback Effects, Their Limitations, and How They Might
Be Facilitated. . . . . *Suzanne Mettler*   30

Limiting Policy Backlash: Strategies for Taming Countercoalitions
in an Era of Polarization . . . . *Eric M. Patashnik*   47

Asymmetric Partisan Polarization, Labor Policy, and Cross-State
Political Power-Building. . . . . *Alexander Hertel-Fernandez*   64

Prescriptions: Climate Change

A New Path for U.S. Climate Politics: Choosing Policies That
Mobilize Business for Decarbonization . . . . *Jonas Meckling*   82

Building Climate Policy in the States . . . . *Samuel Trachtman*   96

Prescriptions: Health Care

Medicaid and the Policy Feedback Foundations for Universal
Healthcare. . . . . *Jamila Michener*   116

Medicare Expansion as a Path as well as a Destination: Achieving Universal
Insurance through a New Politics of Medicare . . . . *Jacob S. Hacker*   135

Prescriptions: Jobs, Wages, and Regional Development

Antitrust Enforcement as Federal Policy to Reduce Regional
Economic Disparities...................................*Robert Manduca*   156

Rebuilding Labor Power in the Postindustrial
United States..*Andrew Schrank*   172

Prescriptions: Criminal Justice

De-Policing America's Youth: Disrupting Criminal Justice Policy Feedbacks
That Distort Power and Derail Prospects ....*Vesla M. Weaver*
and Amanda Geller   190

Feedback Effects and the Criminal Justice Bureaucracy: Officer Attitudes
and the Future of Correctional Reform......................*Amy E. Lerman*
and Jessie Harney   227

FORTHCOMING

Entitlement Reform
Special Editors: JAMES ZILIAK and ROBERT MOFFITT

Fatal Police Shootings
Special Editor: LAWRENCE SHERMAN

Introduction

Policy Feedback in an Age of Polarization

By
JACOB S. HACKER
and
PAUL PIERSON

A large body of research has explored how policies, once enacted, reshape public opinion, governing institutions, and political organizations—a process known as "policy feedback." Yet this productive research agenda has yet to be translated into practical recommendations of the sort regularly provided by other social science research. This volume of *The ANNALS* presents the findings of a major collective effort to do just this. The Policy Feedback Project (PFP) is an effort to develop research-backed arguments about how policy feedback might be harnessed to address collective problems in today's age of partisan polarization and economic inequality. This article orients readers to our collective approach and summarizes some of the contributing authors' findings. In particular, we show how the feedback effects of policies could be used to (1) tackle long-standing public problems that have resisted effective responses, (2) increase the long-term durability of policy initiatives designed to address these problems, and (3) build political momentum and power to facilitate the adaptation and expansion of these initiatives over time.

Keywords: American politics; public policy; policy feedback; interest groups; partisan polarization

The articles in this special issue all emerged out of the Policy Feedback Project (PFP), a unique effort to assist policy-makers seeking to revitalize American democracy and improve public policy. The project was founded with the goal of deepening our understanding of the ways in which policies, once enacted, reshape public opinion, governing institutions, and political organizations—a major area of research in

Jacob S. Hacker is Stanley Resor Professor of Political Science and director of the Institution for Social and Policy Studies at Yale University. He is the author or coauthor of five books and numerous articles on American politics and policy and a fellow of the American Academy of Arts and Sciences.

Correspondence: jacob.hacker@yale.edu

DOI: 10.1177/0002716219871222

political science that has rarely been translated into practical recommendations or policy advice.

In particular, we asked participants in the PFP—all social scientists with extensive policy expertise—to develop research-backed arguments about the ways in which such "policy feedback" might be harnessed to (1) tackle long-standing public problems that have resisted effective responses; (2) increase the long-term durability of major policy initiatives designed to address these problems; and (3) create the potential to build political momentum and power to facilitate continuing efforts to adapt, expand, and improve these initiatives over time. In short, we asked authors to think about how policies might reshape not just American economic and social outcomes but also American politics—in ways that encourage continued efforts to address pressing public problems.

In this introductory article, we first outline the core ideas and aims guiding the PFP. We then discuss how the insights of prior research needed to be updated, given the current political context. Finally, we use this updated understanding to articulate some basic guideposts for policy design, drawing mainly on the articles in this volume that provide general lessons. We also highlight, by way of illustration, a few of the insights that come from the volume's more policy-oriented articles, which offer tailored recommendations for generating positive feedback in key policy areas.

The Policy Feedback Project

Leaders and experts have always considered the political consequences of their policy choices. Yet this thinking has too often been an afterthought. Faced by a pressing problem, the questions usually asked are "Can a law be enacted?" and "Will it effectively address the problem?" As crucial as these questions are, however, another may be just as important: "Will this policy create positive political effects—that is, will it encourage ongoing and, ideally, increasing efforts to address the problem?"

Paul Pierson is John Gross Professor of Political Science at the University of California, Berkeley, and codirector of the Successful Societies Program of the Canadian Institute for Advanced Research. He is the author or coauthor of many articles and five books on American and comparative politics and is a fellow of the American Academy of Arts and Sciences.

NOTE: We thank everyone who provided feedback and guidance at two project workshops: a September 2018 meeting in Cambridge, MA, hosted by the Scholars Strategy Network (SSN); and a February 2019 meeting in Washington, DC, funded by the Washington Center for Equitable Growth. At SSN, Avi Green, Pao Maynard-Moll, Hannah Reuter, and Theda Skocpol were of invaluable assistance. Even before our first meeting, we benefited from the wise counsel of Heather Boushey, Paul Glastris, Jacob Leibenluft, Tara McGuiness, Ellen Nissenbaum, and Felicia Wong. At the American Academy of Political and Social Science, Tom Kecskemethy and Emily Babson made this special issue possible. Thanks also to Yale College student Neeraj Patel for helping to assemble the final papers. Finally, we thank Aaron Goldzhimer for inspiring this project in the first place.

As already mentioned, a substantial and growing body of research has addressed this question, albeit in general and analytic ways. For more than a generation, political scientists and other social scientists have intensively studied how major public policies reshape politics. As a result, we know far more than we once did about the systematic political consequences that policies have and what features of those policies and their political context tend to create one type of effect versus another. Nonetheless, we still have limited ability to translate these findings into informed advice of the sort regularly on offer in economics, decision science, public finance, and the like. This is both because these findings have not generally been translated into *applied* knowledge and because they have not been *updated* to reflect important recent changes in American politics. Indeed, only a handful of articles or books that examine the feedback effects of public policies say anything at all about their implications for contemporary policy design, and those that do provide very limited recommendations. For example, Suzanne Mettler's agenda-setting 2018 book, *The Government-Citizen Disconnect*, devotes five chapters to exploring how American public opinion is shaped by the "submerged" design of U.S. social and educational policies—that is, their reliance on tax expenditures and other indirect forms of public support, rather than direct spending. By comparison, she spends just two pages exploring possible responses, which mostly center on the general recommendation to make policies more visible to citizens.

The need for such application and updating is more pressing than ever. In a highly complex and interdependent society experiencing often rapid and disruptive economic and social change, there is a need to harness public authority to meet collective demands and to adapt prior policy responses to changing circumstances. Yet the American political system is unusually prone to gridlock, and the emergence of intense partisan polarization has made that gridlock even more pervasive. Moreover, the rise of "negative" polarization—an orientation of hostility toward the other side in partisan debates—means not only that it is harder to reach initial consensus, but also that initiatives championed by one side are vulnerable to dismantling or sabotage by the other. Given these circumstances, understanding what allows initial policies to become firmly rooted and then adapt and improve over time is a pressing public matter.

The goal of the PFP is to provide that understanding. Launched in 2017, under the auspices of the Scholars Strategy Network—a national organization of scholars dedicated to offering research-backed advice to policy-makers—the project brought together two groups: social scientists who have studied policy feedback in the past and policy professionals who would like to improve their capacity to make public policies with their potential political consequences in mind. We asked the participating scholars to distill prior research on policy feedback into basic lessons, design principles, and policy recommendations that might help to guide the structure and sequencing of new policy initiatives. In turn, the policy professionals provided their reactions to these arguments and proposals, with an eye toward explaining the general organizational, electoral, and political challenges of contemporary policymaking that the authors may not have considered.

Thus, the authors were asked to focus specifically on how *policy* might remake American politics, not on proposals to change political institutions directly (for example, revision of legislative procedure, election rules, or campaign finance law). The political effects of new policies are the particular focus of research on policy feedback, and such effects have received much less attention in current debates than have proposals for political reform. As all the authors show, moreover, policies are themselves constitutive of the current political landscape, and hence policy changes can themselves be powerful sources of political reform.

From the outset, the project was designed to involve scholars with diverse viewpoints. However, it began with two premises that inevitably shape the prescriptions on offer. First, the purpose was to think about how government could actively address a set of fundamental challenges, including climate change and the strains facing our health care and criminal justice systems. These policy areas were chosen not only because they are associated with significant costs and risks to our society, but also because they are areas *where we have a body of prior research on the political effects of policy that can guide analysis*. We make no claim that these are the most important policy challenges we face, though we believe all are extremely pressing. Nor did we choose them without reference to the character of the proposed responses that currently dominate debate. We chose them because they are areas where we have a significant body of research that can help guide the design of active government policies.

Second, a motivating observation was that *critics* of such active policies have themselves proved adept at using policy to achieve their own preferred ends—often at the state level. For example, a significant body of research has shown that state policies to ban collective bargaining have had profound effects, not just on levels of unionization, but also on *politics* within the affected states. A similar story can be told with regard to efforts to cut taxes aggressively even in the face of significant revenue needs—policies that have changed the politics of public finance in ways that make raising taxes or undertaking new initiatives not just economically difficult but *politically* challenging. A starting goal of the project, therefore, was to think about whether policies with more broadly "progressive" goals might also create such feedback effects.

Policy Feedback and American Governance

Over the last generation, social scientists have developed a sophisticated portrait of a reality that skilled politicians have always recognized: major public policies, such as Social Security, can have substantial political impacts, engendering support that helps those policies to endure. Well-crafted policies do not just address societal problems; they create supportive political dynamics, whether by empowering backers, weakening opponents, making citizens' views of government more favorable, or reducing obstacles to further reform efforts. Drawing on the political scientist E.E. Schattschneider's (1935) seminal insight that "a new policy creates a new politics," social scientists refer to the ways in which policy changes politics as "policy feedback" (Weir and Skocpol 1985; Pierson 1993; Campbell 2002).

Politicians, of course, have long crafted policies with their political consequences in mind. Perhaps the most famous example is FDR's defense of the system of contributory payroll taxes that was a foundation for Social Security. Challenged by an economist on this arrangement, FDR acknowledged,

> They are politics all the way through. We put those payroll contributions there so as to give the contributors a legal, moral, and political right to collect their pensions and their unemployment benefits. With those taxes in there, no damn politician can ever scrap my social security program. Those taxes aren't a matter of economics, they're straight politics. (Schlesinger 1958, 308)

This type of political engineering was at the heart of the New Deal. "Tax and spend" eventually became an epithet, but it was originally FDR advisor Harry Hopkins's well-justified boast. Indeed, the full quote was "tax and tax, spend and spend, elect and elect."

Many of the Democratic achievements of the New Deal, Fair Deal, and Great Society bore out Hopkins's formula. Policies that began as ambitious and risky undertakings evolved to achieve the status of political "third rails." Social Security expanded from a small program covering less than half the population into a universal guarantee of retirement security, adding survivors' and disability insurance along the way. Condemned as "socialized medicine" in the early 1960s, Medicare was untouchable—if not a platform for universal insurance, as its designers hoped—by the early 1970s. In area after area, federal policies that once sparked controversy came to be taken for granted. Social policies expanded, almost never experiencing major retrenchment. New levers of national economic policy, once deployed, were rarely if ever abandoned. Environmental and consumer protections grew, if often through fits and starts. The long arc of history appeared to bend toward successful policy feedback that supported an active "Big Government."

In recent years, however, advocates of active government have seemed less capable of generating such self-reinforcing effects. President Obama, for example, declared in his second inaugural address, "Progress does not compel us to settle centuries-long debates about the role of government for all time, but it does require us to act in our time" (Obama 2013). Yet while the Obama administration and its allies achieved notable policy victories in 2009 and 2010, their record at designing initiatives that met political as well as policy goals was uneven. Some policies never made it to implementation, such as the long-term insurance program embedded in the 2010 Affordable Care Act (ACA; aka "Obamacare")—a provision that was abandoned as unworkable without political complaint. But even when policies were successful, the hand of government was often invisible, sometimes intentionally so, undercutting the prospects for assembling and sustaining strong support coalitions.

Consider the large cut in payroll taxes in the 2009 American Recovery and Reinvestment Act. To boost consumer spending most effectively, it was carefully designed *to attract no notice* (Cooper 2010). Similarly, the Dodd-Frank Wall Street Reform and Consumer Protection Act has not become accepted within corporate circles, and few Americans appear to have grasped its favorable consequences for them. And while the ACA is now producing modestly positive feedback effects, these were perilously slow in coming. Early on, ACA beneficiaries neither reliably perceived the benefits they received nor consistently voted or acted to protect the law (L. Jacobs and Mettler 2016). Worse, the ACA catalyzed a political backlash that not only exacted considerable electoral costs but also left the program struggling to survive.

Setbacks of this sort have prompted much handwringing among these policies' supporters. To date, however, there has been insufficient systematic thinking about which design choices were fundamental and whether alternative choices would have made a difference. More important, there has been little effort to think about how future efforts to address these and similar problems—through legislation, budgets, and executive powers, as well as actions at the state and local levels—could be designed not just to advance key policy goals but to do so in a way that enhances the prospects that reforms, once in place, will endure and expand. Such thinking requires much more than the use of polls or focus groups to assess the immediate popularity of policies, and it requires much more than the cursory consideration of add-ons that might marginally boost the endurance of policies designed solely around technocratic goals. It entails an early and intensive consideration of the multiple ways in which "a new policy makes a new politics."

The articles in this special issue of *The ANNALS* offer such consideration. They review past research on the political consequences of public policies—including, in all cases, research done by the authors themselves—and distill these findings into actionable, straightforward advice. In addition, each article seeks to update prior findings to reflect America's changing politics—above all, the emergence of intense polarization. Feedback research has focused on historical periods in which partisan cleavages were far less prominent than they are today. Absent careful reconsideration, these traditional assessments will provide a poor guide for today's policy-makers.

The articles in this issue can be divided into two broad types. Those that lead the issue focus on *general recommendations*—for example, how to reduce the political backlash that new initiatives inevitably generate. The articles that follow focus on *policy-specific recommendations*. As noted, these policy-oriented articles look at important areas of policy where there has been ample research about policy feedback in the past: health care, climate change, criminal justice reform, and the promotion of better jobs (with a particular focus on regional inequalities and the challenge of ensuring adequate employment in all communities). For each of these areas, there are two articles that present complementary perspectives, whether covering different levels of government, different specific policies, or different aspects of the relevant policies and their politics.

The remainder of this article proceeds as follows. We first discuss the main ways in which policy feedback research must be updated in light of changes in American politics. We then examine the implications of an updated perspective—first for the general problem of harnessing government to address pressing public challenges in the twenty-first century, and then for policy design in specific domains.

Updating Theories of Policy Feedback

Partisan polarization has upended many of our understandings of how American politics works, and processes of policy feedback are no exception. Indeed, it is not too much of an exaggeration to say that polarization and its accompanying changes have shifted us from one political world to another.

In the old world, party attachments were relatively weak, and both parties were cleaved by cross-cutting issues and commitments. In this context, a well-designed program could build support among the extensive groups of voters, organized interests, and opposition party politicians who were politically "available." In turn, this support could ensure a policy's survival irrespective of a party's immediate electoral fortunes and eventually provide a political foundation for future program growth. For example, Medicare passed in 1965 after a decade of coalition building by its advocates, slowly picking up organized supporters and legislative sponsors as it moved closer to enactment. In its final form, it not only included elements recommended by Republicans, but also gained substantial bipartisan support, with seventeen Republicans backing it in the Senate. Once adopted, the program quickly consolidated support: Medicare's popularity rapidly induced most who had initially opposed it to climb on board.

In the new world of hyperpolarization, none of these assumptions can be made. Growing tribalism—the tendency for voters and groups to strongly and almost automatically back one party or the other, coupled with increased animosity toward the other party—has meant that many constituencies once up for grabs are no longer free-floating. It is not just that voters cannot be convinced to vote for the other party; increasingly, it is hard to persuade them to view the other party's proposals sympathetically on *any* prominent issue. This has made it much more difficult to gain broad acceptance for new initiatives that might traditionally have been expected to have strong positive feedback effects. In addition, there is now abundant evidence that general public opinion only weakly constrains opposition policy-makers. Their greatest risk is offending their "base," rather than swing voters or the public as a whole. For example, not a single House Republican voted for the American Recovery and Reinvestment Act of 2009 (aka the "stimulus") at a time that the U.S. economy was in freefall and even though President Obama had made the centerpiece of the law a payroll tax cut.

The new world of American politics is not only politically divided; it is also much more economically unequal (Hacker and Pierson 2010). Economic inequality has compounded political polarization in at least two ways. First, it has weakened the sway of ordinary voters, as opposed to the very affluent and deep-pocketed political organizations. This has made general public opinion even less important as a source of policy durability and expansion. Second, these inequalities have tipped the scales further against new initiatives in many important areas of policy by heightening the blocking power of concentrated interests. Although we focus mostly on polarization in this section, the compounding effects of rising inequality must be kept in mind.

Polarization changes everything

Polarization generates problems for collective problem-solving at all levels of our politics. Parties as organizations increasingly appear to be locked in a zero-sum contest for political dominance. This gives everyone involved—elected and appointed public officials, allied interest groups, activists, and voters—increased incentive to resist initiatives launched by the other side. Case studies of recent policy battles yield a consistent and troubling message: growing polarization has made the task of addressing collective problems vastly more difficult.

Jon Oberlander and Kent Weaver's (2015, 56–57) assessment of the ACA's reception is representative:

> Partisan polarization explains much of the ACA's enduring political problems, as partisans framed debate around ACA's negative impacts, real and imagined, emphasized loss-imposing policy consequences rather than the law's beneficial impacts, and resisted the ACA's implementation at the state and federal level.

Theda Skocpol's (2013) postmortem of the Democrats' failed 2009 "cap-and-trade" legislation to address climate change carries a similar message. Recognizing the Senate as the biggest obstacle to reform, strategists relied on a traditional policymaking logic: leverage the diversity of views and interests within the Republican caucus to build a strong "middle-out" coalition. The goal was to win the support of perhaps a half-dozen GOP senators, providing both needed votes and the coveted branding of bipartisanship.

Needless to say, the gambit failed. Pursuing a tactic that has become increasingly prevalent and effective, powerful interests within and outside the GOP (including right-wing media) countered by intensifying partisan divisions. They defined climate legislation as a Democratic project and effectively marketed this framing to Republican voters. Republican leaders recognized that any bipartisan deal would be politically costly. Along with allied interests, they worked to deter Republican senators from backing anything with Democratic support, no matter how riddled with concessions those Democratic initiatives might be.

Under current conditions, then, the "old world" strategy of middle-out coalitions that rest on bipartisan buy-in holds limited promise, at least at the national level. Even policy designs that contain strong incentives to climb aboard (such as the ACA), and which might have found consolidation relatively easy a generation ago, have encountered fierce partisan resistance. Zero-sum partisan contestation threatens to swamp everything.

It is worth specifying precisely what has changed. The backdrop for the old strategic playbook was a "Madisonian" system that promoted a proliferation of distinct political contexts and interests, which in turn induced cross-cutting cleavages and pluralism. Adages like "where you stand depends on where you sit" or Tip O'Neil's "all politics is local" were broadly accurate portrayals of a political system in which coalitions were loose and fluid, reflecting both national partisan battles and the pull of geographic, sectoral, and cultural constituencies that divided as well as unified partisans.

Over the past few decades, however, this fluidity has given way to an increasingly entrenched partisan divide. In part because of the massive growth of policy activity in Washington, major aspects of American politics—from media environments and interest group structures to party organizations and even state-specific policy battles—have nationalized (Pierson and Schickler 2019). These shifts have created a new kind of partisanship: more cohesive, more consistent, more homogenous, more all-encompassing, and much, much more intense.

These trends have been largely driven by the shifting incentives and activities of political elites. (By "elites," we mean those in and around government who have substantial capacity to shape politics and policy: elected and appointed public officials, interest group and activist leaders, prominent figures in the media, and so on.) Individual politicians, beholden to national organizations, are less free to defect on issues based on local conditions. Interest groups have also increasingly chosen sides. They too operate on a national level, often see one party or the other as far more responsive to their demands, and face incentives to offer political loyalty in return for policy favors. But even voters—relatively late and sometimes reluctant enlistees in the polarization wars—are increasingly attached to national partisan identities and outlooks. Crucially for discussions of feedback, they are also increasingly antagonistic toward politicians, groups, and citizens on the other side of the aisle.

Mass and elite polarization generally work in tandem—for example, the polarization of voters makes it harder for politicians to moderate, and the strategies of elite organization often hinge on creating clear "litmus tests" for pivotal constituencies. Still, it is worth separately taking up the mass and elite sides of the equation before returning to how they simultaneously shape feedback dynamics.

Mass polarization

A growing body of research demonstrates that polarization makes it increasingly difficult to win over voters through policy initiatives if they are not already aligned with a party. Sadly, this remains true even where these voters might benefit significantly from proposed initiatives. This development is especially important to recognize, since analyses of policy feedback have often placed emphasis on the prospects for building support among ordinary citizens who, over time, benefit from and thus become attached to a policy regardless of its partisan origins.

Voters, we know, often have limited awareness of programs. A 1994 poll found, for example, that voters believed the two largest items in the federal budget were "welfare" and "foreign aid"—the former relatively small in budgetary terms (depending on exactly how it was defined), the latter tiny. By contrast, only 15 percent of respondents correctly named Social Security (Kaiser Family Foundation 1994). Yet in our sharply polarized politics, signals or incentives connected to the programs themselves have a much harder time breaking through. Party labels and identities play more and more of a role in how voters interpret even relatively unmistakable realties. Specific policies seem to matter less and less in shaping voters' attitudes and political behavior. While policies do send signals, how those policies are interpreted seems to have changed. Analysts today speak of "negative" or "affective" partisanship, and generally find it is stronger on the GOP side of the aisle (see Abramowitz and Webster 2018). All it may take for "red" Republican voters to recoil is awareness that something is a priority of "blue" Democratic elites. For instance, there is now strong evidence that Republican voters who are primed to link the program to Obama are less likely to sign up for insurance through the ACA (Lerman, Sadin, and Trachtman 2017).

Moreover, many of these voters live in cultural environments where conservative politicians and media dominate political discourse. We know that voters rely heavily on elite cues to form judgments about policies (Zaller 1992; Gilens and Murakawa 2002). Unfortunately, in our polarized climate Republican elites and conservative media have powerful incentives to demonize policy initiatives offered by Democrats. Even if mass polarization is less deep than many assume, it is increasingly overlaid onto geographic divisions between cities and rural areas, thriving metro centers and declining industrial towns, and red and blue states. Taking their cues from oppositional elites and plied with hostile framing in the media, today's more partisan voter may be highly resistant to new initiatives—before and even after the actual effects of those programs materialize.

Elite polarization

At the elite level, growing separation between the parties makes it much more difficult to pursue a standard bandwagon strategy, passing and then consolidating policy by peeling off the more moderate or cross-pressured politicians on the other side. There is ample evidence, moreover, that the problem is particularly acute with regard to the Republican Party. First, most measures of ideological divergence suggest that Republican candidates and officeholders have moved farther right than Democratic elites have moved left (Hacker and Pierson 2015). As a result, there are few if any truly moderate Republicans currently in national elected office—a stark change from a generation ago, when the party was marked by influential northeastern, western, and midwestern moderate factions.

Second, the GOP has been distinctly shaped by the party's increasingly strong performance in rural areas and sparsely populated states, even as Democrats have come to dominate urban regions. Not only does this nonurban edge give Republicans an advantage in the Senate, with its granting of two senators for every state (an advantage that partly carries over to the Electoral College). In addition, it provides a substantial advantage in House elections, since a large share of aggregate Democratic votes are "wasted" in overwhelmingly blue urban districts. The result is that Republicans can capture a larger share of House seats than their share of the overall vote in House elections (an advantage accentuated by partisan gerrymandering, which Republicans, with their outsized strength at the state level, have had greater opportunity to pursue.)

Republicans' sharp movement to the right and their tendency to run for office in safe states or districts—as well as the nature of the interest-group environment discussed next—create very distinct incentives for GOP officeholders. Almost everywhere, GOP politicians find the potential of challenges from their right flank to be their greatest electoral danger. Persuading even potentially reachable politicians to compromise, always difficult, is nearly impossible when they fear well-funded retaliation from their own copartisans.

Another elite-level aspect of polarization concerns interest groups. Achieving positive policy feedback is partly a matter of building a supportive network of organized interests and weakening those groups that constitute powerful bases of resistance. Just as with voters and politicians, however, fewer and fewer groups are free-floating and thus readily available for coalition building. Instead, more and more interests are closely aligned with a party and see their long-term interests as wedded to these alliances.

Major business groups, for example, have become more aligned with the GOP, despite the diversity of perspectives among business leaders themselves (Grumbach and Pierson 2019). Since the 1990s, the biggest corporate organizations—including the Chamber of Commerce and the network of organizations created by billionaire business leaders Charles and David Koch—have simultaneously grown in size and resources and become sharply aligned with the Republican Party (on the Kochs, see Skocpol and Hertel-Fernandez 2016). Since organization is usually essential for influence, this increased partisan tribalism exacts a high potential toll on government initiatives that once would have been expected to elicit active support (as opposed to tacit acceptance) from at least segments of the business community.

Again, the tightening bonds of partisanship make it more difficult to find allies—even for initiatives those groups might be willing or even eager to support in a different partisan climate. Like moderate politicians, interest groups are likely to fear retaliation if they do not stick with their team. They may also calculate that in the long run they suffer more if they do anything that hurts the electoral prospects of their side even when backing specific policies might be beneficial. As with voters and politicians, the search for "middle-out" coalitions based on shared interests may prove fruitless.

These new polarizing dynamics are game-changers for all the elements of American politics that traditionally created opportunities for policy feedback, from the basic foundations of mass political behavior to the commanding heights of elite influence. In the next section, we consider their major implications.

Implications and a Guide to Reading the Articles in This Volume

The contributors to this special volume were asked to focus on three main aspects of policy feedback. These concern what Jacob Hacker, in his article on Medicare expansion in this issue, calls the "three E's": "establishment," "entrenchment," and "expansion."

Establishment. The central issue here is how to minimize and manage what Eric Patashnik, in his article, calls "backlash"—that is, mobilization against a policy during and after its passage that undermines the power of its backers and limits the ability to embed and expand it. Overcoming backlash is not just essential for enactment, since backlash may emerge even before a policy's full effects are felt. It is also a precondition for the *establishment* of policies as going concerns—political "facts on the ground" that opponents must confront, even if they wish those facts were otherwise.

Entrenchment. The question here is what policy designs are most likely to cause policies to "stick," making backsliding less likely. Entrenchment is a process, not a fixed quantity. It occurs when policies strengthen supporters; weaken opponents; create investments by citizens and interest groups; and ultimately swing elites, groups, and the public toward higher and higher levels of support for a policy over time.

Expansion. In addition to establishment and entrenchment, those who design policies often seek their future expansion. The question here is how a policy can create self-reinforcing expansionary dynamics, in which various political actors, groups, and constituencies come to see the updating and expansion of a policy as in their interest, helping to create momentum for further rounds of policy improvement. Entrenchment can occur without expansion—witness the difficulty in expanding Medicare beyond its initial target populations. But since policies require adaptation to changing circumstances, those who design policies hope to generate feedback effects that do not just protect against backsliding, but also facilitate ongoing upgrades.

As noted, these questions were approached by two sets of authors, with each pursuing related but distinct goals. The first set was asked to focus on broad lessons. The second was asked to look at design issues specific to key policy areas. In the remainder of this section, we briefly summarize some of the key findings and recommendations of these complementary analyses, emphasizing the first set's broader conclusions.

The difficulty of mobilizing public opinion through policy success

We begin with a cautionary point. Perhaps the dominant thread of past research on policy feedback traces the capacity of programs to build mass support over time (Campbell 2012). The argument is straightforward: once beneficiaries see concrete benefits from programs, they become a bulwark against backlash or retrenchment. There is no doubt that this has often been a critical dynamic in the past (it lies behind the famous Harry Hopkins quote), and it certainly remains relevant today. Yet while policy designers obviously should do what they can to build such support, a number of contemporary factors point to the difficulty of anchoring policy sustainability in this way.

To begin with, it is simply hard to build popular support across party lines in a context of negative partisanship. Voters outside a party's initial coalition are less likely to be open to positive interpretations of new policies. Moreover, even when a policy benefits them, they are likely to receive very negative cues from conservative elites and media.

An additional difficulty of relying on public opinion is that even if efforts to build mass support have some success, this may have only limited impact on the depth of opposition. As noted, *mass opinion seems to have a much more modest effect on the political behavior of elected officials than commonly believed.* Legislators may be more influenced by powerful concentrated interests—a point we discuss in more detail below.

Based on the partisan asymmetries that we have just discussed, this may be particularly true for the Republican Party. GOP elites may make the reasonable assessment that they can count on the continuing force of negative partisanship to ensure the unwavering support of their "base" irrespective of the party's position on many issues. Both these dynamics were on stark display in 2017 as the Republican majority in Congress came up just short of passing legislation to repeal the ACA (along with introducing other sharp cuts in Medicaid) despite abysmal polling numbers for their proposals. As we have argued elsewhere (Hacker and Pierson 2018), the fact that such historically unpopular repeal legislation could come within a hair's breadth of passing is indicative of the diminishing hold of public opinion on legislators.

Another obstacle to relying on a wave of supportive public opinion to entrench policies is the sharp drop of trust in government over the past generation. Many of the classic examples of positive feedback, such as Social Security and the GI Bill, date from an era when government and public programs were held in much higher esteem. Today, policy-makers face a dilemma, painfully documented in the work of Suzanne Mettler (Mettler 2011, 2018): more and more voters are loath to give government credit for even highly valued benefits. One consequence is that policy designers often "submerge" the role of government to circumvent distrust. In doing so, however, they undermine opportunities to demonstrate the value of government initiatives for citizens, feeding a vicious cycle. In her contribution to this issue, Mettler offers some guidance on how to limit this dynamic. Still, relying on public opinion to institutionalize a new program is unlikely to be a sufficient strategy in most domains.

The need to focus on the interest-group environment

If strategies focused on public opinion now seem less promising, the domain of interest groups may represent a more fertile terrain for positive policy feedback. Organized groups with the capacity to deliver money and votes are critical political players. Policies, along with their political advocates, rise and fall in part because of the ways in which they bolster organized supporters and undermine organized opposition. As Alex Hertel-Fernandez's contribution to this volume stresses, the most important recent *conservative* experiments with policy feedback reflect this understanding. Conservative policy elites have rarely been focused on increasing public support through broadly popular initiatives. Instead, they have aimed directly at shifting the balance of organized power and electoral strength in American politics, often focusing on domains of political contestation (state governments, the courts, regulatory policy), where the independent capacities of public authorities and opposition to conservative activities are both relatively weak.

As Hertel-Fernandez's (2019) work highlights, recent trends have heightened the significance of organized interests in policy development. Rising economic inequality has fueled rising resource inequality among political organizations. In particular, the organized power of the wealthy and large corporations has grown, while that of labor unions has declined dramatically. In many policy areas, including health care and the environment, the entrenched position of concentrated interests who derive big benefits from the status quo has become a formidable obstacle to durable reform.

Policy-makers should pay very careful attention to the likely impact of design choices on interest group environments. Groups are the political actors most intensely focused on, and responsive to, policy. And while polarization has increased the tendency of groups to "pick a team," they are still the political actors most likely to realign their efforts in response to policy developments. Because policies deliver substantial benefits and often powerfully shift incentives, groups can potentially be brought into a coalition—or detached from the other side's coalition.

Thus, for any significant initiative, policy-makers need to consider whether design choices will alienate or incorporate politically important groups. Although it may be tempting to think that mobilizing group support only really matters for getting a policy passed, the research on policy feedback suggests it is vital to approach this question in a dynamic fashion—to think about establishment, entrenchment, and expansion, as well as enactment (Pierson 1993; Patashnik 2008; A. Jacobs and Weaver 2015). Even if a group may not initially support an initiative, it is crucial to think about how to design the policy to encourage agnostic and sometimes even antagonistic groups to "invest" in and adapt to the new program once it is enacted.

At least as important, well-designed policies can have a substantial effect on which kinds of groups thrive or fail. That is, they can change the balance and character of groups contesting a policy. Indeed, policies can even shape what these contesting groups will want in the future. Large-scale government initiatives encourage specific investments by groups—for example, in particular types of technology or the provision of goods and services financed by the public sector—that reshape not just their sense of the possible, but also their priorities.

In short, those seeking to harness government to address collective problems need to be attentive to opportunities to design policy so that it strengthens already supportive groups or induces previously neutral or skeptical groups to reassess their interests once policies are enacted. This type of advance thinking is especially important in the (many) issue areas, such as health care and climate policy, where there are powerful concentrated interests with a large stake in policy design. As noted, concentrated groups who benefit from the status quo have grown stronger in recent decades as rising economic inequality has spilled over into politics.

The need to take such groups seriously is the major message, for instance, of the two articles on climate change by Jonas Meckling and Samuel Trachtman. Both emphasize that even though science suggests bold action by governments is required now, advocates of such action cannot assume away the fierce opposition of extractive and carbon-intensive industries (including labor unions within these sectors). Instead, they will need to design policy in ways that divide and sideline opponents while fostering and bolstering increasingly powerful entities that can challenge them, such as alternative energy producers and consumers. Raising the cost of carbon emissions will not, by itself, do this—or at least not quickly enough to forestall backlash or backsliding. Changing interests and alliances through policy has to be a concerted policy strategy, deployed at both the state and federal levels and designed with political as well economic effects in mind.

A parallel and vital line of thinking urges a greater focus on the impact of policy designs on the *economic* viability of continued political resistance. Analysts should consider whether powerful opponents can be economically marginalized, so their buy-in is not required. As Eric Patashnik argues in his article, some market-utilizing policy reforms (such as airline deregulation) succeeded in rendering the business models of opponents obsolete, leading to a quite rapid and favorable transformation of the interest-group environment. In other areas with large market stakes (health care, climate policies, financial regulation, antitrust), similar strategies may be possible. This market-shaping logic argues for making "structural" change a bigger priority than it often is within expert circles. For example, financial reform has generally focused on changing the incentives of existing firms. Sometimes, however, policies that simply outlaw certain practices or enforce key institutional structures (for example, requiring separation of traditional banking from aggressive financial engineering) may be less subject to backsliding, because they restructure private economic actors along lines that divide or eliminate interest-group opposition.

Of course, the greater threat to these interests posed by structural reforms will also intensify initial resistance. Yet even when resistance is fierce, policies might include backdoor structural changes—provisions that do not pose an existential threat to powerful interests but instead induce them to accommodate rapidly to (that is, make specific investments in) a new policy regime. This is a key feature of various Medicare expansion proposals that seek to move toward, but not all the way to, "Medicare for All," as discussed in Jacob Hacker's article. The idea is to get providers, insurers, and employers to reorient themselves around flows of benefits coming from Medicare, soliciting their buy-in while also increasing the capacity of federal authorities to restructure consolidated insurance and provider markets.

Finally, there is a flip side to the advantages enjoyed by powerful concentrated interests in an era of high inequality. A highly concentrated set of current beneficiaries implies that there is often a very large circle of potential winners from reform. When preexisting policy arrangements are intensely inegalitarian, there may be opportunities to build broad coalitions through reforms that overturn them. In the past, for instance, policy-makers have generally eschewed highly progressive revenue sources because they fear the backlash of (influential) affluent taxpayers. Yet with inequality more and more stark, high-end taxes may sometimes be the path of least political resistance for financing new initiatives. In particular, policies grounded in such financing may well be more durable than broader levies, simply because—in an age of extreme inequality—targeted progressive taxes can finance substantial benefits for a large number of voters and groups. Similarly, as Robert Manduca argues in his article on the benefits of antitrust enforcement as a means of revitalizing declining regions, as corporate power concentrates in fewer and fewer hands, companies may gain political clout but they also become much more politically attractive targets for reform, as the recent travails of Facebook suggest (Frenkel et al. 2018). Moreover, in such a context, changing the behavior or weakening the market power of these dominant companies can have an outsized effect, too.

In the end, no simple, broadly applicable logic dictates when to compromise with a group and when to try to weaken it. Much will depend on the specific design choices available and the particular political context. Yet the fact that our polarized political environment offers diminishing prospects for successful compromise may strengthen the case for a more aggressive, structurally minded approach that seeks to reconfigure the balance of power among organized groups. Where achieving buy-in may be difficult, the case for using policy windows to alter the balance of power in fundamental ways may grow.

Limiting backlash

Patashnik's contribution to our volume focuses on the increasingly evident threat of backlash as a potential (negative) feedback effect. Although such an outcome is always possible for a poorly designed initiative, the risk intensifies in our hyperpolarized context. Partisan opponents and their allies have powerful incentives to make new initiatives a focal point for countermobilization. Opponents of policies (along with opponents of the party enacting them) are certain to exploit features of the contemporary political climate to undercut entrenchment. They will draw on perceived fiscal constraints, low trust in government, and heightened polarization (with its attendant partisan media, culturally insulated voter blocs, and team-oriented politician and interest group alignments) to generate backlash.

Managing backlash is about more than minimizing initial resistance to a policy. (Indeed, as just argued, policies that spark greater initial opposition because they bring about big structural changes may well, if successful, reduce the chance of future backlash.) It does, however, require thinking about how postenactment political dynamics could compromise either the power of a policy's supporters (for example, through electoral losses and investment in counterlobbying) or the durability of a policy (for example, through postenactment sabotage). Put another way, managing backlash is a problem of balancing present and future opposition—of reducing not only the risk that a policy will fail to pass, but also the prospect of countermobilization against it in the future.

In particular, two policy characteristics tend to provoke backlash: very visible financing linked to relatively low-visibility or long-delayed benefits (think of the backlash that led to repeal of the Medicare Catastrophic Coverage Act in the 1980s, discussed by Patashnik) and very direct challenges to the identities or status of people highly reliant on or attached to prereform policy arrangements (think of the backlash of older voters against the ACA, which was effectively demonized as threatening Medicare). The point is not that new initiatives should be deficit-financed, or that reformers should not build on policies that already have claimants; most of the research on feedback argues for seeking a predictable stream of financing and building on existing institutions. The point is that policy design must be mindful of the risk of backlash.

As with a policy's effects on powerful groups, no precise formula dictates how backlash can best be minimized. To lessen backlash from current policy claimants, for example, Patashnik recommends careful attention to their perceptions of the program (for example, as an earned benefit) and how those might be threatened by new initiatives. But Patashnik acknowledges that the exact sources and responses to backlash vary by policy and context. The key point is that policy designers need to put sustainability considerations front and center: to think not just about the exigencies of enactment, but also where organized opposition might come from in the future and how those opponents can be mollified, divided, or undermined. Thus, prescriptions for preventing backlash dovetail with our larger message about organized groups. Often, their preferences and influence—not the public's—are the factor most crucial to success.

Our two articles on criminal justice policies both put considerations of backlash front and center. Both Weaver and Geller, on one hand, and Lerman and Harney, on the other, emphasize the distinctive feedback effects that operate in this domain and make reform extremely difficult. As Weaver and Geller put it, "Criminal justice policies created a new political constituency, strengthening police unions, correctional organizations, prosecutors, and companies attached to the business of managing and housing inmates and cementing their coordination with one another"—a "constituency" that is itself a source of backlash but that also is adept at mobilizing white home owners outside city centers who are pivotal to the formation of criminal justice policies. The two articles offer alternative innovative ideas for reducing backlash: Weaver and Geller call for a new approach that focuses on reducing the toxic interaction between young people and the criminal justice system; Lerman and Harney show how those who work in the correctional system might be harnessed to the cause of criminal justice reform. In both cases, the near inevitability of backlash is taken as a given; the question is how to defuse and redirect it in ways that allow a new set of feedback dynamics to take root.

Utilizing federalism

Much fresh thinking about durable policy design will necessarily concern national policy. Nonetheless, we see a compelling rationale for integrating careful reflection about federalism into these efforts. In our federated political system, national, state, and local policies are deeply interrelated. Those who seek to use government to address collective problems must be attentive to how new initiatives can harness multilevel governance so that it might best contribute to, rather than undercut, long-term success—both in addressing those problems and in fostering a supportive political environment.

A number of the contributors to this volume point out that, in our polarized era, states are increasingly important sites of policymaking. This reflects at least three developments (Grumbach 2018). First, states are much less likely to be gridlocked. Unified partisan control unencumbered by minority vetoes is a situation that national policy-makers almost never face. But it is common in the states, which typically lack supermajority requirements and are increasingly likely to tilt heavily toward one party or the other. Second, states are becoming more economically and demographically diverse, as a century-long trend toward economic convergence has reversed and immigrants have moved into a few key states. As a result, specific states will often provide much more favorable environments than the national government for implementing ambitious initiatives. Finally, and partly for the same reason, states are likely to be sites of countercyclical political action, with at least some vigorously objecting to whatever political constellation is ascendant nationally. Minimizing backlash and building support will almost always rest in part on thinking through how states both allied with and opposed to policy goals will respond.

What are the implications of this increasingly prominent feature of the policy landscape for feedback dynamics? If federalism creates new obstacles to feedback, as the ACA's rocky rollout suggests, how can these obstacles best be managed? Or does federalism create a new opportunity structure in some areas? For example, can policies be advanced and consolidated *in some states* without needing immediately to surmount the obstacles to national policymaking associated with polarization and gridlock? Again, the recent conservative focus on policy at the state level highlighted by Hertel-Fernandez is instructive. National policy-makers may want to pay close attention to whether their initiatives encourage the right kinds of experimentation at the state level.

In a scenario of state-initiated reform, the medium-run effects of such territorially uneven implementation of new policies also needs to be considered. Hertel-Fernandez's article details how conservative success in particular states spills over to shift the balance of political resources in other states, since organized political actors in one set of states often rely on transfers from better resourced allies elsewhere. Samuel Trachtman's article on climate policies argues that those seeking to enact energy and climate reforms can harness these spillovers. He observes that well-designed state initiatives can create administrative capacity and expand supportive constituencies in ways that improve the opportunity structures for further reforms in other states as well as at the national level. So too does Jamila Michener, in her careful consideration of how momentum for Medicaid expansion and improvement can be maintained at the state level, with more ambitious states not only setting the national agenda but also encouraging diffusion of innovative approaches across the states.

Sequencing

In addition to highlighting the balance of state and federal action, both Trachtman and Jonas Meckling (in his complementary article on national climate policies) argue that thinking through policy feedback means thinking about policy *sequence*. If you cannot get from A to Z in one great leap, which policies will get you to, say, G and create political pressures for additional steps that eventually get you to Z? To take an example offered by Meckling, international and cross-state experience suggest that significant new taxes on carbon typically come toward the end of a sequence of reforms that encourage clean energy—precisely because these initial policy departures increase the receptivity of key interests to introducing a price on carbon.

Attention to sequence does not always counsel caution. Even ambitious policy efforts that do not succeed may eventually break through if they plant seeds for the future, increasing the mobilization and power of key groups while making clear who stands in the way of popular initiatives. Nonetheless, policy failures can be extremely costly (as the failure of the Clinton health plan in 1994 suggests), and being on the "right side" of a battle is far better when it is also the winning side. Moreover, the kinds of broad openings for increases in government activism that characterized the 1930s and 1960s—especially the outsized Democratic Party margins that facilitated them—seem highly unlikely to materialize in the near term.

If policy ambitions outstrip political opportunities, however, the best response is usually not retreat but step-by-step advance. Reformers should not only ask what "fallback" reforms are politically feasible and how far toward an ultimate goal they will go. They should also consider how much pressure these reforms will create for future steps in that direction, based on the kinds of feedback effects under discussion. In short, they should analyze how the political effects of policies in round one might affect possibilities in rounds two, three, and beyond.

This kind of thinking, for example, is a central element of Andrew Schrank's proposal for rebuilding worker representation and encouraging better-paid jobs. Schrank argues that the current system of labor law is ill-suited to the present economic context, creating a vicious cycle of policy inaction—punctuated by occasional dramatic retrenchment, as described by Hertel-Fernandez—and the inexorable erosion of traditional labor groups. To create a virtuous cycle, he calls for changing the basic incentives of the labor market through two key regulatory shifts: a higher minimum wage and a new approach to workplace regulation that dramatically improves enforcement. Together, these early steps would create a virtuous, rather than vicious, cycle—in which workers felt freer to join labor organizations and new types of worker organizations gained greater ability to respond to this increased demand. In other words, Schrank argues that relatively modest changes, if done early and well, could create the opportunity for bigger changes down the road, because of the feedback effects they generate. That message, indeed, is conveyed in all the articles in this volume, which remind us that big transformations do not necessarily require big initial policy changes, as long as the feedback effects of those changes are substantial and self-reinforcing.

Conclusion

Efforts to think through issues of policy feedback in the contemporary context will involve a complex range of considerations, and no simple set of principles will be broadly applicable across the range of challenges that policy-makers face. In this article, we have sought to identify and clarify some of the most important considerations that have emerged so far through the work of the PFP. We recognize, however, that this article—and, indeed, this entire special issue—is only a preliminary statement. Although the scholarly literature on policy feedback is now extensive, the examination of how feedback dynamics play out in a climate of high polarization and high inequality is at an early stage. More important, the PFP is the first effort—of hopefully many efforts—to translate an updated understanding of feedback into applied knowledge for contemporary policy-makers.

Still, scholars who have researched how "a new policy makes a new politics" provide ample grounds for thinking that policy design matters for whether policies become established and entrenched and expand over time. Policy-makers who wish to use government to address our nation's serious collective problems should take these lessons to heart.

References

Abramowitz, Alan I., and Steven W. Webster. 2018. Negative partisanship: Why Americans dislike parties but behave like rabid partisans. *Political Psychology* 60 (3): 634–52.

Campbell, Andrea Louise. 2002. Self-interest, Social Security, and the distinctive participation patterns of senior citizens. *American Political Science Review* 96 (3): 565–74.

Campbell, Andrea L. 2012. Policy makes mass politics. *Annual Review of Political Science* 15 (1): 333–51.

Cooper, Michael. 18 October 2010. From Obama, the tax cut nobody heard of. *New York Times*.

Frenkel, Sheera, Nicholas Confessore, Cecilia Kang, Matthew Rosenberg, and Jack Nicas. 14 November 2018. Delay, deny and deflect: How Facebook's leaders fought through crisis. *New York Times*.

Garlick, Alex. 2017. National policies, agendas, and polarization in American state legislatures: 2011 to 2014. *American Politics Research* 45 (6): 939–79.

Gilens, Martin, and Naomi Murakawa. 2002. Elite cues and political decision-making. *Research in Micropolitics* 6:15–49.

Grumbach, Jacob M. 2018. From backwaters to major policymakers: Policy polarization in the states, 1970–2014. *Perspectives on Politics* 16 (2): 416–35.

Grumbach, Jacob M., and Paul Pierson. 2019. Are large corporations politically moderate? Using money in politics to infer the preferences of business. Working Paper.

Hacker, Jacob S., and Paul Pierson. 2010. *Winner take all politics*. New York, NY: Simon & Schuster.

Hacker, Jacob S., and Paul Pierson. 2015. Confronting asymmetric polarization. In *Solutions to political polarization in America*, ed. Nathaniel Persily, 59–72. New York, NY: Cambridge University Press.

Hacker, Jacob S., and Paul Pierson. 2018. The dog that almost barked: What the ACA repeal fight says about the resilience of the American welfare state. *Journal of Health Politics, Policy, and Law* 43 (4): 551–77.

Hertel-Fernandez, Alexander. 2019. *State capture*. New York, NY: Oxford University Press.

Jacobs, Alan M., and R. Kent Weaver. 2015. When policies undo themselves: Self-undermining feedback as a source of policy change. *Governance* 28 (4): 441–57.

Jacobs, Lawrence R., and Suzanne Mettler. 2016. Liking health reform but turned off by partisan politics. *Health Affairs* 35 (5): 915–22.

Kaiser Family Foundation. 1994. Kaiser/Harvard Election Night Survey. Available from https://www.kff.org/health-costs/poll-finding/national-election-night-survey-of-voters-1994-2/.

Lerman, Amy, Meredith Sadin, and Samuel Trachtman. 2017. Policy uptake as political behavior: Evidence from the Affordable Care Act. *American Political Science Review* 111 (4): 755–70.

Mettler, Suzanne. 2011. *The submerged state: How invisible government policies undermine American democracy*. Chicago, IL: University of Chicago Press.

Mettler, Suzanne. 2018. *The government-citizen disconnect*. New York, NY: Russell Sage Foundation.

Obama, Barack. 21 January 2013. Inaugural address. Washington, DC: The White House Archives. Available from https://obamawhitehouse.archives.gov/.

Oberlander, Jonathan, and R. Kent Weaver. 2015. Unraveling from within? The Affordable Care Act and self-undermining policy feedbacks. *The Forum* 13 (1): 37–62.

Patashnik, Eric. 2008. *Reforms at risk: What happens after major policy changes are enacted*. Princeton, NJ: Princeton University Press.

Pierson, Paul. 1993. When effect becomes cause: Policy feedback and political change. *World Politics* 45 (4): 595–628.

Pierson, Paul, and Eric Schickler. 2019. Madison's Constitution under stress: A developmental analysis of political polarization. Unpublished manuscript.

Schattschneider, E. E. 1935. *Politics, pressure and the tariff*. New York, NY: Prentice-Hall.

Schlesinger, Arthur M. 1958. *Coming of the New Deal*. New York, NY: Sentry Books.

Skocpol, Theda. 2013. *Naming the problem: What it will take to counter extremism and engage Americans in the fight against global warming*. New York, NY: Rockefeller Family Fund.

Skocpol, Theda, and Alexander Hertel-Fernandez. 2016. The Koch network and Republican Party extremism. *Perspectives on Politics* 14 (03): 681–99.

Weir, Margaret, and Theda Skocpol. 1985. State structures and possibilities for "Keynsian" responses to the Great Depression in Sweden, Britain and the United States. In *Bringing the state back in*, eds. Peter Evans, Dietrich Rueschemeyer, and Theda Skocpol, 107–68. New York, NY: Cambridge University Press.

Zaller, John. 1992. *The nature and origins of mass opinion*. New York, NY: Cambridge University Press.

General Lessons

Making What Government Does Apparent to Citizens: Policy Feedback Effects, Their Limitations, and How They Might Be Facilitated

By
SUZANNE METTLER

Public policies sometimes generate "policy feedback effects," reshaping public opinion and political participation among beneficiaries or the public generally, often with the effects of generating supportive constituencies that help to sustain the program. Yet such effects do not always occur; in fact, despite that Americans use more social policies than ever, antipathy to government runs high—evidence of a seeming "government-citizen disconnect." Policy design and delivery matters for policy feedback, as policies that make government's role more visible may make more of an impression on beneficiaries; yet political polarization and distrust in government can interfere with such effects. In addition, those who are most aware of the government's role in social provision often participate least in politics, and vice versa. This article considers strategies that public officials and other civic and political leaders can use to facilitate policy feedback effects.

Keywords: policy feedback; social policy; policy design; Affordable Care Act; political polarization; public opinion; political participation

Wwhat a difference a few years can make. In March 2010, President Barack Obama signed into law the Affordable Care Act (ACA), achieving a goal that his party had pursued for decades: health coverage for working-age Americans. Yet when the midterm elections arrived that fall, not only did voters fail to reward the Democrats, but instead they gave the president's party what he himself termed a "shellacking," as Republicans picked up several seats in the Senate and regained control of the House. GOP officials continued, right up through the 2016 election, to rally their voters

Suzanne Mettler is John L. Senior Professor of American Institutions in the Government Department at Cornell University. She is the author of five books, including, most recently, The Government-Citizen Disconnect (Russell Sage Foundation 2018).

Correspondence: suzanne.mettler@cornell.edu

DOI: 10.1177/0002716219860108

through calls to repeal the ACA. After President Trump took office, however, public opinion over the ACA shifted from mostly "unfavorable" to mostly "favorable," as Democrats and independents grew more supportive (Kaiser Health Tracking Polls 2019). Congress proved unable to muster the votes to "repeal and replace" health reform in the Senate, where three Republicans voted against the measure. As Trump and members of his administration threatened to weaken components of the ACA, moreover, the public grew more protective of it. By the time the 2018 midterms arrived, safeguarding the ACA became a winning issue for Democratic candidates, including several in "red" states. Also, voters in some conservative states threw their approval to ballot initiatives that called on state lawmakers to adopt the ACA's expanded Medicaid provisions. In short, the ACA did finally generate "policy feedback effects," but these did not occur immediately or automatically when the law was enacted.

When lawmakers engage in herculean efforts to enact major legislation with far-reaching social, economic, or other effects, it seems reasonable to assume that Americans will take notice, appreciate the new law, and reward its proponents in elections. But it is not that simple. It is not that policies do not matter to citizens: indeed, they do, as people appreciate the specific social policies they use, and rate them highly. But that reaction does not necessarily translate into broader support for those policies, lawmakers, or the party who championed them, or government generally; and it does not guarantee that they will vote or participate in politics in other ways. Still, it can: policy feedback sometimes happens, as policies created at an earlier time influence subsequent political attitudes and behavior. It all depends.

The contemporary polity features what I call a "government-citizen disconnect" (Mettler 2018).[1] On one hand, Americans deeply disapprove of government. Survey data show that Americans' trust in the federal government and their sense that it is responsive to people like them—which ran high during the mid-twentieth century—have plummeted for decades and hover at low levels today. At the same time, Americans in all states and all counties of the nation rely on the federal government more than ever for social benefits that help them to afford health care, housing, higher education, and retirement, and to sustain them in times of economic insecurity. According to data from the U.S. Bureau of Economic Analysis, the portion of the average American's income that comes from federal social transfers has increased from 7 percent in 1969 to 17 percent in 2014 (author's calculations from U.S. Bureau of Economic Analysis 2016). Accounting for both federal social transfers and tax expenditures for the same purposes, I find that use of social benefits is common and widespread, with similar rates of use regardless of income, partisanship, generation, and other divides (Mettler 2018, 54–80). Simply put, we are all beneficiaries of government.

These two trends make for a paradoxical combination. Samuel Lubell, a political scientist writing in the mid-twentieth century, predicted that as public policies gained a larger role in Americans' lives, citizens would become more affirming of government, and politicians who protected social benefits would enjoy an easier path to office (Lubell 1952). But while some evidence of such outcomes exists, so does considerable evidence to the contrary. Over the past 40 years, conservatives have shifted the Republican Party to the Right, and made the dismantling and shrinkage of social policies a top priority. Democrats, meanwhile, have fought to protect such benefits, and despite often-intense opposition, they have largely succeeded; in fact, they have even managed to expand eligibility for several policies and to enact the ACA. Yet even many parts of the country that most rely on social benefits have been sending more conservative politicians to Washington, D.C., including officials who explicitly aim to eviscerate the very policies on which many of their own constituents rely. Take the state of Kentucky, for example. The state elected moderate Democrats to Congress in the 1970s and 1980s, but by the mid-1990s to the present, it chose increasingly conservative Republicans to those positions. Yet over the same time period, the share of the average Kentuckian's income from federal social transfers grew from 10 percent in 1969 to 23 percent in 2015 (Mettler 2018, 14). These developments seem to fly in the face of the expectations of policy feedback theory.

Policy feedback research examines how policies, in addition to producing first-order or intended effects, may also influence politics itself by altering citizens' political behavior. For example, policies may affect citizens' political attitudes, including their support for policies, and they may also shape citizens' rates of political participation, including their likelihood of taking action to advocate for the policies they utilize (Pierson 1993; Skocpol 1992; Schneider and Ingram 1993). Policies can generate supportive constituencies, including groups that mobilize to advocate for and protect them. Some policies, conversely, may undermine citizens' sense of government responsiveness and depress their involvement in politics (Soss, Fording, and Schram 2011). Such developments can affect policy sustainability, and they can also, more broadly, shape citizens' orientations toward government and their civic involvement (Skocpol 1991; Patashnik 2008). The first generation of empirical policy feedback research revealed instances of such occurrences and identified some of the particular forms of participation that ensued. For example, Social Security beneficiaries and recipients of GI Bill education and training benefits subsequently took part in political activities and civic organizations at higher rates, while welfare recipients experienced reduced political efficacy and voted at lower rates (Campbell 2003; Mettler 2005; Soss 1999). More recently, a second generation of scholars has generated new insights by acknowledging that feedback effects do not always occur and specifying the conditions under which they are more or less likely, the motivations that drive them, and the impact of not only policy benefits but also policy burdens (Patashnik and Zelizer 2013; Morgan and Campbell 2011; Mettler 2011). Welfare reform, for example, has not induced the broader public to grow more supportive of aid to the poor, as proponents had predicted it might (Soss and Schram 2007).

Not all policies lead to the creation of supportive constituencies, and feedback effects are unlikely to occur automatically or mechanistically. Policy design and arrangements for delivery matter, as policies that make government's role more obvious are more likely to stimulate supportive responses. Some features of contemporary politics, however, present obstacles to such dynamics. Political polarization and distrust in government spur "motivated reasoning" that can interfere with feedback processes (Taber and Lodge 2006). Conservative antipathy to some policies with visible designs, such as public assistance and food stamps, limits the available policy tools and hinders policy-makers' efforts to showcase government's role. If policy effects are to be spotlighted, therefore, organizations, political parties, and elected officials must take on that task.

In this article, I begin with a brief overview of how the design of social policies matters for policy feedback, focusing particularly on visibility, with some attention to policies that affect both means-tested and non-means-tested social programs. Next, I discuss the factors that can impede policy feedback effects, both with respect to political attitudes and political participation. Finally, I consider strategies and solutions that public officials and other civic and political leaders can use to facilitate policy feedback effects.

Policy Design Matters

Scholars have long argued that policy design influences a policy's capacity to generate effects on citizens' views and behavior. In particular, the visibility of benefits and of government as their sources matters for the effects they will generate (Pierson 1993). For beneficiaries to grow supportive of a policy that benefits them, as well as to take political action in relation to it, first they need to be aware of its existence and its source. Yet many American social benefits obscure government's role as a provider, and some leave people seeing only their own effort in earning resources. When Americans borrow funds to purchase a home and claim the home mortgage interest deduction, for example, they may be unaware that they are reaping a financial advantage that is denied to renters, and few will think of themselves as beneficiaries of a government policy (Mettler 2011, 38, 60–63). Some other policies, such as the GI Bill, Medicaid, and unemployment insurance, more clearly emanate from government largesse.

Tax expenditures is a term that refers to social policies and others that are ensconced within the tax code, so that instead of distributing money or in-kind benefits directly to beneficiaries, government instead collects less in taxes from them. Such policies constitute the lion's share of what I have termed the "submerged state," meaning policies with designs that camouflage government's role as a provider. The cost of U.S. tax expenditures today—meaning the additional dollars that would be collected through the tax system if they did not exist—amounts to $1.5 trillion annually. If such benefits are included with other social spending, the size of the American welfare state as a portion of GDP is on par with those of the most generous among the affluent nations. Most of these policies bestow their benefits disproportionately on more affluent Americans. In the case of the tax-exempt status of employer-provided health and retirement benefits, the upward redistributive bent owes to the fact that more well-off individuals are more likely to be employed in jobs offering such benefits, and this form of inequality has increased over time. Several other tax expenditures subsidize activities that more affluent people are better poised to take advantage of, and low- and moderate-income taxpayers are unlikely to be able to claim enough to reach the threshold for itemizing deductions. While the largest tax expenditures have been around since the early or mid-twentieth century, policy-makers have created many additional ones in recent decades because they have found that their policy design stands a better chance than direct visible benefits of gaining enough bipartisan support to ensure enactment (Michener 2018; Rose 2018; Lerman and Weaver 2014; Lerman, Sadin, and Trachtman 2017; Lerman and McCabe 2017).

Americans typically appreciate these policies, but it is less clear whether they perceive the resources they gain from them to be government benefits. Neither does use of such policies appear to improve their assessments of government, whether the policies are means-tested or not.

The Earned Income Tax Credit (EITC) offers an important test case of these dynamics, because unlike most tax expenditures, it is targeted to the working poor, and it is widely credited with lifting more Americans out of poverty than any other policy today. It has been praised for its impact on social inclusion: a study by Sarah Halpern-Meekin and her collaborators finds that beneficiaries feel that they are treated with dignity and respect when they claim it, typically from a "neat as a pin" office of H&R Block or a similar company, and they appreciate the benefits. Whereas Temporary Assistance for Needy Families (TANF) seems to bestow stigma, the EITC offers claimants a "veritable certificate of deservedness," as they have "no welfare bureaucrats controlling their lives," and "their status as beneficiaries of a cash assistance program is invisible," making it clear only that "they filed their taxes just like every other hardworking American" (Halpern-Meekin et al. 2015, 114, 120). This raises the question of whether the EITC would similarly generate political inclusion.

I find that those who have used EITC, compared to nonbeneficiaries with the same income, education, and other characteristics, are no more likely to think that government has helped them in times of need or has provided them with opportunities to improve their standard of living. By contrast, those who have used TANF or Aid to Families with Dependent Children (AFDC) are 23 percent more likely than others with similar characteristics to think that government has helped them in times of need. The EITC beneficiaries have significantly lower political efficacy than nonbeneficiaries, being more likely to agree that public officials do not care about people like them and that they have no say in what government does. The relationships between policy receipt and income in the case of these attitudes is shown in Figure 1. It is not surprising that political efficacy is related to income, given Martin Gilens's finding about how little responsiveness low-income people receive from policy-makers (Gilens 2012). Yet it is surprising that among low-income people, EITC beneficiaries would be most likely to express such attitudes, given that nearly one out of five tax claimants in recent years utilized the EITC, benefits averaged $2,469 per household, and recipients routinely appreciated the form of policy delivery. TANF, by contrast, now reaches less than 1 percent of the population annually, and its benefits are restrictive and stigmatizing. Evidently, the working poor who are aided by the EITC feel that government has not been very responsive to them; the policy itself, despite its popularity, appears to do nothing to mitigate these views. Its

FIGURE 1
Predicted Probability of Agreement by EITC and AFDC/TANF Users That "Public
Officials Don't Care Much" and "People Like Me Don't Have Any Say," by Income Group

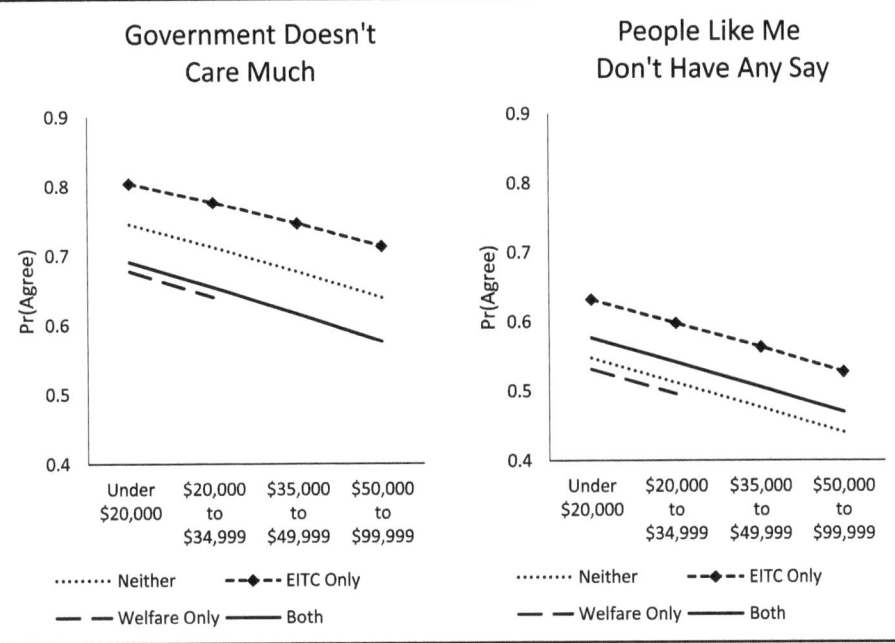

SOURCE: Social and Governmental Issues and Participation Study of 2008 (SGIP).

design, which shrouds government's role as a provider of benefits, appears to account for this disconnect (Mettler 2018, 106–12).

Beneficiaries' responses to higher education policies also indicate that the visibility of social policies may make more of a difference for beneficiaries' political attitudes than whether they are means-tested. Controlling for several other factors, those who have benefitted from the GI Bill were 23 percent more likely than nonbeneficiaries to agree that government provided them with opportunities to improve their standard of living, and Pell Grant recipients were about 10 percent more likely; both policies make government's role fairly visible. By contrast, neither the use of student loans, means-tested Hope and Lifetime Learning tax credits (a precursor to the American Opportunity Tax Credit), nor 529 plans, all policies that obscure government's role, was associated with a significant difference in such views, as seen in Figure 2.

In sum, policies vary in terms of the awareness of government's role they cultivate among beneficiaries, and the degree of visibility in policy design appears to make a difference. Policies that have most easily gained political support in recent decades have often been designed in ways that stymie the capacity for feedback effects. While they may go far to support economic, social, environmental, and other goals, they do little to generate a supportive constituency or support among the public for government generally.

FIGURE 2
Impact of Higher Education Policy Usage on View That Government Provided Opportunities to Improve Standard of Living

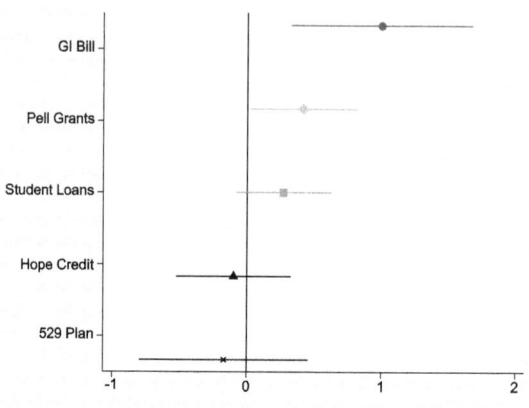

SOURCE: 2008 SGIP.
NOTE: Analysis includes only those with some college or more education.

Deterrents to Feedback Effects on Political Attitudes

While social policies with visible designs are more likely than others to be noticed by beneficiaries and understood by them to emanate from government, there is no guarantee that even these policies will generate positive attitudes about government or support for the policy. Other factors may intervene and overwhelm the impact of policy design.

I considered how individuals' cumulative lifetime usage of different types of policies influenced their views about government, gauged by several different indicators. I divided policies between four types: (1) submerged-means-tested, (2) visible-means-tested, (3) submerged-non-means-tested, and (4) visible-non-means-tested. (By "submerged policies," I mean those that are located in the tax code or channeled through nongovernmental organizations, making government's role in providing them less than obvious.) I controlled for age, race, ethnicity, gender, education, income, partisanship, and views toward welfare. On only one attitude about government was the number of policies people had used associated with more positive views, and that was the view that government had helped in times of need: those who had used more visible-means-tested policies held more positive attitudes. On two measures of perceived government responsiveness, individuals who had used more submerge-means-tested policies actually registered significantly more negative views. It is unlikely that these views were actually caused by policy usage, but rather it seems that the working poor who qualify for such policies likely hold distinctly negative views about government and that the policies themselves are insufficient to mitigate those views (Mettler 2018, 96–106).

If accumulated experiences of social policies do not have much bearing on people's views about government generally, what does? I found, repeatedly, one factor that was highly significant, and that was individuals' attitudes about welfare. Those with unfavorable views of welfare, regardless of how many policies they themselves had used, were significantly more likely to hold unfavorable views of government generally, on all seven different measures I examined. I interpret this to mean that "welfare"—whatever that term may mean to people—functions for some as a microcosm of government, from which they derive broader lessons about how government functions. Exploring the determinants of such views of welfare, I found that both income and racial bias played a role, as groups throughout the entire middle-income spectrum, in households from $35,000 to $100,000, held significantly more unfavorable views, as did whites. The racial bias associated with welfare attitudes has long been observed by scholars (e.g., Gilens 1999). These results also indicate that middle-income people generally resent it, even controlling for race. Many people noted in interviews that they felt they were effectively penalized once they succeeded in earning higher incomes, because it meant that they no longer qualified for means-tested benefits; they regarded that as unfair and deduced from it that government was unresponsive to their struggles.

In short, positive messages about government that these individuals might have derived from social policy usage were in some instances blocked by other messages that have been dominant in political discourse and that they share with people with whom they identify. Recent research has shown that as a society we have become increasingly sorted by income, race, religiosity, and place; and people form their political affiliations particularly through the social bonds and psychological attachments they hold, rather than through a rational, abstract assessment of issue positions (Mason 2015; Achen and Bartels 2016; Cramer 2016). Views about welfare may also be formed through such processes, and then in turn shape broader views about government among some individuals—regardless of their personal experiences of social provision.

In a study of public opinion on the ACA, Larry Jacobs and I detected similar dynamics. We have been conducting a panel study of the ACA since 2010, using an identical questionnaire, with new waves during election season every two years. This permits us to track individuals' views as implementation unfolds. We find that between 2010 and 2014, individuals adopted more positive views that the ACA provided access to health insurance for themselves and their families, controlling for partisanship, trust in government, and several socioeconomic factors. The shift in views was driven by public policy experiences, including usage (by oneself or one's family) of subsidies to pay for health insurance or prescription drug coverage for seniors, shifting from being uninsured in 2010 to insured in 2014, and using government coverage as opposed to private coverage. One group acquired more negative evaluations over time: those who remained uninsured throughout the period. This suggests that people do notice and appreciate

FIGURE 3

Percentage of Beneficiaries Who Are Registered to Vote and Report Voting Regularly

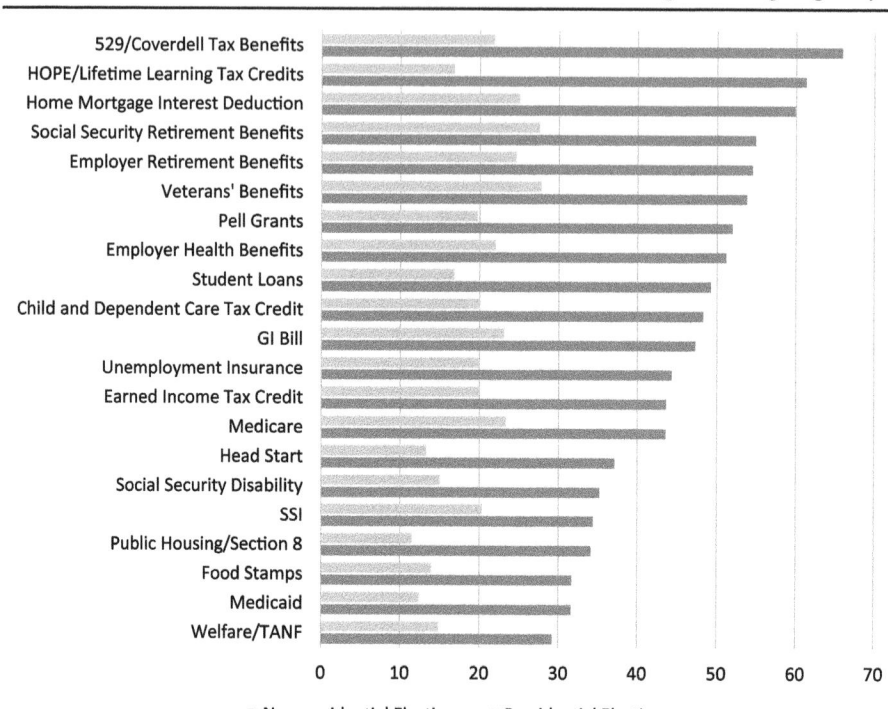

SOURCE: 2008 SGIP.

policies that benefit them, and they may also notice policies that fail to include them (Jacobs and Mettler 2018).

Yet when we considered how those evaluations, in turn, shaped overall assessments of the ACA, we found that the impact of policy experiences grew muted. Rather, partisanship and distrust in government yielded the greatest impact on changed attitudes between 2010 and 2014. The impact of individuals' own personal experiences of policies became diffused by these factors. In short, social and political identities can be more consequential in shaping attitudes in the contemporary political environment than policies themselves, even though respondents clearly appreciate them.

In sum, although many assume that self-interest is a primary driver in politics and that people will be most attentive to policies that benefit them individually or their families in particular, these results suggest that that is not always the case. Citizens may appreciate specific policies and the difference they make in their own lives, but other factors—such as partisanship or views about welfare, for example—may play a more dominant role in shaping their political behavior, impeding the possibilities for a supportive constituency to take shape.

FIGURE 4
Average Rate of Political Participation among Beneficiaries of Social Policies,
by Type of Policy

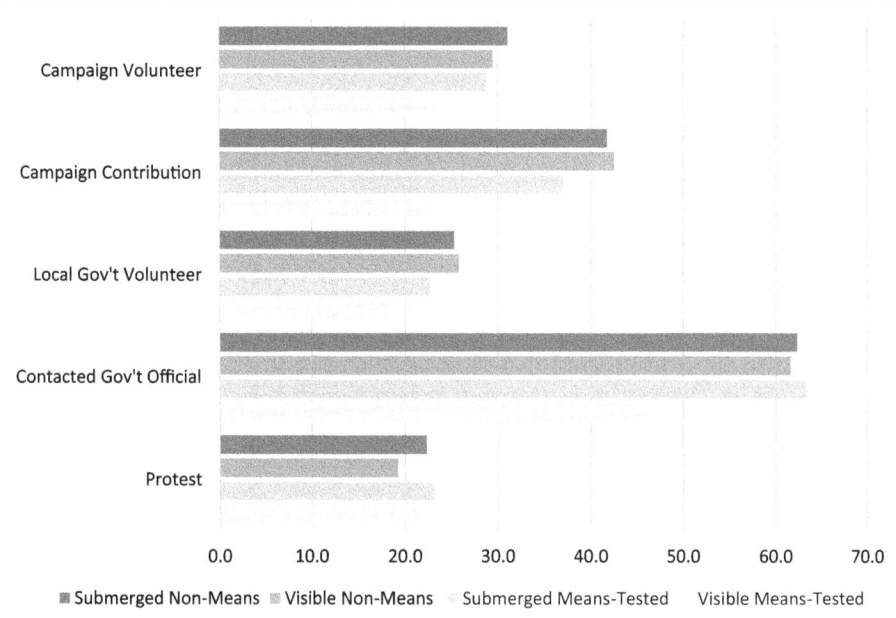

SOURCE: 2008 SGIP.
NOTE: Includes those who have ever received any of the benefits in each policy type.

Despite assumptions that self-interest is a chief determinant of political behavior, many scholars have found that behavior can also be motivated by regard for others, or sociotropism. For example, as people's evaluations of the economy pertain more to their perception of how the country as a whole is faring rather than how they themselves are getting by. Similarly, Jacobs and I find that Americans who over time became more convinced that the ACA was helping the country as a whole also became more supportive of the law, and less concerned about new taxes it would impose. Sociotropism is an underappreciated dimension of policy feedback, one that deserves greater attention (Jacobs and Mettler 2018).

A Participatory Tilt

Some policy feedback research has found that beneficiaries of specific policies participate more in politics, whether to help protect the policies that they themselves benefit from, as in the case of Social Security and Medicare, or because by receiving generous benefits, such as the GI Bill, they have experienced inclusion in the polity and therefore respond as more active citizens. Such analysis identifies differences in the participation rates of individuals who are similar in many characteristics that are associated with political involvement, but who differ in terms of policy usage. In the discussion that follows, I offer more general observations, not ones based on controlling for multiple characteristics, but rather based on associations between general patterns of political participation and types of policy usage.

Scholars of political participation have long established that, generally speaking, individuals with higher socioeconomic status tend to participate more in politics than others. Education serves as a particularly influential determinant, and several other factors can matter as well, including income, race and ethnicity, and gender (e.g., Verba, Schlozman, and Brady 1995). In the contemporary polity, mobilization by organizations or candidates tend to reinforce these patterns, as resources are used efficiently to target those most likely to participate (Schlozman, Verba, and Brady 2012).

These participatory patterns combine with the distribution of differently designed policies to generate a discernable tilt in political involvement: those who take part most frequently are less likely to be aware of how government has benefitted them, whereas those who participate less often are typically more aware of how it has done so. Although government bestows benefits on nearly all Americans, those who are more privileged are most likely to have used primarily non-means-tested policies with submerged designs, which leave them without much of a sense that they have benefitted. These individuals are more likely than others to vote in presidential elections, as seen in Figure 3, and they are highly likely to participate in most other political activities, as seen in Figure 4. By contrast, those who are most aware of how government has aided them are people who have typically used multiple, visible-means-tested benefits, but they are least likely to participate in any political activities with the exception of protest. As a result, public officials are chosen by an electorate tilted toward those less cognizant of government's role as a provider, and once in office they hear more from such individuals than from citizens who are more aware and appreciative of that role. It is worth noting, however, that beneficiaries of some non-means-tested visible policies, such as Social Security and veterans' benefits, do vote at high rates, and as a group they take part in other political activities at rates comparable to those who have used non-means-tested submerged policies (Mettler 2018, 122–30).

The participatory tilt is most striking when we consider it in light of beneficiaries' support for more general social provision. I have explored how lifetime usage of different types of policies relates to support for social provision, controlling for several other factors. In one analysis, I considered determinants of the view that "too little" (as opposed to "too much" or "the right amount") is spent on social policies, measured as an index of eight items including "housing for the poor," "Social Security," "welfare," "aid for poor people," "aid for college students," "health care," "assistance for child care," and "aid for the unemployed." Those who have used more visible means-tested policies are 20 percent more likely to support higher social spending, and those who have used more non-means-tested policies are 30 percent more likely to offer such support; use of submerged policies of either type, by contrast, are not associated with such attitudinal effects. Similarly, I analyzed the determinants of support for the U.S. government guaranteeing health insurance for all citizens, even if it means paying higher taxes. In this case, those who had used more visible means-tested policies were 34 percent more likely to favor such coverage. Considering these results in light of the participatory patterns, this suggests that many of the individuals who are most supportive of more generous social provision—those who themselves have used more visible means-tested policies—are the least likely to take part in elections or to be responded to by policy-makers, because they are less likely to participate (Mettler 2018, 119–22).

Returning to the analysis of the EITC, I considered how its use relates to political involvement. Those who have used the EITC, controlling for several other factors, are significantly more likely to be registered to vote and to vote in nonpresidential elections than others with comparable circumstances. Considering this in light of the earlier findings, this means that such individuals take part in elections while possessing little awareness that government has aided them or been responsive to them. EITC claimants, therefore, like other beneficiaries of tax expenditures, are likely to exercise their political voices but are unlikely to offer policy-makers a message of support for generous social provision (Mettler 2018, 131–33).

In sum, those whose voices are heard most loudly by policy-makers use plenty of social policies themselves, but they are typically policies that obscure government's role, whereas those who use more visible policies, particularly means-tested ones, are more aware of government's role, but they are less likely to be active in politics. This participatory tilt means that policy-makers receive less support for strengthening and expanding social provisions than they would if citizens spoke in politics with equal voices.

These circumstances are not inevitable, however. The ACA, though it has endured scores of death threats by Congress, the courts, and the Trump administration, has managed not only to survive but moreover it appears to be gaining a supportive constituency. In the latest wave of our panel study, conducted in fall 2018, Jacobs, Ling Zhu, and I find that support for the law has grown to its highest point, up 6 percentage points since 2016. Among those who still oppose it, support for repeal has declined by 9 percentage points since 2016; most now favor giving the law time to work and making changes to improve it. The law's supporters, moreover, were more politically engaged in the midterms, exhibiting higher interest in the election (86 percent of supporters voiced "a great deal" or "fair amount" of interest compared to 79 percent of opponents). The supporters were also much more likely to take health care into account in their votes, with 60 percent indicating that it would affect their choice of candidates, compared to only 40 percent among opponents. The ACA, still under serious threat, does appear to be generating feedback effects. Going forward, policy-makers may find that efforts to repeal or decimate it may be increasingly risky for their reelection efforts (Jacobs, Mettler, and Zhu, forthcoming).

Strategies and Solutions

Although social policies do seem to generate policy feedback effects in some instances, perhaps what is more striking in contemporary politics is how infrequently such dynamics are evident. Americans rely on social policies as of this writing more than ever, and policy usage transcends social, economic, and political divisions; and yet the impact of such experiences is often barely perceptible in politics. Rather, the voices of opponents to social provision have been more pronounced.

This suggests that while policy design does have the potential to influence policy feedback effects, such outcomes do not occur automatically or mechanistically. Put differently, lawmakers cannot simply create a new policy and then assume it will generate a greater sense of satisfaction with government among citizens, more supportive constituencies, and more active and engaged citizens generally. Rather, additional steps may be necessary to draw out the potential of policies to foster greater civic involvement. I offer several suggestions here, moving from those that are less likely to be feasible in the near term to those that could be adopted more easily.

A. Enhance policy visibility through design, delivery, and information

Social policies that are designed in a manner that makes the value of benefits more apparent to beneficiaries and government's role as a provider more visible would help to generate greater feedback effects. For the past few decades, proponents of social provision have assumed this is impossible, given the greater political support for new policies with submerged designs paired with the need to build large enough majorities to ensure enactment. During the Obama administration, however, even new social policies that used private delivery mechanisms and tax subsidies garnered little or no Republican support. One-third of the funds in the stimulus bill involved tax expenditures, for example, and many recipients were thus left unaware of the benefits. Proponents of social provision give little heed to how little impression policies in the tax code, such as the EITC, make on beneficiaries. Many policy-makers may assume that policy design does not matter as long as resources are provided, yet proceeding in that manner means that the disconnect between government and citizens will only continue to grow. When opportunities arise in the future to create new policies, lawmakers should aim to use designs that accentuate the visibility of government's role in providing benefits.

New policies might benefit, also, from receiving a **single, identifiable name**. For beneficiaries of Social Security and the GI Bill, the identity of the policy they utilize is unambiguous. For beneficiaries of the ACA, by contrast, it is much less clear. Even those who benefit from the Medicaid expansion may be unaware that their inclusion emanates from the ACA, particularly because that policy goes by different names in different states, such as "Health First Colorado" in Colorado, "Centennial Care" in New Mexico, and "MassHealth" in Massachusetts. For those who purchase health coverage through state-level exchanges, the ACA's role may be less clear, and even less so for those who benefit from changes in the rules by which insurance companies must abide, such as coverage of preexisting conditions. Certainly, it is difficult to imprint a single identity on a complex policy such as the ACA, which combines so many features and builds on existing policies and practices, but policy-makers should give greater attention to surmounting such challenges.

In the interim, policy-makers might consider how government's role in providing benefits in existing policies could be spotlighted more effectively through **policy delivery**. Many EITC claimants go to the offices of private tax preparers for help in attaining their benefits and pay a sizable fee for the service. In some communities, however, AARP (American Association of Retired Persons) volunteers and other members of the community offer their services for free for this purpose; public officials and scholars could work with such groups to find delivery approaches that make more claimants aware of and willing to utilize this cost-free alternative while also better highlighting that the EITC is a public social benefit.

Policy beneficiaries could be provided with **greater information**, for example to make evident the value of the benefits they receive. Some years ago, the Social Security Administration sent annual personal reports to some individuals but not others about the value of the benefits they and their family members would receive if and when they became disabled or retired. A group of political scientists treated this as a natural experiment and examined the impact of the information on recipients' understanding of their benefits and their views about them. They found that such policies enhanced recipients' knowledge of and confidence in the program. They concluded, "Decisions by government officials about the amount, kind, and delivery vehicle for the distribution of information may have a measurable impact on public knowledge and confidence in government" (Cook, Jacobs, and Kim 2010, 409). It is striking how little government does to communicate to citizens about the policies it offers. Compare this to the efforts undertaken by private actors to make sure that those who use their services (many of which are government-subsidized) become and remain keenly aware of them: consider the efforts made by elite private colleges and universities to communicate with their alumni, or of retirement investment and financial services companies to stay in touch with their clients. The Social Security reports offer an example of the impact such information can have.

The relative invisibility of many upwardly redistributive policies in the tax code means that policy-makers need to decide with each **whether it makes more sense to spotlight the value of such policies for beneficiaries or, instead, to scale them back**. Perhaps the first approach is more appropriate for some policies, such as the nontaxable status of health benefits from employers, from which a sizable number of middle-income families benefit. The ACA required new tax forms to be issued that indicate insurance coverage, but an additional form—issued after payment—could make the value of the benefit more apparent by showing how much the subsidy lowered a family's tax bill. Other policies might be better eliminated, making the tax code more progressive and retaining funds that could help average Americans to afford needed resources.

B. Reconnecting citizens and government

While the approaches outlined above might make government's role in some policies more visible, many Americans are already aware that they use government benefits and they appreciate them, but nonetheless they refrain from participating in politics. And others may be unimpressed by efforts to high-light information. It may be at least equally important to find ways to "connect the dots" between citizens' use of social benefits, government's role, and the need to be involved in politics, at least to vote.

Over the past 40 years, even as Americans have relied more on social policies, conservatives have learned effective ways of engaging citizens for purposes that aim to undermine those same policies. Their success in that respect, paired with the results of the research I have summarized here, can be understood through the lens of a classic study about American public opinion conducted a half century ago. In that study, Lloyd A. Free and Hadley Cantril discovered that most Americans espoused conservative values, supporting a "curbing of [f]ederal power," in some respects, but at the same time on practical matters they demon-strated growing liberalism. When Americans were asked abstract questions about government interference, lower taxes, and the sources of poverty, they answered in an ideologically conservative manner, yet when the same individuals were asked about their level of support for specific social policies of the federal govern-ment, they responded as operational liberals (Free and Cantril 1967).

The existence of the "government-citizen disconnect" suggests that conserva-tives have effectively drawn citizens' attention to concerns about abstract issues such as the size of government, the threat of taxes, and the deservingness of recipients of "welfare." Progressives, by contrast, have not managed to direct Americans attention—in a sustained manner—to the value of government ben-efits and the difference they make in individuals' lives.

These findings suggest that proponents of social policies need to find ways to direct attention to how such policies help Americans in their everyday lives. Certainly, this has implications for the messages that party leaders and candidates offer. The impact of such messages should not be exaggerated, however, given our highly partisan environment, the likelihood of some citizens to discount mes-sages associated with the opposing party, and the inclination of others to ignore politics altogether.

It may be valuable for organizations, parties, and elected officials to communicate with Americans about the value of policies that benefit them, what is at stake in elections, and why participation could be worth-while. Organizations, including those that engage with citizens on a personal level in their everyday lives, have an important role to play in this respect. In the mid-twentieth century, labor unions performed these roles for about one-quarter of working Americans and their families, but now those numbers are reduced by more than half. The AARP still communicates effectively to its members in ways that make the value of mobilization on Social Security and Medicare apparent. Contemporary organizations need to play such roles, particularly in the lives of low-income Americans who participate so little in politics, and in states and localities where citizens' reliance on social benefits is especially obscured. Political party organizations at the local level can also play this role, as can elected officials at all levels.

Conclusion

Over the past 40 years, a conservative public philosophy has promoted the idea that the market solves problems and government creates them. Yet, over the same period, the market has offered less than impressive results for many low- and middle-income Americans, who have seen their earnings grow little or stagnate, while job insecurity has increased and employment benefits have become less common. Meanwhile, policy-makers have managed to protect most government social policies and even to expand coverage in some of them. Americans have relied on these policies to help them to weather stagnating incomes and job insecurity, and although policy benefits are often meager, particularly in programs left to individual states to manage, beneficiaries report to pollsters that they find them to be very helpful (Mettler 2018, 84–86). It is an irony, therefore, that many people who benefit from generous policies do not think about them as government benefits, and many others do value their benefits but refrain from taking part in politics. Unlike businesses, however, government does not market or promote its services or remind those who have used them of the value they have derived from them. Neither are most Americans mobilized in ways that would provide them with such reminders. While such circumstances persist, the government-citizen disconnect may only intensify.

Note

1. Here and in several places throughout this article, I draw on my book, Suzanne Mettler, *The Government-Citizen Disconnect* (New York, NY: Russell Sage Foundation, 2018).

References

Achen, Christopher M., and Larry M. Bartels. 2016. *Democracy for realists*. Princeton, NJ: Princeton University Press.

Campbell, Andrea. 2003. *How policies make citizens: Senior political activism and the American welfare state*. Princeton, NJ: Princeton University Press.

Cook, Fay Lomax, Lawrence Jacobs, and Dukhong Kim. 2010. Trusting what you know: Information, knowledge, and confidence in social security. *Journal of Politics* 72 (2): 397–412.

Cramer, Katherine. 2016. *The politics of resentment*. Chicago, IL: Chicago University Press.

Free, Lloyd, and Hadley Cantril. 1967. *The political beliefs of Americans*. New York, NY: Simon and Schuster.

Gilens, Martin. 1999. *Why Americans hate welfare*. Chicago, IL: University of Chicago Press.

Gilens, Martin. 2012. *Affluence and influence*. Princeton, NJ: Princeton University Press.

Halpern-Meekin, Sarah, Kathryn Edin, Laura Tach, and Jennifer Sykes. 2015. *It's not like I'm poor: How working families make ends meet in a post-welfare world*. Berkeley, CA: University of California Press.

Jacobs, Lawrence R., and Suzanne Mettler. 2018. When and how new policy creates new politics: Examining the feedback effects of the Affordable Care Act on public opinion. *Perspectives on Politics* 16 (2): 345–63.

Jacobs, Lawrence R., Suzanne Mettler, and Ling Zhu. Forthcoming. Affordable Care Act: Moving to new stage of public acceptance. *Journal of Health Policy, Politics, and Law*.

Kaiser Health Tracking Polls. 26 March 2019. The public's Views on the ACA. Kaiser Family Foundation. Available from https://www.kff.org/interactive/kff-health-tracking-poll-the-publics-views-on-the-aca/#?response=Favorable—Unfavorable&aRange=twoYear.

Lerman, Amy E., and Katherine T. McCabe. 2017. Personal experiences and public opinion: A theory and test of conditional policy feedback. *Journal of Politics* 79 (2): 624–41.

Lerman, Amy E., Meredith Sadin, and Samuel Trachtman. 2017. Policy uptake as political behavior: Evidence from the Affordable Care Act. *American Political Science Review* 111 (4): 755–70.

Lerman, Amy E., and Vesla M. Weaver. 2014. *Arresting citizenship: The democratic consequences of American crime control*. Chicago, IL: University of Chicago Press.

Lubell, Samuel. 1952. *The future of American politics*. New York, NY: Harper and Brothers.

Mason, Lilliana. 2015. "I disrespectfully agree": The differential effects of partisan sorting on social and issue polarization. *American Journal of Political Science* 59 (1): 128–45.

Mettler, Suzanne. 2011. *The submerged state: How invisible government policies undermine American democracy*. Chicago, IL: University of Chicago Press.

Mettler, Suzanne. 2005. *Soldiers to citizens: The G.I. Bill and the making of the greatest generation*. New York, NY: Oxford University Press.

Mettler, Suzanne. 2018. *The government-citizen disconnect*. New York, NY: Russell Sage Foundation.

Michener, Jamila. 2018. *Fragmented democracy: Medicaid, federalism, and unequal politics*. New York, NY: Cambridge University Press.

Morgan, Kimberly J., and Andrea Campbell. 2011. *The delegated welfare state: Medicare, markets, and the governance of social policy*. New York, NY: Oxford University Press.

Patashnik, Eric M. 2008. *Reforms at risk: What happens after major policy changes are enacted*. Princeton, NJ: Princeton University Press.

Patashnik, Eric M., and Julian E. Zelizer. 2013. The struggle to remake politics: Liberal reform and the limits of policy feedback in the contemporary American state. *Perspectives on Politics* 11 (4): 1071–87.

Pierson, Paul. 1993. When effect becomes cause: Policy feedback and political change. *World Politics* 45 (4): 595–628.

Rose, Deondra. 2018. *Citizens by degree: Higher education policy and the changing gender dynamics of American citizenship*. New York, NY: Oxford University Press.

Schlozman, Kay Lehman, Sidney Verba, and Henry E. Brady. 2012. *The unheavenly chorus: Unequal political voice and the broken promise of American democracy*. Princeton, NJ: Princeton University Press.

Schneider, Anne Larson, and Helen Ingram. 1993. Social construction of target populations: Implications for politics and policy. *American Political Science Review* 87 (2): 334–47.

Skocpol, Theda. 1991. Targeting within universalism: Politically viable policies to combat poverty in the United States. In *The urban underclass*, eds. Christopher Jencks and Paul E. Peterson, 411–36. Washington, DC: Brookings Institution.

Skocpol, Theda. 1992. *Protecting soldiers and mothers*. Cambridge, MA: Harvard University Press.

Soss, Joe, Richard C. Fording, and Sanford Schram. 2011. *Disciplining the poor: Neoliberal paternalism and the persistent power of race*. Chicago, IL: University of Chicago Press.

Soss, Joe. 1999. Lessons of welfare: Policy design, political learning, and political action. *American Political Science Review* 93 (2): 363–80.

Soss, Joe, and Sanford Schram. 2007. A public transformed? Welfare reform as policy feedback. *American Political Science Review* 101 (1): 111–27.

Taber, Charles, and Milton Lodge. 2006. Motivated skepticism in the evaluation of political beliefs. *American Journal of Political Science* 50 (July): 755–69.

U.S. Bureau of Economic Analysis (BEA). 2016. Interactive Data: GDP and Personal Income: Regional Date: Local Area Personal Income and Employment: Personal Current Transfer Receipts (CA35). Washington, DC: U.S. Department of Commerce, Washington, DC. Available from https://apps.bea.gov/itable/iTable.cfm?ReqID=70&step=1.

Verba, Sidney, Kay Lehman Schlozman, and Henry E. Brady. 1995. *Voice and equality: Civic voluntarism in American politics*. Cambridge, MA: Harvard University Press.

Limiting Policy Backlash: Strategies for Taming Counter-coalitions in an Era of Polarization

Policy backlash occurs when people or organizations mobilize against a policy during or after its enactment, diminishing the power of supporters and reducing the likelihood of the policy's subsequent entrenchment and expansion. This article analyzes backlash as a case of negative policy feedback and explores some of the mechanisms through which backlash occurs among elites, organized groups, and mass publics. The main focus is on the politics of "backlash prevention": using strategies to minimize the prospects of countercoalitions against policies serving diffuse or marginalized constituencies in an era of partisan polarization. These strategies include increasing the progressivity of programs after they have become embedded, recognizing that reforms can threaten the social identities and status of constituencies, and increasing reliance on low-visibility taxes. While countercoalitions cannot be completely neutralized in today's contentious political environment, these strategies can load the dice in favor of sustainable change.

Keywords: policy feedback; partisan polarization; policy sustainability; backlash; policy design

Public policies are outputs of the political process, but they are also inputs to it, causing reactions that influence subsequent policy-making (Pierson 1993). As E. E. Schattschneider (1935) famously argued, "new policies create a new politics." Existing policies shape the political agenda, the political participation of citizens, and the activities of policymaking institutions. Public policies, once enacted, can generate their own political durability and

Eric M. Patashnik is Julis-Rabinowitz Professor of Public Policy and Political Science in the Watson Institute for International and Public Affairs at Brown University. He is the author of several books, including Unhealthy Politics: The Battle over Evidence-Based Medicine *(with Alan Gerber and Conor Dowling; Princeton University Press 2017).*

Correspondence: eric_patashnik@brown.edu

DOI: 10.1177/0002716219862511

ANNALS, *AAPSS*, 685, September 2019   47 growth by building mass constituencies and affecting the preferences and capacities of elite actors such as interest groups, elected officials, and bureaucracies (Campbell 2012; Mettler 2005; Hacker 1998; Pierson 1994; Skocpol 1992).

But public policies do not always produce self-reinforcing feedback (Patashnik and Zelizer 2013; Jacobs and Weaver 2015; Baumgartner and Jones 2002; Jones, Theriault, and Whyman 2019). They sometimes endogenously generate *policy backlash*, a strong adverse reaction against a line of policy development. Policy backlash occurs when people or organizations mobilize *against* a policy during or after its enactment, diminishing the power of its supporters and reducing the likelihood of the policy's subsequent entrenchment and expansion. Backlash does not always lead to the reversal of a policy, but it shapes the outcomes of the next round of politics. Backlash may be driven by a perception that a policy will impose material losses on actors, or a belief that a policy is failing to show due respect to a constituency's values, preferences, or status within the society. Examples include the popular uprising in Germany after the country took in millions of asylum seekers (Karnitschnig 2015), white resentment following the passage of civil rights legislation (Edsall and Edsall 1992), and the countermobilization of business power in response to the vast expansion of the American regulatory state in the 1970s (Vogel 1989; Hacker and Pierson 2014).

Backlash can be sparked by policy movements in any direction. However, it is, arguably, a particular threat today to the adoption and sustainability of policies that serve diffuse, marginalized, or otherwise poorly organized constituencies, such as consumers and lower-income Americans. While the targets of general interest or egalitarian policies may lack the incentive or capacity to take part in politics to defend the policies that serve them, their opponents may mobilize potent countercoalitions, pressuring the government to change course and serve more concentrated or advantaged interests (Patashnik 2008; Patashnik and Zelizer 2013; Jacobs and Weaver 2015). As I argue below, the current environment of polarization and intense partisan competition (Binder 1996; Lee 2009) have increased the vulnerability of general interest and redistributive policies to counterlobbying. In sum, reducing the odds and potency of backlash is critical to the political sustainability of activist government.

In this article, I analyze policy backlash as an extreme case of negative feedback. Following a literature review, the article explores some of the key mechanisms through which policy backlash occurs among elite actors, organized groups, and mass publics. My main focus is on the politics of "backlash prevention": using policy design (and other) strategies to minimize the prospects of countercoalitions. I identify and discuss eight strategies that advocates of general-interest and redistributive policies can deploy: (1) increasing the progressivity of programs *after* policy embedding, (2) recognizing that new polices can implicitly threaten the social identities and status of target constituencies, (3) increasing reliance on low-visibility taxes, (4) assessing the potential for backlash and incorporating sustainability considerations into policy design, (5) balancing responsiveness to party bases and marginal supporters, (6) undercutting the institutional bases of support of rent-seeking groups, (7) fragmenting and dividing the interests of those opponent groups, and (8) coopting partisan opponents through postenactment coalition building. While the prospects of countercoalitions cannot be completely neutralized in today's contentious political environment, these strategies can help to load the dice in favor of sustainable policy change.

Backlash as an Extreme Case of Negative Policy Feedback

Backlash is a familiar concept in politics. As law professors Robert C. Post and Reva B. Siegel observe, the term began to be applied to U.S. politics during the civil rights movement, referring to both southern resistance to civil rights laws as well as to a backlash among northern whites (2007, 388–89). Much of the scholarship on backlash has focused on *cultural* backlash—a broad sense of frustration or anger among some people about the general direction of social change. In their 1970 book, *The Politics of Unreason*, Seymore Martin Lipset and Earl Raab defined backlash as the "reaction by groups which are declining in a felt sense of importance, influence, and power, as a result of secular endemic change in the society" (p. 29). More recently, Pippa Norris and Ronald Inglehart (2019) argued that Brexit, the election of Donald Trump, and the rise of authoritarian populism are the manifestations of cultural backlash among traditionalists seeking to "hold back the rising tide of social liberalism" on issues like immigration, women's equality, and gay rights (2019, 145).

While these ideas about backlash are highly suggestive, the backlash concept requires tighter integration with core concepts of the public policy literature (on the lack of analytic precision in the backlash literature, see V. Weaver 2007). A fruitful way to understand backlash is by viewing it through the lens of policy feedback. There are two types of policy feedback: positive (amplifying) and negative (dampening) (see Jervis 1998). Both are essential to the functioning of political systems. Without the momentum of positive feedback, major, durable changes in public policy would not occur. Without the countermobilization unleashed by negative feedback, the political constituencies built as a result of positive feedback "would gather ever-increasing powers until they overwhelmed the entire political system" (Baumgartner and Jones 2002, 10).

Scholars of historical-institutionalism and political behavior have produced a significant body of research on the generation of positive feedback through mechanisms such as path dependence, increasing returns, and processes of self-reinforcement (for excellent literature reviews, see Campbell 2012; Mettler and SoRelle 2018). For example, Social Security built a strong constituency among seniors who actively defended the program against threats (Campbell 2003). Self-reinforcement does not always happen, however. Positive feedback can fail to emerge because of weaknesses in policy design, inadequate or conflicting institutional supports, or inauspicious timing of policy adoption (Patashnik and Zelizer 2013).

Negative feedback often takes the form of a thermostatic response of public opinion to policy (Wlezien 1995). For example, as President Trump has tightened

U.S. immigration policy, the number of Americans who say immigration is a good thing for the country has increased (Nyhan 2018). Negative feedback attenuates a shock to the policy system, "essentially dampening down its effects over time" (Jones, Theriault and Whyman 2019, 134). However, if routine negative feedback is akin to taking the foot off the policy accelerator, policy backlash is like slamming on the brakes (or putting the policy vehicle into reverse). Backlash is thus distinct from the absence of positive feedback; it occurs not when a policy fails to generate lock-in and ever-increasing enthusiasm but, rather, when it engenders rising waves of countermobilization.

Backlash can take a wide variety of forms, from violence, insurrection, and assassination (e.g., the U.S. South in the 1870s) to nullification through illegal action (e.g., the vast flouting of Prohibition).[1] In contemporary, American politics, backlash frequently manifests itself as retrospective punishment of incumbents (see Stokes 2016); social movements (such as the Tea Party); and, most importantly, efforts to repeal, erode, or defund policies (such as the attempt to unravel the Affordable Care Act [ACA]). My analysis of backlash is informed by the literatures on American political development and public policy. A systematic, empirical investigation of the causes and consequences of backlash over the full course of U.S. history is beyond the scope of this article, however.

Research suggests that backlash is frequently triggered in the United States in response to efforts to promote activist, egalitarian government (Hacker and Pierson 2006). Partisan polarization together with the closeness of party competition encourages members of Congress and other party elites to disagree on both sincere *and* strategic grounds over policy reforms that would once have been consensual to differentiate their party brands and tarnish the opposition (Lee 2009; Oberlander and Weaver 2015). The two parties are not mirror images of one another in this struggle. During much of the postwar era, Democrats took the lead in shaping domestic reform legislation, with Republicans often voting for policy expansions on condition that the new laws minimized direct spending, decentralized implementation, and empowered business actors. However, this implicit compromise has frayed in the current era of polarization (Grossman n.d.).

To be sure, congressional lawmaking by some measures remains as bipartisan as it was in the 1970s (Curry and Lee 2019). Yet while historic legislation like the Social Security Act of 1935, the Civil Rights Act of 1964, and the Clean Air Act Amendments of 1990 won support from both parties on final passage, key reforms of the past several decades have been enacted on partisan lines, including the ACA, Dodd-Frank, and the Motor Voter bill (Curry and Lee 2019; Patashnik and Oberlander 2018). When the two parties line up against one another on legislation, the combatants may well continue the battle into the implementation phase. As David R. Mayhew argues, "A party (as opposed to a cross-party coalition) is an organization built exactly to generate messages and mobilize voters. A party that loses on a congressional issue and stays angry may have an incentive to keep the conflict going" (2012, 263). As Oberlander and Weaver (2015, 56) argue,

In a political environment that is both highly polarized and lacking slack resources to provide new benefits to attract voters, negative messaging becomes the major coin of political discourse in both politics and policymaking. These negative messages can undermine the capacity of new policy to become popular and politically institutionalized, leaving program more vulnerable to challenges.

In sum, the high level of partisan conflict and polarization in U.S. politics today lowers the political and organizational costs to ever-present countermobilization.

Mechanisms of Policy Backlash

Policies can generate backlash for multiple and overlapping reasons. Table 1 identifies factors associated with strong countervailing pressure (for similar categorizations, see Jacobs and Weaver 2015; Oberlander and Weaver 2015). The table differentiates between whether backlash occurs among the *mass public* or among *elites and organized groups* (in practice, of course, the two levels are not independent because strategic counterlobbyists may cast a policy as harmful to the public, even if the policy actually makes most people better off). The list of factors encompasses negative feedback on both material and ideational dimensions (does the policy impose large costs or does it threaten actors' values, status, or beliefs about the legitimate role and purposes of government?). It should be emphasized that costs and threats are a matter of *perceptions*, which may or may not correspond to the actual incidence of policy effects (see Wilson 1973; Arnold 1990).

Several mechanisms can stimulate backlash among mass publics. First, while citizens are often poorly informed about the costs and benefits of public policies, they may be mobilized when they are cued by a political candidate or policy entrepreneur to notice losses and when they are able to "trace back" those losses to identifiable government actions, especially when they do not perceive offsetting, traceable gains (Arnold 1990). The perception of losses not only reduces public support for specific policies. It can also reduce public confidence in government as a competent problem-solving institution.

Second, citizens may become angry if they feel that government policy is failing to respect their core values, beliefs, or priorities. While policy-makers' electoral incentives might be expected to prevent this slippage from happening, Morris Fiorina (2017) argues that today's close party balance encourages a "go-for-broke mentality": knowing their hold on authority may be temporary, partisan leaders may seek to leverage their power before it disappears, prioritizing issues important to the party base but less so to others or adopting proposals and positions that are more extreme than those favored by their party's marginal supporters. In sum, policy-makers today possess strong incentives to "overshoot," adopting proposals that contain the seeds of their own countermobilization.

Third, backlash can occur when ordinary voters become resentful of "undeserving" people who receive public assistance without paying their "fair share" or

TABLE 1
Backlash Mechanisms and Strategic Responses

Actor	Mechanism	Strategic Responses
Mass publics	Resentment of "undeserving" beneficiaries; anger over material and political losses	• Increase progressivity of benefits *after* policy embedding • Recognize that policy changes may threaten the identities or status of target constituencies • Expand low visibility taxes
	"Self-undermining" feedbacks	• Forecast potential for backlash and integrate political sustainability considerations into policy design
	Electoral backlash to overreach	• Balance responsiveness to party bases and marginal supporters
Elites and organized actors	Countermobilization to recoup benefits or rents	• Undercut institutional bases of support • Fragment and divide opponents
	Strategic disagreement to differentiate party brand	• Coopt partisan opponents through postenactment coalition building

who are perceived to be the beneficiaries of special governmental treatment, such as public employees who have better pensions, more job security, and more pleasant working conditions than many private sector employees (Cramer 2016).

In contrast to low-information voters, sophisticated elites and groups (including corporations, trade associations, and professional societies) will often notice costs even when they are indirect or temporally distant. These well-organized actors are easily aroused and will countermobilize when their benefits or rents are withdrawn. Elite backlash can also be triggered by policies that challenge the deference such actors often expect when government decisions touch upon their affairs. For example, during the 1990s, medical societies representing spine surgeons who sought to maintain their professional autonomy used their social prestige and Washington connections to attack the Agency for Health Care Policy and Research after it published a report challenging the scientific evidence supporting many back surgeries. As a result of this successful countermobilization, the agency's authority was narrowed and its budget was slashed (Patashnik, Gerber, and Dowling 2017).

Finally, in today's era of polarization and heightened party competition, leaders frequently mobilize against policies simply to "differentiate themselves from their partisan opposition," even with respect to general interest measures their parties have long regarded as unobjectionable on ideological terms (Lee 2009, 3).

In short, elite-led partisan backlash against programs may be fueled not only by sincere conflict over fundamental values but also by strategic disagreement. The GOP's opposition to the ACA (which incorporated many provisions previously supported by conservatives, such as purchasing pools) stems in part from this dynamic.

Strategies to Limit Policy Backlash

By definition, new policies change the status quo, and many people find change stressful and unpleasant. Backlash will predictably occur when new policies impose significant material losses on voters or groups, but countercoalitions can also emerge in reaction to neutral or even beneficial policies that modify preexisting arrangements to which people are strongly attached. No magic bullet exists to lessen backlash against policies that seek to promote more efficient and equitable governance. What works in one policy context may be ineffective in another. In the politics of backlash prevention, trade-offs are often inescapable. For example, a moderate policy design that minimizes the odds of countermobilization may come at the cost of reduced policy effectiveness. Nonetheless, an understanding of the politics of specific issues such as taxation, regulation, and welfare state expansion offers insights into legislative design strategies to increase the odds that policies will endure and expand. While such strategies are not the only factors that shape long-term policy outcomes, I emphasize them because they are the ones most susceptible to policy-makers' control.[2] From a normative perspective, whether advocates should seek to promote positive or negative feedback to a given policy is a question that cannot be answered without projecting the good and bad outcomes that would be produced by the policy's expansion or retrenchment. These outcomes include impacts on civic engagement, equity, and social welfare (Bardach and Patashnik 2015).

Increase the progressivity of programs after policy embedding

One reason why the ACA initially generated backlash among a segment of the public is that many Americans earned too much to be eligible for Medicaid (if they even resided in an expansion state) or to receive subsidies on the exchanges. Yet many of these working- and middle-class citizens faced rising health care costs at a time when their wages were stagnant. While these Americans do receive valuable benefits under the ACA, such as the security that comes from knowing that insurance companies cannot refuse to cover people with preexisting conditions, these benefits are less immediate and direct than the benefits received by Medicaid recipients and other low-income Americans. As a result, some citizens developed a sense of "resentment of 'undeserving' poor people receiving comprehensive benefits" during the ACA's first years of operation (Kliff 2017).

In an era of growing inequality, there is understandable pressure to make social policies as redistributive as possible, as quickly as possible. However, "backlash prevention" arguably should receive early priority. To be sure, any egalitarian policy worth its salt should help the poor, but the allocation of benefits to different income groups can be recalibrated over time as political windows of opportunity open. *Advocates who wish to change the trajectory of government need to play the long game.*

Social Security's political development illustrates this strategy. When Social Security was established in 1935, there was a "moderately close relation" between the amount of benefits retired workers received and the cumulative wages on which they had paid taxes over their careers (Derthick 1979, 227). This arrangement served the "strategic purpose of preserving the public's perception of the program as insurance" (Derthick 1979, 216). As Social Security expanded over the 1950s, the program's emphasis shifted from allocating benefits in proportion to individual tax payments to allocating benefits on the basis of need: "Without disappearing altogether, equity yielded to adequacy" (Derthick 1979, 213). While today's political and economic context is very different from that of the postwar era, a case can be made that building a protective constituency among the working and middle class should be prioritized in expansions of the welfare state. After their support is consolidated, the progressivity of benefit flows can be increased.

Be sensitive to the social construction of target constituencies

Policies may spark backlash among mass publics if they threaten the social identities and status of target constituencies, which are themselves endogenous to previous policy decisions (Schneider and Ingram 1993). Consider the place of various constituencies in the American welfare state. Traditionally, people who receive Social Security and Medicare have been viewed as advantaged and as possessing an "earned" entitlement to benefits on the basis of past payroll tax contributions, in contrast to recipients of means-tested programs like Aid to Families with Dependent Children (AFDC) and Temporary Assistance for Needy Families (TANF). Furthermore, almost all members of the public identify with Social Security and Medicare, believing they will benefit from the programs someday, whereas many people do not think they will ever be on AFDC/TANF (Campbell 2012; Soss and Schram 2007). To be sure, the dichotomy between social insurance and social assistance can be blurry. For example, many formerly middle-class seniors today rely on Medicaid for long-term care benefits after they have depleted their assets (Grogan and Patashnik 2003). Nonetheless, the distinction between "earned" and "unearned" benefits retains a political resonance (Marmor 2018), even though it is possible for means-tested programs to convey positive interpretive effects about the legitimacy of a constituency's claims to governmental assistance (Campbell 2012).

Expansions to social insurance programs thus have the potential to stimulate backlash among advantaged constituencies, who may regard the incorporation of the formerly disadvantaged into their programs as a threat, *even if benefit flows to the advantaged recipients have not been directly cut.* This is one basis for the concern among some that some "Medicare for All" plans could generate backlash among seniors who regard Medicare as *their* program and who "fear—or can be made to fear—that extending the program to others will jeopardize their coverage. They also see Medicare as an earned benefit, and many of them resist extending it to people who they believe haven't earned it" (Starr 2017, 9). To be sure, Medicare expansions could also generate powerful positive feedbacks over time, but programs can be highly vulnerable during their early years before they are consolidated. Policy designers need to recognize that program building not only can cultivate new constituencies but can also unsettle old ones. In sum, political sensitivity is required when policy reforms implicate how an existing mass constituency defines itself and sees its "rightful" place in the polity.[3] *The political risks in a transition from a system in which entitlements are based on contributions to one in which entitlements are rooted in citizenship require close attention.*

Fund programs through low-visibility taxes

In addition to the distribution of public benefits, the structure and visibility of the tax system also influences resentment against recipients of government programs. As U.S. inequality has soared, many reformers have emphasized raising marginal tax rates on the affluent and, more recently, imposing wealth taxes. While progressive taxation regimes can promote key egalitarian goals, such as limiting rent seeking, they also increase the odds of a "tax-welfare backlash" (Wilensky 2012). Progressive tax regimes are politically contentious. As a result, they may not provide stable financing for long-term budget commitments. For example, marginal income tax rates in the United States, unlike payroll tax rates, have risen and fallen with the partisan tides (Patashnik 2000).

To be sure, progressive taxes do combat inequality. But the lion's share of redistribution actually occurs on the *expenditure* side of the budget in all wealthy democracies (Wilensky 2012). While egalitarians in the United States have long advocated for progressive taxation on grounds of fairness, the experience of the Social Democratic parties of Western Europe is that income taxes and property taxes have clear political limits in financing activist government (Wilensky 2012). Wealth taxes generally constitute only a very small share of government revenue in European nations (OECD 2018). Social Democrats in Europe have learned that corporate taxes and taxes on the rich simply do not raise enough money to pay for universal health care, child care assistance, job training, and other major social investments, and that the perceived pain of income taxes and property taxes can trigger countermobilization (Wilensky 2002, 2012). Indeed, cross-national research suggests that the *visibility* of taxes is a more important driver of "tax-welfare backlash" than tax *levels* (Wilensky 2012, 265). It may surprise many Americans to learn that the European nations with the most generous welfare states all have "slightly regressive tax systems" (Wilensky 2012, 265). They use consumption and payroll taxes to pay for government and do the bulk of their redistributing through spending programs.

While the new interest in wealth taxes in the United States is responsive to the current political moment in the United States, an argument can be made for the United States to follow the European example and phase in a federal value-added tax (VAT) over time (Campbell 2011; Wilensky 2012; Starr 2018b). While consumption taxes are somewhat regressive, they are often more acceptable to citizens than income taxes. Well-designed consumption taxes also are much better for economic growth and can include exemptions to protect low- and moderate-income citizens (Gale 2019). Most important, consumption taxes generate significant amounts of revenue that can be used to fund redistributive programs on a politically sustainable basis. While the adoption of a federal VAT is a political nonstarter today, it would clearly help the United States to build and maintain the revenue capacity to meet the challenges of the twenty-first century (Campbell 2011). Sooner or later, this is a taxation strategy that policy-makers will find compelling.

Integrate backlash prevention and political sustainability concerns into policy design

Partisan leaders today can almost always find a basis to criticize their opponents' policies. Republicans cry "socialism" whenever Democrats propose programmatic expansions, and Democrats complain of "unfairness" whenever Republicans call for budget reductions or tax cuts. While elite rhetoric matters, it also makes a huge difference how citizens experience policies in their day-to-day lives. Research suggests that the probability that mass publics will perceive a cost is higher when the cost is larger, occurs sooner, and is more concentrated when an "instigator" is on the scene to help ordinary citizens notice a loss (Arnold 1990; Jacobs and Weaver 2015). Policy-makers who care about long-run policy effects will use policy design strategically to generate positive feedback and minimize backlash (Anzia and Moe 2016).

The backlash against the Medicare Catastrophic Coverage Act (MCCA) of 1988 offers a cautionary lesson of poor design. In contrast to traditional social insurance programs funded by workers' contributions, the MCCA required seniors to self-finance their own benefits and imposed "high, visible, and immediate costs on more affluent Medicare enrollees while delaying benefits" (Oberlander and Weaver 2015, 55; see also Himelfarb 1995; Patashnik 2008). These design features were politically explosive, and the law collapsed. In comparison to the MCAA, the ACA was better designed. It imposed fewer immediate, concentrated costs and offered some modest early order benefits. Still, the ACA did contain several visible costs, including the individual mandate and new payroll and investment taxes on upper-income citizens. These elements probably could not have been eliminated given the severe political and fiscal constraints the ACA's architects faced (Peterson 2018; Oberlander and Weaver 2015).

Yet the ACA's policy design and implementation has also produced a number of highly damaging "self-undermining" feedbacks that might have been avoidable (or at least better managed), including the disastrous rollout of the healthcare.gov website, the cancellation of individual insurance policies, and the ACA's vulnerability to legal challenges (Oberlander and Weaver 2015). Based on in-depth interviews with key congressional actors involved with the design of the ACA,

Burgin (2018, 293) reports that there was insufficient attention to backlash potential:

> The immediate battle to pass reform had consumed aides: they failed to appreciate the value of (and thus did not try to promote) self-reinforcing policy feedback, especially through interpretive effects and institutional supports; they did not recognize the potential of self-undermining feedback dynamics; they overlooked how macro-level coalitional variables (e.g., shifts in partisan governing coalitions and partisan losses) could impact and derail reform; and they did not think about utilizing deck-stacking strategies in an effort to insulate major coverage expansion provisions.

To minimize the risk and potency of backlash, policy designers should give *much* greater attention to concerns about policy sustainability (see R. K. Weaver 2010a; Patashnik 2008). Policy analysts and program administrators should "stress test" their proposals and have on their teams a devil's advocate who tries to think hard of ways that policies could fail to generate a favorable impression on voters due not only to poor design and execution but also as a result of political sabotage—"a party, that is, who can think with 'a dirty mind'" (Bardach and Patashnik 2015, 123).

Balance responsiveness to party bases and marginal supporters

It is not easy to be a politician in the current era of polarization and close party control. An officeholder who fails to energize, satisfy, and solidify her party base will not get nominated, but if an officeholder completely ignores the views, values, and priorities of her marginal supporters, she may lose her seat. Bases and marginal supporters have different outlooks on politics. As Mayhew observes, bases are "astute" and "in it for the long run," while ordinary voters want near-term payoffs like "a good economy right now, a government check in the mail" (2012, 373). In other words, bases typically have much more ambitious expectations of government than do ordinary voters, but ordinary voters have more insistent ones.

Democratic party officeholders in particular thus have a difficult balancing act. They must advance reform projects important to their bases without alienating their marginal supporters. An argument can be made that House Democrats failed to strike the right balance when they prioritized cap and trade climate legislation in the midst of the Great Recession (a period in which many Americans were more worried about their personal finances than about global warming) and designed a bill that seemed to offer few concrete benefits to help ordinary families (Fiorina 2017; Skocpol 2013).

Uproot institutional bases of support

An institutional base of support is a key source of organizational power (Moe 2005). If a policy imposes losses on organized groups, but the groups retain privileged access to political institutions, the groups may be able to reclaim their benefits and erode policy reforms over time.

One effective strategy to control backlash is to uproot the institutions that sustain the influence of narrow interests. For example, a key check on airline carriers' ability to recapture the economic rents they lost as a result of the airline industry's deregulation in 1978 has been the elimination of the Civilian Aeronautics Board (CAB), the independent agency that previously regulated fares and routes. Given its narrow organizational mission and close ties with the industry, the CAB had been highly sensitive to carriers' preferences. After the CAB was terminated, policymaking with respect to the airline industry became subject to much broader influences, including pressure from ideological conservatives opposed to new anticompetitive regulations (Levine 2006; Patashnik 2008).

Weaken and fragment opponents

A second, related reason why the airline industry's ability to recoup lost rents has been checked (despite growing public frustration with the quality of airline service) is that deregulation vastly increased the fluidity and heterogeneity of sector interests as new discount airlines entered the market (and old carriers unable to compete went bankrupt, merged with other airlines, or otherwise disappeared). The effect has been to shake up the industry's roster of players and greatly decrease its political cohesion, making it far more difficult for the industry's main trade association to achieve a consensus position and engage in effective lobbying efforts.

The broader lesson is that fragmenting business groups (either by introducing market forces into a sector subject to regulatory capture or by using policy initiatives to drive wedges between business actors whose activities create distinct social impacts) can be an effective strategy for reducing the potency of backlash in certain cases. In many sectors of the economy, divisions are just waiting to be exploited through smart policy design.

Consider efforts to tax or regulate the oil industry to curb greenhouse gas (GHG) emissions. Over the past few decades, many new "unconventional oils" (e.g., tight oil, oil sands, etc.) have come on line as a result of new technologies like fracking. These unconventional oils vary enormously in their climate impacts (Gordon et al. 2015; Masnadi et al. 2018), but few people outside the industry are aware of this. If GHG emission information from unconventional oils were widely disclosed, it might reconfigure the political economy of the energy sector. Oil companies that produce relatively cleaner oil would be winners under the new transparency regime, while other companies whose oil is dirtier would be losers. The political unity of the oil industry would begin to decay. Industry-wide groups such as the American Petroleum Institute would have a much harder time creating a unified position on petroleum tax and regulatory issues. This step would help to prepare the ground for future environmental reforms at a time when (as the yellow-vest protests in France suggest) mass publics are signaling that the first target for climate change mitigation measures should be producers rather than consumers.

Engage in postenactment coalition building

Prior to the recent increase in party competition and polarization, a key challenge associated with making policies stick was finding ways to ensure that they outlast their enacting coalitions. A large, bipartisan coalition was assumed to exist when a new policy was adopted, but the concern was that policy gains could be undone as old members of Congress departed and new ones entered. A political science literature developed in the 1980s and 1990s focused on strategies to prevent "coalitional drift" (McCubbins, Noll, and Weingast 1987).

Whatever the insights of that literature, it is out of synch with the dynamics of contemporary American politics. While Congress continues to pass most significant laws with broad bipartisan support (Curry and Lee 2019), some of the most ambitious reforms of the past few decades have, nonetheless, passed with few or no Republican votes, meaning that their enacting coalitions were fragile *from the start*. The political sustainability challenge today is less to preserve a policy accomplishment from being undone than to generate a bipartisan base of support among officeholders in the first place (Patashnik, Gerber, and Dowling 2017).

One solution to the lack of Republican buy-in is to make high-level appointments to general interest agencies with an eye not only to technical competence and integrity but also to the imperatives of postenactment coalition building. This solution is most likely to take the edge off of partisan conflict where GOP opposition reflects strategic disagreement, rather than a fundamental ideological battle over taxes, redistribution or cultural values. But this is not a small set of issues (Lee 2009).

Consider the Patient-Centered Outcomes Research Institute (PCORI; see Keller et al. 2018). Established as part of the ACA, PCORI is an independent nonprofit agency that sponsors and funds research on the comparative effectiveness of medical treatments and services. By design, the agency has no authority to make or recommend Medicare or Medicaid coverage or payment decisions, but some experts have hoped that PCORI would over time develop a reputation as a trusted arbiter of medical evidence that would allow it to check the narrow interests of providers and medical device companies and create informational pressure on physicians and purchasers to curb the use of low-value treatments, such as the back surgeries example we mentioned. While Republican and Democratic health care experts alike have long called for increased government support for comparative effectiveness research, the issue got caught up in allegations of "rationing" and "death panels" during the ACA debate. Many Republicans strategically opposed PCORI's creation, and the agency was consequently given a narrow mission (Patashnik, Gerber, and Dowling 2017). PCORI's funding expires in 2019; and while the agency is likely to be reauthorized, it has not yet mobilized patient groups across disease categories, limiting its impact on both public policy and clinical practice (Keller et al. 2018).

The founding director of PCORI was a highly respected physician and public health expert, Joe V. Selby. Selby recently announced his intention to step down. Assuming the agency is reauthorized, a case could be made that his successor should be someone who would help to expand the agency's political base of support, perhaps someone like Gail Wilensky (Patashnik, Gerber, and Dowling 2017). Wilensky was one of the earliest advocates for the establishment of the agency. She had served as director of the Medicare agency under George H.W. Bush as well as John McCain's health care adviser during the 2008 campaign. Of course, this single administrative appointment would not dampen the GOP's continuing opposition to the ACA. But it might send a signal that PCORI has bipartisan roots and that both political parties have a stake in the rationalization of U.S. health care delivery (Patashnik, Gerber, and Dowling 2017).

Conclusion

Advocates of policy change often ignore backlash potential, but this is a mistake. First, backlash is a form of negative feedback, and negative feedback must be part of any theory of policymaking (Baumgartner and Jones 2002; R. K. Weaver 2010b). Even the most popular policies typically grow incrementally rather than exponentially because of negative feedback.[4] Second, backlash not only affects the political sustainability of current policies but establishes precedents that shape subsequent governing possibilities (Skocpol 1992). As Bryan D. Jones, Sean M. Theriault, and Michelle Whyman observe (2019, 264), conservative countercoalitions have shifted the terms of the political debate in the United States since the 1970s, constructing a "new policy terrain on which contests occur." Finally, today's highly competitive and contentious partisan environment makes backlash an increasing threat, even when there is no fundamental ideological dissensus.

The takeaway lesson is not that the prospects for countermobilization should be minimized at all costs. There are always trade-offs in governing, and the advancement of long-term substantive goals, such as promoting equity or social welfare, may require leaders to impose material or symbolic losses on groups and override the preferences of elites and mass publics. Nonetheless, strategic leaders are more likely to retain power, and preserve their policy legacies, if they use policy design to minimize the risk and potency of backlash.

Notes

1. I thank David Mayhew for this insight and for a very helpful correspondence about backlash as a political phenomenon.

2. I thank Tom Burke for this point.

3. To minimize backlash among seniors, Starr's (2018a) "Midlife Medicare" proposal (a much less ambitious reform approach than single-payer, Medicare for All plans) would restrict eligibility for a Medicare buy-in to people aged 55 to 64. These older Americans have already paid Medicare taxes over their working lives and therefore may be viewed as having earned their benefits. Of course, backlash among seniors is not the only possible (or necessarily most important) negative feedback that Medicare expansion proposals could stimulate. Depending on how specific plans are designed, providers, insurance companies, pharmaceutical and medical device companies, and people covered by employer-provided insurance could also form countercoalitions.

4. For example, at the height of Social Security's popularity in the postwar era, Congress was typically willing to increase benefits by only incremental amounts each year. Dramatically larger benefit hikes (say 30 percent) would have triggered sharply negative reactions from workers and businesses, just as large benefits cuts would have produced howls of protests from recipients. On the need to study both positive and negative feedback to understand policy trajectories, see R. K. Weaver (2010b).

References

Anzia, Sarah F., and Terry M. Moe. 2016. Do politicians use policy to make politics? *American Political Science Review* 110 (4): 774–77.

Arnold, R. Douglas. 1990. *The logic of congressional action*. New Haven, CT: Yale University Press.

Bardach, Eugene, and Eric M. Patashnik. 2015. *A practical guide for policy analysis: The eightfold path to more effective problem solving*, 5th ed. Washington, DC: CQ Press.

Baumgartner, Frank R., and Bryan D. Jones, eds. 2002. *Policy dynamics*. Chicago, IL: University of Chicago Press.

Binder, Sarah A. 1996. The disappearing political center: Congress and the incredible shrinking middle. *Brookings Review* 14 (4): 36–39.

Burgin, Ellen. 2018. Congress, policy sustainability, and the Affordable Care Act: Democratic policy makers overlooked implementation, post-enactment politics, and policy feedback effects. *Congress and the Presidency* 45 (3): 279–314.

Campbell, Andrea L. 2003. *How policies make citizens: Senior political activism and the American welfare state*. Princeton, NJ: Princeton University Press.

Campbell, Andrea L. 2011. The 10 percent solution: Why progressives can stop worrying and love a value-added tax. *Democracy* 19 (Winter): 54–63.

Campbell, Andrea L. 2012. Policy makes mass politics. *Annual Review of Political Science* 15:333–51.

Cramer, Katherine. 2016. *The politics of resentment: Rural consciousness in Wisconsin and the rise of Scott Walker*. Chicago, IL: University of Chicago Press.

Curry, James M., and Frances E. Lee. 2019. Non-party government: Bipartisan lawmaking and party power in Congress. *Perspectives on Politics* 17 (1): 47–65.

Derthick, Martha. 1979. *Policymaking for social security*. Washington, DC: Brookings Institution Press.

Edsall, Thomas Bryne. 1992. *Chain reaction: The impact of race, rights, and taxes on American Politics*. With Mary D. Edsall. New York, NY: Norton.

Fiorina, Morris P. 2017. *Unstable majorities: Polarization, party sorting, and political stalemate*. Stanford, CA: Hoover Press.

Gale, William G. 2019. *Fiscal therapy: Balancing today's needs with tomorrow's obligations*. New York, NY: Oxford University Press.

Gordon, Deborah, A. R. Brandt, J. Bergerson, and J. Koomey. 2015. *Know your oil: Creating a global oil-climate index*. Washington, DC: Carnegie Endowment for International Peace.

Grogan, Colleen M., and Eric M. Patashnik. 2003. Universalism within targeting: Nursing home care, the middle class, and the politics of the Medicaid program. *Social Service Review* 77 (1): 51–71.

Grossman, Matt. n.d. Incremental liberalism or prolonged partisan warfare. In *The dynamics of American democracy*, eds. Eric M. Patahsnik and Wendy Schiller. Manuscript under review.

Hacker, Jacob S. 1998. The historical logic of national health insurance: Structure and sequence in the development of British, Canadian, and U.S. medical policy. *Studies in American Political Development* 12 (1): 57–130.

Hacker, Jacob S., and Paul Pierson. 2006. *Off center: The Republican revolution and the erosion of American democracy*. New Haven, CT: Yale University Press.

Hacker, Jacob S., and Paul Pierson. 2014. After the "master theory": Downs, Schattschneider, and the rebirth of policy-focused analysis. *Perspectives on Politics* 12 (3): 643–62.

Himmelfarb, Richard. 1995. *Catastrophic politics: The rise and fall of the Medicare Catastrophic Coverage Act of 1988*. University Park, PA: Penn State University Press.

Jacobs, Alan M., and R. Kent Weaver. 2015. When policies undo themselves: Self-undermining feedback as a source of policy change. *Governance* 28 (4): 441–57.

Jervis, Robert. 1998. *System effects: Complexity in political and social life*. Princeton, NJ: Princeton University Press.

Jones, Bryan D., Sean M. Theriault, and Michelle Whyman. 2019. *The great broadening: How the vast expansion of the policymaking agenda transformed American politics*. Chicago, IL: University of Chicago Press.

Karnitschnig, Matthew. 15 September 2015. Backlash grows against Merkel over refugees. *Politico*.

Keller, Ann C., Robin Flagg, Justin Keller, and Suhasini Ravi. 2018. Impossible politics? PCORI and the search for publicly funded comparative effectiveness research in the United States. *Journal of Health Politics, Policy and Law* 44 (2): 221–65.

Kliff, Sarah. 29 September 2017. Is health care a right? What Ohio and Kentucky teach us. *Vox*. Available from https://www.vox.com.

Lee, Frances E. 2009. *Beyond ideology: Politics, principles, and partisanship in the US Senate*. Chicago, IL: University of Chicago Press.

Levine, Michal E. 2006. Why weren't the airlines reregulated? *Yale Journal on Regulation* 23 (2): 269–97.

Lipset, Seymour M., and Earl Raab. 1970. *The politics of unreason: Right wing extremism in America, 1790–1970*, vol. 5. New York, NY: Harper & Row.

Marmor, Theodore R. 2018. Social insurance and American health care: Principles and paradoxes. *Journal of Health Politics Policy and Law* 43 (6): 1013–24.

Masnadi, Mohammad S., Hassan M. El-Houjeiri, Dominik Schunack, Yunpo Li, Jacob G. Englander, Alhassan Badahdah, Jean-Christophe Monfort, James E. Anderson, Timothy J. Wallington, Joule A. Bergerson, Deborah Gordon, et al. 2018. Global carbon intensity of crude oil production. *Science* 361 (6405): 851–53.

Mayhew, David R. 2012. Lawmaking as a cognitive enterprise. In *Living legislation: Durability, change, and the politics of American lawmaking*, eds. Jeffrey Jenkins and Eric Patashnik, 255–64. Chicago, IL: University of Chicago Press.

McCubbins, Mathew D., Roger G. Noll, and Barry R. Weingast. 1987. Administrative procedures as instruments of political control. *Journal of Law, Economics, & Organization* 3 (2): 243–77.

Mettler, Suzanne. 2005. *Soldiers to citizens: The GI Bill and the making of the greatest generation*. New York, NY: Oxford University Press.

Mettler, Suzanne, and Mallory SoRelle. 2018. Policy feedback theory. In *Theories of the policy process*, 4th ed., eds. Chronopher H. Weible and Paul A. Sabatier, 103–34. New York, NY: Westview Press.

Moe, Terry M. 2005. Power and political institutions. *Perspectives on Politics* 3 (2): 215–33.

Norris, Pippa, and Ronald Inglehart. 2019. *Cultural backlash: Trump, Brexit, and authoritarian populism*. New York, NY: Cambridge University Press.

Nyhan, Brendan. 28 October 2018. How Trumpism actually made Americans more favorable toward immigrants. *Medium*. Available from https://medium.com.

Oberlander, Jonathan, and R. Kent Weaver. 2015. Unraveling from within? The Affordable Care Act and self-undermining policy feedbacks. *The Forum* 13 (1): 37–62.

OECD. 2018. The role and design of net wealth taxes in the OECD. OECD Tax Policy Studies No. 26. Paris: OECD Publishing. Available from https://doi.org/10.1787/9789264290303-en.

Patashnik, Eric M. 2000. *Putting trust in the U.S. budget: Federal trust funds and the politics of commitment*. Cambridge: Cambridge University Press.

Patashnik, Eric M. 2008. *Reforms at risk: What happens after major policy changes are enacted*. Princeton, NJ: Princeton University Press.

Patashnik, Eric M., Alan S. Gerber, and Conor M. Dowling. 2017. *Unhealthy politics: The battle over evidence-based medicine*. Princeton, NJ: Princeton University Press.

Patashnik, Eric M., and Jonathan Oberlander. 2018. After defeat: Conservative postenactment opposition to the ACA in historical-institutional perspective. *Journal of Health Politics, Policy and Law* 43 (4): 651–77.

Patashnik, Eric M., and Julian E. Zelizer. 2013. The struggle to remake politics: Liberal reform and the limits of policy feedback in the contemporary American state. *Perspectives on Politics* 11 (4): 1071–87.

Peterson, Mark A. 2018. Reversing course on Obamacare: Why not another Medicare catastrophic? *Journal of Health Politics, Policy and Law* 43 (4): 605–50.

Pierson, Paul. 1993. When effect becomes cause: Policy feedback and political change. *World Politics* 45:595–628.

Pierson, Paul. 1994. *Dismantling the welfare state? Reagan, Thatcher and the politics of retrenchment*. New York, NY: Cambridge University Press.

Post, Robert, and Reva Siegel. 2007. Roe rage: Democratic constitutionalism and backlash. *Harvard Civil Rights and Civil Liberties Law Review* 42:373–473.

Schattschneider, E. E. 1935. *Politics, pressures, and the tariff: A study of free private enterprise in pressure politics*. New York, NY: Prentice-Hall.

Schneider, Anne, and Helen Ingram. 1993. Social construction of target populations: Implications for politics and policy. *American Political Science Review* 87 (2): 334–47.

Skocpol, Theda. 1992. *Protecting mothers and soldiers: The political origins of social policy in the United States*. Cambridge, MA: Belknap Press.

Skocpol, Theda. 2013. Naming the problem: What it will take to counter extremism and engage Americans in the fight against global warming. Prepared for the Symposium on the Politics of America's Fight against Global Warming, February, Cambridge, MA.

Soss, Joe, and Sanford F. Schram. 2007. A public transformed? Welfare reform as policy feedback. *American Political Science Review* 101 (1): 111–27.

Starr, Paul. 23 March 2017. The Republican health-care unraveling: Resist now, rebound later. *The American Prospect*, 1–11.

Starr, Paul. 4 January 2018 (2018a). A new strategy for health care. *The American Prospect*. Available from https://prospect.org.

Starr, Paul. 28 June 2018 (2018b). The long game on taxes. *The American Prospect*. Available from https://prospect.org.

Stokes, Leah C. 2016. Electoral backlash against climate policy: A natural experiment on retrospective voting and local resistance to public policy. *American Journal of Political Science* 60 (4): 958–74.

Vogel, David. 1989. *Fluctuating fortunes: The political power of business in America*. New York, NY: Basic Books.

Weaver, R. Kent. 2010a. But will it work? Implementation analysis to improve government performance. *Issues in Governance Studies* 32:1–17.

Weaver, R. Kent 2010b. Paths and forks or chutes and ladders? Negative feedbacks and policy regime change. *Journal of Public Policy* 30 (2): 137–62.

Weaver, Vesla M. 2007. Frontlash: Race and the development of punitive crime policy. *Studies in American Political Development* 21 (2): 230–65.

Wilensky, Harold L. 2002. *Rich democracies: Political economy, public policy, and performance*. Berkeley, CA: University of California Press.

Wilensky, Harold L. 2012. *American political economy in global perspective*. New York, NY: Cambridge University Press.

Wilson, James Q. 1973. *Political organizations*. New York, NY: Basic Books.

Wlezian, Christopher. 1995. The public as thermostat: The dynamics of preferences for spending. *American Journal of Political Science* 39 (4): 981–1000.

Asymmetric Partisan Polarization, Labor Policy, and Cross-State Political Power-Building

By
ALEXANDER HERTEL-
FERNANDEZ

As the Republican Party has moved to the Right, conservative politicians have become more comfortable viewing policy as a means of demobilizing their political adversaries. In this article, I show how conservative activists within the Republican Party have leveraged cutbacks to union rights to weaken their political opponents. This case study thus reveals the role of policy feedback strategies in asymmetric partisan polarization. It also illustrates lessons about the conditions under which policy feedback can durably shift the distribution of power in America's fragmented polity. These insights underscore how the success of policy feedback effects depends not just on the initial passage of policies in one city or state, but on the ability of political actors to organize in multiple venues simultaneously. In particular, they highlight the importance of organizing at the *cross-state* level given the substantial political authority of states.

Keywords: policy feedback; labor policy; unions; conservative movement; state policy; federalism

In recent years, the two U.S. political parties have polarized, growing further apart on a range of policy areas (McCarty, Poole, and Rosenthal 2006). Yet this polarization has not been symmetric. As an increasing body of political science and historical scholarship has documented, the Republican Party has grown substantially more conservative than Democrats have grown liberal (Hacker and Pierson 2005; Kabaservice 2012). Conservative ideological extremism is present in both the substance of the issues that right-leaning politicians prioritize, as well as the tactics with which they pursue those policy goals (Mann and Ornstein 2012).

Alexander Hertel-Fernandez is an assistant professor of international and public affairs at Columbia University. His research focuses on American political economy. His most recent book is State Capture: How Conservative Activists, Big Businesses, and Wealthy Donors Reshaped the American States—And the Nation *(Oxford University Press 2019).*

Correspondence: ah3467@columbia.edu

DOI: 10.1177/0002716219862524

ANNALS, *AAPSS*, 685, September 2019

Republican politicians are now substantially more likely to play "hardball"—deploying strategies that are legally within the bounds of constitutional doctrine but violate historical norms of political conduct—than they were in the past and in comparison with Democrats (Fishkin and Pozen 2018). In particular, Republicans have become more comfortable viewing policy as a means of demobilizing or disadvantaging their political adversaries—for instance, by making it harder for Democratic-leaning constituencies to vote or by imposing tax increases on liberal states and institutions (Bentele and O'Brien 2013; Dwyer 2018).

In this article, I consider another way that conservatives have deployed such strategies using policy feedback effects. I show how an increasingly powerful conservative movement within the Republican Party has leveraged cutbacks to union rights to weaken their political opponents even as Democrats have not seen labor policy through this lens. A close examination of this policy area reveals the role of policy feedback strategies in asymmetric partisan polarization. Building on recent scholarship studying scope conditions for feedback processes (e.g., Galvin and Thurston 2017; Jacobs and Weaver 2015; Patashnik and Zelizer 2013), this case study also illustrates broader lessons about the conditions under which political reformers are most likely to be successful in pursuing enduring policy feedback effects that shift the distribution of power in the fragmented American polity. These lessons include:

- organizing at the right levels of government,
- leveraging spillovers between different domains and levels of government so that policy wins in one arena build resources that can be deployed in others,
- ensuring organizational mobilizations that connect feedback processes to the mass public, and
- leveraging a range of proposals viable within different political contexts that make cumulative progress toward the same objective.

Together, these insights underscore how the success of policy feedback effects depends not just on the initial passage of policies in one venue, but instead on the ability of political actors to organize in multiple venues simultaneously before, during, and after policy enactment (cf. Galvin and Thurston 2017). In particular, they highlight the importance of political organizing at the *cross-state* level given the substantial authority of states in the American political system (Grumbach 2018). Before I assess each of these lessons in more detail, I describe the considerable asymmetry that exists between Democrats and Republicans on labor politics and spell out its implications for policy feedback effects.

The Growth of Conservative Advocacy Targeting Labor Unions

Over the past four decades, conservative political activists and donors, often bolstered by private-sector businesses, have built up organizations that have successfully pressed for significant policy changes across the U.S. states (Hertel-Fernandez

TABLE 1
Introducing the Right-Wing Troika

The American Legislative Exchange Council (ALEC; $8–10M per yr.)	The State Policy Network (SPN; $78M+ per yr.)	Americans for Prosperity (AFP; $150M+ per yr.)
• *Thousands of state legislators, hundreds of large companies, & conservative activists/ philanthropists* • Develops and disseminates legislative language through policy task forces • Disseminates examples of introduced/enacted bills to lawmakers (100–200 bills based on ALEC models enacted each year) • Uses regular convenings and the provision of expert advice to encourage lawmakers (who often lack staff) to support the ALEC legislative agenda • Created in 1973	• *Coordinates and supports more than sixty affiliated think tanks in all fifty states* • Testifies for model bills produced by ALEC • Produces media coverage (Op-Eds, interviews, letters) in support of bills • Commissions polls with tailored wording to show public support for bills and regulatory measures • Many of its affiliates participate on ALEC task forces • Created in 1986	• *Nearly 3 M activists and 500+ paid staffers; paid directors in 36+ states* • Active during and between elections • Organizes rallies, petitions, and district contacts with lawmakers • Runs ads supporting and opposing legislators, model bills produced by ALEC • Develops coalitions with other right-wing organizations • Commissions polls with tailored wording to show public support for bills and regulatory steps • Created in 2004

SOURCE: Adapted from Hertel-Fernandez (2019).

2019). These groups, and especially the American Legislative Exchange Council (ALEC), operating since 1973, the State Policy Network (SPN), since 1986, and Americans for Prosperity (AFP), since 2004, have organized in and out of state legislatures to push for right-leaning policies on a range of issues related to unions, taxes, government spending, health care, energy and the environment, and consumer rights. They have also pulled Republican elected officials further to the ideological Right (Hertel-Fernandez 2019; Schlozman and Rosenfeld 2018; Skocpol and Hertel-Fernandez 2016).

Table 1 briefly summarizes the organizational histories of these three groups, which in other work I have dubbed the right-wing "troika" (see Hertel-Fernandez 2019). As Table 1 indicates, ALEC's influence comes from the legislative networks it has assembled and the policy ideas, research assistance, and political strategy it can offer to underresourced legislators pressed for time and staff and who have built relationships with ALEC's staff and corporate and conservative donor-members at regular convenings each year. SPN-affiliated think tanks buttress ALEC's efforts by producing research reports, media commentary, and legislative testimony in support of the model bills that ALEC produces—and in some cases, SPN think tanks serve directly on policy task forces within ALEC. The last member of the troika is the newest, but also in some ways the most expansive. A nation-spanning federated advocacy group at the center of the Koch brothers' political network, AFP combines some 3 million grassroots volunteers with a large campaign war chest and an in-state presence in over thirty states prepared to lobby for local, state, and federal policy change and to intervene in elections to help far-Right Republican candidates at all levels of government.

Although the three networks, and especially ALEC and SPN, enjoyed growing state legislative victories throughout the 1990s and early 2000s, large state-level GOP gains after the 2010 and 2014 elections gave the troika many new opportunities for legislative successes. Take the example of right-to-work laws, which bar unions from collecting fees from nonmembers who benefit from union-negotiated collective bargaining agreements and job protections (known as fair share, representational, or agency fees). The number of right-to-work states—and the proportion of workers living in those right-to-work states—was relatively constant from the 1990s through 2010. Since 2010, however, five states have passed right-to-work laws, bumping the proportion of workers living in right-to-work states to nearly half. Notably, there is strong evidence to suggest that ALEC, AFP, and SPN all played a central role in pushing for the passage of the agency fee rollbacks (Hertel-Fernandez 2019).

It is no coincidence that conservative cross-state lobbying groups and GOP politicians sought right-to-work laws after gaining control of legislatures and governorships. As this article describes, right-leaning advocacy groups and their allies in the Republican Party have prioritized using policy, and above all labor policy, in ways that bolster the political resources of their allies and demobilize the political power of their liberal opponents. The SPN described this strategy of feedbacks to its donors as follows: efforts to curb the power of labor unions like right to work, cuts to public employee collective bargaining, and restrictions on union political activities have the promise of "permanently depriving the Left from access to millions of dollars in dues … every election cycle," which will "defund and defang" one of our freedom movement's most powerful opponents, the government unions" while also "clear[ing] pathways toward passage of so many other pro-freedom initiatives in the states" (original emphasis; Bragdon, n.d.; Pilkington 2018).

Conservatives' intuition about the effects of right-to-work laws on Democrats is borne out by empirical analysis. Examining the passage of agency fee rollbacks across the states from 1980 to 2016, I find in joint work with James Feigenbaum and Vanessa Williamson that right-to-work laws durably disadvantage Democrats and liberal policymaking for years into the future (Feigenbaum, Hertel-Fernandez, and Williamson 2018). The passage of right-to-work laws, we find after comparing neighboring counties straddling state right-to-work lines, lowers Democratic vote shares and turnout up and down the ballot from the presidency down to state government. We show that weaker unions mean that fewer working-class Americans are asked to participate in elections, one of the most important ways in which citizens are mobilized into politics. We further document how campaign contributions from unions to Democrats fall after the passage of those laws. Looking over the longer term, we find that weaker unions also have knock-on effects on other political outcomes. After the passage of right-to-work laws, states are less likely to elect working-class candidates to state legislatures and Congress, and state economic policy moves sharply to the ideological Right. In one especially important example, we find that states are less likely to pass minimum wage increases in the wake of right-to-work laws.

These *negative* effects of policy on the labor movement and the Democratic Party are a mirror image of the initial raft of state laws expanding labor rights for public sector employees in the 1960s and 1970s, which wound up creating a powerful new interest group favoring progressive causes and Democratic candidates (e.g., Anzia and Moe 2016; Flavin and Hartney 2015; Hartney 2014). Yet strikingly, Democrats have in recent decades been reluctant to think about labor policy in the same way as conservatives: as a tool for generating public policy feedback effects to build political power. The Obama administration notably let the Employee Free Choice Act, a bill to support greater labor organizing, fall by the wayside during the short window in 2009 and 2010 when Democrats enjoyed near filibuster-proof majorities in Congress (Meyerson 2010). And just as strikingly, *pro*-union legislation is not typically part of the set of policies pursued by Democrats after they take control of state governments. Put simply, there is no liberal version of state-level right-to-work laws that Democrats have consistently pursued over the years on a scale that matches conservative efforts to retrench labor power.

Democratic ambivalence about union rights has come at a real cost to the party and broader liberal efforts. Even in its weakened state, the labor movement remains an incredibly important part of the Democratic party coalition and a distinctive group in the American political economy. Few, if any, other organized interests have the capacity to move as easily between the economic and political domains, to organize the identities of individuals as workers and as politically engaged citizens, and to represent the interests of working- and middle-class Americans in both elections and public policy battles. There is a long line of work documenting both the post–New Deal anchoring relationship between unions and the Democratic Party, as well as how unions boost workers' political and civic skills and interests; encourage members to participate in politics; provide considerable financing of Democrat political campaigns; and lobby on a range of left-leaning public policy issues at the local, state, and national levels (see, for instance, Dark 1999; Schickler 2016; Schlozman 2015; on unions and other political outcomes, see, for instance, Ahlquist 2017; Ahlquist and Levi 2013; Gilens 2012; Kim and Margalit 2017; Leighley and Nagler 2007; Verba, Schlozman, and Brady 1995).

To put these feedback effects in the theoretical context developed by Paul Pierson, policies that either undermine or bolster the labor movement have the potential to reshape politics at both the interest group and individual levels (Pierson 1993). Stronger unions can act as organized interests in the electoral and policymaking process. But such measures will also make unions more effective as intermediary institutions that themselves can shape individuals' political skills, interests, and identities, and thus their capacities to participate in politics.

Having established the asymmetry in conservative and liberal attention to labor policy and its consequences, I now turn to describing what lessons we can learn about conservative successes in this policy domain for the durability and effectiveness of feedback effects—especially how feedback is contingent on political organization.

Lesson 1: Organizing at the Right Level of Government and across the Whole Country

Even as liberals have not tended to prioritize labor policy, conservatives made defeating unions, especially in the public sector, a central priority. In fact, it was the rise of public-sector unions in the 1960s and 1970, which had begun to organize at the state level, that helped conservative activists to realize that a singular focus on Washington, D.C., would be unproductive given the extent to which states controlled major policy decisions. As one executive director of ALEC lamented, in contrast to the conservative movement, "liberals understood the importance of the states some time ago," and liberal state legislators "are supported by a vast array of special interest groups that have been active in the states for a long time," perhaps most notably public sector unions and especially the "radically liberal National Education Association" (Brunelli 1990).

The irony is that since the 1970s, the tables have turned, and it is liberals, not conservatives, who have ignored the states and focused their attention on either the local or the national levels. That is the first lesson that conservative advocacy against unions reveals about the success (or failure) of policy feedback effects: in the federated American polity, political groups and activists need to organize across the levels of government that have political authority. For instance, as ALEC's executive director noted, it is the states that are responsible for setting important policies over a range of issues. When it comes to labor policy, it is states, not the federal government, that oversee the ability of public-sector unions to organize, collect dues, participate in politics, and collectively bargain (or not). States also have discretion over important aspects of labor market policy, like setting and enforcing the minimum wage or creating paid sick or family leave programs (e.g., Galvin 2016). And states can also use their public contracting activities to set labor standards in ways that encourage (or discourage) strong unions.

Beyond the substantive importance of the states, cross-state political organizing, as savvy political activists have long recognized, gives multiple opportunities to achieve the same goal. "In the states, if you're trying to get [something] passed and you've lost in Kansas, Nebraska and Texas, it's not a total failure. You may well win in Arizona, California and New York that year. You've got 50 shots," stressed one of ALEC's early executive directors in making a sales pitch to potential corporate members (Peirce and Guskind 1984). In addition, moving legislation across the states can pave the way for later national action, too. (I explore both of these benefits to cross-state organizing in more detail in the following section.) As a result, by abandoning the states, progressives are ceding significant ground to conservatives to entrench substantial policy victories over time.

Facing mounting conservative cross-state victories, progressives have shifted their energy to cities, especially on labor issues like the minimum wage through the Fight for Fifteen movement (Rolf 2016). That shift is understandable to the extent that liberal voters are increasingly concentrated in urban areas, making progressive policy change easier in city and municipal governments. Labor activists have similarly pushed for local measures to extend paid sick leave to workers as a condition of employment, given that many workers—and disproportionately low-wage, service sector employees—lack paid sick or family leave.

If the story ended here, it might well provide a strong justification for progressives to abandon cross-state organization in favor of a city-based approach that could lock in policy and political gains through new programs and their supportive constituencies. And indeed, some progressives have doubled down on this thinking. At their 2018 fall conference, members of the Democracy Alliance—the donor club of liberal millionaires and billionaires—attended a session on "City Lights: Rebuilding Progressive Politics One City at a Time" that trumpeted how "cities are primed to be incubators of policy ideas where we can reimagine, rebuild, and implement a progressive vision of government. ... Cities have substantial legal powers and the reach to solve national economic, social, and environmental problems."[1]

But as progressives have tried to pursue more liberal urban initiatives, they have faced two big obstacles. First, they have found that cities have few levers for substantially bolstering union membership or political power, which generally rest at the state and national levels (e.g., Rosenblum 2017). And equally importantly, the troika has responded to local-level progressive initiatives by vigorously embracing state preemption, or when states bar cities from passing measures that exceed the generosity of state level policies. A state with a minimum wage preemption law, for instance, bars cities from passing their own minimum wages that exceed the state law.

Figure 1 plots the share of the U.S. population living in a state with either preemption of local minimum wage rates or local paid sick and family leave programs. It also indicates the year in which ALEC began focusing on preempting local labor market programs through a new model bill push (2011) with the dashed vertical line. Figure 1 shows that an increasing proportion of the U.S. population now lives in states with both kinds of preemption—with an especially big increase after ALEC began focusing on these issues in 2011. In 2000, less than 2 percent of Americans lived in a state preempting local minimum wage hikes. By 2016, that share had increased to nearly six in ten Americans. The trend for preemption of city-wide paid leave initiatives is similarly striking. No state had paid leave preemption on the books in 2000, but by 2016 nearly four in ten Americans lived in a state barring local paid sick leave initiatives unless the state had already created such a program.

In short, the combination of weak city authority over labor policy coupled with state power over preemption severely curtails the ability of blue cities located

FIGURE 1
Conservative Networks Have Rapidly Spread Preemption Laws of Local
Labor Markets, 2000–2016

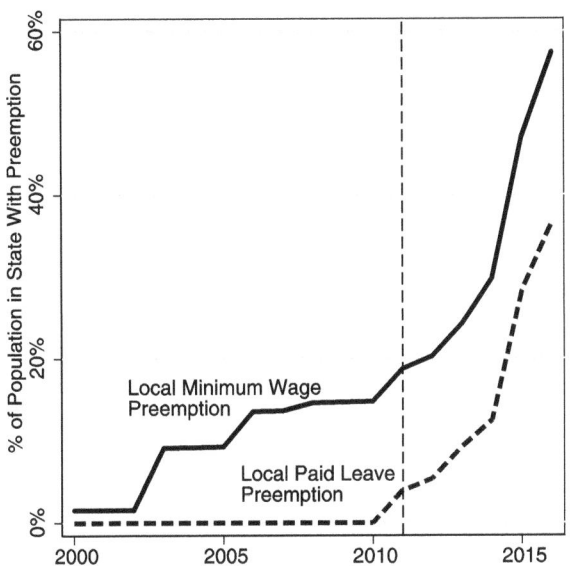

SOURCE: Author's review of state legislation and the U.S. Census Bureau.
NOTE: The figure shows the share of the U.S. population living in states with local minimum wage preemption or local paid or family leave preemption. Dashed vertical line indicates 2011, the year in which ALEC began distributing local labor policy preemption bills to its members.

within red states to take action on their own—foreclosing the possibilities of progressives using control of city government to bolster the labor movement in the ways imagined by many liberals, including many progressive donors. Given the distribution of political power across America's states and cities, then, progressives are substantially disadvantaged by their retreat to urban enclaves. This imbalance thus contrasts with conservatives' wise decision to prioritize state-level organizing, showing the costs of ignoring state-level advocacy for feedback success on the Left.

Lesson 2: Leveraging Interactions between Institutional Venues

If one important lesson conservatives have learned about American politics is how it is not enough to organize only at the local or national level, a second and closely related lesson is how to leverage spillovers between institutional domains. The American political system offers many different venues through which to pursue policy change—like the judiciary, state legislatures, Congress, or the bureaucracy. Crucially, these venues are not independent from one another, and successes in one domain can unleash new resources that activists can use to push reforms in another arena. In the area of labor policy, conservatives have moved seamlessly from litigation into electoral and legislative politics and back again to the courts, all with the goal of retrenching the power of labor unions.

The example of conservative efforts to cut union agency fees is instructive. Conservative networks and activists have pushed for legislation that would curb the right of public-sector unions to collect fees from nonmembers in favorable states under full GOP control (right-to-work bills), using past victories in other states to show potential supporters in later states that such a reform was possible. One ALEC chair who headed up the labor committee argued in an SPN publication that right-to-work in Michigan would not "have happened in 2012 without … Indiana's passage of right-to-work," as his group was able to show wavering Michigan Republicans that "in the election after Indiana passed right-to-work [the Republicans] did not lose a single seat in the state Senate and even picked up nine seats in the House" (Inside ALEC 2013, 21). In this way, the conservative networks leveraged the fact that state politicians are highly attuned to past victories and loses in neighboring states to bolster the passage of agency fee cutbacks in increasingly ambitious terrain.

While full-on right-to-work is at least feasible in states under complete Republican control, such measures are obviously nonstarters in many of the Democratically controlled states with the most powerful public-sector labor unions. In 2014, for instance, more than 40 percent of all public-sector union members worked in just three states: New York, California, and Illinois. Accordingly, to reach unions in these states, conservative activists had to work through the federal courts, which had the power to impose binding rulings in states like New York where legislative action was impossible—providing another example of how the conservative networks have leveraged spillovers between institutional venues.

The 2014 Supreme Court decision in *Harris v. Quinn* (134 S. Ct. 2618) was the first significant victory on this front for conservatives.[2] That case involved a group of workers who provided care to disabled individuals eligible for Medicaid benefits. Although these workers were technically employed by the patients they served, the workers were paid through the federal-state Medicaid program. As a result, the Illinois state government ruled in 2003 that these workers should be considered state employees for the purposes of union representation. A dozen other states followed Illinois' lead in the ensuing years to facilitate the unionization of home health aides. States extended the logic to cover other similar state-reimbursed employees, like day care providers, as well.

Because Illinois is not a right-to-work state, home health aides since 2003 were required to pay fair share fees to their unions even if they were not union members themselves. A group of dissenting workers sued the state to protest this requirement, and the case was eventually heard by the Supreme Court. Appealing to the Court's conservative majority, the plaintiffs in *Harris* successfully argued that Illinois home health aides did not count as full-fledged state employees for the purposes of agency fees. That had the immediate effect of permitting dissenting nonmembers to opt out of paying agency fees to their union. But more ominously, Justice Alito's controlling opinion signaled that the conservative members of the Court were deeply skeptical of the constitutionality of agency fees altogether, inviting further challenges that would invalidate such fees for all public-sector employees.

The way that conservative anti-union activists responded to the decision nicely captures the effectiveness of moving between institutional venues in pursuit of the same outcome. First, right-leaning cross-state organizations launched large publicity campaigns to educate home health aides about their new rights under the *Harris* decision and how they could save money by leaving the union. Think-tanks affiliated with the State Policy Network, for instance, began broadcasting TV spots with sympathetic health aides seated next to the disabled family members they cared for, describing how the workers decided to leave their union to have a little extra money to spend on themselves and their loved ones (Freedom Foundation 2015). The group that aired the spot, the Freedom Foundation, also organized door-to-door drives to the houses of registered health aides and child care providers who were union members (Greenhouse 2016).

Conservative efforts do not stop with appeals to individual members, however. The Freedom Foundation, aided by other right-leaning groups opposed to public-sector unions, have used state and federal litigation to further expand the reach of the *Harris* decision and check union efforts to temper *Harris*'s effects on their membership rolls and coffers. For instance, in the wake of the *Harris* decision, some unions negotiated collective bargaining agreements that required prospective home health aides to attend a mandatory union orientation. The hope was that these orientations could convince aides to voluntarily join the union instead of free-riding off of the union's collective bargaining and job protection efforts. The Freedom Foundation identified plaintiffs who would sue the state to revoke this requirement (Nelson 2017).

In a separate case, the Freedom Foundation sued Washington State to determine the time and location of voluntary union orientation meetings and has begun showing up to those meetings to hand out competing information to workers about why workers should not join the union (Olson 2017; Hayward 2017). And, of course, the most significant follow-up litigation to *Harris* came in the form of the *Friedrichs v. California Teachers Association* (578 U.S. ___, 2016) and then *Janus v. American Federation of State, County, and Municipal Employees, Council 31, et al.* (585 U.S. ___, 2018), which called for an end to agency fees for all public-sector workers. Although the Court deadlocked over *Friedrichs* after the unexpected death of Justice Antonin Scalia in 2016, it ended agency fees using the same logic Justice Alito had laid out in *Harris* in its 2018 *Janus* decision. (The next step laid out for conservative opponents of public-sector unions in *Janus* is to sue unions for agency fees they have charged in the past, which would effectively bankrupt many unions; Scheiber 2018.)

The lesson from conservative networks' advocacy against public union agency fees leading up to and following the *Harris* decision is that it is insufficient for policy feedback activists to focus exclusively on one or two institutional venues alone. Instead, successful policy feedback strategies need to consider the full array of potential tactics that could yield a favorable outcome—and how those tactics can be sequenced in ways that build on one another. In the case of agency fees, the *Harris* decision opened the way for state-based organizing and litigation that could further retrench the power of public unions, even within a Democratically controlled liberal stronghold like Washington State. Separately, however, conservative activists pursued litigation through *Friedrichs* and *Janus* (and now with the agency fee recoupment cases) that would further deal significant blows to unions all across the country.

Lesson 3: Organizing to Connect Feedback Processes to the Mass Public

Aside from emphasizing how durable policy change that reshapes politics requires shifting between institutional venues, the case of public-sector agency fees also underscores how feedback processes are not automatic and require continued investment in political organization and mobilization to register effects, especially in the mass public. As Daniel Galvin and Chloe Thurston explain, "policies do not always, or even very often, generate their own political supports" and instead require active organization to ensure that the feedback loops are closed (Galvin and Thurston 2017, 334).

This is particularly likely to be true when considering feedback effects involving the mass public. For such effects to reverberate throughout the political system, individuals need to perceive a policy's benefits and how their own lives are affected by the policy (Arnold 1990; Mettler 2011). Individual citizens are less likely to be closely monitoring the political landscape for these details than are organized interest groups whose main work involves lobbying or political advocacy, and so these mass-level feedback effects are especially likely to require organizational drives that help citizens to make the necessary links to complete feedback loops.

Anti-union conservative activists recognized these limitations of mass feedback effects, and instead of ending their work with the 2014 court victory in *Harris*, they took to the public, literally going door to door as we saw to help home care workers to understand the implications of the decision and how those workers could opt out of paying dues to their unions while still benefiting from their union's collective bargaining agreements and job protections. This canvassing and mobilization thus closed the feedback loop, weakening unions and Democratic politics more broadly by helping workers to take advantage of their newly obtained opt-out rights.

Beyond the specific case of home health aides, conservative activists have taken a similar approach in right-to-work states with the National Employee Freedom Week initiative. The annual event, cosponsored by AFP, ALEC, and many individual SPN affiliates, involves "a national effort to inform union employees about the freedoms they have to opt out of union membership and let them make the decision that's best for them"[3] Affiliated organizations pledge to reach out to workers with information on how much money they could be saving if they stopped paying union dues while still benefiting from union-negotiated provisions (as is permissible in right-to-work states), including the necessary paperwork that workers can print out and mail to their union to sever their memberships.

Perhaps the most ambitious drive, however, has unfolded in the wake of the *Janus* decision, which SPN has billed as "the opportunity of a lifetime" to defund the public-sector labor movement. "Imagine tens, even hundreds, of millions of dollars currently used to push damaging left-wing causes and candidates vanishing," the Freedom Foundation described in a donor proposal about the upcoming *Janus* opt-out campaigns that they had planned (Brooks 2018). One journalist reported that the Freedom Foundation had trained eighty canvassers to start knocking on the doors of public-sector workers in California, Oregon, and Washington to convince those workers to opt out of their unions (Eidelson 2018). The Freedom Foundation's ambitious goal was to shrink membership rolls in those three states by 127,000 members, and it had been planning for the *Janus* decision for months by acquiring lists of public employees and conducting grassroots activist trainings. SPN affiliates in Illinois, Michigan, Ohio, and Pennsylvania are leading large-scale targeted opt-out campaigns with the support of the national network as well (Brooks 2018).

In sum, activists seeking to entrench their own policy feedback effects would be wise to draw from this experience and not simply assume that a legislative or judicial victory signifies the end of a political battle (see also Patashnik 2008, Patashnik and Zelizer 2013). For policy changes to register effects, especially in the mass public, activists have to stay on the ground to show citizens how those policies affect their lives and connect the policies to concrete political actions.

Lesson 4: Adapting Reforms to Varying State Political Contexts

The final lesson that policy feedback scholars and activists can learn from conservative offensives against unions involves taking advantage of varying political contexts to achieve the same policy objective in multiple states at once. Despite that conservative networks are seeking the same objective of weaker unions, especially in the public sector, not all groups pursue the same policies in service of that goal. As the SPN has summarized in a "tool kit" for its affiliates, advocates of "responsible, limited government reforms" need to select "the best reform based on [their] state's political and cultural environment," stressing that "SPN's extensive research on successful and unsuccessful union reforms nationwide shows that the only way to curb union influence is through systematic reform efforts targeting multiple states. Success does not hinge on a single reform tactic" (Bragdon, n.d.).

To that end, SPN called for activists to pursue union recertification requirements (like those passed in Iowa and Wisconsin) in states that have "legislative majorities and executive branches that support union reform," opt-out campaigns in right-to-work states for private-sector workers (and before *Janus*, public-sector workers) in states where conservatives lacked full control of the legislature and the governorship but where state laws permit SPN affiliates to request lists of public employees and union members through public record laws, and right-to-work laws in states where conservatives enjoyed veto-proof majorities in the legislature and a strong ally in the executive.

In other writing, SPN and ALEC have also emphasized how smaller reforms can pave the way for larger ones within the same state. Measures to cut back the power of public labor unions, for instance, can then make it easier to pass other reforms to the private sector, as the case of Wisconsin exemplifies well. This logic also extends to nonlabor legislation, too; weaker unions can then make it easier to pass other "free-market reforms," as SPN has explained to its allies. The case of Iowa is relevant here: after retrenching public-sector union collective bargaining and organizing rights, the GOP-controlled state government was able to pursue a number of cuts to other labor market regulations and social programs, including preempting local-level minimum wage increases.

By tailoring their ambitions to the local political climate, SPN was able to rack up additional wins that they would not have achieved pushing for all-or-nothing proposals. That is important for narrower concerns of organizational maintenance for conservative advocacy groups because it provides concrete evidence to donors and supporters of victories even in states under full Democratic control in government. And these incremental victories slowly chipped away at the power of organized labor across the country as a whole, too. That is because unions, and especially public unions, transfer revenue from "blue" states with stronger memberships to "red" states with weaker members. On average, for instance, around 20 percent of the budgets of state National Education Association affiliates in right-to-work states comes from transfers from wealthier unions in non-right-to-work states. Cuts to the budgets of those wealthier unions because of membership declines thus reduce the possibilities of redistribution to boost the power of unions in less favorable political climates.

All told, scholars of feedback effects ought to take away the lesson that reformers do not need to pass the same legislation in all states to achieve the same objective. Instead, reformers should focus on figuring out what policies are viable in different contexts that can produce political gains within and across the states—and make other policy objectives more viable.

Understanding Feedback Effects in the Fragmented American Polity

As this article has made clear, conservatives have built up a strategy for using policy feedbacks to durably disadvantage unions—and Democrats—over many decades. This strategy is bound up in the increasingly polarized Republican Party, with conservative activists coming to view policy as means of reshaping power and dismantling their opponents (cf. Fishkin and Pozen 2018; Mann and Ornstein 2012). These feedbacks have been quite successful, weakening labor unions' political clout, with knock-on implications for the ability of Democrats to win and hold elected office and for the fate of other liberal policy priorities. But beyond helping us to understand why conservatives have managed to have so much success capturing control of state government in recent years, this analysis has also illuminated deeper theoretical features of policy feedback effects relevant for scholars of public policy and political reformers from across the ideological spectrum.

A close study of conservative labor policy victories shows how it is not enough to simply enact policies and expect to reap political dividends, as those policies change the preferences and resources of key interest groups and the mass public. Instead, in the fragmented American polity—with political power spread across different institutional arenas and decentralized among the federal, state, and local levels—political reformers need to think carefully about their control of state-level governments, tailoring their policy proposals to the unique political contexts in each state. Moreover, reformers are most likely to be successful when they are able to use the overlapping venues of policymaking to their advantage, leveraging victories in one venue (say, the courts) to build power in others (say, state legislatures). And political activists need to close the feedback loops by organizing on the ground to ensure that the *effects* of policy are registered by the mass public. Together, these lessons can help scholars of public policy to understand why we see feedback processes succeed in some areas and not others—and might also inform efforts to rebuild labor union clout in the years and decades to come in response to conservative victories.

Notes

1. Author's record of Democracy Alliance program.

2. This followed a narrower 2012 Supreme Court decision in *Knox v. Service Employees International Union* (567 U.S. 298), which ruled that public-sector unions needed to obtain affirmative consent from workers to collect special assessments. Justice Alito crucially laid the groundwork for a First Amendment challenge to public-sector agency fees more generally in this decision that litigants would pursue in *Harris* and then *Janus*.

3. "National Employee Freedom Week," available from https://web.archive.org/web/201712310 15745/http://employeefreedomweek.com.

References

Ahlquist, John S. 2017. Labor unions, political representation, and economic inequality. *Annual Review of Political Science* 20:409–32.

Ahlquist, John S., and Margaret Levi. 2013. *In the interest of others: Organizations and social activism.* Princeton, NJ: Princeton University Press.

Anzia, Sarah F., and Terry M. Moe. 2016. Do politicians use policy to make politics? The case of public-sector labor laws. *American Political Science Review* 110 (4): 763–77.

Arnold, R. Douglas. 1990. *The logic of congressional action*. New Haven, CT: Yale University Press.

Bentele, Keith G., and Erin E. O'Brien. 2013. Jim Crow 2.0? Why states consider and adopt restrictive voter access policies. *Perspectives on Politics* 11 (4): 1088–1116.

Bragdon, Trevor. n.d. *State workplace freedom toolkit*. Arlington, VA: State Policy Network.

Brooks, Chris. 2 July 2018. How corporations plan to use Janus to turn workers against their own unions. *In These Times*.

Brunelli, Sam. 1990. *State legislatures: The next conservative battleground*. Washington, DC: The Heritage Foundation.

Dark, Taylor. 1999. *The unions and the Democrats: An enduring alliance*. Ithaca, NY: Cornell University Press.

Dwyer, Paula. 21 August 2018. Trump's war against blue states. *Bloomberg*.

Eidelson, Josh. 27 June 2018. Koch brothers-linked group declares new war on unions. *Bloomberg*.

Feigenbaum, James, Alexander Hertel-Fernandez, and Vanessa Williamson. 2018. From the bargaining table to the ballot box: Political effects of right to work laws. National Bureau of Economic Research Working Paper No. 24259, Cambridge, MA.

Fishkin, Joseph, and David E. Pozen. 2018. Asymmetric constitutional hardball. *Columbia Law Review* 118 (3): 915–82.

Flavin, Patrick, and Michael T. Hartney. 2015. When government subsidizes its own: Collective bargaining laws as agents of political mobilization. *American Journal of Political Science* 59 (4): 896–911.

Freedom Foundation. 2015. Freedom Foundation launches cable TV ad featuring homecare worker who opted out of SEIU. Freedom Foundation. Available from https://www.freedomfoundation.com/press-release/freedom-foundation-launches-cable-tv-ad-featuring-homecare-worker-who-opted-out-of-seiu/.

Galvin, Daniel J. 2016. Deterring wage theft: Alt-labor, state politics, and the policy determinants of minimum wage compliance. *Perspectives on Politics* 14 (2): 324–50.

Galvin, Daniel J., and Chloe N. Thurston. 2017. The Democrats' misplaced faith in policy feedback. *The Forum* 15 (2): 333–43.

Gilens, Martin. 2012. *Affluence and influence: Economic inequality and political power in America*. Princeton, NJ: Princeton University Press.

Greenhouse, Steven. 10 March 2016. The door-to-door union killers: Rightwing foundation takes labor fight to the streets. *The Guardian*.

Grumbach, Jake M. 2018. From backwaters to major policymakers: Policy polarization in the states, 1970–2014. *Perspectives on Politics* 16 (2): 416–35.

Hacker, Jacob S., and Paul Pierson. 2005. *Off center: The Republican revolution and the erosion of American democracy*. New Haven, CT: Yale University Press.

Hartney, Michael T. 2014. Turning out teachers: The causes and consequences of teacher political activism in the postwar United States. Doctoral disseration, University of Notre Dame, South Bend, IN.

Hayward, Matthew. 2017. We are taking the message of freedom to the front line. Freedom Foundation. Available from https://www.freedomfoundation.com/labor/we-are-taking-the-message-of-freedom-to-the-front-line/.

Hertel-Fernandez, Alexander. 2019. *State capture: How conservative activists, big businesses, and wealthy donors reshaped the American states – and the nation*. New York, NY: Oxford University Press.

Jacobs, Alan M., and R. Kent Weaver. 2015. When policies undo themselves: Self-undermining feedback as a source of policy change. *Governance* 28 (4): 441–57.

Kabaservice, Geoffrey. 2012. *Rule and ruin: The downfall of moderation and the destruction of the Republican Party, from Eisenhower to the Tea Party*. New York, NY: Oxford University Press.

Kim, Sung Eun, and Yotam Margalit. 2017. Informed preferences? The impact of unions on workers' policy views. *American Journal of Political Science* 61 (3): 728–43.

Leighley, Jan E., and Jonathan Nagler. 2007. Unions, voter turnout, and class bias in the U.S. electorate, 1964–2004. *Journal of Politics* 69 (2): 430–41.

Mann, Thomas E., and Norman J. Ornstein. 2012. *It's even worse than it looks: How the American constitutional system collided with the new politics of extremism*. New York, NY: Basic Books.

McCarty, Nolan, Keith T. Poole, and Howard Rosenthal. 2006. *Polarized America: The dance of ideology and unequal riches*. Cambridge, MA: MIT Press.

Mettler, Suzanne. 2011. *The submerged state: How invisible government policies undermine American democracy*. Chicago, IL: University of Chicago Press.

Meyerson, Harold. 20 February 2010. Under Obama, labor should have made more progress. *The Washington Post*.

Nelson, Maxford. 2017. DSHS aiding SEIU misinformation of home care workers. Freedom Foundation. Available from https://www.freedomfoundation.com/labor/dshs-aiding-seiu-misinformation-of-home-care-workers/.

Olson, Stephanie. 2017. DSHS violated public records act to aid its union friends. Freedom Foundation. Available from https://www.freedomfoundation.com/litigation/dshs-violated-public-records-act-to-aid-its-union-friends/.

Patashnik, Eric. 2008. *Reforms at risk: What happens after major policy changes are enacted*. Princeton, NJ: Princeton University Press.

Patashnik, Eric, and Julian E. Zelizer. 2013. The struggle to remake politics: Liberal reform and the limits of policy feedback in the contemporary American state. *Perspectives on Politics* 11 (4): 1071–87.

Peirce, Neal R., and Robert Guskind. 13 October 1984. The new Right takes its political show on the road to win power in the states. *The National Journal*.

Pierson, Paul. 1993. Review: When effect becomes cause: Policy feedback and political change. *World Politics* 45 (4): 595–628.

Pilkington, Ed. 15 May 2018. Exclusive: How rightwing groups wield secret "toolkit" to plot against U.S. unions. *The Guardian*.

Rolf, David. 2016. *The fight for fifteen: The right wage for a working America*. New York, NY: New Press.

Rosenblum, Jonathan. 2017. Fight for $15: Good wins, but where did the focus on organizing go? *Labor Studies Journal* 42 (4): 387–93.

Scheiber, Noam. 18 July 2018. Trump nominee is mastermind of anti-union legal campaign. *The New York Times*.

Schickler, Eric. 2016. *Racial realignment: The transformation of American liberalism, 1932–1965*. Princeton, NJ: Princeton University Press.

Schlozman, Daniel. 2015. *When movements anchor parties*. Princeton, NJ: Princeton University Press.

Schlozman, Daniel, and Sam Rosenfeld. 2018. The long new Right and the world it made. Paper prepared for the 2018 American Political Science Association meetings.

Skocpol, Theda, and Alexander Hertel-Fernandez. 2016. The Koch network and Republican Party extremism. *Perspectives on Politics* 14 (3): 681–99.

Verba, Sidney, Kay Lehman Schlozman, and Henry E. Brady. 1995. *Voice and equality: Civic voluntarism in American politics*. Cambridge, MA: Harvard University Press.

Vernuccio, F. Vincent. March/April 2013. Right-to-work in Michigan: The untold story. *Inside ALEC*, 21.

Prescriptions: Climate Change

A New Path for U.S. Climate Politics: Choosing Policies That Mobilize Business for Decarbonization

By
JONAS MECKLING

What policies could mobilize business support for progressive and durable national climate policy in the United States? I examine the climate policy experiences of U.S. states and propose that a national clean energy standard combined with carefully allocated public investment in clean energy infrastructure and innovation could mobilize economic interests in support of decarbonization. Further, I argue that the more entrenched clean energy and infrastructure become, the more likely it becomes that comprehensive climate policies can be passed in the future. This includes performance and deployment mandates beyond the electricity industry, including in the transport and building sectors. These initial steps may also help to build a winning coalition for progressive federal carbon pricing, as opposed to an accommodative coalition in support of weak carbon pricing.

Keywords: climate policy; carbon pricing; clean energy; business power; policy feedback

The challenge of climate policy has long been understood as one of internalizing negative externalities. In other words, we have viewed climate policy largely as the need to regulate the negative effects of fossil fuel production and consumption. Policy proposals have tended to focus on economically optimal solutions, centered on carbon pricing in the form of either carbon taxes or cap-and-trade systems. By and large, economists see these pricing instruments to be first-best policy options in terms of cost-effectiveness

Jonas Meckling is an assistant professor of energy and environmental policy at the University of California, Berkeley. His latest book is Carbon Coalitions: Business, Climate Politics, and the Rise of Emissions Trading *(MIT Press 2011). Previously, he served as senior advisor to the German Minister for the Environment.*

NOTE: I am grateful for comments by participants of the Policy Feedback Project Workshop at Harvard University and the Technology-Policy Feedback Workshop at ETH Zurich.

Correspondence: meckling@berkeley.edu

DOI: 10.1177/0002716219862515

(Fischer and Newell 2008), an approach that draws on the particular success of the U.S. sulfur dioxide trading program, which helped to address acid rain at low cost in the 1990s. Liberals and environmentalists have also broadly supported pricing as the main pillar of climate policy in the past.

Increasingly, however, the climate challenge has been recast as one of energy systems transformation—from a high-carbon to a low-carbon energy system (Geels et al. 2017). The particular attribute of energy systems is that they exhibit a high degree of positive reinforcement. "Carbon lock-in" refers to the inertia resulting from mutually reinforcing physical, economic, political, and social dynamics. Energy systems are particularly prone to lock-in and path dependency given their high capital costs, long capital turnover times, and interrelationships between socioeconomic and technical systems (Seto et al. 2016). Politically, lock-in of energy systems empowers incumbent actors, in particular fossil fuel indus-tries and energy-intensive manufacturing industries. As a result, policies that directly impose costs on fossil fuel industries and large energy consumers mobi-lize strong and sustained opposition to pricing initiatives (Ciplet, Roberts, and Khan 2015). From the perspective of system change, climate policy that only incentivizes process improvements within the existing energy system, like low-level carbon pricing, is unlikely to unleash political dynamics in favor of transfor-mation. "Unlocking" the fossil fuel energy system calls for policies that create economic winners and, thus, support reform coalitions and mitigate backlash from economic losers or weaken them. The history of climate policy offers some initial lessons on what kinds of policies can mobilize business support.

The reality of climate policy has proven to be one of broad climate policy mixes, rather than carbon pricing silver bullets. These policy mixes include regu-latory policies, such as carbon pricing systems and performance standards (e.g., fuel economy standards), alongside various distributive policies, such as subsidy schemes for clean energy technologies (Rogge and Reichardt 2016; Edmondson, Kern, and Rogge 2018). Carbon pricing includes carbon taxes and cap-and-trade systems, a policy that caps emissions and creates a market for tradable permits. These policy mixes have evolved over time: policies that provide benefits to clean energy companies and households emerged before policies were adopted that impose costs on polluters (Meckling, Sterner, and Wagner 2017; Pahle et al. 2018). For example, California adopted its first renewable portfolio standard, a policy that requires utilities to provide a certain share of their electricity from renewable sources, in 2002. In this early phase, the state also adopted renewable energy subsidies (Meckling and Jenner 2016). California only introduced a cap-and-trade system, which put a price on greenhouse gas (GHG) emissions, in 2013.

Clean energy policies have proliferated much more widely than carbon pricing policies, although economists consider them second best in terms of cost-effectiveness (Fischer and Newell 2008). Such policy often entails a portfolio of different targeted instruments, including support for research and development, deployment subsidies, tax rebates, loan guarantees, and deployment mandates for renewable energy. In the electricity sector, at least 132 countries and subna-tional jurisdictions, such as states and provinces, had enacted either a feed-in tariff or a renewable portfolio standard by 2014. In the United States, twenty-nine states have adopted a renewable or alternative energy portfolio standard.

Carbon-pricing policy has been spreading globally since 2003, when the EU Emission Trading System was adopted. In total, fifty-one carbon-pricing systems have been implemented or are scheduled for implementation, making it much less prevalent than clean energy policies. Prices have remained very low, significantly below the level needed to achieve emission reduction commitments under the Paris Agreement (World Bank 2018). In the United States, only twelve states have adopted carbon pricing, and, with the exception of California's, those state policies only cover the electricity sector.

In the electricity sector, clean energy incentives and mandates preceded the introduction of carbon pricing in two-thirds of all jurisdictions with carbon pricing. Similarly, in the transport sector, clean energy policies preceded carbon pricing in 58 percent of all cases (Meckling, Sterner, and Wagner 2017).[1]

The history of climate policy thus reveals a trade-off between political feasibility and cost-effectiveness. The cost-effective policy solutions favored by economists and environmentalists alike only get adopted at later stages and often with low stringency. Actual climate policy has evolved as a policy mix, in which clean energy policies have proliferated more widely and often preceded regulatory policy such as carbon pricing. Carbon pricing systems increasingly serve as an insurance policy for emission reductions achieved with various targeted clean energy policies (Burtraw 2016). They prevent backsliding of policy progress by avoiding increases in GHG emissions. But clean energy policies are the main driver of emission reductions.

Policy-makers face two primary challenges in building long-term political support for climate policy: developing policy that expands economic opportunities for decarbonization and, thus, creates supportive coalitions—across firms, workers, and citizens—and formulating policy that mitigates potential backlash from economic losers or weakens incumbent industries.

Climate policy, thus, first needs to help grow political interests and coalitions in favor of developing a low-carbon energy system. If policy can create opportunities for incumbent actors to invest in clean energy, it can mobilize well-organized and powerful interests. As firms invest in clean energy infrastructure, feedback dynamics can emerge around a low-carbon energy system (C. Roberts et al. 2018). This resembles the dynamics observed in social policy, in which voters who receive benefits get vested in the future success of the policy in question. A classic case is how the provision of Social Security mobilizes senior citizens to vote (Campbell 2002). Climate policy, however, also differs from social policy (C. Roberts et al. 2018). For instance, government support for low-carbon technologies is meant to be temporary. As the cost of low-carbon technologies drops, government support needs to be retrenched. Policy feedback is thus a double-edged sword: it helps to expand the ambition and the scope of policy, but it can also result in rent-seeking of clean energy companies that may actually not facilitate continuous emission reductions.

Climate policy also needs to address the direct and indirect costs it creates for various groups to avoid or limit backlash. Renewable energy subsidies, for example, impose direct costs on taxpayers or rate payers. Renewable energy policies also create indirect costs for fossil fuel industries as these lose market share or for homeowners who experience a loss of property value as a result of, for instance, a wind power plant. As these costs mount, political pushback by those bearing the costs is likely to grow. This suggests a growing need to focus on cost containment in mature policy mixes—next to providing benefits to constituencies—to avoid political backlash. It also suggests strategies to mitigate unavoidable backlash by compensating or weakening the opposition.

Mobilizing Business Support through Policy Design

The ability of climate policies to grow support depends on the benefits they offer to political groups, including business and voters. Throughout the history of climate politics, business has proven particularly influential in shaping policy outcomes in the United States and internationally (Falkner 2008; Layzer 2012). This section focuses on how policies can create and expand business support for climate policy, with some discussion of benefits for households.

Two attributes of climate policies affect their ability to mobilize durable political support: the extent of benefits they generate and the types of investments they trigger. The more concentrated, visible, and sustained the benefits are, the more likely companies and voters will be to support the policy over time. The more concentrated the costs are, the more likely they will be to oppose the policy. In addition, policies vary in terms of the capital investment that they incentivize, resulting in different levels of "stickiness" of business support. Various climate policy designs perform differently on these two criteria.

Carbon pricing policy tends to impose concentrated costs on the powerful few—well-organized firms—and to provide diffuse benefits in the form of climate mitigation to the weak many, that is, the broader public (see Table 1, lower left). This has consistently mobilized strong opposition from incumbent energy firms against ambitious carbon pricing. In some cases, fossil fuel industries supported weak forms of carbon pricing as a form of political accommodation (Meckling 2011; Ball 2018). More recently, the design of some cap-and-trade systems has evolved to include the auctioning of emission allowances and to use the revenues to support clean energy investments. This is a promising avenue to combine regulatory and distributive policy, shifting the distributional implications from concentrated costs and diffuse benefits to one of concentrated costs for polluters and concentrated benefits for clean energy companies (see Table 1, upper left). This improves the political feasibility and durability of the instrument compared to cap-and-trade systems without redistribution (Rabe 2016).

The main advantage of cap-and-trade lies in incentivizing least-cost adjustments to achieve emission reductions. This often entails changes to the production process, such as fuel switching from coal to gas, rather than investments in clean energy technology infrastructure. As such, carbon pricing—in particular with low emission caps—does not lead to sticky political interests. For example,

TABLE 1
The Distributional Effects of Climate Policies

		Costs	
		Concentrated	Diffuse
Benefits	Concentrated	Carbon pricing with redistribution (auction revenues for clean energy investments)	Clean energy policies (feed-in tariff, tax credits + clean energy standard)
	Diffuse	Carbon pricing without redistribution (cap-and-trade with grandfathering)	

the EU's cap-and-trade system mobilized London's financial community to support the policy and to enter the carbon market business. The financial services industry created its own lobbying group, which supported stringent emission caps alongside environmental groups (Meckling 2011). Yet when the emissions market slumped due to overallocation, these firms quickly scrapped their carbon business and exited the business. Their capital investment had been relatively low. Both of these characteristics of carbon pricing—the lack of concentrated benefits for business and the lack of incentives for high, long-term capital investments—limit the potential for policy feedback in carbon pricing.

Clean energy policies, mostly subsidies and tax credits, tend to provide concentrated benefits for clean energy companies, while imposing diffuse costs on taxpayers or rate payers (Table 1, upper right). This has made them highly politically salient, resulting in desired policy feedback dynamics in a number of instances (Aklin and Urpelainen 2013; Laird and Stefes 2009). In particular, clean energy subsidies, such as the feed-in tariff, mobilize strong constituencies (Bayer and Urpelainen 2016). A feed-in tariff provides a long-term subsidy for renewable electricity generation. While the feed-in tariff is the dominant electricity-related clean energy policy employed outside of the United States, tax credits in combination with renewable portfolio standards are the dominant policy approach in the United States. While critics have been concerned that green subsidies would lead to perpetual rent-seeking by clean energy industries, governments in Europe and the United States have, in fact, proven to be able to reduce subsidies as technology costs decline. The German government, for instance, moved from a fixed feed-in tariff to auctioning. In the same vein, the U.S. federal solar tax credit is set to expire for household installations in 2022.

Clean energy policies create sticky interests by incentivizing multidecade investments in clean energy infrastructure, such as solar and wind farms or electric vehicle infrastructure. This is particularly the case if they are targeted and send direct, high-leverage policy signals rather than broad and shallow ones (Meckling et al. 2015). Companies will be interested in maintaining government support given the long payoff times for energy infrastructure investments, making them more likely to lobby for policy support than to exit the market. Renewable portfolio standards in U.S. states—combined with federal tax credits—have resulted in policy feedback by growing business constituencies under certain conditions (Stokes 2015). As they invest in renewable energy technologies, clean energy industries can emerge as supporters of renewable energy policy specifically but also broader emission reduction goals more generally (Biber 2013). Renewable portfolio standards can be combined with net metering policies that allow households to reduce their electricity bills by feeding self-produced solar power into the grid. Campaigns to repeal state-level renewable portfolio standards have failed in a number of cases given the entrenched interests of clean energy industries and voters (Stokes 2015).

A National Clean Energy Standard and Infrastructure Investment

In this section, I propose that federal policy follow the path of state-level climate policy by first strengthening clean energy policies—subsidies combined with technology mandates—before advancing carbon pricing. I suggest a national clean energy standard—as opposed to a renewable portfolio standard—and increased public investment in energy infrastructure and spending that addresses systemic challenges of energy system transformation. The national debate on a Green New Deal engages with versions of these policies, as federal climate politics in the United States is undergoing a shift. For decades, the national policy debate was focused on carbon pricing. Now, it shows greater openness to a variety of instruments. Here, I focus on how to design these policies to strategically mobilize business in support of decarbonization.

A national clean energy standard

Growing clean energy interests in the electricity sector and beyond is central to reconfiguring the interest group politics of climate change (Schmidt and Sewerin 2017). Clean energy policies at the state level have partially achieved this. Renewable portfolio standards have been the most widely adopted state-level climate policy, though standards vary significantly in ambition levels and several portfolio standards are at risk of retrenchment or stagnation (Stokes 2015). About two-fifths of U.S. states do not yet have a deployment standard. Also, total clean energy investment in the United States has largely been stagnant since 2015 (Bloomberg New Energy Finance 2018). Scaling up state-level clean energy policies through a national standard and expanding the scope of eligible technologies holds promise to grow and broaden business coalitions for climate policy. Different versions of a national clean energy standard have been introduced in Congress since 2002 (Bochner 2014). Since these earlier attempts, three factors, in particular, have changed. First, the renewable energy lobby, including technology providers and project developers, has grown significantly in the wake of state-level renewable energy policy implementation. Some Republican-led states such as Arizona and Texas now have significant clean energy interests. Second, the cost of solar and wind power has plummeted, being or becoming cost-competitive with coal and gas in a number of U.S. states. And third, the majority of voters has come to support renewable portfolio standards, though this depends on framing and policy design (Stokes and Warshaw 2017).

A national clean energy standard could differ from existing state-level renewable portfolio standards by turning it from a "renewable energy" to a "low-carbon" standard. This could bring a number of technologies, such as nuclear energy, carbon capture and storage, biomass, and waste-to-energy, under the standard. Proposals for a national clean energy standard have been made in the past and again recently as of this writing (Aldy 2011; Gillis and McBride 2018; Cleary, Palmer, and Rennert 2019). The advantage would be threefold. First, both types of technologies are increasingly seen as essential to reducing emissions in the United States. Second, it could potentially mitigate the opposition of powerful business lobbies, particularly the coal and gas industries and electric utilities. Third, allowing for a large set of lower-carbon technologies would mobilize a broad alliance of energy industry interests for a national clean energy standard, possibly avoiding some political battles within clean energy interests (D. Roberts 2019).

For example, nuclear energy is, at 20 percent of annual electricity generation, the largest source of low-carbon power in the United States (U.S. Energy Information Administration 2019). At the same time, nuclear plants are increasingly losing the competition with natural gas. Since 2013, five nuclear plants have closed and others are at risk of closure (Fitzpatrick et al. 2018). A clean energy standard that includes nuclear energy could help to extend the lifespan of existing nuclear plants. This may play an important role in containing the continued expansion of gas infrastructure. Gas power plants and gas pipelines are highly capital-intensive investments, with a lifetime of multiple decades. Such investments thus create sticky interests, which may present political barriers to deeper emission reductions in the medium to long term.

The Intergovernmental Panel on Climate Change (IPCC) expects that any pathway to emission reductions that would prevent catastrophic climate change requires the removal of carbon dioxide from the atmosphere (IPCC 2014). The 2018 IPCC report "Global Warming of 1.5°C" has brought the need for negative emission technologies, technologies that extract carbon dioxide from the atmosphere, to the fore. A core technology is likely to be carbon capture and storage (CCS). For decades, CCS was not deployed widely and remained locked in high costs. In February 2018, Congress significantly expanded a tax credit for CCS. This has been seen as a boon for an aging oil industry, which deploys CCS for enhanced oil recovery.[2] A national clean energy standard that considers coal-fired electricity generation combined with CCS as eligible could potentially help to integrate CCS into a reformist climate agenda. Environmentalists are wary of extending the lifeline of the oil and gas industry. Yet the deployment of CCS depends on the infrastructure of that very industry (Buck 2018). In addition, building on existing business models, such as enhanced oil recovery, allows policy-makers to scale up the deployment of CCS to begin to drive down the cost of the technology, which to date has been prohibitive.

A broad national clean energy standard would promote low-carbon interests among business. Yet the experience of state-level renewable energy policies shows that broadening the low-carbon coalition beyond business to voters matters. It remains to be explored how this could be done best. Infrastructure spending, as discussed below, could help with it. But a national clean energy standard could also be designed to ensure that some benefits go directly to households by, for instance, including some form of household payments for solar. These would provide incentives for households to generate their own solar-powered electricity. Such benefits have shown to mobilize Republican voters who were attracted by libertarian ideas on energy choice (Stokes 2015). Georgia's Green Tea Alliance between the Tea Party and the Sierra Club is such an example. A major recent opinion poll shows that net-metering is popular with voters across the ideological spectrum: even among "very conservative" voters, 62 percent support net-metering (Simon and Mills 2017). It remains to be explored what federal policy-makers could do to support household payments for solar. A net-metering carve-out provision in a national clean energy standard could possibly be one option, but such a measure would have to be weighed against flexibility criteria. At a basic level, policy-makers could frame a national clean energy standard as an opportunity to develop household solar policies that afford consumer choice on energy.

Investment in infrastructure and innovation

The growth of renewable energy in U.S. states is the result of deployment mandates and subsidies. Public spending on clean energy infrastructure remains in many cases central to making clean energy technologies competitive with fossil fuels. It easily mobilizes investors as a political constituency, including both firms and households. These effects can be long-lasting given the multidecade life of energy infrastructure investments. It can also mobilize workers, depending on the magnitude and durability of the employment effects of investments. In the short term, this calls for an extension of existing subsidies, including the Investment Tax Credit, the Production Tax Credit, and federal tax credits for electric vehicles. It also makes the case for broader long-term public government investment to advance low-carbon technological change across sectors to reconfigure economic interests in favor of decarbonization. Yet designing an infrastructure and innovation package that is both politically and environmentally effective is a grand challenge.

Allocating funds of a public investment package in energy infrastructure also requires critical political decisions. Three political aspects, in particular, may be important for government investment to have positive feedback that enables more progressive climate policy at a later stage: mobilizing new industry players, allying with labor, and geographic distribution. Old industries—including utilities, oil and gas, auto companies, and heavy industries—hold significant political power and need to be mobilized to invest in low-carbon technologies to broaden the alliance for decarbonization. In some cases, old industries need to be weakened. In other cases, old industries have important industrial and technological capabilities that can be leveraged for a low-carbon development path. An infrastructure package also raises the question of how to mobilize labor unions that often have members across dirty and clean energy industries. An important component to engage labor will likely be a strong workforce development component to allow workers in polluting industries to transition into emerging sectors. Finally, infrastructure investment can help to reshape interests in laggard states on clean energy technology deployment. For the long-term viability and effectiveness of federal climate policy, it may be critical to carefully channel visible projects to laggard states.

Our understanding of how to design long-term public investment programs to achieve political feedback is limited. Yet recent history offers a major case study in the 2009 American Recovery and Reinvestment Act (ARRA), which provided $90 billion for energy projects (Carley 2016). While a renewed infrastructure investment program would need to have a longer lifetime and greater scope than ARRA, there are important lessons to be learned from how the stimulus package succeeded or failed in mobilizing green constituencies in the energy sector. This includes the distribution of types of projects and the exploration of what types of financial instruments could best mobilize investment. In developing a public investment program, policy-makers and experts may want to conduct a detailed assessment of ARRA to inform funding decisions.

A public clean energy investment package could mobilize green constituencies but still fail to make a dent in GHG emissions. To be environmentally effective, government investment would need to focus on systems transformation—such as a flexible grid—to allow for deeper emission cuts and stimulate technological innovation in areas where GHG emissions are particularly hard to achieve, including heavy industries and negative-emission technologies. An expanded infrastructure package would need to address the systemic challenges of clean energy transitions. So far, state-level renewable energy policies have driven a wedge of renewable power into the U.S. electricity mix. To accommodate growing amounts of intermittent electricity, the United States needs to invest more in flexibility options, including grid expansion, electricity storage, and demand management (Mitchell 2016). In the transport sector, accelerating the deployment of electric vehicles depends on the expansion of charging infrastructure. To improve energy efficiency, investments in smart grids and efficient technologies are central (Carlock, Mangan, and McElwee 2018).

Public spending on deployment of clean energy technologies has relatively immediate effects on political mobilization. Spending on innovation in the form of public research, development, and demonstration (RD&D) funding is politically less salient in the short term but is likely to have important long-term political effects. Significantly expanding low-carbon RD&D is central to developing lower-cost technologies that will allow for deeper emission reductions in the mid- to long-term future (Cunliff 2018). Otherwise, rising costs could result in significant political backlash at a later stage. In addition, negative emission technologies, which the IPCC deems necessary for avoiding catastrophic climate change, need to be developed. The Information Technology & Innovation

Foundation, an innovation think tank, lays out six major research missions: advanced nuclear energy; long-duration grid storage; carbon-neutral fuels; carbon capture, utilization, and storage; carbon dioxide removal technology; and basic energy research. In addition, investment may target technological solutions in heavy industries, including cement, steel, and energy-intensive manufacturing, where emission reductions have proven particularly challenging.

Political Consequences and Future Policy Options

The policies proposed in this article promise the potential to mobilize business support that enables more ambitious federal climate policy in the future. The future policy options discussed here are not meant to be seen in a strict temporal sequence.

Expanding clean energy coalitions across U.S. states

A national clean energy standard combined with an infrastructure and innovation package has the potential of taking the story of U.S. states with progressively expanded renewable portfolio standards to the national level. In particular, it would help to shift the geography of low-carbon interest groups by developing green constituencies in states with weak or no state-level renewable portfolio standards. A critical question will be the extent to which these alliances are not just made up of new—and politically weak—clean energy firms but also incumbent firms. These can be established firms in other industries that expand into the production or installation of renewable energy technologies. It can also include utilities. Making CCS projects count toward compliance may mitigate the opposition of some electric utilities. In the medium to long term, this could develop positive spillovers into federal climate politics more broadly. As low-carbon interests grow and expand to veto states, they are likely to support more ambitious climate reduction goals and enable more stringent regulatory policy reforms. Given the breadth of interests among low-carbon electricity firms, particular attention needs to be paid to a broad national clean energy standard so that it does not lead to a fractured climate lobby.

Enabling regulatory mandates beyond electricity

The strength of clean energy coalitions varies significantly by sector. We have witnessed growing political support for clean energy in the electricity sector, in the wake of the growth of renewable energy. This may make the adoption of a national clean energy standard possible in the next few years. In other sectors, including transport, the reconfiguration of economic interests is at an earlier stage. Yet as public investment in, for example, clean energy transport systems such as charging infrastructure expands the alliance of firms, workers, and households vested in a low-carbon transport future, sufficient political support may materialize for stronger regulatory reforms, including the passage of performance and deployment mandates. For example, U.S. federal policy could follow the example of some U.S. states by adopting a zero-emission vehicle standard. Already today the Trump administration's pushback on fuel economy standards has led to protests by automakers that have started investing in low-carbon future options. Similarly, stringent efficiency standards for the building sector, such as a net-zero building energy standard, may be politically possible in the wake of a targeted investment program for building efficiency. Both performance and deployment mandates create and expand market opportunities, while also closing down markets for dirty technologies. They thus have the potential to not only strengthen firms invested in clean energy but also to divide and weaken incumbents invested in fossil fuel technologies. Lobbies in the fossil fuel, transportation, and utility sectors remain a much more well-resourced force than renewable energy firms, making a case for policy strategies that divide the opposition (Brulle 2018). For example, the Environmental Protection Agency's mercury rule of 2011 closed down the construction of new coal plants, weakening the coal industry and dividing the coal and gas lobbies.

Enabling carbon pricing as an insurance policy

As the cost of public investment in clean energy grows and clean energy technology costs decline, political pressure to reduce subsidies is likely to mount. Much depends on how visible the costs are. This could present a challenge to policy stability if technology costs have not yet dropped sufficiently and clean energy interests are not yet strong enough. It could, however, also offer a political opportunity to add more efficient pricing policies to the climate policy mix.

Clean technology firms are likely to begin to support carbon pricing, as subsidies become politically unsustainable. For example, in Germany, carbon pricing did not have much of a constituency for the longest time. It was largely tolerated as a policy imposed by the European Commission. Yet as the cost of the feed-in tariff, the linchpin of the country's clean energy policy, has grown and led to consumer backlash and cutbacks of government subsidies, the national renewable energy association has begun to support carbon pricing. This suggests that carbon pricing coalitions at a later stage in climate policy development may be made up of interests that align with stringent and effective climate policy. Instead, carbon pricing alliances at an earlier stage of climate policy development are often polluting industries that seek minimal policy intervention.

In current U.S. climate politics, accommodative and progressive carbon pricing coalitions are competing to set the agenda. The oil industry–backed Climate Leadership Council suggests a less stringent pricing scheme that is tied to regulatory rollback. Its proposal was developed by former Republican Secretaries of State James Baker and George Shultz. It aims to eliminate several of the complementary measures that have helped clean energy industries to emerge and are central to an effective climate policy mix, though it has not yet decided on the full extent of rollback (Lavelle 2019; Kaufman 2018). The Energy Innovation and

Carbon Dividend Act sponsored by Representatives Ted Deutch (D-FL) and Francis Roones (R-FL) is more ambitious and does not aim at regulatory rollback of, for instance, state-level renewable energy policies. The grassroots group Citizens' Climate Lobby is its primary supporter, while industry support seems largely absent. This coalitional landscape suggests that at this point no broad alliance that includes core economic interests exists for progressive carbon pricing in the United States. The time for carbon pricing is right when a winning coalition emerges that seeks progressive carbon pricing in addition to complementary policies.

In this scenario, carbon pricing would be an insurance policy, complementing a range of sectoral investments and mandates, not a substitute for all other climate policies. Carbon pricing would ensure that emissions do not increase again and introduce more efficient pricing signals to help reduce the cost of mitigation. Experience with state-level carbon pricing suggests that a policy with some form of redistribution of revenues to households and/or clean energy industries may exhibit the greatest political salience (Klenert et al. 2018; Rabe 2016; Skocpol 2013).

Conclusion

Addressing climate change requires policy expansion and reform over decades. This article suggests policy-makers view climate policy development as progressive coalition-building, in particular with powerful economic interests. Drawing on the path taken by U.S. states, I argue that a national clean energy standard and public investment in infrastructure and innovation may mobilize business support. They could pave the path toward regulatory reforms such as deployment and performance mandates and carbon pricing in future rounds of policymaking. This proposal thus resonates with ongoing debates on a Green New Deal, while highlighting the importance of policy design for the sustained mobilization of business for climate policy.

Notes

1. Only a few countries have started officially to price carbon emitted from transport fuel use, the majority of which are Scandinavian countries that did so in the early 1990s.

2. Enhanced oil recovery, or EOR, is a technology that involves injecting carbon dioxide into aging oil wells to produce more oil.

References

Aklin, Michael, and Johannes Urpelainen. 2013. Political competition, path dependence, and the strategy of sustainable energy transitions. *American Journal of Political Science* 57 (3): 643–58.

Aldy, Joseph. 2011. *Promoting clean energy in the American power sector*. Washington, DC: Hamilton Project, Brookings Institution.

Ball, Jeffrey. July/August 2018. Why carbon pricing isn't working. *Foreign Affairs*.

Bayer, Patrick, and Johannes Urpelainen. 2016. It is all about political incentives: Democracy and the renewable feed-in tariff. *Journal of Politics* 78 (2): 603–19.

Biber, Eric. 2013. Cultivating a green political landscape. *Vanderbilt Law Review* 66 (2): 399–462.

Bloomberg New Energy Finance. 2018. *Clean energy investment trends, 2017*. London: Bloomberg New Energy Finance.

Bochner, Francesca F. 2014. Water, wind, and fire: A call for a federal renewable portfolio standard. *Duke Environmental Law & Policy Forum* 25:201–25.

Brulle, Robert J. 2018. The climate lobby: A sectoral analysis of lobbying spending on climate change in the USA, 2000 to 2016. *Climatic Change* 149 (3–4): 289–303.

Buck, Holly Jean. 24 July 2018. The need for carbon removal. *Jacobin*.

Burtraw, Dallas. 2016. The Supreme Court's CPP ruling: Likely a small impact on emissions. Available from https://www.resourcesmag.org/common-resources/the-supreme-court039s-cpp-ruling-likely-a-small-impact-on-emissions/.

Campbell, Andrea L. 2002. Self-interest, Social Security, and the distinctive particpation patterns of senior citizens. *American Political Science Review* 96:565–74.

Carley, Sanya. 2016. Energy programs of the American Recovery and Reinvestment Act of 2009. *Review of Policy Research* 33 (2): 201–23.

Carlock, Greg, Emily Mangan, and Sean McElwee. 2018. *A green new deal: A progressive vision for environmental sustainability and economic stability*. Washington, DC: Data for Progress.

Ciplet, David, J. Timmons Roberts, and Mizan R. Khan. 2015. *Power in a warming world*. Cambridge, MA: MIT Press.

Cleary, Kathryne, Karen Palmer, and Kevin Rennert. 2019. *Clean energy standards*. Washington, DC: Resources for the Future.

Cunliff, Colin. 2018. *An innovation agenda for deep decarbonization: Bridging gaps in the federal energy RD&D portfolio*. Washington, DC: Information Technology & Innovation Foundation.

Edmondson, Duncan L., Florian Kern, and Karoline S. Rogge. 2018. The co-evolution of policy mixes and socio-technical systems: Towards a conceptual framework of policy mix feedback in sustainability transitions. *Research Policy*. doi:10.1016/j.respol.2018.03.010.

Falkner, Robert. 2008. *Business power and conflict in international environmental politics*. Basingstoke: Palgrave Macmillan.

Fischer, Carolyn, and Richard G. Newell. 2008. Environmental and technology policies for climate mitigation. *Journal of Environmental Economics and Management* 55 (2): 142–62.

Fitzpatrick, Ryan, Jameson McBride, Jessica Lovering, Josh Freed, and Ted Nordhaus. 2018. *Clean energy standards: How more states can become climate leaders*. Washington, DC: Third Way and Breakthrough Institute.

Geels, F. W., Benjamin K. Sovacool, Tim Schwanen, and Steven Sorrell. 2017. Sociotechnical transitions for deep decarbonization. *Science* 357 (6357): 1242–44.

Gillis, Justin, and Jameson McBride. 14 August 2018. Here's how to cut greenhouse gas emissions without taxing them. *New York Times*.

Intergovernmental Panel on Climate Change (IPCC). 2014. *Climate change 2014 synthesis report: Summary for policymakers*. Geneva: IPCC.

Kaufman, Noah. 2018. *A comparison of the bipartisan Energy Innovation and Carbon Dividend Act with other carbon tax proposals*. New York, NY: Columbia Center on Global Energy Policy.

Klenert, David, Linus Mattauch, Emmanuel Combet, Ottmar Edenhofer, Cameron Hepburn, Ryan Rafaty, and Nicholas Stern. 2018. Making carbon pricing work for citizens. *Nature Climate Change* 8 (8): 669–77.

Laird, Frank N., and Christoph Stefes. 2009. The diverging paths of German and United States policies for renewable energy: Sources of difference. *Energy Policy* 37 (7): 2619–29.

Lavelle, Marianne. 7 March 2019. Carbon tax plans: How they compare and why oil giants support one of them. *Inside Climate News*.

Layzer, Judith A. 2012. *Open for business: Conservatives' opposition to environmental regulation*. Cambridge, MA: MIT Press.

Meckling, Jonas. 2011. *Carbon coalitions: Business, climate politics, and the rise of emissions trading.* Cambridge, MA: MIT Press.

Meckling, Jonas, and Steffen Jenner. 2016. Varieties of market-based policy: Instrument choice in climate policy. *Environmntal Politics* 25 (5): 853–74.

Meckling, Jonas, Nina Kelsey, Eric Biber, and John Zysman. 2015. Winning coalitions for climate policy: Green industrial policy builds support for carbon regulation. *Science* 249 (6253): 1170–71.

Meckling, Jonas, Thomas Sterner, and Gernot Wagner. 2017. Policy sequencing toward decarbonization. *Nature Energy.* doi:10.1038/s41560-017-0025-8.

Mitchell, C. 2016. Momentum is increasing towards a flexible electricity system based on renewables. *Nature Energy* 1 (February): 1–6.

Pahle, Michael, Dallas Burtraw, Christian Flachsland, Nina Kelsey, Eric Biber, Jonas Meckling, Ottmar Edenhofer, and John Zysman. 2018. Sequencing to ratchet up climate policy stringency. *Nature Climate Change* 8 (10): 861–67.

Rabe, Barry G. 2016. The durability of carbon cap-and-trade policy. *Governance* 29 (1): 103–19.

Roberts, Cameron, Frank W. Geels, Matthew Lockwood, Peter Newell, Hubert Schmitz, Bruno Turnheim, and Andy Jordan. 2018. The politics of accelerating low-carbon transitions: Towards a new research agenda. *Energy Research & Social Science* 44:304–11.

Roberts, David. 17 January 2019. Here's one fight the Green New Deal should avoid for now. *Vox.* Available at https://www.vox.com.

Rogge, Karoline S., and Kristin Reichardt. 2016. Policy mixes for sustainability transitions: An extended concept and framework for analysis. *Research Policy* 45 (8): 1620–35.

Schmidt, Tobias S., and Sebastian Sewerin. 2017. Technology as a driver of climate and energy politics. *Nature Energy* 2 (6): article no. 17084.

Seto, Karen C., Steven J. Davis, Ronald B. Mitchell, Eleanor C. Stokes, Gregory Unruh, and Diana Ürge-Vorsatz. 2016. Carbon lock-in: Types, causes, and policy implications. *Annual Review of Environment and Resources* 41 (1): 425–52.

Simon, Nicholas, and Sarah B. Mills. 2017. A majority of Americans support net energy metering. In *National survey on energy and environment.* Ann Arbor, MI: University of Michigan. Press

Skocpol, Theda. 2013. *Naming the problem: What it will take to counter extremism and engage Americans in the fight against global warming.* Cambridge, MA: Harvard University Press.

Stokes, Leah C. 2015. Power politics: Renewable energy policy change in US states. PhD diss., Massachusetts Institute for Technology, Cambridge, MA.

Stokes, Leah C., and Christopher Warshaw. 2017. Renewable energy policy design and framing influence public support in the United States. *Nature Energy* 2 (8). doi:10.1038/nenergy.2017.107.

U.S. Energy Information Administration. March 2019. Nuclear energy overview. Available from https://www.eia.gov/totalenergy/data/monthly/pdf/sec8_3.pdf.

World Bank. 2018. *State and trends of carbon pricing.* Washington, DC: World Bank.

Building Climate Policy in the States

By
SAMUEL TRACHTMAN

Large-scale carbon emissions reductions in the United States likely require national-level policy, but political and institutional constraints restrict the scope of policy that can be enacted in Washington. State governments, on the other hand, have demonstrated a remarkable willingness to enact climate policies, despite the global nature of the problem. Although it is limited in directly reducing carbon emissions, state policy has the potential to make the terrain of U.S. climate politics more fertile for future policy. I discuss mechanisms by which climate *policies* enacted at the state level can influence climate *politics* across the states and at the national level. Finally, I make policy and political strategy recommendations that take these multilevel policy feedback dynamics into account.

Keywords: climate change; subnational; state policy; policy feedback; multilevel feedback; federalism

The scientific evidence is clear: policy choices in the next decade will be crucial to averting the worst effects of climate change (Masson-Delmotte et al. 2018). Because it is both a large emitter and a global leader, the United States will play a key role in either driving a global response or impeding one. Recent developments at the national level do not inspire optimism. Even with control of the presidency and a supermajority in Congress in the early Obama years, the Democrats were unable to push through substantial climate legislation (Skocpol 2013). What is more, the Trump administration has rolled back Obama's modest executive actions on climate (Milman 2018).

Samuel Trachtman is a PhD candidate in political science at the University of California, Berkeley. He studies public policy in American politics, focusing on climate change, healthcare, federalism, and state policy. Prior to Berkeley, he worked in public policy at the Congressional Budget Office and at Southern California Edison.

Correspondence: sam.trachtman@berkeley.edu

DOI: 10.1177/0002716219865173

Climate optimists look to the state and local levels, where governments have been highly active in enacting policies to mitigate climate change despite the global nature of the problem. Indeed, since 1990 twenty-eight states have adopted renewable portfolio standards (RPS). Liberal-leaning states have responded to federal climate inaction in the Trump era by further ramping up policy and declarations. In addition to passing a slew of state-level policies, twenty-four governors have agreed to implement policies to advance the goals of the Paris Agreement through the U.S. Climate Alliance (Wallach 2019).

The optimism is tempered, though, by concerns about the effectiveness and sustainability of relying on subnational policy to address climate change. Even as advocates press for policy advances at the state and local levels, there is general agreement that large-scale carbon emissions reductions in the United States will require national-level policy (e.g., Saha 2014). Because national-level policy is needed to address climate change, it is crucial to consider the feedback effects of subnational policies on politics at multiple levels of government.

Although state policy is, for reasons I discuss, generally an inefficient mechanism for directly reducing carbon emissions, state policies have the potential to make the terrain (Hacker and Pierson 2014) of U.S. politics more fertile for large-scale climate policies in the future. In this article, I highlight the particular ways in which climate *policies* enacted by one state can influence climate *politics* in that state, in other states, and at the national level. These types of *multilevel* policy feedback effects can help to counteract the collective action problems inherent in addressing climate change. They also help to resolve the mismatch between the economically optimal level of policy—the national or international level (Nordhaus 2015)—and the more politically feasible level of policy—the subnational level.

In addition to highlighting mechanisms of positive feedback, I also highlight potential for backlash, or negative feedback (Jacobs and Weaver 2015). As Eric Patashnik discusses in this volume, the intense partisan politics of the current era makes policies more vulnerable to backlash, so policy designers should consider mechanisms of negative feedback. Finally, I highlight a number of empirical questions. At this point we have only qualitative and anecdotal evidence for many of the policy feedback dynamics I discuss, since scholars have not developed strategies for quantitatively evaluating policy feedback effects in climate, much less estimated cross-state and state-national feedback effects. That said, lack of empirical evidence should not be interpreted as evidence of a null effect, especially given the challenges of causal identification in policy feedback research.

A Turn to the States

In an ideal political scenario, reducing carbon emissions would be addressed through policy almost entirely at the national and international levels. The drive for an international response stems from the reasoning, derived from economic models of collective action, that national or subnational actors would be reluctant to reduce emissions absent an international agreement (Nordhaus 2015). Yet international negotiations have failed to produce binding emissions restrictions, and the international climate framework has shifted from "top-down" to "bottom-up" with the 2015 Paris Agreement (e.g., Robiou du Pont and Meinshausen 2018).

If a political solution is not to come from the international level, the next best alternative is the national level. Large nations such as the United States contribute enough to global emissions that, according to rational choice models that account for the costs and benefits of emissions reductions, they have an incentive to reduce emissions despite the collective action problem (Nordhaus 2015).[1] This collective action problem might then be mitigated at the international level through "pledge and review" processes or climate clubs (Victor 2011).

However, in the U.S. case, large-scale national-level climate policy seems far out of reach. While overall public support for addressing climate change is strong, it has not improved considerably over time.[2] Meanwhile, other political trends, layered on the United States's unique political institutions, are unfavorable to large-scale national-level climate policy. First, Congress is increasingly gridlocked. While American political institutions were designed to privilege the status quo, polarization expands the "gridlock interval," preventing Congress from addressing major issues like climate change (Binder 2015).

Second, the institutional structure of Congress is biased against proclimate interests. In addition to privileging the status quo, the design of Congress privileges rural areas, which have grown more opposed (relative to urban areas) to climate policy over time.[3] The rural bias of the Senate, with its overrepresentation of small-population states, is well-known. However, as Democrats have become clustered in urban areas, the House has also developed a rural bias, in many cases worsened due to partisan gerrymandering (Chen and Rodden 2013).

These institutional barriers would not be so prohibitive if climate change were less divisive along partisan lines. But consistent with general polarization, while the Democratic Party has grown more bullish on addressing climate change, the Republican Party is increasingly responsive to groups opposed to addressing it (Skocpol 2013). This was not always the case. The parties took similar stands on general environmental issues until the mid-1990s. Moreover, as recently as 2008, leading Democrats and Republicans jointly called for climate action.[4] Since then, the parties, both at the elite and individual levels, have moved ever further apart on climate policy (Kim and Urpelainen 2017; Egan and Mullin 2017). Greater climate polarization makes national-level policy less likely, both due to gridlock and rural bias in representation.

Moreover, due to the overwhelming power of party attachments and elite cues, large-scale shifts in public sentiment are unlikely to occur absent signals from Republican Party elites (Green, Palmquist, and Schickler 2004; Lenz 2013). Indeed, Skocpol (2013) argues that a major mistake of climate advocates in the cap and trade push of 2010 was the failure to account for the power of anticlimate forces within the Republican Party.

Unable to win national-level legislation, climate advocates have turned much of their attention to the state (and local) level. While the Democrats' federal-level cap and trade proposal crashed in former President Obama's first term, California and a coalition of Northeast states have grown their respective carbon trading schemes. Meanwhile, a growing number of governors have responded to President Trump's withdrawal from the Paris Agreement by acting as U.S. climate representatives in international talks.[5] State-level climate action, however, has generally been restricted to states controlled by Democrats, while Republican-controlled states have generally stagnated and in some cases retrenched climate policies (e.g., Stokes 2015).

While Democrat-controlled states have led the way, survey evidence supports the notion that most citizens, in both Democrat- and Republican-controlled states, want their state governments to do more on climate. According to the Yale Program on Climate Change Communication's 2018 survey data, more than 54 percent of respondents in states under Democratic governors supported their governors doing more (compared to just over 53 percent in states under Republican governors), while only between 15 and 16 percent of respondents in both Democrat- and Republican-governed states advocated for their governors to do less. Meanwhile, the percentage of respondents advocating additional action was an even higher 57 percent in unified Democrat-controlled states—the states currently doing the most on climate.

Limitations of State Policy

While states have shown a remarkable willingness to adopt aggressive climate policies, state policy is inherently limited in addressing climate change. First, states are limited by the collective action problem. It is unclear what costs citizens in liberal states will be willing to bear in the long run to reduce emissions while coal plants fire off in other parts of the country. Indeed, legislative efforts to establish a carbon tax have stagnated in liberal strongholds such as Vermont and Massachusetts, while a high-profile ballot initiative establishing a carbon tax failed in Washington State in 2018 (Meyer 2018).

In addition to the collective action problem, there are other more direct barriers to effective state climate policy. One is carbon leakage, a dynamic by which emissions regulations introduced in one jurisdiction lead to increases in emissions in other jurisdictions (e.g., Fowlie and Reguant 2018). Scholars generally recognize two mechanisms of leakage: first, where carbon-intensive industrial activity is shifted to regions with less stringent regulation; and second, where regulations reduce demand for carbon intensive inputs, lowering their price, increasing their consumption, and thereby raising emissions elsewhere.

Carbon leakage is particularly worrisome for subnational policy. In an integrated electricity market, if one state requires more of its electricity to be sourced through renewable power sources, this might increase the availability of existing dirtier power sources for states with less aggressive policy, a dynamic known as "resource shuffling" (Cullenward 2014). Moreover, the common national market makes it easier for energy intensive industry to shift production and emissions to lagging states. Research suggests leakage continues to erode the effectiveness of state climate policies, despite the actions states have taken to mitigate it (Caron, Rausch, and Winchester 2015; Rabe 2018).

Finally, even if state policy were highly effective in reducing carbon emissions, it is unlikely that enough states will be controlled by climate policy–friendly politicians in the near future to make a serious dent in U.S. emissions. One reason is that the areas of the country where liberal candidates tend to perform well are not highly carbon intensive. In the 2018 elections, the number of Democratic "trifectas" (where one party controls both chambers of the legislature and the governor's office) grew to fourteen states. While these fourteen states account for around 35 percent of the population and 35 percent of GDP, they only contributed 25 percent of total emissions as of 2015.

State Policy as a Political Tool

The optimal level at which government should intervene for effective climate policy—the national level—does not align with the level of government at which there is political capacity for addressing climate change—the state and local levels.[6] How should climate advocates respond to the mismatch? One way is to consider the ways that state climate policies can help to build political capacity for policy expansion within states, across states, and at the national level.

Depending on their design, public policies can reshape future politics, a dynamic that political scientists call "policy feedback" (e.g., Pierson 1993). For instance, Campbell's (2003) seminal work demonstrated that the advent of Social Security markedly increased the participation of seniors in politics, redirecting the trajectory of U.S. politics and policy.

Scholars have long recognized the vital role of these types of path dependencies in energy systems. Unruh's (2000) influential paper coined the phrase *techno-institutional complex* to describe the various feedback mechanisms between technology and society that make it difficult to move away from a carbon-intensive production system. More recently, scholars have considered how policy can produce political feedback that chips away at fossil fuel's techno-institutional complex (e.g., Levin et al. 2012). Building on these theoretical advances, scholars have proposed strategic policy sequencing to leverage policies like green industrial supports, which are politically attractive but not particularly effective in reducing emissions, into policies like carbon pricing, which are politically unattractive but effective at reducing emissions (e.g., Meckling et al. 2015; Pahle et al. 2018). This strand of literature has recognized that resolving a long-term issue like climate change requires policy that is not only sustainable but also capable of ratcheting up over time. Therefore, policies designed to promote positive feedback are essential.

This general feedback framework must be tweaked for the particular institutional context of the U.S. states. State policy is limited in its effectiveness at emissions reductions, so exploiting feedback processes to ramp up policy in one state is likely to have a minor overall effect on emissions. On the other hand, feedback effects from state policy could be quite powerful to the degree that they influence politics in other states and nationally.

There are several reasons why cross-state and state-national feedback are particularly consequential in this context. First is decreasing marginal returns. Ratcheting up an already-strict carbon pricing scheme is likely to carry a high cost per ton of emissions abated, while introducing a modest carbon pricing scheme might price out coal plants, abating a large amount of emissions at a low cost. As a result, policies in leading states that influence politics (and ultimately, policy) in lagging states would be particularly impactful. Second, cross-state feedback can reduce carbon leakage, sharpening the emissions-abating effects of policies in the leading state. For instance, to the degree that California's policies produce positive political feedback in Arizona, they might lead to the adoption of stricter climate policies there. If Arizona adopted stricter policies, less carbon would "leak" from California to Arizona. Third, cross-state feedback effects could jump-start within-state feedback processes. Green industrial policy in California might encourage the adoption of green industrial policies in Arizona, mobilizing Arizonan renewable interests that subsequently advocate for policy maintenance or expansion.

Although climate is a global public good, due to the institutional and political factors discussed, U.S. policy progress on climate change is more feasible at the subnational level. To the degree that state climate policies make the terrain (Hacker and Pierson 2014) of national politics more fertile for broader climate action, they might have effects on the long-term trajectory of climate change that go far beyond direct emissions reductions.

Policy Recommendations

Utility-scale green industrial policy

Policies like RPS or feed-in tariffs (FiT) that mandate or incentivize adding renewable generation capacity have played an important role in driving growth in wind and solar generation (Carley et al. 2018). By promoting the development of renewable capacity, these policies can produce within-state, across-state, and state-national positive feedback.

Green industrial policies can construct and empower political interests like clean energy firms that often advocate to defend and expand those policies that benefit them (Meckling et al. 2015). This feedback mechanism is not necessarily limited to the states where policies are passed. RPS are satisfied through the purchase of renewable energy credits (RECs), which are submitted to regulators by load-serving entities (generally utilities). Most states allow a certain percentage of RECs to be submitted "unbundled," or purchased separately from the associated electricity produced (Carley et al. 2018). Strict RPS policies increase the demand for RECs, which can spur the development of renewables projects in other states (Hollingsworth and Rudik 2019). For instance, it seems that the strong RPS in California has spurred the growth of wind power in Wyoming (Barringer 2008).

To the degree that local wind energy interests are active in Wyoming politics, this is a clear mechanism of cross-state policy feedback. Moreover, since states are subject to national law, the green industries constructed through state policy also have a stake in national-level policy debates. While they are still vastly out-muscled by fossil fuel interests in Washington, state green industrial policies have undoubtedly enhanced the power of the clean energy lobby in Washington.

Another mechanism by which green industrial policy can produce multilevel positive feedback is the development of technology. Recent evidence suggests that market-stimulating policies were a key factor driving down the cost of solar panels (Kavlak, McNerney, and Trancik 2018). Expanding green industrial policies in leading states can lead to efficiency gains in technologies like solar panels, in addition to other technologies like advanced storage and smart grids that allow a power system to accommodate significant intermittent renewable resources. The development of these technologies reduces the cost to other states of adopting strict RPS policies. For instance, to the degree that a strong RPS in California drives the development of more efficient storage technology, this would lower the cost to other states of imposing a stricter RPS.

Advocates must exercise caution, though, since green industrial policies might also generate negative political feedback. The biggest potential source of negative feedback is constituent backlash to higher electricity prices. Policies like RPS and FiT (as generally designed) tend to increase electricity rates, especially at higher levels of penetration (Weiss 2014). One way to mitigate this effect is by sequencing green industrial policies after energy efficiency policies that reduce electricity usage overall. Lower electricity usage means that price increases are less likely to lead to large increases in electricity bills.[7]

These dynamics motivate several recommendations, which are presented in Table 1. First, in general, policies that promote the development of green energy should be pursued or ratcheted up whenever possible. In addition, in "leading states," loosening within-state generation requirements can reduce the economic cost of ratcheting up RPS, while potentially generating positive cross-state feedback.

Different strategies might be required in "lagging," more conservative states, where RPS requirements are generally nonexistent, weak, or under attack (Stokes 2015). In these states, advocates might consider a feed-in tariff instead. While RPS requires a specified proportion of total electric power to come from renewable sources, feed-in tariffs set a price (generally higher than wholesale electricity rates) at which renewable generators can sell power to the grid. Since they tend to encourage the development of generation from independent power producers (IPPs), as opposed to utilities, FiT may be more likely to produce a supportive constituency, especially in rural areas (Bayer and Urpelainen 2016).

Distributed generation policy

In addition to promoting the development of utility-scale renewable generation, state policies also have huge implications for the development of distributed

TABLE 1
Green Industrial Policy Recommendations

Recommendation	Positive Feedback	Negative Feedback	Empirical Question
Loosen within-state generation requirements	Build renewable interests in lagging states	Less within-state generation might reduce within-state feedback	Do renewable producers advocate in states where located even if benefit from policies in another state?
Ramp up RPS	Build renewable generation; incentivize development of complementary technologies like storage	Higher electricity prices	Magnitude of positive feedback from building renewables? Sensitivity of consumers to prices?
Advocate for FiT in lagging states	Build renewable generation more likely to be owned by IPP's vs. utilities	Higher electricity prices	Magnitude of positive feedback from building renewables? Sensitivity of consumers to prices?

generation (DG), mainly rooftop solar. There are two key policy levers by which states can influence the development of DG.[8] First is pricing. In many states, rooftop solar is promoted through a pricing scheme known as net energy metering (NEM), which allows individuals and businesses that install distributed power (like rooftop solar) to sell any excess electricity generated to the utility at the full retail rate. Opponents argue that NEM produces a cross-subsidy from general ratepayers to owners of rooftop solar systems, although estimates of the size of the subsidy are disputed and depend on the amount of distributed generation on the grid (Barbose 2018). Regardless, policies like NEM that value electricity produced behind the meter at a high rate are essential to the growth of rooftop solar (Carley 2009).

Second is interconnection, or the rules for how a distributed generation system can connect to the grid.[9] Consistent, rooftop solar–friendly interconnection standards are essential to the development of rooftop solar (Carley 2009). In addition to declines in the price of solar panels, rooftop solar–friendly state policies have led to rapid growth in rooftop solar installations.[10]

The most basic potential feedback mechanism from pro–rooftop solar policy is mobilization of program beneficiaries (rooftop solar owners) to protect and expand those policies that benefit them. However, there are reasons we might expect a minimal effect in this case. First, NEM pricing is generally not highlighted in utility bills, so people may not see themselves as beneficiaries (Mettler 2011). Moreover, a large portion of installations are leased to customers by firms such as Sunrun and Vivint, which, depending on the terms of the lease, would bear the cost of policy changes. More research is required to determine how rooftop solar affects the political behavior of policy beneficiaries. This research

TABLE 2
Distributed Generation Policy Recommendations

Recommendation	Positive Feedback	Negative Feedback	Empirical Questions
Maintain or expand NEM, especially in high-potential, low-penetration states	Beneficiary and employee feedback; industry feedback (especially cross-state)	Electricity prices	Individual and employee beneficiary? Magnitude of cross-state feedback from industry? Sensitivity of consumers to prices?
In leading states, introduce designs to reduce rate impacts, like allocating general revenue or revenue from carbon pricing	Electricity prices		Sensitivity of consumers to prices?
Expand community solar programs	Construct beneficiaries		Advocacy of beneficiaries?

might pay particular attention to organizations working to mobilize rooftop solar owners such as the Solar Rights Alliance. Advocates might also consider strategies to increase the salience for beneficiaries of policies like NEM that support rooftop solar.

Pro–rooftop solar policies might also influence politics by mobilizing those employed in the sector. The rooftop solar industry generates considerable employment.[11] Anecdotal evidence suggests those employed in the sector will mobilize to defend policies that keep business flowing. Furthermore, there is some evidence that employment in rooftop solar might increase support for climate policy more broadly (e.g., Tvinnereim and Ivarsflaten 2016).

Pro–rooftop solar policies also support business interests that have been strong advocates for the maintenance and expansion of these policies. These effects can take hold at multiple levels and sites of government. The most profitable territory for large installer firms such as Sunrun and Vivint are sunny states with prosolar policies. Since the number of viable homes is limited in these states, long-term expansion for rooftop solar companies requires the take-up or maintenance of prosolar policies in other states. For this reason, large installers have been on the front lines of battles to preserve or expand policies like NEM in Arizona, Nevada, and South Carolina. These companies were empowered by aggressive renewables policies in early adopting states such as California and Hawaii, but spend resources lobbying for policy maintenance and expansion elsewhere (e.g., Whieldon 2015).

The feedback framework suggests several broad recommendations, which are laid out in Table 2. To start, climate advocates might push for expansion of pro–rooftop solar policies, especially in low-penetration, high-potential states.

Focusing on low-penetration states reduces the risk of large increases to electricity rates, which might produce negative feedback. Moreover, expanding the policy to low-penetration states might allow clean energy interests to get a foothold.

In leading states, advocates might consider design changes that reduce rate impacts of policies such as NEM at higher penetrations. For instance, instead of financing the program through a ratepayer cross-subsidy, states might allocate revenue from carbon trading programs or severance taxes on oil and gas extraction to fund rooftop solar supports.

Advocates might also focus on promoting community solar programs, which allow individuals to invest in a local solar generation facility and receive credits on their energy bills (Coughlin et al. 2010). These programs tend to be more cost-effective than NEM, since community solar sites capture economies of scale (Brehm, Koch Blank, and Mosier 2018). Moreover, community solar allows renters and homeowners without suitable roofs to participate, expanding the pool of potential beneficiaries.

Carbon pricing

Carbon pricing policies have been more difficult to enact than green industrial policies at the state level. Unlike green industrial policies, carbon pricing tends to impose concentrated costs while delivering diffuse benefits (Rabe 2018). Despite this, California has established and expanded its cap and trade program, while the Regional Greenhouse Gas Initiative (RGGI), the northeast states' cap and trade program for power plants, has grown over time. In addition to reducing emissions,[12] carbon pricing (in the form of either a carbon tax or cap and trade) has the potential to produce within-state, across-state, and state-national positive feedback.

First, carbon pricing schemes that produce revenue and fund programs can generate beneficiaries (Marron and Morris 2016). Research shows that program beneficiaries often mobilize politically to defend those policies that produce their benefits (e.g., Pierson 1996). Revenue from carbon pricing programs is, in many cases, directed toward organizations working in clean energy and energy efficiency.[13] For instance, in Connecticut, RGGI funds are invested in energy efficiency and renewable energy programs managed by organizations such as the Connecticut Green Bank. In California, revenues from the cap and trade program established under Assembly Bill (AB) 32 have funded a number of community organizations throughout the state.[14] It is not hard to imagine that these groups would advocate for the continuation and expansion of cap and trade programs, although research documenting these effects is needed.

In addition to eroding the power of the fossil fuel industry, evidence suggests carbon pricing programs can also soften business opposition over time. Once a business has incurred the costs of adapting to an unfavorable policy, its preferences might change to neutral or even favorable (Meckling 2015). Eric Biber documents this process with respect to Proposition 23 in California (Biber 2013). Proposition 23, brought up in 2010, would have suspended the implementation

TABLE 3
Carbon Pricing Policy Recommendations

Recommendation	Positive Feedback	Negative Feedback	Empirical Questions
Expand where possible, focusing on states with strong green industrial policy	Soften business opposition; change preferences for national policy; erode opposition power	Electricity prices	How does carbon-intensive industry respond to carbon pricing? Sensitivity of consumers to prices?
Visible spending of auctioned permits	Construct beneficiaries		Advocacy of beneficiaries?

of AB 32—legislation that established California's cap and trade program. The proposition ended up losing badly in both Democratic- and Republican-voting parts of the state. Biber (2013) discovers a remarkable difference in the interest group landscape between AB 32 and Proposition 23. The California business community, led by the Chamber of Commerce and the large California-based oil company Chevron, mobilized strongly against AB 32. Four years later, though, the business community was mostly neutral. The process of adapting to AB 32 led California businesses to soften their opposition to climate policy down the road.

Moreover, state-level carbon pricing schemes can influence the preferences of firms for national level policy in a multilevel feedback dynamic. California utilities such as Pacific Gas and Electric (PG&E), while not always supportive of within-state climate policies, supported Obama's failed national-level carbon pricing initiative. The preference of California utilities for stricter national-level regulation is consistent with an economic motive. Carbon pricing policies increase electricity rates, which is harmful for large customers such as manufacturers. These customers may be inclined to shift production to other states, threatening utilities' business in the long run. Having stricter national-level policy reduces the disparity in policy stringency across state lines, which makes fleeing leading states for lagging states less appealing. These avenues of feedback motivate the recommendations put forth in Table 3.

An important and unresolved question is how best to use revenues from carbon pricing programs to generate positive feedback. It is clear that policy-makers should avoid using revenue in a nonvisible way, like paying down debt (Mettler 2011). But it is less clear whether revenues should be used to fund programs with concentrated beneficiaries (Oye and Maxwell 1994), or to fund diffuse (but visible) benefits like a per-capita dividend. A recent review article argues that the optimal choice might vary based on political context. According to Klenert and coauthors (2018), revenues can be tailored to address obstacles to climate policy expansions. For instance, where the main obstacles are distributional concerns, revenues can be transferred to the poor; but where the main obstacles are efficiency and competitiveness, reimbursing firms might be preferable.

Product standards

Product standards have proven in the past to generate powerful positive cross-state and state-national policy feedback. For instance, California's auto emissions standards have been adopted by a number of other states and strongly influenced the standards set by the Obama administration (Sullivan 2009).[15] Due to the size of California's vehicle market, manufacturers are inclined to produce a line of vehicles that satisfy its requirements. Preferring a unified market, those manufacturers are then more likely to advocate for the harmonization of standards at the stricter level (Vogel 1997). California's appliance and equipment efficiency standards on a variety of other products have also become national standards through similar processes.

Climate advocates can use product standards strategically to take advantage of the political geography of climate change in the United States. While Democrat-controlled states do not emit much carbon, they account for a sizable portion of economic output. As mentioned previously, Democratic "trifectas" account for around 35 percent of GDP but 25 percent of total emissions (as of 2015). By influencing standards in these locales, climate advocates can influence the preferences of manufacturers, who then can become allies in advocating for the diffusion and upward migration of standards. Moreover, product standards shift a substantial portion of the cost of emissions reductions to producer regions (e.g., Bolwig et al. 2013). Strategically shifting the cost of compliance to other states is one way of dealing with the collective action problem inherent in addressing climate change.

Bureaucracy

Successful policy can rely on strong administrative capacity, which itself is often produced as a result of prior policy decisions (e.g., Skocpol and Finegold 1982). The development of the California Air Resource Board (CARB) exemplifies the key role of policy in building bureaucratic capacity. Originally formed in 1967 to implement air quality policies, CARB's capacity grew as California adopted increasingly aggressive air quality measures. As California politicians have grown more concerned with climate change, CARB's mission and expertise has evolved accordingly (Vogel 2018). California's landmark 2006 carbon pricing law delegated the nuts and bolts of the policy to CARB, specifying only the timetable for emissions reductions and the requirement that market mechanisms be used to produce those reductions. A similar pattern occurred in the Northeast, where, as Barry Rabe (2018) argues, the long history of state coordination on air quality standards through Northeast States for Coordinated Air Use Management (NESCAUM) provided an important base for the development of RGGI. By stimulating the development of administrative capacity, state policies can open doors for more complex or administratively burdensome policies down the road.

Moreover, administrative capacity developed by one state can be used by other states through regional compacts. For instance, establishing a regional emissions trading program lowers the costs for other states in the region to price emissions.

According to a conversation with a Vermont program administrator, it is very unlikely Vermont would have priced its power plant emissions without the regional establishment of RGGI.[16]

While the national government is perhaps less likely to borrow administrative capacity from the states, development of administrative capacity in the states can also matter to the extent that state bureaucracies act as lobbyists and sites of policy expertise. For instance, CARB has emerged at the center of the political and legal battle against the Trump administration's plans to terminate California's ability to set its own fuel economy standards (Marshall 2018). This battle has consequences for California policy as well as policy in the thirteen states, plus Washington, D.C., that have adopted California's standards.

This suggests that, in crafting state policy, climate advocates should not necessarily advocate for solutions that minimize bureaucracy (Morgan and Campbell 2011). Moreover, advocates might promote policies that build bureaucratic capacity in environment-focused agencies, even if they have negligible direct effects on climate change mitigation.

Climate education

Climate education is another policy area that does not directly influence emissions but might affect climate politics in the future, in this case by influencing public receptivity to climate science. The states have recently been active sites of policymaking regarding climate education. In 2017, Idaho lawmakers removed parts of science education standards that referred to climate change, while similar bills have passed in Alabama and Indiana (Worth 2017). Climate advocates should be attentive to laws targeting climate education in lagging states and defend against them when possible. Climate advocates in liberal states might consider advocating for the addition of climate-change-related material to educational curricula and making sure teachers are sufficiently prepared to provide students with an understanding of the gravity of the issue (Kirk 2017).

Severance taxes

Severance taxes, longstanding policies in many states, levy taxes on the extraction of natural resources such as oil and gas (Rabe and Hampton 2015). While severance taxes can have meaningful effects on emissions (Erickson and Lazarus 2018), current levels seem mostly nonpartisan, with California's rate lower than Texas's. This may change, though, as California lawmakers have come under increased pressure to sharpen supply-side carbon policies (Wheeling 2018).

While severance taxes do not have the same potential to build interests that green industrial policies do, they can erode the power of entrenched opposition like oil companies, thereby generating positive feedback for the climate movement. Moreover, revenue can be used to fund programs and potentially generate political allies. Severance taxes should be expanded where possible, but climate advocates should be careful to avoid negative feedback from loss of employment

TABLE 4
Other Policy Recommendations

Recommendation	Positive Feedback	Negative Feedback	Empirical Questions
Expand and defend product standards	Firms advocate for diffusion and upward migration		Firm responses to product standards in U.S. for various products?
Administer programs publicly	Increases scope for future policy; regional compacts; national-level lobby		Amount of federal lobbying by state bureau- crats?
Develop and promote climate education curricula. Be atten- tive to reverse in lag- ging states	Improve receptivity to climate commu- nication in future	Parental resistance	Effects of climate education on receptivity to com- munication/atti- tudes
Expand and defend severance taxes	Erode power of fos- sil fuels; program beneficiaries	Employment effects	

in highly extractive areas. Harmful employment effects may be softened through geographically targeted economic development programs. Policy recommenda- tions in the areas of severance taxes, climate education, bureaucratic capacity, and product standards are laid out in Table 4.

National Policy

The feedback framework has implications for national policy in addition to state policy. In this volume, Jonas Meckling discusses the potential for policies like a national clean energy standard to mobilize business support for future climate policy advances. In addition, climate advocates might consider the ways in which national policy can complement state policies to produce multilevel cycles of positive feedback. Existing policies like the investment tax credit (ITC) and pro- duction tax credit (PTC), by subsidizing renewable generation, reduce the cost to states of enacting green industrial policies. State-level green industrial policies, in turn, can produce positive political feedback at the national level. Indeed, anecdotal evidence suggests that one reason the PTC and ITC were preserved in the 2017 tax bill was the importance of green industry in states such as Iowa and Nevada (Plumer 2018). Green industry would not be as strong in these states absent state policies; but, also, perhaps states would have been less likely to adopt strong green industrial policies absent incentives offered from the federal gov- ernment through the PTC and ITC.

Conclusion

While state climate policies have limited capacity to directly reduce emissions, the structure of U.S. federalism means that they have significant potential to make the terrain of national-level politics more fertile for future large-scale climate policy. In this article, I outlined a number of mechanisms by which different types of climate-related state policies might "feed back" into the political system in the states in which they are enacted, in other states, and at the national level. Due to a lack of empirical research, a number of questions remain regarding how systematic and how large these potential effects are. Limited existing empirical work makes it difficult to provide confident estimates of effect sizes, but theoretical work allows for some general hypotheses.

First, I would expect group-level effects to be stronger than individual-level effects. Climate policies, because they generally do not engage directly with individual citizens, might be less likely to mobilize individuals than, for instance, health policies (Clinton and Sances 2018). Moreover, even to the degree that they do engage directly with citizens, they may not do much to change people's attitudes on climate. Especially on polarized issues like climate, political attitudes are so strongly tied to partisan identity that policy experiences may not move them (Green, Palmquist, and Schickler 2004). What is more, to the degree that policy uptake is itself polarized (Lerman, Sadin, and Trachtman 2017), Republicans might be less likely to put themselves in a position to benefit from climate policy. Finally, even if policy beneficiaries mobilize to protect those policies that benefit them, it is unclear the degree to which beneficiaries would mobilize more broadly for climate policies (Galvin and Thurston 2017). For instance, we might expect rooftop solar owners to mobilize to protect NEM, but not to establish carbon pricing.

On the other hand, the nature of climate policy and the energy transition suggests interest group (including business) effects might be quite impactful. While the energy system remains dominated by fossil fuels, renewable sources like wind and solar have grown rapidly in recent years (Weaver 2019). Successful climate policy will entail at least partially replacing fossil-fuel intensive energy production systems with renewable energy production systems (e.g., Huberty and Zysman 2010). This replacement will both dislodge entrenched anticlimate interests such as fossil fuel companies and empower interests such as renewable power producers that stand to benefit from stricter carbon controls, a powerful combination for sustainable reform (Patashnik 2008).

To the degree that empirical work supports the potential effects discussed, the proposed framework has important implications for political strategy around climate policy in the United States. Different types of climate policies will be feasible in different types of states. Policies that lead to marginal emissions reductions, especially in conservative-leaning states that have lagged behind, might have significant political implications in the future. Taking forward-looking policy action in the states can help to ensure that the next time climate-friendly lawmakers have power in Washington, advocates will be successful in promoting the strong national-level policy likely needed to avoid climate crisis.

Notes

1. The collective action problem stems from the fact that the global climate is a public good, so each individual country would, absent an international agreement, reduce emissions less than the socially optimal amount.

2. See "American Public Opinion on Global Warming" (Political Psychology Research Group at Stanford University), available from https://pprggw.wordpress.com/fundamentals/.

3. "Visualizations & Data" (Yale Program on Climate Change Communication, n.d.), available from http://climatecommunication.yale.edu/visualizations-data/.

4. "Pelosi and Gingrich Unite for Climate Protection," *Grist* (2008), available from https://grist.org/article/nancy-newt-sittin-on-a-couch/.

5. "Seventeen Governors in U.S. Climate Alliance Mark One-Year Anniversary with New Wave of Climate Actions" (United States Climate Alliance, 2018), available from https://www.usclimatealliance.org/publications/oneyearanniversary.

6. I mainly consider state policy here, although a similar analysis could be performed for local policies. Local policies are potentially less powerful since localities have less constitutional authority than states and can be preempted by states.

7. This is one reason why aggressive climate policies in California have not generally led to large bill increases (Daniels 2017).

8. Although other policies like incentive schemes and RPS carve-outs are also important.

9. IREC Editors, "IREC Released Update to Highly Influential Interconnection Model Procedures" (Interstate Renewable Energy Council, 26 April 2019), available from https://irecusa.org/2013/04/irec-releases-update-to-highly-influential-interconnection-model-procedures/.

10. "Solar Industry Research Data" (Solar Energy Industries Association, 2019), available from https://www.seia.org/solar-industry-research-data.

11. A survey by the Advanced Energy Economy Institute found over 500,000 jobs in advanced energy in California (Nichols 2017). While this figure could be an exaggeration, the number is likely quite large regardless.

12. Although some recent evidence suggests the emissions-reducing effects of carbon taxes, at current rates, are marginal (Pretis 2019).

13. "The Investment of RGGI Proceeds in 2016" (The Regional Greenhouse Gas Initiative, 2018).

14. "CARB Awards $10 Million in Cap-and-Trade Funding to Help Communities Curb Air Pollution," (California Air Resources Board, 2018), available from https://ww2.arb.ca.gov/news/carb-awards-10-million-cap-and-trade-funding-help-communities-curb-air-pollution.

15. The Clean Air Act grants California a waiver to establish its own auto emissions standards, which other states are permitted to follow. The 1990 amendments allowed other states to adopt California's standards.

16. Conversation with Vermont administrator in January 2019.

References

Barbose, Galen. 2018. *Putting the potential rate impacts of distributed solar into context*. Washington, DC: U.S. Department of Energy. Available from https://doi.org/10.2172/1469160.

Barringer, Felicity. 11 November 2008. A land rush in Wyoming spurred by wind power. *New York Times*.

Bayer, Patrick, and Johannes Urpelainen. 2016. It is all about political incentives: Democracy and the renewable feed-in tariff. *Journal of Politics* 78 (2): 603–19.

Biber, Eric. 2013. Cultivating a green political landscape: Lessons for climate change policy from the defeat of California's Proposition 23. *Vanderbilt Law Review* 66:399–462.

Binder, Sarah. 2015. The dysfunctional Congress. *Annual Review of Political Science* 18 (1): 85–101.

Bolwig, Simon, Lone Riisgaard, Peter Gibbon, and Stefano Ponte. 2013. Challenges of agro-food standards conformity: Lessons from East Africa and policy implications. *European Journal of Development Research* 25:408–27.

Brehm, Kevin, Thomas Koch Blank, and Leah Mosier. 2018. Progress and potential for community solar. Rocky Mountain Institute. Available from http://www.rmi.org.

Campbell, Andrea Louise. 2003. *How policies make citizens: Senior political activism and the American welfare state*. Princeton, NJ: Princeton University Press.

Carley, Sanya. 2009. Distributed generation: An empirical analysis of primary motivators. *Energy Policy* 37 (5): 1648–59.

Carley, Sanya, Lincoln L. Davies, David B. Spence, and Nikolaos Zirogiannis. 2018. Empirical evaluation of the stringency and design of renewable portfolio standards. *Nature Energy* 3 (9): 754–63.

Caron, Justin, Sebastian Rausch, and Niven Winchester. 2015. Leakage from sub-national climate policy: The case of California's cap and trade program. *Energy Journal* 36 (2). Available from https://doi .org/10.5547/01956574.36.2.8.

Chen, Jowei, and Jonathan Rodden. 2013. Unintentional gerrymandering: Political geography and electoral bias in legislatures. *Quarterly Journal of Political Science* 8:239–69.

Clinton, Joshua D., and Michael W. Sances. 2018. The politics of policy: The initial mass political effects of Medicaid expansion in the states. *American Political Science Review* 112 (1): 167–85.

Coughlin, Jason, Jennifer Grove, Linda Irvine, Janet Jacobs, Sarah Johnson Phillips, Leslie Moynihan, and Joseph Wiedman. 2010. *A guide to community solar*. National Renewable Energy Lab. Washington, DC: U.S. Department of Energy.

Cullenward, Danny. 2014. How California's carbon market actually works. *Bulletin of the Atomic Scientists* 70 (5): 35–44.

Daniels, Jeff. 2017. California has glut of electricity, but residents still pay 40% more than national average. CNBC. Available from https://www.cnbc.com.

Egan, Patrick J., and Megan Mullin. 2017. Climate change: US public opinion. *Annual Review of Political Science* 20 (1): 209–27.

Erickson, Peter, and Michael Lazarus. 2018. *How limiting oil production could help California meet its climate goals*. Seattle: Stockholm Environment Institute. Available from https://www.sei.org/wp-content/uploads/2018/03/sei-2018-db-california-oil2.pdf.

Fowlie, Meredith, and Mar Reguant. 2018. Challenges in the measurement of leakage risk. *AEA Papers and Proceedings* 108:124–29.

Galvin, Daniel J., and Chloe N. Thurston. 2017. The Democrats' misplaced faith in policy feedback. *The Forum* 15 (2). Available from https://doi.org/10.1515/for-2017-0020.

Green, Donald P., Bradley Palmquist, and Eric Schickler. 2004. *Partisan hearts and minds: Political parties and the social identities of voters*. Hartford, CT: Yale University Press.

Hacker, Jacob S., and Paul Pierson. 2014. After the "master theory": Downs, Schattschneider, and the rebirth of policy-focused analysis. *Perspectives on Politics* 12 (3): 643–62.

Hollingsworth, Alex, and Ivan Rudik. 2019. External impacts of local energy policy: The case of renewable portfolio standards. *Journal of the Association of Environmental and Resource Economists* 6 (1): 187–213.

Huberty, Mark, and John Zysman. 2010. An energy system transformation: Framing research choices for the climate challenge. *Research Policy* 39 (8): 1027–29.

Jacobs, Alan M., and R. Kent Weaver. 2015. When policies undo themselves: Self-undermining feedback as a source of policy change. *Governance* 28 (4): 441–57.

Kavlak, Goksin, James McNerney, and Jessika E. Trancik. 2018. Evaluating the causes of cost reduction in photovoltaic modules. *Energy Policy* 123 (December): 700–10.

Kim, Sung Eun, and Johannes Urpelainen. 2017. The polarization of American environmental policy: A regression discontinuity analysis of Senate and House votes, 1971–2013. *Review of Policy Research* 34 (4): 456–84.

Kirk, Karin. 2017. Teachers digging in to teach climate change. *Yale Climate Connections*.

Klenert, David, Linus Mattauch, Emmanuel Combet, Ottmar Edenhofer, Cameron Hepburn, Ryan Rafaty, and Nicholas Stern. 2018. Making carbon pricing work for citizens. *Nature Climate Change* 8 (8): 669–77.

Lenz, Gabriel S. 2013. *Follow the leader? How voters respond to politicians' policies and performance*. Chicago, IL: University of Chicago Press.

Lerman, Amy E., Meredith L. Sadin, and Samuel Trachtman. 2017. Policy uptake as political behavior: Evidence from the Affordable Care Act. *American Political Science Review* 111 (4): 755–70.

Levin, Kelly, Benjamin Cashore, Steven Bernstein, and Graeme Auld. 2012. Overcoming the tragedy of super wicked problems: Constraining our future selves to ameliorate global climate change. *Policy Sciences* 45 (2): 123–52.

Marron, Donald B., and Adele C. Morris. 2016. How to use carbon tax revenues. Tax Policy Center. Available from https://doi.org/10.2139/ssrn.2737990.

Marshall, Aarian. October 2018. California is fighting the Trump administration on car emissions. *Wired*. Available from https://www.wired.com.

Masson-Delmotte, V., P. Zhai, H. O. Pörtner, D. Roberts, J. Skea, P. R. Shukla, A. Pirani, W. Moufouma-Okia, C. Péan, R. Pidcock, S. Connors, J. B. R. Matthews, Y. Chen, X. Zhou, M. I. Gomis, E. Lonnoy, T. Maycock, M. Tignor, and T. Waterfield, eds. 2018. Summary for policymakers. In *Global warming of 1.5°C*. Geneva: World Meteorological Organization.

Meckling, Jonas. 2015. Oppose, support, or hedge? Distributional effects, regulatory pressure, and business strategy in environmental politics. *Global Environmental Politics* 15 (2): 19–37.

Meckling, Jonas, Nina Kelsey, Eric Biber, and John Zysman. 2015. Winning coalitions for climate policy. *Science* 349 (6253): 1170–71.

Mettler, Suzanne. 2011. *The submerged state: How invisible government policies undermine American democracy*. Chicago, IL: University of Chicago Press.

Meyer, Robinson. March 2018. Maybe blue states won't take serious action on climate change. *The Atlantic*. Available from https://www.theatlantic.com.

Milman, Oliver. 21 August 2018. How the Trump administration is rolling back plans for clean power. *The Guardian*.

Morgan, Kimberly J., and Andrea Louise Campbell. 2011. *The delegated welfare state: Medicare, markets, and the governance of social policy*. New York, NY: Oxford University Press.

Nichols, Chris. June 2017. Do California's clean energy jobs equal 10 times the nation's coal mining jobs? *Politifact*. Available from https://www.politifact.com.

Nordhaus, William. 2015. Climate clubs: Overcoming free-riding in international climate policy. *American Economic Review* 105 (4): 1339–70.

Oye, Kenneth A., and James H. Maxwell. 1994. Self-interest and environmental management. *Journal of Theoretical Politics* 6 (4): 593–624.

Pahle, Michael, Dallas Burtraw, Christian Flachsland, Nina Kelsey, Eric Biber, Jonas Meckling, Ottmar Edenhofer, and John Zysman. 2018. Sequencing to ratchet up climate policy stringency. *Nature Climate Change* 8 (10): 861–67.

Patashnik, Eric M. 2008. *Reforms at risk: What happens after major policy changes are enacted*. Princeton, NJ: Princeton University Press.

Pierson, Paul. 1993. When effect becomes cause: Policy feedback and political change. *World Politics* 45 (4): 595–628.

Pierson, Paul. 1996. The new politics of the welfare state. *World Politics* 48 (2): 143–79.

Plumer, Brad. 22 January 2018. Tax bill largely preserves incentives for wind and solar power. *New York Times*.

Pretis, Felix. 2019. Does a carbon tax reduce CO2 emissions? Evidence from British Columbia. Available from https://papers.ssrn.com/abstract=3329512.

Rabe, Barry. 2018. *Can we price carbon?* Cambridge, MA: MIT Press.

Rabe, Barry G., and Rachel L. Hampton. 2015. Taxing fracking: The politics of state severance taxes in the shale era. *Review of Policy Research* 32 (4): 389–412.

Robiou du Pont, Yann, and Malte Meinshausen. 2018. Warming assessment of the bottom-up Paris Agreement emissions pledges. *Nature Communications* 9 (1). Available from https://doi.org/10.1038/s41467-018-07223-9.

Saha, Devashree. 2014. Sub-national climate change actions prevail over national politics. Brookings (blog). Available from https://www.brookings.edu.

Skocpol, Theda. 2013. Naming the problem: What it will take to counter extremism and engage Americans in the fight against global warming. Paper prepared for the Symposium on the Politics of America's Fight against Global Warming, Cambridge, MA.

Skocpol, Theda, and Kenneth Finegold. 1982. State capacity and economic intervention in the early new deal. *Political Science Quarterly* 97 (2): 255–78.

Stokes, Leah C. 2015. Power politics: Renewable energy policy change in US states. MA thesis, Massachusetts Institute of Technology, Cambridge, MA.

Sullivan, Colin. 20 May 2009. Vow of silence key to White House-Calif. fuel economy talks. *New York Times*.

Tvinnereim, Endre, and Elisabeth Ivarsflaten. 2016. Fossil fuels, employment, and support for climate policies. *Energy Policy* 96 (September): 364–71.

Unruh, Gregory C. 2000. Understanding carbon lock-in. *Energy Policy* 28 (12): 817–30.

Victor, David. 2011. *Global warming gridlock*. New York, NY: Cambridge University Press.

Vogel, David. 1997. *Trading up: Consumer and environmental regulation in a global economy*. Cambridge, MA: Harvard University Press.

Vogel, David. 2018. *California greenin'*. Princeton, NJ: Princeton University Press.

Wallach, Philip A. 22 March 2019. Where does U.S. climate policy stand in 2019? Brookings (blog).

Weaver, John. January 2019. EIA: Wind and solar will be fastest growing sources of electricity in 2019 and 2020. *Pv Magazine USA*.

Weiss, Jurgen. 2014. Solar energy support in Germany. The Brattle Group. Available from https://www.seia.org/sites/default/files/resources/1053germany-closer-look.pdf.

Wheeling, Kate. May 2018. How California undercuts its efforts to combat climate change. *Pacific Standard*.

Whieldon, Esther. December 2015. Solar blowback hits Reid's Nevada. *Politico*.

Worth, Kate. May 2017. A new wave of bills takes aim at science in the classroom. *Frontline*.

Prescriptions: Health Care

Medicaid and the Policy Feedback Foundations for Universal Healthcare

Public policies are products of politics, but they also *feed back* into the political system by shaping the actions and attitudes of members of the polity. To date, scholarly examinations of feedback processes have been mostly concerned with understanding the relationship between public policy and democracy; relatively little attention has been paid to connecting policy feedback to the practical questions that animate politics. This article examines policy feedback as it applies to efforts aimed at achieving universal health coverage in the United States—a widely held policy goal shared by a majority of American voters across partisan lines. I argue that in the contemporary political context, Medicaid—a pillar of the American healthcare system and the primary mechanism for insuring low-income and disabled citizens—can produce negative feedbacks that demobilize political action, destabilize advocacy groups, and deter coalition building. Together, these feedbacks undermine future possibilities for universal healthcare. After detailing these democratic dilemmas, I outline strategies for proactively addressing them.

Keywords: policy feedback; Medicaid; universal healthcare; negative feedback

By
JAMILA MICHENER

Public policies can affect the trajectory of politics. This intuitive and astute observation forms the basis for a body of scholarship that systematically charts the political effects of public policy—a process known as *policy feedback* (Béland 2010; Campbell 2003, 2012; Lerman and Weaver 2014; Mettler 2005; Mettler and Soss 2004; Michener 2018; Patashnik and Zelizer 2013; Pierson 1993; Skocpol 1992; Soss 2000). Ideally, insights about policy feedback processes can be thoughtfully applied to illuminate pressing problems in the world. Yet even as scholarly

Jamila Michener is an assistant professor in the Department of Government at Cornell University. She is author of Fragmented Democracy: Medicaid, Federalism and Unequal Politics *(Cambridge University Press 2018).*

Correspondence: jm2362@cornell.edu

DOI: 10.1177/0002716219867905

knowledge of policy feedback grows in nuance and scope, it may not translate into relevant or useful information beyond the pages of academic books and journals. The translational prospects of policy feedback research depend on the extent to which scholars make their findings legible to wide audiences and relevant to real-world dilemmas (Hacker 2010). This article is one step in that direction. I leverage ideas from the policy feedback literature to think prospectively about how contemporary Medicaid politics is laying the groundwork for the future of health policy. This move from academic theorization and measurement to practical engagement with the world—though fraught in some ways—is a productive effort to confront "the problems and questions that govern our horizons as scientists of politics and policy in a nation whose tradition, language, and aspirations claim to be democratic" (Farr, Hacker, and Kazee 2006, 586).

In view of that goal, I argue that after the Affordable Care Act (ACA) became U.S. law, Medicaid politics prompted (at least) three negative feedback processes. If exacerbated and neglected, this negative feedback can hinder future efforts to expand access to healthcare. These matters have clear partisan implications. However, negative feedback is crucial for reasons that transcend strategic partisan calculations. Policy feedback that stymies political engagement, weakens political organizations, and hampers coalition building risks subverting (small-d) democratic policy outcomes. My arguments in this article hinge on the presupposition that, irrespective of any particular partisan implications, undermining participatory democracy is undesirable. In light of that assumption, I end the article with suggestions for strategies to counteract negative Medicaid feedback effects.

The Goal of Universal Healthcare: Why Medicaid Matters

According to a recent national survey by the Pew Research Center, six in ten Americans say that it is the federal government's responsibility to make sure all Americans have healthcare coverage (Kiley 2018). Perhaps even more strikingly, a 2018 Reuters-Ipsos survey found that 70 percent of Americans now support "Medicare for all," including 85 percent of Democrats and 52 percent of Republicans (Stein, Cornwell, and Tanfani 2018). Notwithstanding such bipartisan support, universal coverage policies are commonly perceived as politically infeasible (Brooks 2019; Faris 2017; Hiltzik 2016; Kelly and Alesci 2019; Robinson 2019; Siegel 2018; Stolberg and Pear 2019; Waldman 2018). Certainly, practical barriers like costs and administrative complexity make universal coverage a daunting goal. Nonetheless, many analysts agree that the most crucial dynamics of health policy are determined by politics (Hacker 2008, 2018; Grogan and Park 2017b; Mayer, Kenter, and Morris 2015; Rigby, Clark, and Pelika 2014; Rigby and Haselswerdt 2013; Roper 2007). Policy feedback scholars can thus contribute useful knowledge about the path toward universal healthcare by thinking critically about how existing policies create politics.

To that end, this article focuses on the policy feedback implications of Medicaid. Medicaid is a pillar of the American health care system. As the single largest public health insurer in the United States, Medicaid provides health coverage for upwards of 72 million Americans (Centers for Medicaid & Medicare Services 2019). Given its size and scope, the future of any healthcare policy transformation likely pivots on the current-day status and effects of Medicaid policy. The political effects of Medicaid are especially germane. Recent research demonstrates that Medicaid affects political outcomes such as voting, participating in political groups, and policy attitudes (Clinton and Sances 2018; Haselswerdt 2017; Haselswerdt and Michener 2019; Hopkins and Parish 2018; Michener 2017, 2018). Medicaid policy shapes the political attitudes and actions of both individuals and organizations (Michener 2018). Given its role in producing the political conditions that structure the trajectory of health policy, Medicaid is central to assessing a route toward a robust universal healthcare system in the United States. Importantly, Medicaid's intergovernmental design, its development in the wake of the ACA, and its status in the larger healthcare system pose distinct policy feedback dilemmas. In the pages that follow, I outline these challenges and describe how the post-ACA context risks eroding the political foundation on which Medicaid rests and, thereby, makes universal healthcare a heavier political lift. I offer both offensive and defensive approaches to addressing this predicament. The problems I point to are difficult, and silver bullet solutions do not exist. Still, I sketch three strategies for diffusing negative policy feedback and generating positive feedback. I primarily emphasize states but also keep an eye toward national policy and politics.

Contemporary Healthcare Politics and Medicaid Policy Feedback

The politics of healthcare has grown even more explosive and polarized in the wake of the 2010 ACA. This is especially true with regard to Medicaid, a policy that reflects both the promise and peril of healthcare in the United States. In the last few years, we have seen vigorous efforts at the national and state levels to erode Medicaid. The 115th Congress attempted to advance a parade of unpopular "repeal and replace" policies. Though these policies had quite anodyne names such as the "American Health Care Act" and the "Better Care Reconciliation Act," they were each marked by a forceful drive toward large cuts to Medicaid. According to projections from the Congressional Budget Office, the repeal and replace policies would have led to tens of millions of people being uninsured, many as a result of reductions in Medicaid coverage via the imposition of per capita caps or block grants (Jost 2017). In response to threats to Medicaid funding, there was striking pushback from a wide range of stakeholders who stood to lose substantially if Medicaid were weakened (Cancryn 2017; Cancryn and Demko 2017; Michener 2018; Sarlin 2017; Stein 2017; Subberwal 2017). Such groups included program beneficiaries, doctors, hospitals, insurance companies, and organizations representing disabled and elderly Americans who count on Medicaid for their survival and long-term care.

The partisan political episodes around "repeal and replace" efforts made it pointedly clear that neither Medicaid's entrenchment nor its popularity will secure its political viability. Threats of cuts have loomed large even as Medicaid garners support from 74 percent of Americans, including 65 percent of Republicans.[1] Medicaid is an undoubtedly vital lifeline for tens of millions of Americans. Researchers have quantified the number of lives it saves and measured its effects on outcomes ranging from poverty to education to crime (Cohodes et al. 2016; Hu et al. 2016; Miller and Wherry 2018; Sommers and Oellerich 2013; Wen, Hockenberry, and Cummings 2017; Zewde and Wimer 2019). Seventy percent of Americans have had a direct personal connection to Medicaid.[2] Still, the program remains vulnerable. Given that the fate of universal healthcare is linked to the fate of Medicaid, the interplay between Medicaid policy and politics—and the resulting feedback—warrants close attention.

To date, the leading story of policy feedback and Medicaid in the era of the ACA is positive. Several studies find that the ACA's Medicaid expansion was a boon for voter turnout (Haselswerdt 2017; Clinton and Sances 2018). This research is valuable, but it focuses solely on the short-term participatory effects of the recent Medicaid expansion. A broader look at Medicaid policy feedback reveals a more complex set of political forces. For example, federalism gives states and localities marked influence over the contours of Medicaid. This makes for a "many-headed" policy that takes very different forms in different places and has direct implications for politics (Michener 2018; Sanger-Katz 2015; Sparer 1996; Thompson 2012). Federalism can fragment the politics of Medicaid, splinter policy coalitions and interest groups, raise barriers to political coordination across locales, impede democratic accountability, and differentially demobilize policy beneficiaries as well as those who live in communities alongside them (Michener 2017, 2018; Haselswerdt and Michener 2019). All in all, increased voting in the immediate aftermath of Medicaid expansion is but one potential feedback effect in this bigger picture. Others include (1) effects on the advocates and activists attempting to organize and mobilize in the realm of healthcare; (2) effects on those Americans insured via state marketplaces who may become disenchanted with their coverage relative to the perceived benefits of Medicaid; and (3) effects of Section 1115 waivers—institutional mechanisms that provide states with leeway to depart from federal statute and test new Medicaid policies—and other administrative interventions into Medicaid. Unlike Medicaid expansion, these feedbacks are negative, potentially demobilizing Medicaid beneficiaries and stigmatizing the program more broadly. Below, I consider the implications of each of these three policy feedback dilemmas in more detail.

Feedback Dilemma #1: Demobilizing Policy Advocates and Activists

The first source of negative policy feedback in the current healthcare landscape has to do with how the ACA shapes the political context in which policy advocates and activists operate.[3]

The ACA has profoundly polarized the politics of healthcare, creating marked incentives for a wide variety of stakeholders to become more intensely involved with health policy (Béland, Rocco, and Waddan 2015; Hertel-Fernandez, Skocpol, and Lynch 2016; Gray, Lowery, and Benz 2013; Rocco and Haeder 2018). On the ground, this makes for a more fraught policy process. In particular, this shifts the contours of health policy for advocates and interest groups seeking to move the healthcare system toward an expansive, equitable, and universal structure. As battle lines have been drawn over "Obamacare," organizations that might have otherwise been focused on making forward progress in terms of the quality, scope, and equity of healthcare are instead engaged in a constant series of political skirmishes largely oriented around defending the ACA.

In the last several years, during the process of writing a book about Medicaid and since the publication of that book, I have engaged extensively with the leaders of health policy organizations across the country. I have given presentations at their annual meetings, consulted them on the politics of Medicaid, helped them to craft surveys, and had in-depth conversations with them about the work that they do. Along the way, I have observed that the politics of the ACA has twofold consequences for political organizations focused on improving healthcare access and equity. On one hand, fighting for the ACA can energize these organizations, provoking action and coordination. On the other hand—and especially over the long run, as ACA-related political battles rage on—the politics of the ACA can destabilize, distract, and dishearten policy advocates. For example, in a recent phone conversation, the leader of a healthcare advocacy organization in an embattled southern state described policy advocates in her state as being "discouraged" by the fight against Medicaid work requirements. After a long effort to expand Medicaid, the prospect of yet another barrier to care was dispiriting. In 2010, when the ACA was passed, many health policy advocates celebrated the prospect of expanding Medicaid. Since then, they have been compelled to fight harder than ever simply to defend the status quo against retrenchment. Although such political actors continue to push back as each new hurdle is erected, doing so absorbs energy that might otherwise be useful for mobilizing more broadly and deeply, thinking beyond the most immediate political challenges and organizing affirmatively—not just against regressive change but for positive change. Many of the phone calls, meetings, and consultations I have been a part of for the last few years have been focused on how to protect Medicaid, while comparably few have been geared toward farsighted envisioning of ways that Medicaid can play a part in a larger move toward universal care. While taking a defensive posture at this political moment makes sense for Medicaid advocates, doing so constrains the capacity building and imagination necessary to move toward a different future.

Relatedly, the language, tactics, and action that political organizations take have been altered by the hyperpolarized post-ACA politics (especially in conservative states). This can generate organizational fissures and divisions. For example, I have seen policy advocates divided over whether to accept and support Medicaid expansion accompanied by work requirements or whether to reject expansion when such strings are attached. More pragmatic advocates view expansion as a fast track to vital gains for tens of thousands of people and are, thus, willing to compromise. Less sanguine advocates worry that opening the door to conditional coverage lays the foundation for a weakened program and imperils the health of the people who would be left behind under work-oriented Medicaid regimes. Organizations that would otherwise work together can thus find themselves at odds over this disagreement (and others). As a result, cooperation and collaboration among policy coalitions can be elusive.

Another adverse upshot of the tough policy environment that many state healthcare advocacy organizations currently face concerns changes in the regulatory and bureaucratic environment of state and local health policy. The ACA has placed a spotlight on Medicaid. While this is a good development in some ways, it also has disadvantages. Particularly in politically "red" or "purple" states, as government officials contemplate implementing Medicaid expansion or as they actually begin to expand, they also often search for ways to "reform" Medicaid to make it more efficient, less costly, and more politically palatable. The search for routes to reform opens up possibilities that were otherwise not included in the repertoire of policy options (Weaver 2010; Jacobs and Weaver 2015), some of which are subtle and bureaucratic but nonetheless important. Most people are unaware of such developments, but advocacy organizations are tasked with responding to them on the frontlines—and they expend scarce resources and time to do so. For instance, in Kentucky, amid high-profile contention over Medicaid expansion, Medicaid bureaucrats decided to more strictly interpret a rule requiring Medicaid beneficiaries to have up-to-date addresses. They required that Medicaid enrollees verify their addresses and flagged beneficiaries whose mail was returned to sender. They then disenrolled people for violating this technicality.[4] In the wake of disenrollment related to address mismatches, advocacy organizations had to reroute energies toward tackling this matter. In this way, resistance to Medicaid expansion (even in states that decide to expand) generates barriers to access for Medicaid beneficiaries and levies a tax on health advocacy organizations that must most directly confront such barriers.

In sum, the policy issues and polarization that dominate ACA-era health politics can lead to splintering, narrowing, cautiousness, and resource depletion among health policy organizations seeking to expand access and improve equity.

Feedback Dilemma #2: Failed Insurance Marketplaces Breed Resentment

The second negative policy feedback I address concerns the failures (real and perceived) of the ACA. Though Medicaid is the main emphasis here, it does not exist in isolation from the other parts of the ACA. Instead, the other major pieces of the ACA work in tandem with Medicaid expansion and sometimes at cross-purposes with it. Take state insurance marketplaces, for example. While Medicaid expansion has emerged as the centerpiece of the ACA, state marketplaces have struggled. The insurance marketplaces have been "buffeted in many states by high premium increases, sicker-than-expected risk pools, and insurer withdrawals" (Oberlander 2017). Crucially for policy feedback, the class politics of this problem pits would-be allies in the healthcare realm against one another. The marketplaces were designed as an option for lower-middle- and middle-income Americans. Many of those intended constituents now face disappointment over the skyrocketing prices of premiums and the instability of the marketplaces (Semanskee, Claxon, and Levitt 2017). In 2017, 69 percent of Americans surveyed in a Kaiser Health Tracking Poll said that it was "extremely" or "very" important to pass legislation to stabilize ACA insurance markets.[5] The observable discontent of marketplace consumers is too easily juxtaposed with the salient expansion of Medicaid and the perception that it is a better option than others. In 2018, 52 percent of Americans (including 50 percent of Republicans) reported believing that Medicaid was "working well for most low-income people covered by the program."[6] In the eyes of "working"- or "middle"-class Americans, their primary option for receiving care has fallen short, while the benefits that flow to Americans living in poverty seem high quality and ever expanding (of course, reality is much more complicated than that). This arrangement risks cultivating a political environment ripe for vilifying Medicaid in the eyes of better-resourced Americans who are struggling to pay for health insurance and facing frustration over the limits of state marketplaces. The feedback challenge at stake here has to do with the politics of intergroup class dynamics given the variable success of different parts of the ACA, some of which map onto insurance coverage for particular socioeconomic groups. Overlaying these class dynamics are equally important racial dynamics (Michener 2019). The perception that Medicaid beneficiaries (read: poor black people) are getting stuff while hardworking Americans (read: "working-class" white people) lose out, however misguided, can produce a more toxic racialized health politics than we already have and prevent cross-class, cross-race mobilizing that could secure universal healthcare in the long run (Grogan and Park 2017b; Tesler 2012).

Feedback Dilemma #3: Section 1115 Waivers Demobilize and Stigmatize

The third negative feedback possibility I consider involves the broadening of states' policy options through Section 1115 waivers. Such waivers have long existed, but ACA politics has given states an incentive to push the bounds in terms of the design of waivers, and the presidential administration of Donald J. Trump has encouraged such stretching. The most salient waivers impose work requirements on Medicaid beneficiaries. Even beyond that, waivers are wide ranging. Pending and approved waivers include lockout penalties that prevent beneficiaries from accessing care for some prescribed period of time after non-compliance with a given eligibility condition; drug screening, allowing states to

FIGURE 1
Landscape of Approved and Pending Section 1115 Medicaid Demonstration Waivers

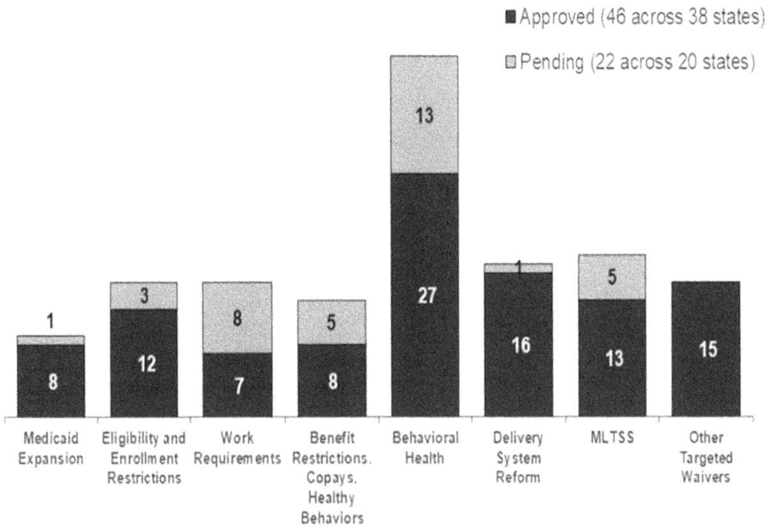

■ Approved (46 across 38 states)
▫ Pending (22 across 20 states)

1	3	8	5	13	1	5	
8	12	7	8	27	16	13	15

Medicaid Expansion | Eligibility and Enrollment Restrictions | Work Requirements | Benefit Restrictions, Copays, Healthy Behaviors | Behavioral Health | Delivery System Reform | MLTSS | Other Targeted Waivers

SOURCE: Kaiser Family Foundation Medicaid Waiver Tracker (as of January 23, 2019).
NOTE: MLTSS = Medicaid Managed Long Term Services and Supports.

implement screening for substance abuse disorders among beneficiaries; "reasonable promptness" provisions that allow states to delay the start of coverage until after the first premium is paid; the elimination of retroactive coverage so that new beneficiaries are not covered for the limited period immediately before formal enrollment; the elimination of transitional medical assistance so that beneficiaries who find work (or better work) lose benefits due to increased income without a transition period; elimination of presumptive eligibility so that hospitals cannot proceed with providing care on the presumption that certain patients are eligible; and more (see Figures 1–3).

The overarching theme of these waivers is that they limit coverage, introduce administrative burdens, and increase the likelihood that people will lose benefits (Herd and Moynihan 2019). Such waivers can produce negative feedback in numerous ways. Most proximately, by politically demobilizing Medicaid beneficiaries. Political demobilization can happen if waivers lead to substantial disenrollment from Medicaid because disenrollment can lead to decreased voting (Haselswerdt and Michener 2019). More generally, disenrollment limits the reach and effectiveness of Medicaid during a time when building political capital for more expansive healthcare requires extending the reach of health programs and improving their effectiveness.

Political demobilization as a result of waivers can also happen in response to the negative experiences they produce for Medicaid beneficiaries (Michener

FIGURE 2
Section 1115 Medicaid Waivers: Work Requirements

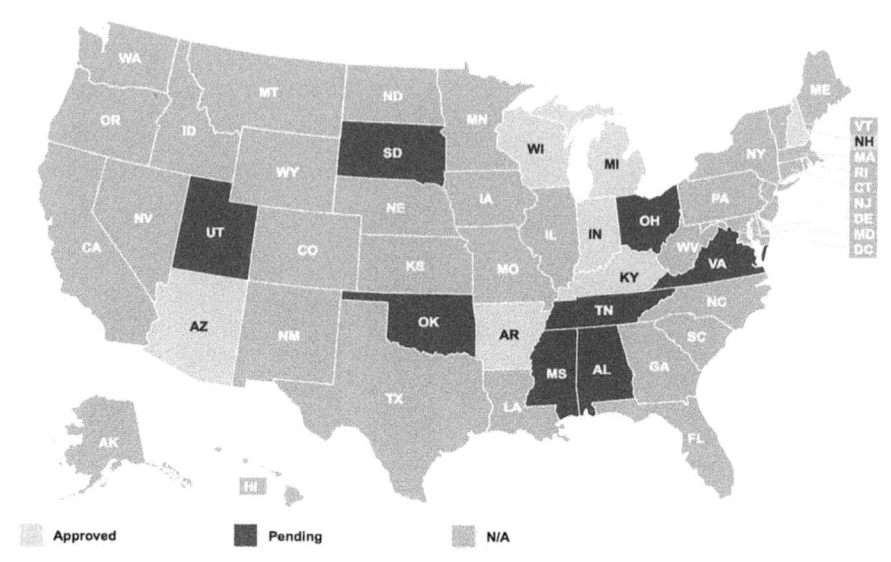

SOURCE: Kaiser Family Foundation Medicaid Waiver Tracker (as of January 23, 2019).

FIGURE 3
Section 1115 Medicaid Waivers: Eligibility and Enrollment Restrictions

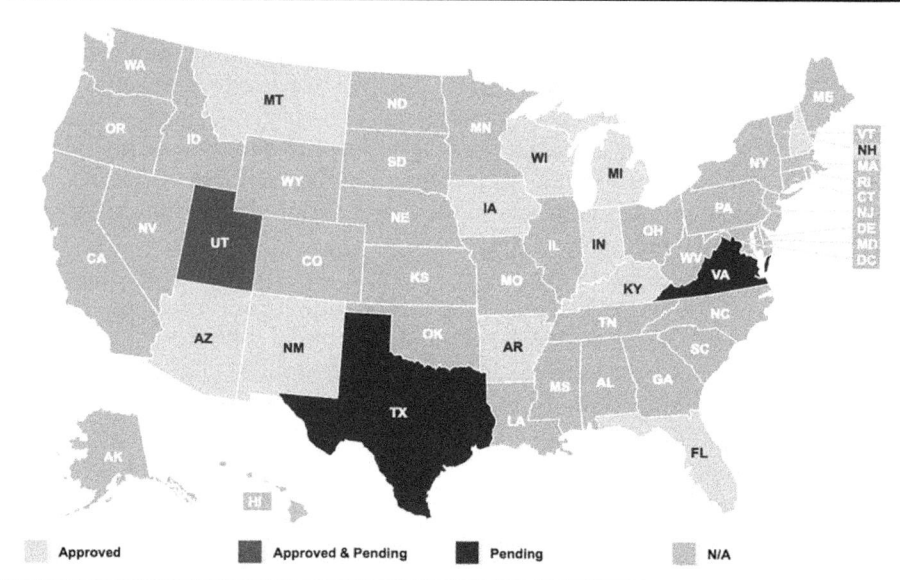

SOURCE: Kaiser Family Foundation Medicaid Waiver Tracker (as of January 23, 2019).

2018). Especially perniciously, the administrative burden associated with waivers will target the "most advantaged" among Medicaid beneficiaries (i.e., people in the expansion population who are slightly less poor, less unhealthy, and more connected to the labor market). Waivers therefore risk alienating the beneficiaries who are closest to the "working" and middle classes and who could otherwise build a stronger bridge for cross-class coalitions. Looking beyond beneficiaries, waivers can fuel the stigmatization of Medicaid. They may signal to the broader public that Medicaid beneficiaries must be policed, controlled, and watched (Schneider and Ingram 1993; Soss and Schram 2007). Medicaid is a program that is closely connected to many Americans, and at present, it is not intensely stigmatized among the general public (Grogan and Park 2017a). Waiver policies risk reversing that course by codifying and reinforcing stereotypes about the kinds of people who rely on Medicaid (nonworkers) and the necessity of social control for subsets of the Medicaid population (nonworking able-bodied adults).

Countering Negative Feedbacks and Generating Positive Feedbacks

With these policy feedback dilemmas in mind, I propose three strategies for counteracting the democratic erosion that they threaten. Admittedly, these strategies come with their own challenges, and their feasibility will vary depending on state contexts and federal political developments. My objective is to highlight courses of action that have the potential to cultivate a more democratic polity and an equitable healthcare system.

Build political momentum for health care at the state level

I recently talked to a state health policy advocate who told me that "everyone wants national solutions but we forget that every good thing that has ever happened at the national level started in the states." If the "good thing" one seeks nationally is political power to create an equitable universal healthcare system, then advancing toward that goal begins at the state level. Building political momentum in the states is an offensive strategy for eventual national change. Of course, there are many rounds of politics required to propel the progression from state to national, and I cannot lay all of them out here. Nonetheless, I recommend two distinct kinds of efforts: (1) broad coalition building and (2) visionary agenda setting.

As intimated above, the ACA has intensified the degree to which state-level organizations are mired in a complex policy environment that continually distracts, destabilizes, and discourages them from working optimally. Furthermore, the uneven success of the ACA risks splintering the interests of healthcare consumers along lines of class and race. Together, these negative feedback processes can dampen coalitional possibilities by straining the organizations that might work to forge coalitions and dividing those with the most at stake. To generate positive policy feedbacks, health advocacy organizations, healthcare providers, and other relevant groups must coalesce. Particularly important is that such groups organize with attentiveness to bridging class, race, and issue-based subgroups. Advocacy and other organizations must create opportunities for the most sympathetic and publicly supported health consumers (e.g., people with preexisting conditions, people with disabilities) to make common cause with the least-supported health consumers (e.g., nonworking able-bodied adults). The hardest task of coalition building will be to cut through the many issue-based, ideological, and partisan silos that characterize the health policy arena to systematically enlarge the size and power of healthcare constituencies.

In practice, this will require organizations across the spectrum of health policy interests to build political capacity. That process will be different in each state. Some states have already undertaken campaigns that required building coalitions (e.g., states that have mobilized to get Medicaid expansion passed via ballot initiative). In those places, organizations must continue to see beyond short-term campaigns, holding together coalitions and expanding them even during times where health policy issues seem more dormant than previously. Lawmakers will have to craft policies that cut across healthcare consumer subgroups and are relevant to as many organizations and individuals as possible. Policy-makers and organizations can work together to identify synergies, as organizations can alert policy-makers to opportunities to develop and push legislation that has the most expansive possibilities for organizing. This is possible even in politically conservative states where such policy may be very difficult to pass. Whether or not policies are passed, the policy process itself can create opportunities for state coalitions to organize together, to test the political waters, and to see what is feasible given developing configurations of coalitions. Any policy passed is a boon for such coalitions; and with careful expectation management, even policies with widespread coalitional support that do not pass can be made into a political liability for recalcitrant politicians who refuse to respond to their constituents.

Ultimately, only better-resourced, higher-capacity organizations can afford to look beyond the immediate political context to build toward more expansive possibilities. Providing state policy advocates with financial and political resources to enable them to build organizing capacity is, therefore, crucial. At the same time, having a broader vision does not mean overlooking the nuts and bolts of what many state advocacy organizations do well. A complementary way to build capacity is to achieve and highlight very local gains (like changes in burdensome administrative practices). When organizations engage in smaller political battles for the purposes of fighting against immediate barriers to care, it is more than small potatoes. Their core constituencies should know about it and be engaged for "small" winnable battles that reinforce infrastructure and morale as building blocks for larger efforts. Integrating both macro (going after state-level policy change) and micro (going after local or particularistic bureaucratic changes) policy approaches into a larger plan for coalition building across wide swaths of health consumer groups is a path toward generating positive feedback effects.

Policy-makers and bureaucrats are potential partners in the organizational capacity building efforts described here. They have opportunities to interact with a wide range of organizations, can productively connect such organizations to one another, can devise legislative or bureaucratic channels to distribute resources to such organizations, and can brainstorm about how to structure policy in such a way as to promote the broadest coalitions possible. Local media are also potentially key actors in this regard because they can make the work of local organizations salient, inform the public about otherwise unnoticed fights that such organizations continually wage, and amplify the messages and voices of organizations that do not have the capacity to manage public relations or shape public discourse.

Set an expansive agenda

The core idea here is simple: states that have the power to do so should take big, bold steps toward expanding healthcare on a state level. This logic applies to localities (indeed, the mayor of New York City recently committed to a plan for providing comprehensive health care for all city residents including undocumented immigrants). Bold policy progress will only be possible in a few places, but it is nonetheless a key step in leveraging states and localities as the "laboratories of democracy" that they are so often purported to be. Major state and local policy advances can demonstrate that policy approaches now perceived as infeasible are indeed possible. Of course, great care is warranted here. If states and localities implement policies that are bold failures, they risk stifling the effort to demonstrate the feasibility of these policies on the national stage. Moreover, if states advance policies that represent some progress, but those policies retain many of the more profound limitations of the current system (e.g., limited attentiveness to long-term care, insufficient mechanisms to control costs and pricing, marked class or race inequities), then even the "success" of such policies can be limiting by perpetuating the existing problems in the system and setting a ceiling for future policy advances. In short, one cannot assume that any bold action on the state and local levels will suffice. To forfend against making things worse, states with the political majorities necessary to take bold action must think beyond the state level and look beyond the moment. Those states should explicitly confer with other states as well as with national organizations to reasonably evaluate the long-term implications of their policy choices. This means strategizing about how any policy under consideration fits into a broader national path toward universal coverage. Applying this lens—a multilevel policy feedback perspective—will be difficult, but it can change the calculus for more forward-thinking states looking to take the lead. If a critical mass of states and localities make intrepid progress that is also strategically designed as part of a longer-term national focus, there will be more evidence useful for designing and justifying bold policies at the national level. Moreover, diffusion effects could create cross-state patterns that generate positive feedback at both the state and national levels.

Create policy and administrative protections to reinforce Medicaid

This set of recommendations focuses on defensive strategies that limit negative feedbacks associated with the ACA. On a national level, the best (medium term) policy protection against fueling politically damaging antipathy toward Medicaid is to strengthen the other aspects of the ACA by stabilizing the insurance marketplaces and securing protections for preexisting conditions. As noted earlier, Medicaid is not at its strongest if the policies targeting the middle-class flounder. Such an arrangement can sow seeds of cross-class divisions that risk hindering broad-based coalition building at the state and national levels. National policy-makers should pursue policies that offset the failures of the marketplaces. Federal policies with these aims are already on the table, but a feedback-oriented perspective sheds a different light on this sort of defensive legislation in at least two ways. First, though protecting the ACA may seem like a narrow endeavor given more stirring calls for "Medicare for All," the two efforts can be part and parcel of a policy feedback perspective. Constituents who perceive the ACA as a disaster because of negative experiences with the health insurance marketplaces may be even less trusting of government and thus even less amenable to calls for universal coverage. For similar reasons, people may also be more hostile toward Medicaid and its beneficiaries. Preventing such negative feedbacks in the present means short-term "fixes" like marketplace stabilization. Such interventions do not foreclose more expansive future possibilities. A second important insight that follows from the vantage point of feedback effects is that efforts to shore up the ACA must be public, identifiable, and comprehensible to the public. The minutiae of the ACA, the exchanges, and the rules around preexisting conditions can easily distance the average constituent and hide the role of the government (Mettler 2011). Along with passing legislation focused on stabilization, a major goal of national policy-makers should be to make the concrete implications of such legislation very salient.

On the state level, steps to protect Medicaid via bureaucratic administration are important. Such efforts include closely monitoring and evaluating the administrative implementation of Medicaid expansion to constrain the political side effects of regressive waivers. Some political organizations are already evaluating the effects of waivers or planning to do so. Supporting such efforts financially and through bureaucratic mechanisms for policy evaluation is a first step, and doing so is justifiable across ideological contexts. Understanding how waivers are unfolding is crucial for assessing their effects. A secondary and politically relevant upshot of formally assessing the effects of waivers is that measurement and assessment are crucial for making a legal case against waivers when there is evidence that they are harmful.

Finally, to protect and reinforce Medicaid on both the state and national levels, elected officials, bureaucrats, media, academics, and anyone in a position to shape policy discourse should think carefully about how to talk about Medicaid and its beneficiaries, what other programs to connect it with, which populations to highlight, and which aspects of Medicaid policy they emphasize. This may seem small, but policy discourse and political communication matter, especially for building long-term change (Gillion 2016; Levine 2015; Scrase and Ockwell 2010). Emphasizing the wide reach of Medicaid is key given that people with closer connections to the policy are more supportive of it (Grogan and Park 2017a). Linking the fate of Medicaid to the fate of the health system more broadly (and specifically the fate of interests relevant to middle-class Americans) is also crucial. At the same time, caution is in order on two counts. First, downplaying Medicaid's role in supporting low-income Americans and depicting it as a "middle-class" program is not a sustainable strategy. If the goal is to build cross-class coalitions, then middle-income Americans need to value a program that disproportionately benefits people living in poverty, not eschew it. This is why rhetoric and framing that links the fate of low-income Medicaid beneficiaries, middle-income long-term care and disabled beneficiaries, and other (non-Medicaid) healthcare consumers (like people with preexisting conditions) is optimal. Second—and most concrete for policy purposes—practices around talking about Medicaid programs are easy to overlook, but important. The preferable course of action is to advocate for program names, descriptions, and public-facing language (on websites, in pamphlets, etc.) that center the value and sources of Medicaid benefits and decenter technocratic language about eligibility and costs. When Medicaid programs have names that obscure the resources that the program offers and highlight its burdens (e.g., Arizona's Medicaid agency is called the Arizona Healthcare Cost Containment System) and when public officials and public-facing materials emphasize costs, eligibility limitations, and scarcity, there may be negative long-term consequences for how the public views the program. Even Medicaid advocates tend to fall into these rhetorical patterns, so there is a need for the widescale adoption of language and framing that is more sensitized to the feedback processes that might be set in motion by political discourse.

Extend the reach and function of Medicaid

This final set of recommendations is based on a core observation: positive feedback effects will proliferate as Medicaid works better for more people with more visibility that is explicitly linked to policy decisions and politics (Campbell 2003; Mettler 2005, 2011). The ACA expansion has been one part of this, but strengthening Medicaid politically and building from that strength to achieve further gains requires continuing to expand the reach and role of Medicaid. I suggest at least three ways of doing this.

First, make existing Medicaid coverage as accessible to as many people as possible through increased funding (at the state and national levels) for outreach and enrollment via intermediaries like healthcare navigators, social workers, and community health workers. My interviews with Medicaid beneficiaries and community health workers alike reveal that these actors can play an important role in making experiences with Medicaid more positive, by lightening administrative burden and preventing disenrollment. Such positive experiences make it more likely for Medicaid to exert positive feedback effects in ways that support future transformative change. Between 2017 and 2018, federal funding for health navigator programs that support enrollment and outreach was cut by 84 percent (Keith

2018). To the extent that national policy-makers can reverse this direction, positive feedbacks may be more likely. States can also devote more funding to such efforts.

Second, pursue an expanded public health model of state Medicaid policy-making and administration that focuses on the social determinants of health. Doing so can extend the reach and role of Medicaid in people's lives, further entrenching it, creating more positive feedback effects, and providing evidence that more health care support is both morally and fiscally responsible. Some states are already leading the way in this regard by using Medicaid funds to cover costs such as housing, transportation, medical-legal partnerships, and more. States should look for creative ways to use existing Medicaid resources to these ends. Medicaid waiver demonstrations are already used for the purposes of supporting housing, legal services, and other crucial resources to Medicaid beneficiaries. As of this writing, three states (Delaware, Hawaii, and Maryland) provide supportive housing services as part of Section 1115 waivers, and at least six states use Section 1915(c) waivers to deliver housing-related services such as supports to transition into community-based living, home modifications, and one-time moving expenses (Jopson and Regan 2016; Musumeci 2017). Some of these waivers are in politically conservative states. For example, the Louisiana Department of Health operates a permanent supportive housing program financed through state funding streams that include Medicaid. Other Section 1915(c) waivers help the state to provide pretenancy, tenancy crisis, and tenancy-maintenance services. These and other policies help to support Medicaid beneficiaries in more and varied ways, stabilizing them and making positive policy feedback more viable among them. States should not lose sight of the benefits of waivers focused on leveraging Medicaid to address the social determinants of health that impede the economic and political lives of Medicaid beneficiaries.

Third, state and federal policy-makers should increase support for institutions that inform and empower healthcare consumers. Such institutions already exist in some states (e.g., the office of the healthcare advocate in Connecticut, the office of the patient advocate in California). Expanding support for and creating more nonpartisan state institutions that can help to inform and engage health constituencies is a potentially valuable step toward engendering positive policy feedbacks. Such institutions could assist in ensuring that Medicaid beneficiaries and other healthcare consumers have the best possible experiences with government programs, that they are empowered to defend their social rights and navigate otherwise alienating bureaucratic frustrations. The infrastructure for these institutions already exists in some places, but it can be extended, solidified, and made more salient. In other places, no such institutions exist, but they can be created via collaborative efforts (for example, Vermont's health care advocate project is operated through Vermont legal aid) and with state and national support. State health consumer advocacy institutions are achievable but not minor; they could play a role in creating an infrastructure of support that promotes the democratic inclusion of healthcare constituencies of all kinds.

Conclusion

The observations proffered here apply research on policy feedback to contemporary political dilemmas. The suggestions that followed illuminate potential mechanisms for generating positive policy feedback or neutralizing negative feedback. State capacity building catalyzes the political groundwork useful for mobilizing political resources in support of desired change. Bold state action sets nationally relevant precedent. Policy and administrative backstops attend to the weaknesses of the ACA, increasing chances for fruitful cross-class mobilization (or at the very least, stemming the tide undermining such possibilities). Extending the reach and functions of Medicaid by making existing programs more accessible, being more attentive to policy concerning the social determinants of health, and further developing consumer advocacy institutions are steps that make Medicaid more politically inclusive. Ultimately, I do not highlight these strategies for partisan purposes. I do so in view of an unoriginal yet compelling principle: "Political science has a unique ability, and even perhaps a special obligation, to engage with issues of democratic choice that fundamentally affect the life circumstances of citizens" (Farr, Hacker, and Kazee 2006, 579).

Notes

1. These numbers are from the Kaiser Family Foundation Health Tracking Poll (February 2018). The polling data are available online from https://www.kff.org/health-reform/poll-finding/kaiser-health-tracking-poll-february-2018-health-care-2018-midterms-proposed-changes-to-medicaid/.

2. Ibid.

3. It is important to note that state political environments vary significantly. Key sources of variation to consider include (1) whether states have adopted Medicaid expansion; (2) the density and power of health interest groups, which varies significantly across states (Gray, Lowery, and Benz 2013); and (3) healthcare expenditures per capita, which range from very high (D.C. spends $11,944) to much lower (Utah spends $5,982).

4. Here is an example of a letter describing the new policy that was sent to Kentucky health care providers: https://www.caresource.com/documents/member-address-mismatch-disenrollment/. Here is another example describing some of the details and detailing the actions that healthcare providers must take to prevent disenrollment: http://passporthealthplan.com/wp-content/uploads/2015/08/08-18-PROV51713-Member-Disenrollment.pdf.

5. Kaiser Family Foundation Health Tracking Poll (September 2017): https://www.kff.org/health-reform/poll-finding/kaiser-health-tracking-poll-september-2017-whats-next-for-health-care/?utm_campaign=KFF-2017-September-Tracking-Poll&utm_source=hs_email&utm_medium=email&utm_content=2&_hsenc=p2ANqtz–pbtZgGfclYLHnR762ynztwF9i1j2qZa1febywFuMGu5TVPXajfPgbVdvT-FrHpNh18NwmhIZdnoSKCkhKFRM-yjHhoBw.

6. Kaiser Family Foundation Health Tracking Poll (February 2018). The polling data are available online from https://www.kff.org/health-reform/poll-finding/kaiser-health-tracking-poll-february-2018-health-care-2018-midterms-proposed-changes-to-medicaid/.

References

Béland, Daniel. 2010. Reconsidering policy feedback: How policies affect politics. *Administration and Society* 42 (5): 568–90.

Béland, Daniel, Philip Rocco, and Alex Waddan. 2015. Polarized stakeholders and institutional vulnerabilities: The enduring politics of the Patient Protection and Affordable Care Act. *Clinical Therapeutics* 37 (4): 720–26.

Brooks, David. 4 March 2019. "Medicare for All": The impossible dream. *New York Times.*

Campbell, Andrea Louise. 2003. *How policies make citizens: Senior political activism and the American welfare state.* Princeton, NJ: Princeton University Press.

Campbell, Andrea Louise. 2012. Policy makes mass politics. *Annual Review of Political Science* 15:333–51.

Cancryn, Adam. 25 September 2017. Protesters dragged out of Senate hearing on Obamacare repeal. *Politico.*

Cancryn, Adam, and Paul Demko. 27 June 2017. Emboldened industry lobbyist try to scale back Medicaid cuts. *Politico.*

Centers for Medicare & Medicaid Services. 2019. December 2018 Medicaid and CHIP enrollment data highlights. Available from https://www.medicaid.gov/medicaid/program-information/medicaid-and-chip-enrollment-data/report-highlights/index.html.

Clinton, Joshua D., and Michael W. Sances. 2018. The politics of policy: The initial mass political effects of Medicaid expansion in the states. *American Political Science Review* 112 (1): 167–85.

Cohodes, Sarah R., Daniel S. Grossman, Samuel A. Kleiner, and Michael F. Lovenheim. 2016. The effect of child health insurance access on schooling: Evidence from public insurance expansions. *Journal of Human Resources* 51 (3): 727–59.

Faris, David. 28 March 2017. Why "Medicare for all" is easy to say and near impossible to do. *The Week.*

Farr, James, Jacob S. Hacker, and Nicole Kazee. 2006. The policy scientist of democracy: The discipline of Harold D. Lasswell. *American Political Science Review* 100 (4): 579–87.

Gillion, Daniel Q. 2016. *Governing with words: The political dialogue on race, public policy, and inequality in America.* New York, NY: Cambridge University Press.

Gray, Virginia, David Lowery, and Jennifer K. Benz. 2013. *Interest groups and health care reform across the United States.* Washington, DC: Georgetown University Press.

Grogan, Colleen M., and Sunggeun Park. 2017a. The politics of Medicaid: Most Americans are connected to the program, support its expansion, and do not view it as stigmatizing. *Milbank Quarterly* 95 (4): 749–82.

Grogan, Colleen M., and Sunggeun Park. 2017b. The racial divide in state Medicaid expansions. *Journal of Health Politics, Policy and Law* 42 (3): 539–72.

Hacker, Jacob S. 2008. Putting politics first. *Health Affairs* 27 (3): 718–23.

Hacker, Jacob S. 2010. The road to somewhere: Why health reform happened: Or why political scientists who write about public policy shouldn't assume they know how to shape it. *Perspectives on Politics* 8 (3): 861–76.

Hacker, Jacob S. 3 January 2018. The road to Medicare for everyone. *The American Prospect.*

Haselswerdt, Jake. 2017. Expanding Medicaid, expanding the electorate: The Affordable Care Act's short-term impact on political participation. *Journal of Health Politics, Policy and Law* 42 (4): 667–95.

Haselswerdt, Jake, and Jamila Michener. 2019. Disenrolled: Retrenchment and voting in health policy. *Journal of Health Politics, Policy and Law* 44 (3): 423–54.

Herd, Pamela, and Donald P. Moynihan. 2019. *Administrative burden: Policymaking by other means.* New York, NY: Russell Sage Foundation.

Hertel-Fernandez, Alexander, Theda Skocpol, and Daniel Lynch. 2016. Business associations, conservative networks, and the ongoing Republican war over Medicaid expansion. *Journal of Health Politics, Policy and Law* 41 (2): 239–86.

Hiltzik, Michael. 8 January 2016. The dream of Medicare for all: Here's why the Sanders health plan is more hope than change. *Los Angeles Times.*

Hopkins, Daniel J., and Kalind Parish. 2018. The Medicaid expansion and attitudes toward the Affordable Care Act: Testing for a policy feedback on mass opinion. Available from http://dx.doi.org/10.2139/ssrn.2990576.

Hu, Luojia, Robert Kaestner, Bhashkar Mazumder, Sarah Miller, and Ashley Wong. 2016. The effect of the Patient Protection and Affordable Care Act Medicaid expansions on financial wellbeing. National Bureau of Economic Research Working Paper No. 22170, Cambridge, MA.

Jacobs, Alan M., and R. Kent Weaver. 2015. When policies undo themselves: Self-undermining feedback as a source of policy change. *Governance* 28 (4): 441–57.

Jopson, Andrew, and Carol Regan. 2016. *Bringing independence home: Housing-related provisions under Medicaid 1915(c) home- and community-based services waivers*. Boston, MA: Center for Consumer Engagement in Health Innovation and Community Catalyst. Available from https://www .communitycatalyst.org/resources/publications/document/Bringing-Independence-Home_Housing_ Released_HCBS-1915c-Waivers.pdf.

Jost, Timothy. 20 July 2017. The latest CBO score of the better care Reconciliation Act leaves 22 million uninsured by 2026. Health Affairs Blog. Available from www.healthaffairs.org/do/10.1377/ hblog20170720.061145/full/.

Keith, Katie. July 2018. CMS announces even deeper navigator cuts. *Health Affairs Blog*. doi:10.1377/ hblog20180712.527570.

Kelly, Caroline, and Cristina Alesci. 29 January 2019. Michael Bloomberg: Medicare-for-all would bankrupt us for a very long time. *CNN Politics*.

Kiley, Jocelyn. 2018. *Most continue to say ensuring health care coverage is government's responsibility*. Washington, DC: Pew Research Center. Available from https://www.pewresearch.org.

Lerman, Amy E., and Vesla M. Weaver. 2014. *Arresting citizenship: The democratic consequences of American crime control*. Chicago, IL: University of Chicago Press.

Levine, Adam Seth. 2015. *American insecurity: Why our economic fears lead to political inaction*. Princeton, NJ: Princeton University Press.

Mayer, Martin, Robert Kenter, and John C. Morris. 2015. Partisan politics or public-health need? An empirical analysis of state choice during initial implementation of the Affordable Care Act. *Politics and the Life Sciences* 34 (2): 44–51.

Mettler, Suzanne. 2005. *Soldiers to citizens: The GI bill and the making of the greatest generation*. New York, NY: Oxford University Press.

Mettler, Suzanne. 2011. *The submerged state: How invisible government policies undermine American democracy*. Chicago, IL: University of Chicago Press.

Mettler, Suzanne, and Joe Soss. 2004. The consequences of public policy for democratic citizenship: Bridging policy studies and mass politics. *Perspectives on Politics* 2 (1): 55–73.

Michener, Jamila. 2017. People, places, power: Medicaid concentration and local political participation. *Journal of Health Politics, Policy and Law* 42 (5): 865–900.

Michener, Jamila. 2018. *Fragmented democracy: Medicaid, federalism, and unequal politics*. New York, NY: Cambridge University Press.

Michener, Jamila. 2019. Policy feedback in a racialized polity. *Policy Studies Journal* 47 (2): 423–50.

Miller, Sarah, and Laura R. Wherry. 2018. The long-term effects of early life Medicaid coverage. *Journal of Human Resources*. doi:10.3368/jhr.54.3.0816.8173R1.

Musumeci, Mary Beth. 2017. *Key themes in Medicaid Section 1115 behavioral health waivers*. Washington, DC: Kaiser Family Foundation. Available from http://files.kff.org.

Oberlander, Jonathan. 2017. The end of Obamacare. *New England Journal of Medicine* 376 (1): 1–3.

Patashnik, Eric M., and Julian E. Zelizer. 2013. The struggle to remake politics: Liberal reform and the limits of policy feedback in the contemporary American state. *Perspectives on Politics* 11 (4): 1071–87.

Pierson, Paul. 1993. When effect becomes cause: Policy feedback and political change. *World Politics* 45 (4): 595–628.

Rigby, Elizabeth, Jennifer Hayes Clark, and Stacey Pelika. 2014. Party politics and enactment of "Obamacare": A policy-centered analysis of minority party involvement. *Journal of Health, Politics, Policy and Law* 39 (1): 57–95.

Rigby, Elizabeth, and Jake Haselswerdt. 2013. Hybrid federalism, partisan politics, and early implementation of state health insurance exchanges. *Publius: The Journal of Federalism* 43 (3): 368–91.

Robinson, Nathan J. 26 February 2019. Ignore all arguments about what is "politically feasible." *Current Affairs*.

Rocco, Philip, and Simon F. Haeder. 2018. How intense policy demanders shape postreform politics: Evidence from the Affordable Care Act. *Journal of Health Politics, Policy, and Law* 43 (2): 271–304.

Roper, William L. 2007. Here we go again—Lessons on health reform. *Health Affairs* 26 (6): 1551–52.

Sanger-Katz, Margaret. 28 January 2015. The goal was simplicity; instead, there's a many-headed Medicaid. *New York Times*.

Sarlin, Benjy. 5 May 2017. Deep Medicaid cuts drive backlash to health care bill. *NBC News*.

Schneider, Anne, and Helen Ingram. 1993. Social construction of target populations: Implications for politics and policy. *American Political Science Review* 87 (2): 334–47.

Scrase, J. Ivan, and David G. Ockwell. . 2010. The role of discourse and linguistic framing effects in sustaining high carbon energy policy—An accessible introduction. *Energy Policy* 38 (5): 2225–33.

Semanskee, Ashley, Gary Claxon, and Larry Levitt. 2017. *How premiums are changing in 2018.* San Francisco, CA: Henry J. Kaiser Foundation.

Siegel, Marc. 4 August 2018. "Medicare for all" is a pipe dream. *The Hill.*

Skocpol, Theda. 1992. *Protecting mothers and soldiers: The political origins of social policy in the United States.* Cambridge, MA: Belknap Harvard Press.

Sommers, Benjamin D., and Donald Oellerich. 2013. The poverty-reducing effect of Medicaid. *Journal of Health Economics* 32 (5): 816–32.

Soss, Joe. 2000. *Unwanted claims: The politics of participation in the US welfare system.* Ann Arbor, MI: University of Michigan Press.

Soss, Joe, and Sanford F. Schram. 2007. A public transformed? Welfare reform as policy feedback. *American Political Science Review* 101 (1): 111–27.

Sparer, Michael S. 1996. *Medicaid and the limits of state health reform.* Philadelphia, PA: Temple University Press.

Stein, Jeff. 22 June 2017. "No Cuts to Medicaid!" Protesters in wheelchairs arrested after release of health care bill. *Vox.*

Stein, Letitia, Susan Cornwell, and Joseph Tanfani. 2018. Party Crashers: Inside the progressive movement roiling the Democratic Party. *Reuters Investigates.* Available from https://www.reuters.com/investigates/special-report/usa-election-progressives/

Stolberg, Sheryl Gay, and Robert Pear. 18 March 2019. Medicare for All is divisive (in the Democratic Party). *New York Times.*

Subberwal, Kaeli. 25 July 2017. As Senate advances on Obamacare repeal, protesters fight for Medicaid. *Huff Post Politics.*

Tesler, Michael. 2012. The spillover of racialization into health care: How President Obama polarized public opinion by racial attitudes and race. *American Journal of Political Science* 56 (3): 690–704.

Thompson, Frank J. 2012. *Medicaid politics: Federalism, policy durability, and health reform.* Washington, DC: Georgetown University Press.

Waldman, Paul. 10 December 2018. If you want Medicare-for-all, prepare for a long and bloody fight. *Washington Post.*

Weaver, Kent. 2010. Paths and forks or chutes and ladders? Negative feedbacks and policy regime change. *Journal of Public Policy* 30 (2): 137–62.

Wen, Hefei, Jason M. Hockenberry, and Janet R. Cummings. 2017. The effect of Medicaid expansion on crime reduction: Evidence from HIFA-waiver expansions. *Journal of Public Economics* 154:67–94.

Zewde, Naomi, and Christopher Wimer. 2019. Antipoverty impact of Medicaid growing with state expansions over time. *Health Affairs* 38 (1): 132–38.

Medicare Expansion as a Path as well as a Destination: Achieving Universal Insurance through a New Politics of Medicare

By
JACOB S. HACKER

Growing interest in "Medicare for All" has revived hopes for universal health insurance. Yet serious disagreements remain over *how* to expand Medicare and *how far* to move toward a universal Medicare system. In this article, I consider these disagreements in light of what we know about "policy feedback"—the ways in which policies, once enacted, reshape public opinion, governing institutions, and political organizations. Rather than focusing on the "political feasibility" of proposals for Medicare expansion, I focus on their "policy sustainability": whether proposals, once enacted, can be *established* in place, *entrenched* over time, and *expanded* and improved as circumstances change. Achieving these "three E's," I argue, requires a flexible approach that builds on the current system (and hence falls short of Medicare for All) but also contains a universal coverage guarantee and other provisions designed to create strong feedback effects conducive to the expansion of Medicare over time.

Keywords: health care; health insurance; Medicare; policy feedback; American politics; Affordable Care Act

Growing interest in "Medicare for All" has revived hope for universal health insurance, after a decade of debate over the Affordable Care Act (ACA). Yet despite a near consensus among advocates of expanded coverage that Medicare should be the foundation for future coverage expansions, serious disagreements remain over *how* to expand Medicare and *how far* advocates can and should move toward a universal Medicare system in the relatively near term. Plans for expanding Medicare range from categorical expansions (for example, 55- to 65-year-olds) to various types of

Jacob S. Hacker is Stanley Resor Professor of Political Science and director of the Institution for Social and Policy Studies at Yale University. He is the author or coauthor of five books and numerous articles on American politics and policy and a fellow of the American Academy of Arts and Sciences.

Correspondence: jacob.hacker@yale.edu

DOI: 10.1177/0002716219871017

Medicare buy-in proposals to single-payer national health insurance—each with influential proponents within the health policy community.

In keeping with the goal of this special issue, this article considers these alternative policy ideas in light of what we know about "policy feedback"—the ways in which policies, once enacted, reshape public opinion, governing institutions, and political organizations over time. In particular, I focus on what I term *policy sustainability*, which should be distinguished from the more common phrase *political feasibility*. Feasibility usually concerns whether a policy can be enacted. Sustainability, by contrast, refers to whether policies, once enacted, can be *established* in place, *entrenched* over time, and *expanded* and improved as political and economic circumstances change. These "three E's"—establishment, entrenchment, and expansion—are fundamentally political outcomes. Moreover, they are political outcomes that we should expect to be heavily influenced by policy design, as the large and growing scholarship on policy feedback demonstrates.

Thus, my analysis of proposals for Medicare expansion really gets going where most policy analyses end, with the question of what happens *after* a policy gets passed. I start with (and hopefully justify) the premise that moving from our current system to Medicare for All in one "big bang" will be difficult to achieve and, even if achieved, vulnerable to backlash. But the core of this article concerns how to design reform proposals so that they (1) move as close as possible to the elusive aim of universal Medicare and (2) create feedback effects conducive to further movement toward that goal—that is, to establishment, entrenchment, and expansion.

The Opportunity—and Challenge

Advocates for fundamental reform have embraced Medicare for three good reasons. First, while the ACA has produced tremendous achievements—cutting the share of Americans without health insurance roughly in half, extending new protections to almost everyone with private insurance (for example, requiring coverage for preexisting conditions), and helping to moderate medical inflation—it has not lived up to expectations in one critical area: providing affordable health insurance to those without workplace protections or access to Medicaid (a problem more glaring because of the judicially imposed incompleteness of the ACA's Medicaid expansion). Nor has the ACA created the kind of strong support coalition associated with other landmark social policies. Though political buy-in has increased and may well have been decisive in repelling legislative assaults in 2017, possibilities for *expansion* have seemed more modest. Enthusiasm for building on Medicare is partly a reflection of these lessons.

Second, Medicare has looked better and better relative to private insurance. It provides valuable and valued coverage through a simple enrollment and financing system. Coverage is not contingent on whether someone has the wherewithal or means to navigate a complex eligibility gauntlet; all eligible

Americans are enrolled more or less automatically. What is more, the prices that Medicare pays providers are lower and more consistent across services, regions, and providers (Cooper et al. 2018). And the gap has been growing, as doctors and hospitals increasingly consolidate into large medical systems demanding premium prices. In recent years, Medicare's overall tab has risen with the retirement of the baby boom generation. Yet its spending per enrollee, which is what really matters, has been essentially flat, rising less quickly than either economic growth or inflation (Bivens 2018).

Third, and perhaps most important, Medicare is not only effective; it is overwhelmingly popular (Norton, DiJulio, and Brodie 2015). Republican and Democratic voters alike embrace the program (though the former are much less keen on expanding it to new groups), and everyone knows what it is and roughly how it works. This helps to explain why a number of proposals that envision new systems that are fairly different from the current Medicare system use the label "Medicare for All" (U.S. Congress 2018, 2019).

In short, a much-expanded Medicare program is desirable. It is also arguably more feasible than other equally ambitious proposals. The popularity of Medicare—as well as some of its familiar features that account for its popularity, such as broad access to providers—buffers reform plans that are based on it against some of the harshest political counterwinds. Advocates of affordable, quality coverage for all have very good reasons to make Medicare a cornerstone of their efforts.

Still, Medicare for All will be a heavy political lift. To say that is to state the obvious, and it should not be confused with claims about desirability. If we were building a system for broad coverage and cost control from scratch, the argument for universal Medicare would be extremely strong. But we are not starting from scratch (Hacker 2019a). The exorbitant costs and maddening fragmentation of our health care framework greatly bolster the case for reform. They also greatly increase the likelihood that highly resourced and powerful groups and those with good coverage will be effectively mobilized against it.

How, then, can Medicare be expanded? How can we overcome the formidable hurdles that have stood in the way of affordable universal insurance in the past, especially backlash from powerful vested interests and already-insured Americans? How can we increase the chance of initial *establishment* of a new law and encourage it to become increasingly *entrenched* over time? And how can we maximize the chance that these steps will lead to further ones—to *expansion* as well as establishment and entrenchment?

The key, I argue, is to think about reform as a path, not simply a destination: as a sequence of policy moves, flexible to changing circumstances, that are designed to enhance the power of those sympathetic to further moves, while weakening, sidelining, co-opting—and, yes, in some cases, buying off—opponents. Economists speak of a world of "second bests," in which ideal measures are off the table, either because they do not exist or because they are unattainable. What policy feedback research adds to this familiar refrain is a positive spin: second bests differ a lot with regard to their political effects, and the best of them—the first-best second-best, if you will—have a greater chance of creating positive political forces that foster establishment, entrenchment, and enactment.

The proposal I have developed—and presented at extended length elsewhere (Hacker 2001, 2007, 2019b)—is meant as a constructive contribution to such a discussion. It draws from my own work on the topic beginning in the early 2000s, as well as many current plans for improving the ACA and expanding Medicare. Moreover, it is meant to be open to adaption and modification in several key areas.

In brief, this proposal would make Medicare the default source of coverage for everyone, but then allow people to obtain insurance through employment-based plans—and perhaps high-quality state Medicaid programs—if they met high (and rising) standards. Initially, at least, younger Americans would have their own part of Medicare, which I call "Part E." But the goal would be to spark a flexible step-by-step process that as quickly as possible united everyone without secure insurance within a single public pool. In short, this approach is designed to create a reform path that unites crucial stakeholders and constituencies, fragments or appeases critical organized interests, and yet still puts in place the conditions for effective cost control and continued expansion of Medicare.

Go Big or Go Home?

The struggle over health care has always been about politics as much as policy. The evidence that the American model is inferior is overwhelming (Squires 2015; Papanicolas, Woskie, and Jha 2018). No other country spends as much as we do per capita, but the United States is the only rich democracy without universal insurance, and its health outcomes (including outcomes that are closely linked to the performance of the medical system) are middling to poor (Hacker and Pierson 2016). The problem is not coming up with ideas for reform that would be far better than this policy dumpster fire. The problem is figuring out how to overcome the political barriers to pursuing those ideas—not only to get them passed, but to ensure that they foster the political conditions for continuing improvement.

As already indicated, these challenges can be grouped into three broad categories, which I call the "three E's": the challenge of establishing a policy, especially in the face of likely backlash; the challenge of entrenching it over time, that is, getting beneficiaries and stakeholders to see it as valuable and invest in its continuance; and the challenge of expanding it, which requires not just forestalling a major counterpush against the law but also attracting new allies, gaining stronger allegiance from initial supporters, and creating new opportunities for constructive legislative or executive action.

One important point to emphasize up front is that policy approaches that minimize one set of risks may accentuate others. In particular, provisions designed to ensure quick establishment of a law may not create strong enough institutional foundations or vested interests to ensure entrenchment, much less foster expansion. On the other hand, overcoming initial backlash is a precondition for doing anything else. The first consideration, therefore, must be how to tackle the major sources of initial backlash—both during and after legislative debate—in ways that do not compromise future success.

In health care, the most fundamental of these sources emerge out of the path-dependent development of American health insurance (Hacker 2002). Our nation's costly patchwork quilt of coverage both enriches powerful organized interests and makes middle- and upper-income Americans highly sensitive to perceived new costs or risks. Backlash from these groups (actual or expected) has repeatedly thwarted efforts to achieve universal insurance, and, indeed, it is why Medicare was limited to the elderly in the first place.

As noted, Medicare for All faces a tough climb here. First, it envisions displacing workplace insurance, through which half of Americans receive coverage. Past debates have repeatedly demonstrated that those with such protections can be frightened by the argument that their coverage will be taken away or undermined. Polling shows that support for Medicare for All drops precipitously when the elimination of employment-based insurance is mentioned and, in fact, that many who support a universal Medicare system think they could keep their employment-based coverage under it (Kirzinger, Muñana, and Brodie 2019).

Second, because it replaces employer coverage, Medicare for All involves enormous up-front spending and thus enormous new revenues. There is no need to debate the specifics, since everyone agrees on the basics: American tax levels would have to rise from their current low levels in cross-national perspective to something much closer to the international norm. (My back-of-the-envelope calculation is that annual federal health spending would have to go up by at least 8 percent of GDP: fully financed, this would roughly move the United States up to the German level of taxation.)

To be sure, these new taxes are likely to be lower in the aggregate than existing private payments, leaving most households better off. But they will also be much more visible than today's hidden sources of financing, such as the reduced take-home pay of workers who receive employment-based benefits and the higher taxes that all Americans pay because of tax breaks for these benefits. As a result, many insured Americans will perceive that they are being made worse off—especially after the stakeholders whose interests will be threatened demonize the plan.

In short, political realities and policy requisites collide. Medicare for All would get us to universal coverage and effective cost control. But expecting the breakthrough necessary to pass it could be the political equivalent of waiting for Godot.

Hence the interest in partway proposals—not Medicare for All but "Medicare for More." A large number of such plans have been proposed in the past few years. Among health policy specialists, there has been extensive discussion of the policy differences among these plans and some of the political judgments that lay behind these differences, as well as of some of the economic incentives they might set up over time—such as whether a partial Medicare expansion would be a "glide path" to Medicare for All, as employers enrolled their workers in a lower-cost public plan (Neuman, Pollitz, and Tolbert 2018).

What has not received virtually any attention, however, is the *political* effects each proposal might create. For example, would a buy-in be seen as fallback coverage and shunned by middle-class Americans (especially healthy middle-class Americans) or encounter fierce opposition from current Medicare beneficiaries, worried about their coverage or resentful of new enrollees? Would a proposal that was not designed to achieve universality at first actually create political forces conducive to its achievement, or would movement toward this vital goal stall out (or even reverse), as it has so many times before? The policy differences do not look all that large, but lurking behind sometimes-technical distinctions—or left out altogether—are a number of crucial design choices that are likely to have big political effects.

The remainder of this article is about those choices and which provisions I think have the best chance of resolving them. The basic message is simple: different paths have different likelihoods of reaching an attractive destination because of the political effects they are likely to generate. If Medicare for All might mean "Waiting for Godot," some proposals for expanding Medicare remind me of the old refrain "You can't get there from here." They might be vast improvements, but they are not likely to unleash dynamics that lead to universal coverage or effective cost control. How such a path might be constructed—and where, roughly, we should want it to take us—is the next topic.

Achieving the International Standard

Medicare is an attractive foundation for expanding coverage in part because it upholds the shared cross-national template for successful health policy (White 1995): it covers everyone who is eligible more or less automatically, and it restrains prices without impeding access (indeed, while offering the biggest provider "network" in the world). For almost everyone outside Medicare, either one or both of these elements of the international standard are absent, despite the great advances made by the ACA.

To be sure, there are many outcomes we should care about beyond coverage and costs. But universality and effective price control are both deeply dependent on each other and preconditions for almost every other health policy aim. A proposal for which it is clear that these goals will remain elusive even after enactment, establishment, and entrenchment—that you cannot get there from here—is not a good path to follow.

Of course, forecasting the feedback effects of new policies is difficult. Those who designed Medicare thought it would be a stepping stone to universal insurance. If political conditions had remained as favorable as they were in 1965, perhaps it would have been. But two negative feedback effects probably could have been foreseen (Hacker 2002).

First, Medicare's designers were so focused on finding a political inroad that they basically took the most sympathetic and hard-to-insure groups out of the employment-based system. (The congressional addition of physicians' insurance to Medicare and the last-minute decision to combine Medicaid with Medicare only accentuated this.) Second, the desire to establish the program over provider resistance led to massive cost overruns, coloring perceptions of the program and eating up resources for potential expansions (Oberlander 2003). For both these reasons, Medicare never moved much beyond its original beneficiaries. Indeed, those beneficiaries have resisted new benefits they see as hurting theirs.

Medicare's story suggests not only that feedback effects may be hard to predict but also that there are tensions between establishment and entrenchment, on one hand, and expansion, on the other. Focusing on sympathetic constituencies and providing generous transition payments may facilitate the former but impede the latter. Nonetheless, a generation of work on policy feedback—updated for current hyperpolarized realities—suggests a few general conclusions about reform trajectories that are likely to arc toward universality and cost control.

- *Preventing backlash comes first.* In today's politics, backlash is a certainty— the question is how serious it will be. Unified opposition from partisan opponents, at least at the national level, is a given. Two more variable sources of backlash are medical industry actors and those who have relatively good coverage. The quicker they can be brought on board, or at least partly appeased, the better.
- *Move it or lose it.* Everyone knows windows of opportunity for passing laws are short. So too, however, are windows for establishing them. Quickly getting operations up and running and delivering benefits to key constituencies is vital—at the very least, to weather backlash. By the same token, messing up early can create lasting effects, both perceptual (this program does not work) and material (accommodating to this program is not worth my political or financial capital).
- *Start as big as possible.* A corollary proposition is that it rarely makes sense to have a slow ramp-up of policy operations that are designed in law to be big. Organized opponents just have more time to head things off. For proposals like Medicare expansion where size really matters—small program, small effects—you want to achieve the maximum feasible dimensions as quickly as possible.
- *Structure over specifics.* Though not always true, most policies rise or fall based on a few key structural questions—three, in particular: (1) Does a policy have the basic means to deliver promised benefits? (2) Does it have an adequate revenue stream? (3) And is it designed so that the answers to (1) and (2) will remain affirmative even if lawmaking is stalemated? Structure also shapes the most basic issue: What does this policy look like? If you want a policy to be recognized and its success to create self-reinforcing enthusiasm about what it does, it needs to be relatively visible and simple—at least to key political actors—and it has to create clear enough lines of accountability so that its architects and defenders are given credit for their work and its opponents can be held responsible for their attacks.

Based on these considerations, there is reason to worry that some of the present plans will not get there from here. In particular, proposals that would simply create a Medicare buy-in option or add Medicare to the individual marketplaces do not seem well poised to either become established and entrenched or create expansionary pressures.

The main problem is scale: the public plan envisioned in these proposals just would not cover a lot of people. Small scale is a policy liability, increasing the chance the plan would end up attracting people with disproportionately high health costs and decreasing its leverage to control costs. It is also a major political liability, since these policy problems and the lack of a strong support constituency or serious stakeholder investment would likely quell opportunities for expanding the public plan to a substantial share of the population.

Proposals for categorical expansion raise similar difficulties, though, depending on their design, they could cover a much larger group. The case for expanding Medicare to 55- to 65-year-olds—what Paul Starr calls "midlife Medicare" (Starr 2017)—is strong: this is a group that has faced increasing vulnerability in the labor market and has paid into Medicare for a good chunk of time. It is also a group that bears great similarity to those currently covered by Medicare: enrolling the "near elderly" in Medicare would pose much less threat to the identity of current beneficiaries than adding younger groups.

But these advantages of categorical expansions are counterbalanced by a major disadvantage: the serious risk that such proposals will stall out, leaving us with a bigger Medicare program but not a clear path to further expansions. We only have to look to Medicare's history to see how a policy can create a robust beneficiary group but not strong political dynamics for further expansion. Midlife Medicare would build on the current understanding of the program as an entitlement for retirees and near retirees based on years of work and contributions. Partly for this reason, it might make it even harder to achieve reforms built on different understandings.

A more technical issue that nonetheless really matters is how to integrate a new Medicare plan with employment-based insurance. Buy-ins and public option plans largely assume that such insurance will be minimally touched, at least at the outset, which is one reason why they are unlikely to deliver universal coverage. But a categorical expansion of Medicare forces the question: is everyone in the category in, and if not, how do we ensure that they get covered? On the one extreme, we could just lower the eligibility age for Medicare, full stop. This would require coming up with the revenues to replace displaced coverage and managing the inevitable backlash caused by that displacement—a mini version of the Medicare for All conundrum. On the other extreme, we could have a Medicare buy-in restricted to this group, which might be a "here" even farther from "there" than most buy-ins and public option plans, since it would make the new Medicare option available only to a particular, and potentially small, segment of the workforce.

The Imperative of Enrollment

The foregoing discussion of how coverage expansions might stall out points to an important conclusion: if we want universality, we have to build it into the structure of proposals. Even if we do not think it is achievable in round one, what we put in place in round one should give us the best chance of achieving it in round two (or three or four). If a categorical expansion is just about covering one group, that is not an issue. But if it is about getting to universality, as it should be, it is a big one.

The upshot, I have come to believe, is that all Medicare expansion plans should contain the foundations for universal, automatic enrollment. Without such provisions, proposals are basically designed to give up before the game begins, to accept a world of insecurity in which too many Americans are uninsured or at risk of becoming uninsured. Putting in place the foundations for guaranteed universal coverage does not mean achieving it immediately, or even in a single round. But policies should have a clear path to it.

In the case of categorical expansions, this would most likely entail including provisions that integrate Medicare with employer-sponsored insurance, so that eligible Americans still in the workforce would be assured of either workplace coverage or Medicare. (More in a moment on the general issue of how to allow employment-based insurance to continue without countenancing a world of health insecurity.) A categorical expansion might stall out, and indeed I fear it would, but at least it would ensure coverage of all who were newly eligible.

Guaranteed enrollment would respond to almost every one of the imperatives already discussed. It would create quick, visible effects, promoting political support and ramping up the size of the public plan quickly. It would also reduce the ability of opponents to undermine a Medicare expansion by stealth, deterring enrollment by stigmatizing beneficiaries or cutting funding for marketing and outreach.

Medicare is the gold standard for automaticity: you are 65 or permanently disabled, you are in.[1] Medicaid and marketplace coverage are both more hit or miss: roughly 30 million Americans remain uninsured and the number appears to be rising (Garfield, Orgera, and Damico 2019). The difficulty is twofold: (1) eligibility is complex and varies based on income and other factors; and (2) there is no single "touch point" where people are signed up (and reenrolled when necessary). If the destination is universality and the path is Medicare expansion, both problems must be tackled.

Given the role of employers in the current system, the natural place to begin is the workplace. So long as employers are still providing coverage to some workers, universality will be elusive if there is not a mechanism for (1) determining whether workers get coverage at their place of employment and (2) signing them up for Medicare if they do not. In addition, there is a strong political argument for (3) requiring some contribution toward the cost of that coverage, as I discuss here.

The ACA does not do this: its coverage requirement only applies to larger employers (at least 50 full-time workers), the penalty for noncompliance is not a contribution to the cost of coverage, and the requirement only applies if the worker receives subsidies for private individual coverage through the regulated marketplaces. Most important, there is no process for automatically enrolling workers in coverage if their employer does not provide it. Add on top of this that many eligible for Medicaid do not get signed up—whether because they are unaware they could be covered; they are cycling between jobs or moving between states; or they are deterred by complex, burdensome, and stigmatizing eligibility rules—and it is clear our current system is very far from having the foundations for guaranteed coverage.

The Medicare Part E proposal I have outlined would guarantee coverage in a few ways. Most important, it would change the ACA's "play-or-penalty" approach into a true "play-or-pay" system. Employers would still have to provide insurance ("play") or make a payment to the federal government. But these payments made in lieu of providing coverage would be considered *contributions* rather than penalties, with workers whose employers made the contribution automatically enrolled in Part E. (The design of these contributions is discussed later in this article, as it is closely related to Part E's over-time expansion.) And if employers did provide insurance, their coverage would have to meet high minimum standards, including automatic enrollment of workers. To ensure the federal government has an accurate record of all employment-based coverage, firms of all sizes would need to report if they covered their workers.[2] However, smaller firms would not necessarily have to pay a contribution, and contributions could be nominal to nonexistent for smaller, lower-wage firms. Similarly, the contribution requirement would have to extend to independent contractors and other self-employed workers (who would pay the contribution directly, as with Social Security taxes).

A play-or-pay requirement of this sort would essentially reach everyone who worked or lived in a family with a worker, including the self-employed. As a result, all but a tiny slice of Americans would have the opportunity to be automatically enrolled within a short period of time (Lewin Group 2008). To reach this small slice would require additional steps: signing people up when they receive other public benefits, or file their taxes, or seek care without insurance. But just as important as signing people up will be making sure they remain signed up. Today, most insurance requires that subscribers establish their eligibility up front and cuts them off if they fail to establish it or do not pay their premiums. Guaranteed coverage requires the opposite: sign people up and keep them signed up as long as they do not have a qualified alternative, and only in that context figure out what and how they can pay.

The debate over Medicare expansion is mostly focused on *what* will be expanded—Medicare, or something close to it. To really move to universal coverage, however, we need to know *how* people actually get covered by this expanded system. This is particularly true of plans that fall short of universal Medicare. After all, Medicare for All has an answer to the coverage question: you are born, you are in. Those who advocate a partial Medicare expansion have to answer the question as well, even if their path to universality may be longer and less direct.

From Us versus Them to Them versus Us

The most effective attack on universal health care is relatively simple: you want to help "them" (lower-income Americans who lack coverage) at the expense of "us" (higher-income Americans who have it). This is a smear, of course, and it is a smear that easily becomes racially laden, since the first group is much more likely to be nonwhite than the latter. But it is a smear that works because it contains some truth. In health care, progressive reforms *have* tended to provide the most visible direct benefits to Americans of modest means. The persistent fiscal constraints created by tax cutting push advocates to fixate on incremental federal costs and focus on those most likely to be uninsured. At the same time, the insurance arrangements of middle-class and affluent Americans, however flawed, have deep-pocketed defenders in the corporate and medical worlds.

The result is a vicious circle: the path of least resistance leads to cash-strapped reforms that leave millions uninsured while protecting the costliest segments of the system. This means that many Americans who are *not* low-income remain deeply insecure and that federal dollars spent on health care buy much less than they would in a system with reasonable costs. It also means that the minority of Americans younger than 65 who see government insurance as essential to their well-being lack the political heft or cohesion to defend what they have, much less advocate for more. It is hard to imagine a political dynamic more corrosive of solidarity than this.

Thus, a central imperative of Medicare expansion—perhaps *the* central imperative—is to foster communities of shared interest. Medicare has to be seen as a source of health security for many more nonelderly Americans. At the same time, both Medicare beneficiaries and those who remain in employment-based health plans have to see a direct link between a broader Medicare program and better benefits for themselves.

This imperative has at least three implications. First, Medicare has to be improved for older and disabled Americans if it is to be expanded to the rest of Americans. If the fight over the ACA carries any lesson, it is that Medicare beneficiaries need assurances that their benefits are secure and improving. It should not take two or three elections for them to find out that Medicare benefits are better and death panels are a conservative bogeyman.

Fortunately, smart politics is also good policy. For all its popularity and success, Medicare has significant gaps (Cubanski and Boccuti 2015). Addressing these shortcomings may not be sufficient to assuage beneficiaries' concerns, but if the upgrades are substantial and rapid, they should minimize the kind of backlash seen in the 2010 to 2014 interregnum.

Second, and by the same token, a Medicare expansion needs to provide something tangible to workers whose employers continue to provide insurance. To be sure, it will provide the security of knowing that if you lose or change jobs, you will have a simple, affordable option that is the same nationwide. Given the weaknesses of the marketplaces, the promise of fallback coverage provided by the ACA is much less reassuring.

Still, any proposal that envisions a good chunk of Americans remaining in employment-based coverage has to make workplace plans work better for the tens of millions of Americans who remain vulnerable to high medical bills and unexpected insurance gaps (Sawyer, Cox, and Claxton 2017; Claxton et al. 2017). The ACA's standards are simply not high enough, a reflection of the narrow political window it had to pass through and the determination not to displace employment-based insurance. These standards need to be upgraded in a way that is visible, impactful, and directly linked to the expansion of Medicare.

In Medicare Part E, these linked imperatives would be achieved by upgrading Medicare for all beneficiaries, older and younger alike, and making this new benefit standard a floor for private coverage. To meet the play-or-pay requirement, in other words, employer plans would have to be as generous as Medicare. Thus, Medicare Part E would not only provide a guaranteed source of coverage; it would also set a floor for benefit generosity outside Medicare. Medicare would thus provide a high level of coverage for all its beneficiaries, and the quality of insurance would also improve for those whose employment-based coverage was below Medicare's new standard.

The third implication is that Medicaid has to be integrated more fully with Medicare and workplace plans. Medicaid has evolved tremendously in the past half century—from a marginal program of welfare medicine into the nation's largest insurer. And it has proven more resilient than many experts, myself included, expected. Nonetheless, it remains highly variable in generosity from state to state, is facing severe political and fiscal pressures, and pays doctors and hospitals so little that many providers refuse to accept it. The biggest problem, of course, is the continuing unwillingness of some states to expand their programs. But there are also millions of Americans who are eligible for Medicaid yet fall through its cracks, deterred by burdensome rules and the stigma the program still carries. What is more, a number of GOP-controlled states—with the imprimatur of the Trump administration—are increasing both the burdens and the stigma, which makes mainstreaming Medicaid all the more vital.

It will not be easy, as Jamila Michener's article in this special issue makes clear. Medicaid has its own political defenders, who understandably worry its beneficiaries will be harmed more than helped by folding the program into a national plan. Meanwhile, opponents will use this specter to frighten those currently on Medicare. And Medicaid is comparatively cheap—upgrading its payments and ensuring everyone eligible for it gets covered will raise the price of reform. But it is a price worth paying. No policy will reach universality if it keeps Medicaid as-is, and consigning the disadvantaged to a wholly separate system will only perpetuate the vicious cycle of us versus them.

At a minimum, Medicaid enrollment should be shifted to be automatic. In Medicare Part E, for example, when people were enrolled in Part E—whether through the workplace or through other efforts—federal authorities could check whether they qualified for Medicaid and, if so, transfer their coverage to state offices. In turn, states could be required to tell the federal government whom they covered through Medicaid and to inform the federal government whenever that coverage lapsed for whatever reason, so those affected could be covered by Part E. This alone would transform Medicaid from a program people scramble to get into—and frequently get knocked off of—into something much closer to the Medicare model, in which those who are eligible are automatically insured.

If there is going to be division, it has to be between a big us and a small them—everyone who has come to see Medicare and the standards it sets as critical to their health security and the deep-pocketed defenders of our exorbitant system who stand in the way of this goal.

Cost Control without (Too Much) Backlash

These deep-pocketed defenders are not particularly popular, which makes them an attractive target for reformers. They are, however, politically powerful. Organized interests that reap outsized rewards from lucrative pockets of American health care are perhaps the biggest wild cards in any reform fight. They will be against big changes, that much is sure, but how deep and prolonged their opposition is will matter greatly not just for enactment, but also establishment, entrenchment, and expansion.

The general advice from policy feedback research is that forestalling backlash and building communities of interest require spending generously and rapidly at the outset. But this advice raises the obvious rejoinder: how? New spending might not have to be paid for initially, but it will have to be eventually. Sustainable programs need sustainable revenues. And other progressive policies, such as infrastructure investment, have much greater claim to our deficit dollars.

Supporters of Medicare for All have proved reluctant to answer this question (wisely, I think—but they cannot remain silent forever). The basic approach, however, is clear: on one hand, replace premiums and a good chunk of out-of-pocket payments with taxes; on the other, generate major savings to ensure those taxes are not exorbitant. And, in theory, near-instant savings of considerable magnitude are possible: Medicare for All universalizes coverage within a single public insurance pool, lowering administrative costs, eliminating profits, and giving the federal government the leverage to cut prices.

The rub is that all this will provoke major opposition. Tax resistance has already been mentioned. But no less daunting is the prospect of quickly ratcheting down prices to Medicare levels, much less to international norms. The familiar adage that every dollar of health spending is someone's income is *literally* true when it comes to physicians, who make much more than doctors in other rich nations (especially specialists). But it is essentially true for every part of our medical-industrial complex: drug companies, hospitals, medical device manufacturers, and on and on. Only insurers, perhaps, do not have a lot at stake if prices come down. But by proposing to basically do away with them, Medicare for All would give them plenty of reason to fight, too.

So the two-part answer embodied in Medicare for All—raise taxes and cut prices—is at odds with what will almost certainly need to be done to get a new policy enacted and established. No country has gotten to universal insurance without making huge concessions to powerful private interests, and no country has had to deal with providers so consolidated and costly, drug manufacturers so insulated from competition and accountability, or insurers so free to make profits for doing what most countries consider a routine public function (Hacker 1998). The question is not whether concessions will be made; the question is what they will be.

A word of caution: 'tis the season of legislative sponsorship, when visions of precise legislative language dance through policy-makers' heads. Savvy bargaining may entail holding back some concessions that almost certainly will have to be granted. But it is a mistake to confuse current bills with future bargaining. Some sponsors of current legislation are incorporating the bargains they think will happen; others may be anticipating them but offering what is in effect their opening bid. Both approaches have merit, but neither is what will happen as an actual legislative package wends its way toward enactment. When we are pondering policy strategy rather than preparing legislative text, we should try to be clear about what we *expect* to happen as opposed to what we would like to happen.

What I expect to happen is relatively generous treatment of the medical industry in round one, but ideally a law that also puts in place the structural features that will ensure serious savings in the future. Expanding but not universalizing Medicare has many defects, but it does mean that major interests would not suddenly see their reimbursements for everything plunge to Medicare levels. At the same time, if the public plan is sufficiently big—refer back to the earlier discussion—a lot more people would still be covered by Medicare, which would mean more services financed at Medicare rates. Meanwhile, private insurers selling their services to employers that still offer coverage would face competitive pressure to demand lower prices so employers would not see it as a better deal to switch their workers into Medicare, too.

What about private plans that participate in Medicare Advantage and now enroll roughly a third of current beneficiaries? To minimize backlash, it seems wise to allow them to continue to operate within Medicare (with ongoing refinement of how these plans are paid to reduce overpayments). For one, Medicare patients like these options. Think how easy it will be to create resistance from current beneficiaries if reformers tell older and disabled Americans who are in private plans that they are no longer available. For another, it is hard to see how private options can be preserved for older and disabled Americans but blocked for new enrollees in Medicare. And given that a fair number of people will be moving from private employment-based coverage into Medicare, it seems wise to reassure workers that they will be available, too.

But the public is not the real problem; *insurers* are. The biggest companies are deeply invested in Medicare Advantage. Ensuring they still had a role in a postreform world—especially when it was lessened in other parts of the market— would reduce their inevitable opposition. Indeed, Medicare is much more attractive than the ACA marketplaces to the largest insurers, which have largely failed to jump into them.

Many progressive advocates are rightly critical of Medicare Advantage. But the program was improved by the ACA, which reduced plan payments to better reflect the true cost of providing benefits. Most plans actually pay rates close to Medicare's (Medicare Payment Advisory Commission 2017). This is, in large part, because they operate in a market in which their main competitor is Medicare. Thus, they can pay Medicare-like rates and still get providers to participate in their networks. (This, by the way, is one reason why privatizing Medicare would be a disaster; without the bargaining clout of the traditional program, private plans would be paying the exorbitant prices they pay in the rest of the market.)

Expanding Medicare to a large number of younger Americans might even give private plans additional leverage over providers. After all, even the most consolidated and costly provider systems accept Medicare rates for older patients. Once Medicare was expanded, these lower rates would be paid on behalf of many younger Americans, too. For providers, the alternative to private payments would increasingly be Medicare rates for younger as well as older patients. As result, private plans might well be able to lower what they paid for nonelderly patients and still attract providers.

The general rule of thumb is that reformers should try to minimize up-front losses for powerful stakeholders. The exception is when such losses—read: revenues and savings—are integral to the design of the proposal and, in particular, to creating a sustainable revenue stream. In Medicare Part E, for example, the payroll-based contributions by employers fall into this category. They help to fund Part E and create a link between contributions and benefits, as in Social Security. Those newly enrolled in Medicare should also pay a modest premium. As in Part B, these premiums should cover only a small fraction of the total cost, and vary by income, with lower-income enrollees paying a minimal amount. Similarly, improved benefits for current Medicare beneficiaries could be financed in part by increasing the Medicare tax paid by workers.

None of this is to minimize the difficulty of raising the necessary revenue. (Ironically, the 2017 tax cuts could help with the problem, since ending them would be a popular way to raise revenues.[3]) Still, because most Americans who receive employment-based insurance would continue to do so and because employers would be required to contribute something, the additional new taxes needed would be much more modest than those for Medicare for All.

Two potential sources of *savings* are also critical enough to risk backlash: regulated provider payments and price bargaining for prescription drugs. In each case, the goal should be to begin with arrangements generous enough to blunt opposition yet that embody the capacity for future restraint. For example, providers could be required to treat newly enrolled Medicare patients if they accept traditional Medicare, but initial payments could contain a bonus of some sort, phased out over time. Even a partial move toward Medicare rates would produce major savings.

With drug manufacturers, price bargaining could begin with frequently used and high-cost drugs that have few substitutes and gradually move to a formulary of the sort most nations use. Initially, prices could be negotiated on behalf of private Part D plans, before moving to allow direct coverage of prescription drugs through Medicare itself. These changes will encounter serious opposition, but the cost savings from allowing Medicare to bargain for lower drug prices and provide a drug benefit directly are so substantial that significant pushback is worth courting.[4]

These examples illustrate the balance that will have to be struck between establishment and entrenchment. If a plan is really to be a "glide path" to universal affordable health care, it is going to need a fair amount of altitude at the outset and a relatively low-angle descent. It will also need some power—self-reinforcing dynamics that foster expansion.

Fostering Expansion

If backers of Medicare for All have to explain how it passes, advocates of Medicare for More have to explain how it grows: how does their plan expand into affordable health care for all?

In our joint article in this special issue, Paul Pierson and I call this "sequencing." If complete transit is unlikely, how much pressure will each step in a sequence of reforms create for the next? Sequencing should be distinguished from "staging": the steps laid out in a bill for implementing specific provisions over time. Medicare for All bills, for example, often include some initial moves toward that goal. But these early provisions are staged, not sequenced, and opponents will inevitably focus on the final stage: universal Medicare. In the best case, staging gives advocates time to get things right and create buy-in. In the worst, it gives opponents time to undermine or reverse the policy.

Sequencing, by contrast, involves multiple rounds of policymaking in which each policy ideally creates momentum for the next. And it has to be at the heart of any evaluation of plans to expand but not universalize Medicare. Such plans need to provide a focal point for expansion, easily understood and defended. They need to offer cost-saving opportunities for employers, states, and individuals so they buy in. In short, they need to embody a step-by-step process (flexible to changing circumstances) that unites crucial stakeholders and constituencies, fragments or appeases opposition forces, and yet still puts in place the conditions for effective cost control and continued expansion of Medicare.

Although the ACA finally appears well established, its ability to create such expansionary forces has proven mixed. More and more states are expanding Medicaid, but the ACA has not generated the kind of middle-class buy-in that has made Medicare so popular and resilient. To the contrary, many Americans still see the law as a threat to their benefits, despite the many ways in which it improved Medicare and private plans.

Such scare tactics will be harder when benefits are provided directly by Medicare. Medicare is familiar, and people know they have it because of government. In addition, if Medicare becomes the benefit floor for private plans, Medicare expansion would encourage privately insured workers to believe they had a stake in the program, too.

Employers' role is pivotal in this regard. If they see Medicare as an attractive means of insuring their workers, they are much more likely to climb on board. In the past, business opposition to social programs withered once employers realized they were a good deal. Although such dynamics are likely to be more muted today, a Medicare expansion could appease or fragment key parts of the business community if designed correctly.

In my proposal for Medicare Part E, for example, the employer contributions are meant to be significantly lower than the full cost of coverage, in part to minimize corporate resistance, in part to encourage enrollment in Medicare. They should be in there to encourage large employers to continue to provide insurance on their own (which would also decrease initial backlash by reducing revenue needs and coverage dislocations). But they should be modest and raise only a small share of the total cost of expanded Medicare coverage.

A similar set of considerations arise with regard to Medicaid. For example, a reform plan could give states strong incentives to cover low-income families through Medicare. States would not be allowed to simply "dump" Medicaid beneficiaries into Medicare, but they could be given a fairly generous deal, so those ambivalent about managing coverage see gains in transferring it to the federal government. Of course, this would also make it more likely that low-income Americans would enjoy seamless coverage through Medicare.[5]

One of the virtues of Medicare Part E is that its core components could be pursued sequentially. Indeed, many of them have already been established by the ACA—preexisting coverage protections, limits on lifetime benefit caps, coverage of young adults under their parents' employer plans—while others build on the ACA's provisions, such as the shift from a play-or-penalty to a play-or-pay requirement.

Consider the following sequence. First, Medicare could be upgraded and employers given the option of buying in to cover their workers. At the same time, the standards for employment-based plans could be raised. Then, the penalty under the ACA could be transformed into a contribution requirement—first for larger employers, then for all employers. Each of these steps would be popular, do much good, and create momentum for further action.

The test with any sequenced approach is whether each step will increase the pressure for more. As I have argued, simply adding Medicare to the marketplaces or even expanding Medicare to new categorical groups might not meet that test. I think Medicare Part E does meet it—that is, it is likely to get us to guaranteed universal coverage through a self-reinforcing process.

Conclusion

Advocates of fundamental health reform will continue to debate the best way forward. Such disagreements, however, should not obscure shared principles: that affordable health care coverage should be guaranteed for everyone and that the bargaining power of a democratically accountable government can and should be used to restrain costs.

The disagreements that remain are real, but many reflect issues of political feasibility—and, in particular, differing assessments of whether we can almost immediately replace the current employment-based patchwork framework (and especially all employment-based plans, which cover approximately 150 million Americans) with a single system that replaces the bulk of current private financing with new federal taxes. The hopes of advocates of universal insurance are mostly shared. Their assessments of what is politically possible are not.

In this article, I have sought to add issues of *sustainability* to the conversation: how can we establish a policy, entrench it, and create expansionary pressures over time? These three E's, I have argued, need at least as much consideration as the challenge of enactment.

For those who think my proposal is still too timid, I hope that this article will at least help them to think through what kinds of fallback options *would* be acceptable, with "acceptable" meaning capable of achieving their ultimate goals. For those who find my approach more attractive, I hope that my discussion will encourage them to broaden their thinking, too. All who believe in affordable quality health care for everyone need to move beyond easy critiques and start talking about how shared goals can be achieved—if not in a single enactment, through a sequence of self-reinforcing steps.

Notes

1. Though, technically, Part B is voluntary, nobody in his or her right mind would choose to disenroll, given the modest premium.

2. As under the ACA, I think employers should be allowed to distinguish between full- and part-time workers—if they chose to provide insurance only to full timers, they would make the contribution just for part timers, who would be enrolled in Medicare Part E.

3. Indeed, a perverse benefit of the tax cuts is that they allow coverage expansions to be financed by simply failing to continue prior giveaways, without running afoul of rules against deficit spending. This means that many of the components of Medicare Part E should be passable through the budget process, which prevents a Senate filibuster.

4. Allowing Medicare to provide a direct drug benefit would have another payoff, too: it would level the playing field between Medicare and Medicare Advantage plans. Today, only private plans are allowed to cover prescription medicine alongside other services, which is one big reason beneficiaries enroll in them. (Beneficiaries of traditional Medicare have to enroll in private Part D plans to receive drug benefits.) Sweeten Medicare, and Medicare Advantage plans lose this unfair advantage.

5. Moreover, what is good politically and programmatically might also be good constitutionally. The Supreme Court's ostensible problem with the ACA's Medicaid expansion is that it was too coercive. Though an increasingly conservative court will be ginning for a fight, more generous terms may forestall a successful challenge.

References

Bivens, Josh. 2018. *The unfinished business of health reform.* Washington, DC: Economic Policy Institute. Available from https://www.epi.org/files/pdf/152676.pdf.

Claxton, Gary, Matthew Rae, Michelle Long, and Anthony Damico. 2017. 2017 Employer Health Benefits Survey. Washington, DC: Kaiser Family Foundation and Health Research and Education Trust. Available from www.kff.org.

Cooper, Zack, Stuart V. Craig, Martin Gaynor, and John Van Reenan. 2018. The price ain't right? Hospital prices and health spending on the privately insured. *Quarterly Journal of Economics* 134 (1): 51–107.

Cubanski, Juliette, and Cristina Boccuti. 2015. Medicare coverage, affordability, and access. *Generations* 39 (2): 26–34.

Garfield, Rachel, Kendal Orgera, and Anthony Damico. January 2019. The uninsured and the ACA: A primer – Key facts about health insurance and the uninsured amidst changes to the Affordable Care Act. Washington, DC: Kaiser Family Foundation. Available from https://www.kff.org.

Hacker, Jacob S. 1998. The historical logic of national health insurance: Structure and sequence in the development of British, Canadian, and U.S. medical policy. *Studies in American Political Development* 12 (1): 57–130.

Hacker, Jacob S. 2001. Medicare Plus: Increasing healthcare coverage by expanding Medicare. In *Covering America: Real remedies for the uninsured*, eds. Jack A. Meyer and Elliot K. Wicks, 73–100. Washington, DC: Economic and Social Research Institute.

Hacker, Jacob S. 2002. *The divided welfare state: The battle over public and private social benefits in the United States*. New York, NY: Cambridge University Press.

Hacker, Jacob S. 11 January 2007. Health care for America: A proposal for guaranteed, affordable health care for all Americans building on Medicare and employment-based insurance. Economic Policy Institute Briefing Paper No. 180, Washington, DC.

Hacker, Jacob S. 2019a. *The great risk shift*. 2nd ed. New York, NY: Oxford University Press.

Hacker, Jacob S. 3 January 2019 (2019b). The road to Medicare for everyone. *American Prospect*. Available from www.prospect.org.

Hacker, Jacob S., and Paul Pierson. 2016. *American amnesia: How the war on government led us to forget what made America prosper*. New York, NY: Simon & Schuster.

Kirzinger, Ashley, Cailey Muñana, and Mollyann Brodie. 23 January 2019. KFF Health Tracking Poll – January 2019: The public on next steps for the ACA and proposals to expand coverage. Washington, DC: Kaiser Family Foundation. Available from www.kff.org.

Lewin Group. 2008. *Cost impact analysis for "Health Care for America" proposal*. Washington, DC: Economic Policy Institute. Available from http://www.sharedprosperity.org/hcfa/lewin.pdf.

Medicare Payment Advisory Commission. 2017. Status report on the Medicare Advantage Program. In *Report to the Congress: Medicare payment policy*. Washington, DC: MedPAC. Available from www.medpac.gov.

Neuman, Tricia, Karen Pollitz, and Jennifer Tolbert. October 2018. *Medicare-for-All and public plan buy-in proposals: Overview and key issues*. Washington, DC: Kaiser Family Foundation. Available from www.kff.org.

Norton, Mira, Bianca DiJulio, and Mollyann Brodie. July 2015. *Medicare and Medicaid at 50*. Washington, DC: Kaiser Family Foundation. Available from www.kff.org.

Oberlander, Jonathan. 2003. *The political life of Medicare*. Chicago, IL: University of Chicago Press.

Papanicolas, Irene, Liana R. Woskie, and Ashish K. Jha. 2018. Health care spending in the United States and other high-income countries. *JAMA* 319 (10): 1024–36.

Sawyer, Bradley, Synthia Cox, and Gary Claxton. 4 October 2017. *An analysis of who is most at risk for high out-of-pocket spending*. Washington, DC: Kaiser Family Foundation. Available from www.health-systemtracker.org.

Squires, David. 8 October 2015. *U.S. health care from a global perspective*. New York, NY: The Commonwealth Fund. Available from www.commonwealthfund.org.

Starr, Paul. 23 March 2017. The next progressive health agenda. *The American Prospect*.

U.S. Congress. 2018. Senate. Medicare for All Act of 2017. S 1804. 115th Cong. Available from https://www.congress.gov.

U.S. Congress. 2019. House. Medicare for All Act of 2019. HR 1384. 116th Cong. Available from https://www.congress.gov.

White, Joseph. 1995. *Competing solutions: American health care proposals and international experience*. Washington, DC: Brookings Institution Press.

Prescriptions: Jobs, Wages, and Regional Development

Regions of the United States have seen their incomes diverge dramatically over the last four decades. This article makes the empirical and political case for treating regional economic disparities as a national phenomenon best resolved through federal policy, rather than exclusively as a matter of local responsibility. It then considers reinvigorated antitrust enforcement as an example of a federal policy that would strengthen local economies while benefiting from policy feedback effects.

Keywords: inequality; regional disparities; antitrust; policy feedbacks

Antitrust Enforcement as Federal Policy to Reduce Regional Economic Disparities

By
ROBERT MANDUCA

The last 40 years have seen a dramatic widening of economic disparities between regions of the United States. A handful of rich coastal metros have seen their incomes grow substantially, while large regions of the country struggle with unemployment and stagnation. This regional inequality is uniquely consequential for U.S. politics because political power is distributed geographically, meaning that unlike other social groups, struggling places are guaranteed to keep their representation.

In this article, I argue that rising regional inequality should be thought of first and foremost as a consequence of national economic policy—that is, it stems from political decisions made at the federal level. In addition to being an accurate reflection of the forces that have buffeted many parts of the United States since 1980, this framing will help to generate the political will to address regional divergence, particularly from within struggling regions themselves.

Robert Manduca is a PhD candidate in Sociology and Social Policy and a doctoral fellow in the Multidisciplinary Program in Inequality and Social Policy at Harvard University.

Correspondence: rmanduca@g.harvard.edu

DOI: 10.1177/0002716219868141

Second, I explore the policy feedback dynamics in one national policy area with important regional implications: antitrust enforcement. There is a growing movement to strengthen antitrust policy in light of rapid corporate consolidation in recent years. Here I describe why antitrust enforcement has important implications for regional economies and how a new antitrust regime could benefit from policy feedback effects that would help to entrench and expand its impact once established. I also highlight some advantages that may make antitrust enforcement easier to enact than other federal regional development policies, as well as some strategic considerations in the initial enactment.

The Geographic Concentration of Prosperity

One of the most wrenching social and economic shifts to hit the United States over the past 40 years has been the geographic concentration of prosperity. Since 1980, the income gap between the richest and poorest regions of the country has widened by 50 percent, a reversal of more than 100 years of economic convergence (Ganong and Shoag 2017). A handful of metro areas have seen concentrations of wealth almost unprecedented in human history, while a much larger set has seen their jobs evaporate and their economic bases contract. In addition to the direct economic pain this causes, it likely contributes to family instability (Autor, Dorn, and Hanson 2017; Wilson 1996), diminished mobility prospects for children (Sharkey 2013; Sharkey and Faber 2014), and declining social and political cohesion (Beramendi 2012).

The size of the change is shown in Figure 1, which plots mean family income by commuting zone (a definition of metro area comprising a central city and surrounding suburban counties) as a fraction of the national mean family income in 1980 and 2013. In 1980, the picture is one of relative consistency across most of the country. New York (specifically the New Jersey suburbs) and Washington, D.C., stand out as cities with mean incomes more than 20 percent higher than the nation as a whole, while rural parts of the Southeast and Southwest had incomes substantially lower than average. Across the rest of the country, average incomes fell into a tight band between 80 percent and 120 percent of the national mean.

By 2013, this was no longer true. Most of the East Coast had joined New York and D.C. in the highest income category, as had northern California and Minneapolis-St. Paul. At the same time, rural economies across the country had hollowed out, with most rural parts of the Pacific Northwest, the Midwest, and California joining those in the Southeast and Southwest in the bottom income category. In total, whereas just 12 percent of the U.S. population in 1980 lived in commuting zones with mean family incomes more than 20 percent higher or lower than the national average, by 2013 the share had climbed to 31 percent.

FIGURE 1
Commuting Zone Mean Family Income as a Fraction of the National Average,
1980 and 2013

A: 1980

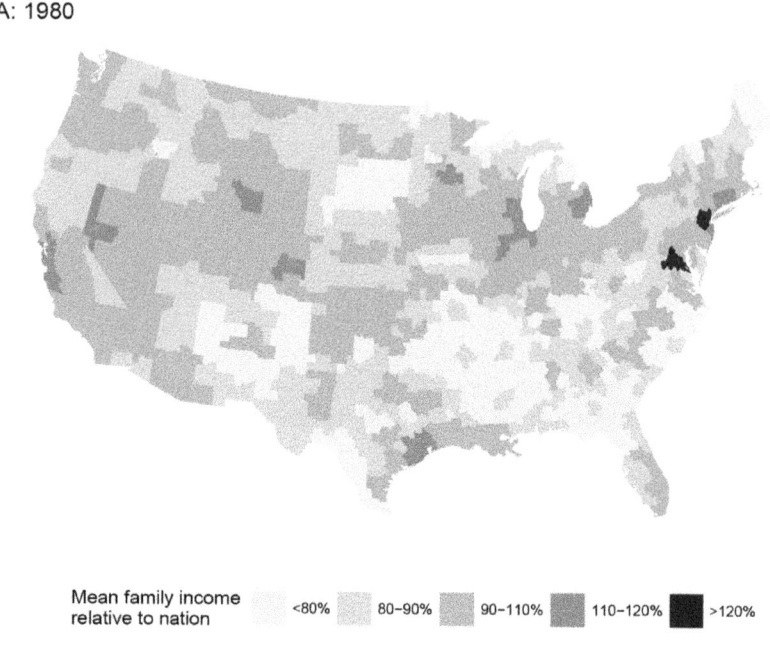

B: 2013

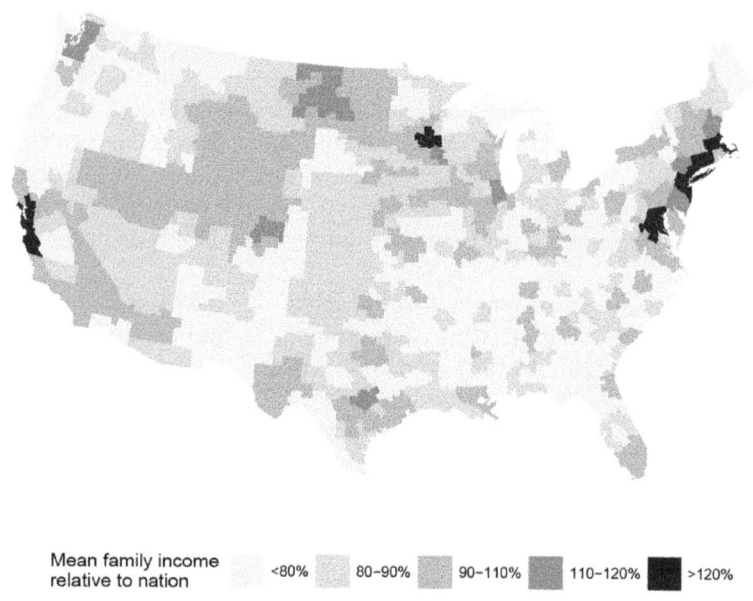

SOURCE: Reproduced from Manduca (2019).

The unique political consequences of inequality between regions

Inequality between places is uniquely consequential for U.S. politics because declining areas retain their political representation. No matter how much a state's population shrinks, it keeps its two Senate seats. And while House districts are redrawn every 10 years, they are drawn based on residential, not voting, population. Because voting is strongly correlated with income (Leighley and Nagler 2013), this means that poor places maintain a political voice that poor people as individuals often do not. For example, in 2018 just 175,000 voters participated in the contested election for WV-03, a district with a median income of $36,000. This is fewer than half of the 370,000 votes cast in MO-02, another close election, but one held in a district with a median income of $79,000 (Golshan and Mark 2018). Yet both districts have equal representation in Congress. This means that the federal government is structurally predisposed to address the concerns of districts like WV-03 out of proportion to either their financial resources or political mobilization.

The geographical apportionment of representation should lead the federal government to spend disproportionate effort addressing the challenges facing struggling regions, all else equal. But such action has been largely absent. In part, this is because local economic performance is not typically discussed as a national political issue, but rather as the responsibility of local governments and civic leaders. This article argues that local economic performance should be treated as a national issue on both empirical and political grounds.

Local Economic Performance Is a National Political Issue

At first glance, it is not necessarily apparent that the economic performance of local regions should be thought of as a national issue. Just as an individual's economic success in the United States is often attributed primarily to his or her personal actions and character traits, so regional economic success is frequently described as stemming predominantly from local actions. Conversely, regional economic difficulties are often attributed to local failings.

This "local responsibility" view of regional economic development pervades much of the writing, both academic and popular, that examines the plight of struggling regions. Popular writers have profiled successful regions in the hope that other places can adopt the strategies they have taken (Fallows and Fallows 2018). Academic researchers, too, have sought to identify the local characteristics that predict economic success, using both case studies (Saxenian 1996; Storper et al. 2015) and large-sample quantitative analyses (Benner and Pastor 2012; Kemeny and Storper 2012). Some findings of this literature have emphasized the importance of developing tightly knit "clusters" of interrelated industries (Porter 1998). Other studies have encouraged regions to develop urban amenities that can attract the highly skilled workers who currently command high wages (Clark et al. 2002; Florida 2002; Glaeser, Kolko, and Saiz 2001), while a third set has highlighted the role of interconnected leadership networks that allow diverse groups of local stakeholders to jointly solve local problems (Benner and Pastor 2015; Storper et al. 2015).

These recommendations are typically aimed at local policy-makers, suggesting actions that can be undertaken independently by individual regions. There are good reasons for this approach: in the absence of a concerted national effort, individual places can only control what goes on within their borders, and some places have been remarkably effective at navigating the twenty-first-century economy. But as a diagnosis of why so many places are currently struggling, and as a proposal for fixing this problem at scale, the local responsibility view is incorrect empirically and misguided politically.

Empirics: Regional disparities largely result from national trends

The local responsibility view of regional economic development, and the associated focus on restoring prosperity by improving local competitiveness, fundamentally misunderstands the changes that have caused regional disparities to increase. There has always been a vigorous economic competition between cities in the United States—nineteenth-century civic boosters make that abundantly clear. But for more than 100 years up to the 1970s, poor regions still gained on rich ones on average (Barro and Sala-i-Martin 1992). Starting in the late 1970s, some aspect of the competition changed, and rich regions began pulling further ahead. The core question about regional divergence, then, is not why some regions do better than others economically. It is why the gap between winners and losers suddenly started increasing in the late 1970s.

Much of the research studying this reversal has attributed it to a change in the spatial distribution of different types of workers. Starting around 1980, college-educated workers in particular began to cluster in a relatively small number of cities (Moretti 2012). Possible explanations for this concentration include the rise of industries with strong economies of agglomeration (Diamond 2016; Kemeny and Storper 2012), the increasing importance of urban amenities to high-income workers (Clark et al. 2002; Florida 2002; Glaeser, Kolko, and Saiz 2001), or the implementation of increasingly restrictive zoning and occupational licensing laws that make it more difficult for people to move to prosperous areas (Schleicher 2017; Ganong and Shoag 2017). In line with these findings, the most prominent policy proposals to reverse regional divergence have focused on undoing this sorting and spatially redistributing high-paying jobs and skilled workers back to struggling areas. Some would do this by subsidizing employment in struggling regions (Austin, Glaeser, and Summers 2018), while others would make it easier for lower-income workers to move to thriving metros (Avent 2011; Yglesias 2012), or directly relocate institutions and government agencies away from coastal metros (MacGillis 2010; Yglesias 2016).

These policies are unlikely to have success on their own because they misunderstand the core driver of regional economic divergence. While there has indeed been a spatial concentration of college educated workers, and a sorting of people across metro areas by income, its contribution to divergence is relatively small. A more important factor has been rising income inequality at the national level. If there had been no income sorting whatsoever, rising income inequality alone would still have increased the economic disparities between regions by more than half as much as actually occurred. But if income inequality had been kept constant, the observed amount of sorting would have only increased disparities between regions by about a quarter of the true amount (Manduca 2019). The widening gap between rich and poor regions is thus first and foremost a reflection of the widening gap between rich and poor people. And while the causes of rising inequality are hotly debated, they almost certainly include many changes to national economic policy made beginning in the 1970s and 1980s (Hacker and Pierson 2010).

Thus, purely as a matter of policy, reinvigorating the economies of struggling regions and reducing the gaps between rich and poor places are likely to require national action. Framing regional divergence as a national policy decision rather than a matter of local responsibility is also more likely to generate the political will needed to address it.

Political consequences of treating regional divergence as a national policy issue

In addition to being empirically accurate, framing regional disparities as the consequence and responsibility of federal economic policy rather than local failings is likely to be a potent political message. Rather than telling rural or rust belt voters that their hometown economic struggles are their fault and that their cities need to "shrink to greatness" (Glaeser 2010), this approach would rightly attribute economic difficulties to national policy changes made largely outside their control. It is far less condescending, more likely to match voters' lived experiences, and gives a clear direction for action: updating national economic policy to meet the needs of the regions it has left behind (Glastris 2019).

As commentators (e.g., Catte 2019; Kelloway 2019) have noted, while rural and rust belt areas are often viewed as conservative, that hides a strong strain of economic populism (Levitz 2019). Individual progressive economic policies can do very well in red states: Missouri decisively rejected a right to work referendum in 2018, just as Oklahoma rejected a so-called right to farm referendum in 2016. A platform of economic populism that explicitly draws the line between national economic policy and local economic struggles would likely be compelling to voters in these areas.

Addressing regional divergence with national policy is a promising strategy as a matter of both policy and politics. The remainder of this article considers one possible national policy with important regional effects: reinvigorated antitrust enforcement. It outlines how the lack of effective antitrust enforcement has contributed to regional divergence, how a renewed antitrust movement might build on itself through policy feedback effects, and how advocates of a new antitrust regime might design it to maximize its chance of success.

Antitrust Enforcement as Federal Regional Convergence Policy

An increasing number of scholars and policy-makers recognize that many American companies have gotten too big (Wu 2018). In industry after industry, the major players have consolidated until only a handful of firms control the large majority of the market. Some conglomerates, most infamously Amazon, have attained dominant positions in multiple markets simultaneously and adeptly use their position in one market as leverage over competitors in another (Khan 2017).

The result of this consolidation has been a rise in economic inequality. At the most fundamental level, when a firm acquires a competitor, it reduces the number of alternatives available to its employees, customers, and suppliers, increasing its power over anyone who interacts with it (Emerson 1962; Coleman 1982). As a result, firms in concentrated markets are able to hold down wages (Wilmers 2018; Azar et al. 2018). This is a core reason that the share of national income going to labor has declined by 6 percentage points since 1980 (Autor et al. 2017; Barkai 2016).

The negative consequences of market concentration for regional economies can be especially severe (Salerno 2017). The waves of corporate consolidation over the past four decades have deprived many cities and towns of the corporate headquarters and local businesses that used to be a source of high-paying jobs and demand for professional business services (Longman 2015). The loss of these jobs is amplified by economic multipliers: the local spending of each accountant or lawyer may support two or three restauranteurs or gas station attendants. Beyond strictly economic effects, local business owners are often a key source of charitable donations and civic leadership, roles that absentee owners do not continue at the same levels (Brunell 2006). More broadly, local business ownership is a strong predictor of community and civic health on a number of indicators (Tolbert et al. 2002; Tolbert, Lyson, and Irwin 1998).

For rural areas, often dominated by a small number of employers or industries, the consequences of consolidation have been particularly devastating. Consider the case of agriculture. In the 1980s, 37 percent of every dollar consumers spent on food ended up with the farmer who produced it. Today, the farmer receives less than 15 percent (Kelloway 2019). Taking economic multipliers into account—agriculture often forms the economic base of rural areas—that change alone can plausibly account for a substantial portion of rural America's struggles. It has come largely because of consolidation among both farmers' suppliers and their customers. Where there used to be dozens of seed companies, now there are just three (Charles 2016). Prices for seed have risen accordingly. And where there were once many buyers for farm products, now there are just a handful: in meatpacking, for instance, four companies control 85 percent of the market for beef (Leonard 2014). This consolidation was a direct result of changes to the interpretation of antitrust law, and it could be reversed through updated policy.

Agriculture is just one sector where the results of consolidation have been especially pernicious for regional economies. Another example is air travel, which has been felt most noticeably by midsize cities. The number of major airlines has fallen steadily since deregulation in the 1970s, from more than twenty to just four as of this writing. As a result of consolidation, air service has become more concentrated in major cities, with connectivity to small and midsize airports dropping substantially since 2007 (Wittman and Swelbar 2014). The lack of convenient air service is a major constraint on cities' economic competitiveness and is often cited as a reason that corporate headquarters leave smaller cities and towns (Longman and Khan 2012).

The lack of effective antitrust enforcement over the past 40 years has been a major contributor to economic stagnation in many parts of the country, and a reinvigorated approach to enforcement offers a promising route to help restore prosperity across the country. If implemented carefully, with attention to potential policy feedbacks, a renewed antitrust movement could maintain and expand itself over time.

Policy Feedback Considerations in the Development of New Antitrust Policy

There are several features of antitrust enforcement as a political issue that make it a particularly promising federal regional development policy. These features occur with respect to all of the "three E's" that Jacob Hacker mentions in his article in this issue (Hacker, this volume). Its bipartisan appeal to voters, potential to attract business support, and logistical ease of enactment make the *establishment* of a reinvigorated antitrust regime likely to be easier than many other regional development policies. Once established, initial successful antitrust actions are likely to change the politics of the issue in ways that make its *entrenchment* and *expansion* more likely. Here I briefly describe these attractive features and potential for policy feedbacks, along with certain strategic recommendations related to sequencing and the use of federalism in the initial establishment phase.

Note that two types of regulatory action form the core of the antitrust toolkit. One is to block proposed mergers, preventing new monopolies from being created. The second is to break up currently existing companies with excess market power into their component parts. Both types of enforcement would benefit from the promising political considerations facilitating the establishment of a renewed antitrust movement. But many of the most promising feedback effects related to the entrenchment and expansion of such a movement will be felt most strongly with the successful breakups of currently existing firms. For this reason, a revitalized antitrust movement should strongly consider pursuing such breakups whenever possible, even though regulators have been hesitant to pursue them in the past (Wu 2018).

Features of antitrust enforcement that make its establishment more likely

Among possible federal regional development policies, reinvigorated antitrust enforcement stands out in several ways that make its establishment as a policy more likely. First, it is salient and familiar to voters. Most voters have encountered monopolies in their daily lives, whether they be airlines, utilities, internet providers, or tech platforms. Almost everyone has had a negative experience with a company too large or omnipresent to avoid in the future. Breaking such companies up offers a response to angry customers who would otherwise not have any way to express their frustration.

Moreover, aggressive antitrust enforcement has a long history in the United States, and it was widely practiced within the lifetimes of many voters. It has been a stated principle of capitalist economics since Adam Smith (Smith 1827), albeit one that has often been honored in the breach. In the United States specifically, antitrust enforcement fits with a longstanding American skepticism toward "bigness" (Lemann 2016; Rosen 2016). Perhaps for these reasons, the current antitrust movement has managed to find support among both liberals and conservatives. A poll conducted in September 2018, for instance, found that 65 percent of Americans—and 54 percent of Trump voters—think the government "should do more to break up corporate monopolies" (Dayen 2018). And leading proponents of antitrust enforcement in Congress and the media are found on both sides of the aisle (Crane 2018).

Perhaps more important than its broad appeal among voters, antitrust enforcement has the potential to attract support, or at least avoid opposition, from a wide range of organized interest groups. Of particular note is the potential for corporate ambivalence on this issue. Unlike many progressive economic policies, many companies—including quite powerful ones—stand to benefit from a reinvigorated antitrust regime. Yelp, for instance, has been a major critic of Google's abuse of its search monopoly for several years (Dougherty 2017). When AT&T attempted to acquire T-Mobile in 2010, some of the most vocal opposition came from competitor Sprint (Singel 2011), though that did not stop Sprint from initiating its own bid for T-Mobile recently. Even Walmart, the largest retailer in the country, recently joined with other brick and mortar retailers to call on the Federal Trade Commission (FTC) to examine "persistent oligopolies in other parts of the retail system," specifically singling out the market power of Amazon and Google (Dodge 2019). Companies like these could potentially become strong supporters of specific antitrust enforcement actions or a new antitrust movement in general.

This potential to attract corporate support is a key advantage of antitrust enforcement as a regional development policy. A major question will be whether proponents of the new enforcement regime will be able to secure support, or at least neutrality, from overarching corporate lobbying organizations like the U.S. Chamber of Commerce. As I discuss, choosing initial enforcement targets to maximize the possibility of such support or neutrality is a strategic imperative for the new antitrust movement.

A third advantage of antitrust enforcement relative to many potential federal redevelopment policies is the comparative ease with which it could be enacted. For the most part, the current antitrust movement is calling for better enforcement of laws already on the books, by agencies that already exist. This means that large parts of the policy could be implemented without creating new government entities or requiring large increases in federal spending, and perhaps even without new legislation.

These three features of reinvigorated antitrust enforcement—its widespread support among voters, potential for ambivalence from corporations, and legislative ease of enactment—suggest that it may be easier to establish than many other federal regional development policies. Should initial enforcement actions be successful, they are also likely to entrench the policy and lay the groundwork for further expansion.

Entrenchment and expansion: The finality of breaking up companies

Should initial enforcement actions succeed—and specifically should existing oligopolistic companies be broken apart—they are likely to alter the political landscape in ways that entrench the new antitrust regime and promote future regional development efforts in general.

When a company is successfully split apart, it no longer exists as an independent entity capable of political action. That in itself may remove the single biggest source of potential backlash to a given enforcement action—as Patashnik describes in his contribution to this issue, sometimes the most effective way to reduce backlash is to fragment the organizations most likely to mobilize such backlash (Patashnik, this volume).

The entrenchment effects of breaking up existing monopolies extend beyond their particular enforcement action. Monopoly rents are a key source of political donations, either from the companies themselves or from the individuals who own them (Skocpol and Williamson 2012). Reducing those rents through increased competition will thus decrease the money available to fund future anti-enforcement lobbying.

Beyond reducing the availability of monopoly rents to fund future advocacy, successful enforcement actions may reduce the political clout of targeted industries by changing the number and nature of corporate players. In the case where one company is split horizontally into several competitors, this would occur by increasing the total number of actors that need to be coordinated for industry-wide lobbying, which is likely to make such coordination more difficult. In the case where a company is split vertically into firms that each occupy different stages in the chain of production, the successor firms may have policy interests that directly conflict. Amazon the online market platform and its client Amazon the bookseller are likely to have a tense relationship and might end up on opposite sides of debates about Internet policy.

A particularly promising dynamic, which is plausible though by no means guaranteed, would be if the successor companies created by one round of trust-busting become agitators for the next round. Firms in some cases pursue mergers and acquisitions defensively in response to observed or anticipated consolidation in their own or related industries (Gorton, Kahl, and Rosen 2009; Ahern and Harford 2014). This process can lead to vertical or horizontal merger waves where all tiers of an industry's supply chain quickly consolidate. If some of these mergers were undone, the resulting smaller companies might push for further antitrust enforcement up or down their supply chain to even the playing field once more. That could create a virtuous cycle in which the successor companies from one enforcement action lobby for the next action.

Should a more assertive antitrust regime become established, it is quite possible that it will induce beneficial feedback effects that could entrench and expand it relatively quickly. It is important to note that many of these feedback effects would stem from the changes to the marketplace and political arena that result from breaking up firms that are currently consolidated vertically or horizontally into their component pieces. This dynamic suggests that proponents of the new enforcement regime would be wise to push for the full breakup of consolidated companies rather than simply imposing fines or attempting to regulate them through consent decrees. A powerful firm that has just been hit with a major fine is likely to redouble its efforts at political influence; a firm that is split in two will likely find that its successor companies have both less total power and conflicting goals.

Strategic Considerations in Establishing a Reinvigorated Antitrust Regime

Despite the many features that make antitrust enforcement a promising candidate for establishment, it is important that advocates pursue the issue carefully and strategically. Here I briefly discuss some strategic considerations related to the initial establishment of a reinvigorated antitrust regime. These recommendations include embracing the political nature of antitrust enforcement, thinking carefully about the sequencing of enforcement actions, and taking advantage of federalism to force progress at the state level if federal regulators continue with a lax approach.

Embrace the political nature of antitrust

Antitrust policy is fundamentally a political issue. It centers on questions about resource distribution and power that are at the core of any political system. This means that any attempts to remove it from public debate and treat it as a purely technical question are likely to fail: entrenched interests will continue to correctly see it is as vitally important to their interests, and without a countermobilization bureaucrats will almost certainly succumb to their lobbying.

Rather than searching for an illusory econometric magic bullet, supporters of stronger antitrust enforcement should fully embrace its political nature. This means building an antitrust movement that mobilizes a large number of people, uses high-visibility platforms to describe the problems of consolidation—and even the specific harms caused by specific companies—and pressures public figures, both elected and unelected, to take clear stances in favor of competition. Antitrust is an issue with great power to energize everyday consumers and voters, and that power should be utilized.

A corollary to the political nature of antitrust is that, as with other political issues, fighting for greater enforcement and campaigning against predatory companies may result in political progress even in instances where the immediate objective is defeated. Just as an initial electoral loss can lay the groundwork for future victories, so each attempt to fight a merger or break up a monopoly moves the national conversation forward, generates awareness of the harms of consolidation, and makes further merger attempts appear more costly to businesses.

Careful sequencing to build momentum

Because a new antitrust enforcement regime is likely to face substantial pushback from entrenched interests, the initial targets for enforcement actions should be carefully chosen for political as well as legal viability. Enforcers should aim to set precedent and build momentum by choosing targets for enforcement that are in politically precarious positions and that offer the possibility of dividing corporate lobbies.

Companies that are already distrusted by consumers and politicians are in a politically weak state that may make them easier targets for initial enforcement. Facebook offers a potentially useful example. It is increasingly disliked by consumers after a multitude of hacking, fake news, and privacy scandals (Liao 2018). At the same time, it is distrusted by conservative politicians for its perceived liberal bias. This weak position means that government intervention to protect Facebook's customers may face less skepticism than similar action against a more popular company—the need for some sort of corrective action is widely apparent. Equally important, while industry lobbying groups might be concerned about the implications of a successful dismantling of Facebook, they may hesitate to face the political consequences of aligning themselves with an unpopular company.

As described above, an important feature of antitrust enforcement is that many companies stand to benefit from it alongside consumers and workers. Antitrust advocates would do well to choose initial enforcement targets that maximize the chance of gaining support from other corporations and keeping industry- or economy-wide business lobbying groups on the sidelines. The most promising cases will be ones that have relatively powerful interests on both sides, such as Walmart and Amazon, mentioned above, or Google and News Corp, who recently squared off in Australia (Meade 2018).

By picking initial targets that are politically weak or have strong corporate opponents, antitrust enforcers will be more likely to win their initial cases in the courts of law and public opinion. Once some initial victories are achieved, further enforcement actions can build on their precedent and benefit from the more favorable political landscape.

Federalism and the advantageous position of state attorneys general

A third strategic consideration concerns the level of government at which to pursue establishment of a new antitrust regime. Ideally, aggressive enforcement should be pursued concurrently wherever possible, be that through the FTC, the U.S. Department of Justice (DOJ), Congress, or the states. However, action may not always be possible at the federal level, and in recent years the FTC and DOJ have generally looked favorably on mergers (Tepper 2019). Thus, it may be advantageous to initially pursue enforcement at the state level. A number of state attorneys general (AGs) have already begun investigations into Google and Facebook (Romm 2019), and ten state AGs recently sued to block the proposed merger between T-Mobile and Sprint (Harding McGill 2019).

Besides the possibility of short-term action, state AGs have a number of advantages as antitrust enforcers. The most important of these is that in most states they are elected politicians. This means that they are well equipped to treat antitrust as a political issue—they have more reason than career bureaucrats to consider the political optics of particular stances and are more likely to be adept at communicating with the media and the public. They also stand to see personal electoral benefits from popular enforcement actions and are directly susceptible to pressure from organized advocates. State AGs thus occupy a unique position. Unlike federal enforcers at the DOJ or FTC, they are elected politicians who know how to mobilize voters and can be directly pressured to adopt procompetition stances. But unlike members of Congress, they have direct enforcement power.

A state-level strategy also offers the possibility of building enforcement momentum piecemeal. It may prove easier for antitrust advocates to secure the support of a handful of AGs, perhaps from states that are especially harmed by a particular conglomerate or potential merger, than to convince the FTC or DOJ to reverse several decades of harmful policies. As a suit progresses, other states or federal agencies may join in.

Conclusion: National Action for a National Problem

This article has considered the problem of economic divergence between regions of the United States. Over the past four decades, the United States has bifurcated economically, with increasing fractions of the population living in both exceptionally poor and exceptionally rich places. Many of the biggest challenges facing the country are intricately tied to this bifurcation, including the basic question of whether national political cohesion can be maintained. Here I have argued that the growing economic disparities among regions of the United States should be treated first and foremost as a national policy issue. This view is accurate because it takes into account the changes that have pulled regions apart, and it is valuable because it offers pathways to political action that might address the problem.

As an example of a national policy with important effects on regional economies, I have considered antitrust enforcement. Though difficult to quantify directly, the lax antitrust enforcement of the past few decades has likely contributed to the economic struggles of many cities and towns nationwide. A reinvigorated antitrust movement would thus likely disproportionately benefit those parts of the country that have been left behind. In addition to having unique characteristics that make its establishment more likely in this era of polarization and negative partisanship, antitrust offers the possibility of beneficial feedback effects that may make it easier to entrench and expand.

Antitrust is just one of many areas in which national policy shifts starting in the 1970s and 1980s exacerbated economic gaps among regions. Other policy areas include the devolution of welfare program administration from the federal government to the states (Rodríguez-Pose and Gill 2004); the relaxing of financial and telecommunications regulations; and the end of federal revenue sharing with state and local governments, which led to a dramatic increase in the fiscal stakes of regional economic competition (Pacewicz 2016). Policy-makers seeking to address regional disparities today would do well to remember the role federal action had in creating those disparities and to recognize its potential for reducing them.

References

Ahern, Kenneth R., and Jarrad Harford. 2014. The importance of industry links in merger waves. *Journal of Finance* 69 (2): 527–76.

Austin, Benjamin, Edward Glaeser, and Lawrence H. Summers. 2018. Saving the heartland: Place-based policies in 21st century America. In *Brookings Papers on Economic Activity*, Spring: 151–232. Washington DC: Brookings Institution Press.

Autor, David H., David Dorn, and Gordon Hanson. 2017. When work disappears: Manufacturing decline and the falling marriage-market value of men. National Bureau of Economic Research Working Paper 23173, Cambridge, MA.

Autor, David H., David Dorn, Lawrence F. Katz, Christina Patterson, and John Van Reenen. 2017. The fall of the labor share and the rise of superstar firms. National Bureau of Economic Research Working Paper 23396, Cambridge, MA.

Avent, Ryan. 2011. *The gated city*. Seattle, WA: Amazon Digital Services.

Azar, José, Ioana Elena Marinescu, Marshall Steinbaum, and Bledi Taska. 2018. Concentration in U.S. labor markets: Evidence from online vacancy data. National Bureau of Economic Research Working Paper 24395, Cambridge, MA.

Barkai, Simcha. 2016. Declining labor and capital shares. Stigler Center for the Study of the Economy and the State New Working Paper Series No 2, Chicago, IL.

Barro, Robert J., and Xavier Sala-i-Martin. 1992. Convergence. *Journal of Political Economy* 100 (2): 223–51.

Benner, Chris, and Manuel Pastor. 2012. *Just growth: Inclusion and prosperity in America's metropolitan regions*, 1st ed. London: Routledge.

Benner, Chris, and Manuel Pastor. 2015. *Equity, growth, and community: What the nation can learn from America's metro areas*. Berkeley, CA: University of California Press.

Beramendi, Pablo. 2012. *The political geography of inequality: Regions and redistribution*. New York, NY: Cambridge University Press.

Brunell, Richard M. 2006. The social costs of mergers: Restoring "local control" as a factor in merger policy. *North Carolina Law Review* 85:149–221.

Catte, Elizabeth. 2019. Finding the future in radical rural America. *Boston Review*.

Charles, Dan. 6 April 2016. Big seed: How the industry turned from small-town firms to global giants. *Morning Edition*. NPR.

Clark, Terry Nichols, Richard Lloyd, Kenneth K. Wong, and Pushpam Jain. 2002. Amenities drive urban growth. *Journal of Urban Affairs* 24 (5): 493–515.

Coleman, James S. 1982. *The asymmetric society*. Syracuse, NY: Syracuse University Press.

Crane, Daniel A. 2018. Antitrust's unconventional politics. *Virginia Law Review* 104:118–35.

Dayen, David. 28 November 2018. Attacking monopoly power can be stunningly good politics, survey finds. *The Intercept*.

Diamond, Rebecca. 2016. The determinants and welfare implications of U.S. workers' diverging location choices by skill: 1980–2000. *American Economic Review* 106 (3): 479–524.

Dodge, Brian. 30 June 2019. It's time to protect consumers and competitive markets. Available from https://www.rila.org.

Dougherty, Conor. 1 July 2017. Inside Yelp's six-year grudge against Google. *New York Times*.

Emerson, Richard M. 1962. Power-dependence relations. *American Sociological Review* 27:31–41.

Fallows, James, and Deborah Fallows. 2018. *Our towns*. New York, NY: Vintage.

Florida, Richard. 2002. *The rise of the creative class*. New York, NY: Basic Books.

Ganong, Peter, and Daniel Shoag. 2017. Why has regional income convergence in the U.S. declined? *Journal of Urban Economics* 102 (November): 76–90.

Glaeser, Edward L. March 2010. Shrinking Detroit back to greatness. *New York Times*.

Glaeser, Edward L., Jed Kolko, and Albert Saiz. 2001. Consumer city. *Journal of Economic Geography* 1 (1): 27–50.

Glastris, Paul. 2019. Editor's note: Check your coastal urban privilege. *Washington Monthly*.

Golshan, Tara, and Ryan Mark. 19 November 2018. Live election results: Top House races. *Vox*.

Gorton, Gary, Matthias Kahl, and Richard J. Rosen. 2009. Eat or be eaten: A theory of mergers and firm size. *Journal of Finance* 64 (3): 1291–1344.

Hacker, Jacob S. 2019. Medicare expansion as a path and a destination: Achieving universal insurance through a new politics of Medicare. *The ANNALS of the American Academy of Political and Social Science* (this volume).

Hacker, Jacob S., and Paul Pierson. 2010. *Winner-take-all politics*. New York, NY: Simon & Schuster.

Harding McGill, Margaret. 11 June 2019. State AGs sue to block T-Mobile-Sprint merger. *Politico*.

Kelloway, Claire. 2019. How to close the Democrats' rural gap. *Washington Monthly*.

Kemeny, Thomas, and Michael Storper. 2012. The sources of urban development: Wages, housing, and amenity gaps across American cities. *Journal of Regional Science* 52 (1): 85–108.

Khan, Lina. 2017. Amazon's antitrust paradox. *Yale Law Journal* 126 (3): 564–907.

Leighley, Jan E., and Jonathan Nagler. 2013. *Who votes now? Demographics, issues, inequality, and turnout in the United States*. Princeton, NJ: Princeton University Press.

Lemann, Nicholas. 21 March 2016. Notorious big. *The New Yorker*.

Leonard, Christopher. 4 March 2014. Meat racket excerpt: How Tyson keeps chicken prices high. *Slate*.

Liao, Shannon. 26 March 2018. New survey finds Americans' trust in Facebook continues to decline. *The Verge*.

Longman, Phillip. 28 November 2015. Bloom and bust. *Washington Monthly*.

Longman, Phillip, and Lina Khan. 2012. Terminal sickness. *Washington Monthly*.

MacGillis, Alec. 25 July 2010. The case for breaking up Washington—and scattering government across America. *Washington Post*.

Manduca, Robert A. 2019. The contribution of national income inequality to regional economic divergence. *Social Forces*. Available from https://doi.org/10.1093/sf/soz013.

Meade, Amanda. 4 May 2018. Google, Facebook not playing by the rules, News Corp tells ACCC. *The Guardian*.

Moretti, Enrico. 2012. *The new geography of jobs*. Boston, MA: Houghton Mifflin Harcourt.

Pacewicz, Josh. 2016. *Partisans and partners: The politics of the post-Keynesian society*. Chicago, IL: University of Chicago Press.

Patashnik, Eric M. 2019. Limiting policy backlash: Strategies for taming countercoalitions in an era of polarization. *The ANNALS of the American Academy of Political and Social Science* (this volume).

Porter, Michael E. 1998. Clusters and the new economics of competition. *Harvard Business Review*.

Rodríguez-Pose, Andrés, and Nicholas Gill. 2004. Is there a global link between regional disparities and devolution? *Environment and Planning A* 36 (12): 2097–2117.

Romm, Tony. 15 March 2019. Facebook, Google and other big tech giants are about to face a "reckoning," state attorneys general warn. *Washington Post*.

Rosen, Jeffrey. 3 June 2016. The curse of bigness. *The Atlantic*.

Salerno, Lillian. 20 April 2017. Want to rescue rural America? Bust monopolies. *Washington Post*.

Saxenian, AnnaLee. 1996. *Regional advantage*. Cambridge, MA: Harvard University Press.

Schleicher, David. 2017. Stuck! The law and economics of residential stagnation. *Yale Law Journal* 127 (1): 78–154.

Sharkey, Patrick. 2013. *Stuck in place: Urban neighborhoods and the end of progress toward racial equality*. Chicago, IL: University of Chicago Press.

Sharkey, Patrick, and Jacob W. Faber. 2014. Where, when, why, and for whom do residential contexts matter? Moving away from the dichotomous understanding of neighborhood effects. *Annual Review of Sociology* 40 (1): 559–79.

Singel, Ryan. 6 September 2011. Sprint files own lawsuit against AT&T, T-Mobile merger. *Wired*.

Skocpol, Theda, and Vanessa Williamson. 2012. *The Tea Party and the remaking of Republican conservatism*. New York, NY: Oxford University Press.

Smith, Adam. 1827. *An inquiry into the nature and causes of the wealth of nations*. Edinburgh: University of Edinburgh Press.

Storper, Michael, Thomas Kemeny, Naji Makarem, and Taner Osman. 2015. *The rise and fall of urban economies: Lessons from San Francisco and Los Angeles*. Palo Alto, CA: Stanford University Press.

Tepper, Jonathan. 9 January 2019. Why regulators went soft on monopolies. *The American Conservative*.

Tolbert, Charles M., Michael D. Irwin, Thomas A. Lyson, and Alfred R. Nucci. 2002. Civic community in small-town America: How civic welfare is influenced by local capitalism and civic engagement. *Rural Sociology* 67 (1): 90–113.

Tolbert, Charles M., Thomas A. Lyson, and Michael D. Irwin. 1998. Local capitalism, civic engagement, and socioeconomic well-being. *Social Forces* 77 (2): 401–27.

Wilmers, Nathan. 2018. Wage stagnation and buyer power: How buyer-supplier relations affect U.S. workers' wages, 1978 to 2014. *American Sociological Review* 83 (2): 213–42.

Wilson, William Julius. 1996. *When work disappears: The world of the new urban poor*. New York, NY: Vintage.

Wittman, Michael D., and William S. Swelbar. 2014. Capacity discipline and the consolidation of airport connectivity in the United States. *Transportation Research Record* 2449 (1): 72–78.

Wu, Tim. 2018. *The curse of bigness: Antitrust in the new gilded age*. New York, NY: Columbia University Press.

Yglesias, Matthew. 2012. *The rent is too damn high: What to do about it, and why it matters more than you think*. New York, NY: Simon & Schuster.

Yglesias, Matthew. 9 December 2016. Let's relocate a bunch of government agencies to the Midwest. *Vox*.

Rebuilding Labor Power in the Postindustrial United States

Workers in the United States have lost their voice (or influence) in Washington and the workplace. Industrial unions are ill-suited to the postindustrial economy, and alternative organs of representation and influence (i.e., "alt-labor") are trapped in a vicious circle of vulnerability and volatility that limits their likely growth. As a result of this, power is increasingly skewed toward employers and their political allies, who add to labor's difficulties by eliminating and evading remaining labor protections. The federal government could help to restore a balance of power between workers and employers by establishing and enforcing a robust wage floor: (1) a $15 an hour minimum wage, (2) a nationwide hotline for workers who believe that their rights had been violated ("911 for workers"), and (3) a database that would allow regulatory agencies and worker organizations to rationalize and coordinate labor and employment law efforts. Doing so would produce a positive feedback loop so workers regain their voice on the job and in politics.

Keywords: organized labor; unions; workers; labor law; minimum wage; regulation

By
ANDREW SCHRANK

Workers in the United States have lost their voice. Union membership hovers at approximately 10 percent of the labor force, down from a postwar peak of more than 30 percent. Congress and the courts have banned nonunion alternatives—like works councils and joint consultation committees—that engage in bilateral negotiations with employers. The result is a "voice gap" (Adler 2003, 372; Colvin 2003, 712; Kaufman 2012, 466; Kochan et al. 2019, 3) that depresses wages and benefits, and aggravates inequality, by altering the balance of

Andrew Schrank is Olive C. Watson Professor of Sociology and International and Public Affairs at Brown University. His research has appeared in leading journals in political science, sociology, international development, and Latin American studies. He is the coauthor (with Michael Piore) of Root-Cause Regulation: Protecting Work and Workers in the Twenty-First Century *(Harvard University Press 2018).*

DOI: 10.1177/0002716219868672

power between workers and employers on the job and in the broader political sphere (Krueger 2018).

Observers of this dynamic part company over solutions that might help America's workforce to regain its voice. Some look to the New Deal for ideas and push for legislation designed to revitalize the traditional labor movement (Compa 2016; Elk 2018). They hold that unions are down but not out and that judges and politicians are the principal obstacles to their success. Others hold that labor law reform is neither likely nor sufficient in an era of deindustrialization, automation, and austerity (Theodore 2016, 160; Milkman and Luce 2017, 159; Hirsch and Seiner 2018, 1731), and they look to "a deeper, pre-New Deal past" (Cowie 2016, 15) for inspiration. They place their faith in alternative labor (alt-labor) arrangements—including immigrant rights organizations, worker centers, and nonprofit law firms—that allegedly demand less state support.

I try to stake out a middle ground that restores worker voice and redresses inequality not by bypassing but by building upon existing labor and employment legislation. In particular, I hold that by raising the minimum wage established by the Fair Labor Standards Act (FLSA) of 1938 to $15 an hour, establishing a hotline for workers who believe that their rights at work have been violated ("911 for workers," or 911-4w), and building a database that would allow regulatory agencies and worker organizations to use the data collected to rationalize and coordinate their enforcement efforts, the federal government could establish and enforce a robust national wage floor (Economic Policy Institute [EPI] et al. 2019) that would simultaneously protect, embolden, and empower workers on the job and in politics.

The key is to recognize and exploit the potentially positive feedback loop between exit and voice (Hirschman 1970): when workers are able to demand statutory protections and their enforcement, they are more likely to be better paid in the labor market as a whole; when they are better paid in the labor market as a whole, they are better able to threaten or survive exit from their incumbent employers; when they are better able to threaten or survive exit from their incumbent employers, they are better able to exercise voice in politics and the workplace; and when they are better able to exercise voice in both arenas, they are better able to demand statutory protections that further boost wages and benefits and their enforcement. Taken together, therefore, an enforceable wage floor should not only turn bad jobs good but simultaneously foster the growth of a virtuous circle of (potential) exit and (actual) voice at the firm and societal levels down the road.

I make the case for a meaningful wage floor in five principal sections. First, I describe the limits to the New Deal model in an era of deindustrialization, automation, and decentralized production. Industrial unions presuppose an industrial economy, I argue, and large-scale industry is a thing of the past. Second, I discuss the achievements and limitations of alt-labor against the backdrop of the New Deal model. While alternatives to industrial unions are long overdue, in light of the breakdown of mass production and the growth of the service sector, they are unlikely to achieve their goals by sidestepping the political process or embracing the "militant voluntarism" (Cowie 2016, 37; see also Duff 2014, 874; Jacobs 2018,

13) of the Progressive Era. Third, I discuss the benefits of a national wage floor that builds on the achievements of the FLSA by increasing the minimum wage, establishing a hotline for distressed workers, and incorporating the information that hotline collects into a database designed to facilitate a rational approach to enforcement generally. Workers who have both the right to a living wage and ready access to regulatory agencies are less likely to fall victim to poverty and exploitation, I argue, and correspondingly are more likely to contribute to campaigns to rein in rogue employers—whether directly, by joining forces with alt-labor; or indirectly, by contributing to a database that allows regulators and their allies to crack down on tens of thousands of employers who routinely violate multiple labor laws (General Accounting Office [GAO] 1988; Bernhardt, Spiller, and Theodore 2013). Fourth, I discuss the feasibility of the proposal in an era of political polarization and fiscal constraints (Hacker and Pierson 2018). Minimum wage increases are broadly popular, greedy businesspeople and white-collar criminals are decidedly unpopular, and information technology should lower the cost of 911-4w and data integration. And, finally, I conclude by reiterating the case for a wage floor underpinned by old laws and new technologies. A wage floor has relatively low upfront costs, is politically palatable, and should simultaneously reward and reinvigorate workers and their allies.

Setting the Stage: The Decline of the New Deal Model of Industrial and Labor Relations

The problem in the U.S. labor market lies less in the *quantity* than the *quality* and *distribution* of jobs. There are not enough *good* jobs. The poverty rate is three times the unemployment rate. And a vastly disproportionate share of the good jobs that are available are held by white, male workers who are fortunate enough to be well educated—leaving women, minorities, and the less educated at risk of both mind-numbing labor and occasional or ongoing poverty (Sauter 2018; Thrush 2018).

The problem is in large part the product of a vicious circle: absent bargaining power, workers cannot do much to improve their situations; and in their current situation, workers tend to lack bargaining power (Sussman 2016; Krueger 2018). Survey data suggest that at least half of all workers report a gap between their desired and actual levels of input into their "benefits, compensation, promotion, job security, technological change, and protections against harassment" (Kochan et al. 2019, 14), for example, and that almost half of all nonunionized workers would vote for a union if given the opportunity—a sharp uptick from prior surveys (Kochan et al. 2019, 20). But the best-known solutions to the voice gap—for example, repealing the Taft-Hartley Amendments to the Wagner Act, or adopting the Employee Free Choice Act, in an effort to eliminate barriers to union certification that undermined the New Deal equilibrium—seem politically unrealistic and economically naïve in today's decentralized, volatile global economy.

After all, the New Deal system went from strength to strength. Mass production allowed unskilled workers to consolidate their power at the proverbial point of production. Industrial unions translated their efforts into collective bargaining contracts and progressive reform. Productivity gains allowed industrial enterprises to comply with the contracts and reforms that the unions had extracted at relatively low cost. And the whole system could be overseen by specialized agencies (e.g., the National Labor Relations Board, the Wage and Hour Division of the Department of Labor, and later the Occupational Safety and Health Administration [OSHA] and Equal Employment Opportunities Commission), which could plan their regulatory efforts in a relatively stable macroeconomic environment; and enforcement personnel, who reaped economies of scale by covering thousands of at least nominally homogeneous workers every time they entered the field, entered a judgment, or made a ruling (Piore and Schrank 2018).

In other words, the scale economies that made modern factories profitable also left them vulnerable. Unions could organize tens of thousands of workers in a single campaign. Regulators could address their needs in a single factory visit. Judges could defend their rights with a single ruling. And companies could lose more than they had to gain by resisting organization and regulation—at least in the short run.

The system did not produce Shangri La. There were differences in pay and status within the factories and unions. They were often racialized and gendered (see, e.g., Greer 1976). And unorganized workers, who were disproportionately female and/or minority, were relegated to second-class citizenship (Piore 1980, 404).

The problem with the New Deal system, however, was not just that it was inequitable but that it was unsustainable. Employers who wanted to escape the clutches of the system had several options available, including divide-and-conquer strategies made possible by the very inequalities that the system had aggravated, hard bargaining by oligopolies in tight northern labor markets, and the retreat to the South—where the Wagner Act had been diluted, if not necessarily defanged, by "right-to-work" campaigns and the like even before the passage of Taft-Harley (see, e.g., Cowie 1999; Gross 2011; Lichtenstein 2011).

These problems would in all likelihood be aggravated today, moreover, by deindustrialization, the deceleration of productivity growth, and the decentralization of production—which together raise the costs and undercut the efficiency of specialized enforcement agencies. After all, the specialized enforcement personnel who oversaw the New Deal system were costly and inflexible, but the demand for their specialized services was relatively predictable in the Bretton Woods era, and they reaped a large return on the government's investment by addressing the needs of hundreds—or perhaps thousands—of workers each time they entered a factory or entered a judgment. When their descendants enter a workplace or a judgment today, however, they cover a few workers or overlook countless violations that fall outside their jurisdictions but are sitting under their noses, thus leaving money lying on the table (Piore and Schrank 2018).

The decentralization of employment poses a similar challenge to collective bargaining. Unions still win most elections that occur under the National Labor Relations Act (i.e., the Wagner Act); however, the elections themselves tend to occur in smaller bargaining units, meaning that organizers and administrators are running to stay in place independently of the better-known hurdles imposed by employer opposition (Compa 2016, 23).

Positive policy feedbacks have thus turned negative for workers and their families in the United States. Today's wage-earners are too diffuse, diverse, and precarious to be organized and protected by traditional institutions, which were designed for a homogeneous, stable, and centralized workforce; and in the absence of organization and protection they will grow ever more diffuse, vulnerable, and precarious.

Consider, for example, the differences between large employers in the mid-twentieth century, when industrial giants like General Motors, General Electric, and U.S. Steel employed tens of thousands of relatively homogeneous workers in stand-alone plants (Freeman 2018); and today, when cities across the country are competing for Amazon fulfillment centers that employ an average of 1,700 heterogeneous workers (Steiner 2017), retail outlets like Wal-Mart and Costco are considered large establishments with even fewer employees, and both brick-and-mortar retailers and their online competitors are selling products made in factories overseas—and demanding public subsidies to do so.

Sparrows Point in Baltimore offers an evocative example. The Bethlehem Steel mill there once employed more than thirty thousand members of the United Steelworkers Union (Henry 2002; see also Reutter 2004, 397); but it closed in 2012 and is currently being redeveloped into a logistics hub with a host of heavily subsidized tenants ranging from Amazon, with a target of fifteen hundred workers, to smaller retailers and restaurants with just a few workers (Simmons 2016; Wood 2018a, 2018b).

Organizing these workers would be incredibly costly. Bargaining contracts and filing grievances on their behalves would be more so. And enforcing their legal protections would be an inefficient nightmare—with understaffed, specialized agencies such as OSHA and the Wage and Hour Division (WHD) of the Department of Labor making separate trips to the same establishment on different days at great expense. Where union representatives or regulatory agents could address the needs of tens of thousands of workers a day in the 1950s, they would cover a few hundred on a very good day in the current climate. On a bad day, they would find that their targets had shut their doors or reopened down the block under a different name (Levine 2018).

Unions, regulators, and labor lawyers are effectively fighting a twenty-first-century war with twentieth-century weapons. The war is a campaign against small, decentralized employers in highly competitive industries who have both an incentive and the ability to cut corners as well as costs, in part by exploiting workers who are vulnerable to division and abuse. The weapons are high-cost, specialized bureaucracies that presuppose scale economies and stability that no longer exist.

It is no wonder, therefore, that the United States faces an epidemic of labor and employment law violations. Survey data suggest that more than a quarter of all low-wage workers in the country's largest cities are paid less than the legally mandated minimum wage (Bernhardt, Spiller, and Theodore 2013; Galvin 2016). Overtime violations are rampant. We have one of the highest rates of occupational fatality—not to mention *the* highest rate of child labor—among the high-income members of the OECD. Union activists are threatened and intimidated with near impunity (Piore and Schrank 2018). And employment discrimination is so widespread that members of minority groups—African American men in particular—have trouble finding jobs, let alone good jobs, in the first place (Pager and Western 2012). The nontraditional campaigns pursued by alt-labor are therefore long overdue and well-suited to the times.

Beyond the New Deal Model: The Rise of Alt-Labor

Alternatives to industrial unions are not, however, emerging in a political vacuum. On the contrary, they presuppose and propel political action including movement building, advocacy, litigation, and lobbying on behalf of reforms designed to help low-wage workers (Lee 2016, 524). What most clearly differentiates alt-labor from traditional labor, therefore, is less an aversion to politics or public authority per se than a tendency to pursue political as well as shop-floor action flexibly and opportunistically. Where traditional unions performed a relatively narrow range of tasks for a large—and largely homogeneous—workforce, and thus exploited economies of scale, alt-labor groups pursue a variety of goals with a diverse array of workers (Gottheil 2014, 2248–52; Hirsch and Seiner 2018, 1779), and thus pursue economies of scope.[1] One observer goes so far as to compare them to new economy start-ups that "try a lot of things, fail fast, and when things work, lean-in" (Weissbourd 2018, 12–13); she goes on to draw a contrast between "lean" labor organizations and "traditional unions" that are more focused and less flexible. Examples of the former would include the aforementioned "worker centers," which "provide services and advocate on behalf of non-union workers" (Hirsch and Seiner 2018, 1748); law firms and legal advocacy groups that take labor and employment cases on behalf of low-wage workers in particular (Quigley 2016); organizations that defend workers with distinct jobs (e.g., day laborers, taxi drivers) or identities (e.g., immigrants); and alliances of different groups or stakeholders in the alt-labor community (see, e.g., Steinkopf-Frank 2019).

Organizations like these could lay the foundation for a new model of labor and employment relations. But to do so they will have to go from strength to strength, just as industrial unions did in the mid-twentieth century—when victories helped the movement to grow, and growth helped the movement to achieve more victories. In other words, alt-labor would have to foster increasing returns through "positive feedback" loops (Pierson 2000) that are arguably more difficult to build and sustain in today's polarized, cynical, and austere environment than in an era of Democratic hegemony based in part on white male hegemony in the North and, all the more so, the South (Hacker and Pierson 2018; see also Cowie 2011).

One finds pockets of positive feedback like this in alt-labor. Consider, for example, the Working Hands Legal Clinic (WHLC) in Chicago, which used regular legal work and referral fees to underwrite support for worker centers in the early twenty-first century—before eventually being absorbed into a larger alliance of alt-labor organizations. "In addition to direct representation services," explains law professor Bill Quigley, "WHLC worked on policy issues related to employment in low-wage jobs and fights to remove barriers to low-wage workers exercising their rights and being paid for their work" (Quigley 2016; see also Bobo and Casillas Pabellón 2016, 271; Carrillo 2017, 101). The results included not only more extensive protections against wage and hour violations but rules that make fee-shifting between attorneys and alt-labor groups more straightforward. "In Chicago now," explains the clinic's founder, "it is pretty standard for law firms to share fees with such nonprofit organizations, including worker centers" (Williams quoted in Quigley 2016).

Examples like these speak to the *possibility* of postindustrial policy feedback. The lawsuits generate legal fees. The legal fees fund the lobbying. The lobbying shapes the legislation. The legislation makes more successful lawsuits possible. And the plaintiffs and policy advocates join forces and build power over time.

But WHLC is the exception to the rule. Most alt-labor organizations are trapped in a vicious circle of low funding and limited reach: in the absence of resources, they are unable to offer extensive services let alone policy advocacy; and without more legal and political victories, they are unable to raise funds that would support worker defense and reform campaigns. In many cases, moreover, they are dependent on foundation grants—and thus subject to onerous reporting requirements, at best, and capture by elite donors, at worst (Avins, Larcom, and Weissbourd 2018, 60; see also Compa 2015, 11).

To build the new economy, of course, start-ups had to break out of a similar circle. They could not develop viable products without capital, and they could not get capital without viable products. While private investors take much of the credit for turning the vicious circle into a virtuous one in places like Silicon Valley, federal agencies took the lead by offering start-ups and scientists seed funding and subsidies before venture capitalists and investment banks got involved (Schrank and Whitford 2009; Block and Keller 2011). The question, therefore, is whether the federal government could play a similar role for alt-labor, and the answer is likely to be found in the debate over the minimum wage.

Building a Wage Floor: F15, 911-4w, and Regulatory Rationalization

The so-called Fight for 15 (F15) campaign brought the possibility of a large-scale increase in the federal minimum wage to national attention for the first time in history. But the origins of F15 are controversial, and the campaign to "give

America a raise" arguably predates the eponymous movement in any event, dating at least to the publication of David Card and Alan Krueger's landmark study of the effects of the New Jersey minimum wage increase on employment in the state's fast food industry in the early 1990s (Card and Krueger 1994). While mainstream theory predicted that employers in New Jersey would respond to the wage shock by laying off workers, Card and Krueger (1994) found that they actually hired more workers than their counterparts in neighboring Pennsylvania, where the lower federal minimum prevailed.

Other scholars have challenged Card and Krueger's results to be sure (see, e.g., Neumark and Wascher 2000), but the "overwhelming weight of the evidence" (DeLong 2015; see also Schmitt 2013) supports their position; and doubts about the employment costs of minimum wage legislation have, if anything, grown further with the appearance of real-world experiments in cities and states across the country. More than half of the U.S. population now lives in a state or municipality that mandates a minimum wage higher than the federal standard of $7.25 an hour, and "by 2022, 17 percent of Americans will live in a city or state with a $15 minimum wage" (Gill 2018). Given that the $7.25 federal standard prevails in a number of key purple states (e.g., Pennsylvania, Virginia, and Wisconsin), moreover, the issue could prove salient in the 2020 election.

Imposing a $15 minimum wage at the national level would have an array of normative and distributive advantages. Evidence suggests that the *direct* beneficiaries of minimum wage laws are disproportionately—if by no means exclusively—likely to be women and minorities who would experience rising wages, declining poverty, and less need (and perhaps eligibility) for public assistance programs such as food stamps (Reich, Jacobs, and Bernhardt 2014); that is, the very workers who were relegated to the periphery of the New Deal system. But the *indirect* beneficiaries would potentially include frustrated workers in different regions, classes, and communities who would rejoin the labor force as their expected earnings grew; taxpayers who would no longer have to bear the costs of social programs that in effect subsidize low-road employers; and vulnerable workers who would gain voice and bargaining power as their own costs of job loss declined.

The growth of voice is by no means obvious, however, for voluntarists on the Left have at times been as skeptical of minimum wages as radicals on the Right, albeit for different reasons. While conservatives worried that wage standards would destroy jobs by pricing labor out of the market, voluntarists worried that they would destroy voice by rendering collective bargaining unnecessary—and Samuel Gompers, the founding president of the American Federation of Labor, famously opposed a statutory minimum wage on the grounds that "the minimum tends to become the maximum" over time (Samuel 2000, 34).

Remnants of "Gompersian voluntarism" (Schlozman 2015, 8) are found among some champions of alt-labor. But history and scholarship have largely put paid to their views (Mishel and Walters 2003, 4), and contemporary experts therefore see the minimum wage and worker voice as complements rather than substitutes—*if* minimum wage laws are enforced.

In that respect, the F15 is being carried out at an ironic moment in American labor history. On one hand, there is a groundswell of support for a dramatic expansion in the federal minimum wage, and perhaps for worker protection more generally. On the other hand, public officials are having trouble enforcing labor and employment laws that are already on the books. Minimum wage violations are rampant. Enforcement personnel are in short supply. Cognate labor and employment laws are violated with near impunity. And unions are near extinction—especially in the private sector (Piore and Schrank 2018).

Part of the problem lies in the aforementioned mismatch between the regulatory system established during the New Deal (and bolstered by the Great Society) and the shape of the contemporary economy. The former was designed with mass production in mind. The modal worker was assumed to be a semi-skilled white male who worked in a factory, belonged to a union, and relied on a collective bargaining contract overseen by the National Labor Relations Board (NLRB); insofar as there were gaps in the system (e.g., nonunionized workers, African Americans, women), moreover, they would be filled by similarly specialized laws (e.g., the Fair Labor Standards Act in the 1930s and eventually Title VII of the Civil Rights Act) and agencies (e.g., WHD, OSHA, Equal Employment Opportunity Commission [EEOC]), but the latter would backstop rather than underpin the system as a whole.

In other words, the regulatory system that protected the factory labor force required no less specialization than the factory itself. The NLRB oversaw collective bargaining. The WHD took responsibility for wages and hours. And eventually OSHA and EEOC joined the mix, along with a host of smaller federal, state, and local agencies.[2]

What this meant in practice was that the system as a whole presupposed stability and scale. Both the fixed costs of running that many agencies and the variable costs of dealing with their different targets (e.g., visiting firms, hearing testimony, making rulings, etc.) are enormous. If they are to reap a meaningful return on the government's investment in their establishment and administration, therefore, these agencies have to make sure that their personnel either pursue economies of scale by reaching huge audiences with each visit, ruling, or decree, and do so on a near-constant basis; or pursue economies of scope by joining forces to defray upfront costs and reach the worst offenders who violate more than one law or regulation (GAO 1988). Otherwise, they are running up the down escalator.

Reaching huge audiences was broadly feasible in the industrial era, when inspectors could cover hundreds or perhaps thousands of workers with each factory visit; administrative agencies and courts could set precedents for millions of allegedly homogeneous workers with each decree or ruling; and a relatively stable macroeconomic environment allowed public officials to plan their campaigns accordingly (i.e., to maximize the utilization of case processing resources). But the organizational and spatial decentralization of production have conspired with automation to undermine these assumptions, leaving the existing enforcement agencies in limbo. Their targets are too small to permit economies of scale in case processing. Their jurisdictions are too narrow to allow them to compensate by pursuing economies of scope (i.e., covering more ground with each investigation, visit, or ruling). And their specialties are frequently ill-suited to a rapidly changing economy.

What is to be done about the decline of regulatory authority? The U.S. federal government is unlikely to merge OSHA, WHD, and EEOC, let alone to adopt the "one inspector(ate) per firm" approach recommended by the International Labour Organization (Piore and Schrank 2018), but improvements can be made at relatively low cost short of a complete overhaul by thinking about enforcement gaps from both the supply and the demand sides. On one hand, enforcement resources are in short supply. They are neither sufficient in number nor efficiently allocated. To take but one example, the average workplace will be visited by a wage and hour investigator no more than once every 50 years—and once there, the investigator will pay no attention to safety and health, employment discrimination, or union-busting, despite the fact that violations tend to travel in packs (Piore and Schrank 2018). On the other hand, the demand for redress is insufficient. Workers are not only scared to lose their jobs if they complain but unsure where to complain in the first place. "To which of the nine agencies listed on the bulletin board in the breakroom do I turn? And what happens if I do so?"

We could address the first problem by creating a national database of labor law violators and asking or compelling all enforcement agencies to contribute their data, much as U.S. police departments were pushed toward "data integration" (La Vigne et al. 2017, 6) in the aftermath of September 11 and the manufacturing extension centers funded by the National Institute of Standards and Technology (NIST) are compelled to contribute their data to NIST's systems (Brandt, Schrank, and Whitford 2018). Employers who showed up repeatedly and/or violated multiple statutes could be flagged for additional screening, much like suspicious passengers in airports, and agencies might be given incentives to carry out joint investigations. Argentina has not only created a database of labor law violators but linked it to data on government subsidies and contracts, depriving firms on the former from access to the latter; the country has seen a rapid drop in informality and related forms of noncompliance.[3] The United States could easily do the same.[4]

We could also boost the demand for redress by establishing and advertising an anonymous clearinghouse and telephone number for reports of workplace abuse. Rather than trying to figure out whether the mistreatment they had suffered was covered by one of the myriad notices on the bulletin board in the breakroom, workers could call a single number in search of the advice they needed, and their calls could be routed to the appropriate agency or agencies. Crime reports skyrocketed with the advent of the 911 emergency response system (Burnham 1996), and we could expect a similar spike following the introduction and advertisement of 911-4w; that is, a rapid response system for workplace abuse. If regulatory and enforcement agencies responded to the spike by carrying out joint investigations informed by their newly integrated data, moreover, they could compensate for the economies of scale (i.e., covering more workers per visit) that were lost with the breakdown of large-scale industrial employment by exploiting economies of scope (i.e., covering more violations per visit) in an era of concentrated violations (GAO 1988; Piore and Schrank 2018).

The conjunction of a higher minimum wage and improved enforcement would thus produce a new virtuous circle that would at least partly replace the one broken by the demise of the industrial economy. Workers would feel empowered and knowledgeable enough to exercise voice at the workplace; their organizations would help to aggregate their knowledge and influence; rogue employers would be on notice; their responsible counterparts would reap the competitive rewards; and conditions across the labor market—not only in terms of wages but in regard to safety and health, overtime, collective bargaining, employment discrimination, and the like—would improve accordingly. Consider the broader externalities or feedback effects:

- Workers who are less worried about losing their jobs are more likely to undertake organizing campaigns, thereby creating more unions, workplace committees, and worker centers.
- Employers who are compelled to comply with overtime law are likely to spread employment over more workers, thereby creating more jobs.
- Workers who are less tired are less likely to suffer on-the-job accidents, thereby taking the pressure off safety and health investigators and insurance rates.
- Employers who are forced to pay higher wages, and who recognize the benefits of a healthier, happier workforce, will undertake productivity-enhancing improvements that leave everybody better off.

And the virtuous circle produced by alt-labor, F15, and 911-4w will lock in over time. It is obviously impossible to know whether such a scenario would come to pass, since at this point it is entirely speculative. But we can gain some insight into the potential synergy between protective legislation and worker voice by considering the history of alt-labor, and worker centers in particular, at the state level.

Worker centers emerged in hostile environments, where employers held the cards and labor legislation was minimal (Galvin 2016, 334). In fact, Janice Fine holds that the first wave arose in the late-twentieth-century South "in response to institutionalized racism in employment, the rise of manufacturing and 'big box' retail, and the absence of labor unions as a vehicle for organizing" (Fine 2006, 9). But the mean minimum wage is nonetheless $9.23 an hour in thirty states and the District of Columbia where she and her colleagues found worker centers in 2005 (Fine, Doan, and Werberg 2005; U.S. Department of Labor 2019) and just over $8 an hour in states where they did not, including several northern states that have surprisingly low minimum wages.[5]

Obviously, these are mere correlations; they say nothing at all about causality, which would be hard to unpack under the best of circumstances. But they are at least consistent with the idea that worker voice fuels protective legislation and vice versa in a positive feedback loop, which is also consistent with an abundance of case study material to that effect (see, e.g., Fine 2006; Garrick 2014; Galvin 2016, 342).

Political Feasibility: Labor Politics and Policy in an Era of Polarization and Austerity

Jacob Hacker and Paul Pierson portray political polarization as the most vexing obstacle to policy reform in the current era and worry that it is aggravated by fiscal constraints in an era of federal deficits. "All else equal," they argue, "policy designs that do not severely worsen these problems are more likely to gain a secure foothold" (Hacker and Pierson 2018, 7). Examples of reforms that fail to meet their test are easy to come by: universal preschool and free college poll well but cost a fortune, for instance, and Medicare for All is more controversial and costly still. Unlike most entitlements, however, raising and enforcing the minimum wage would seem to fit the bill. It is broadly popular and relatively cheap.

Most Americans support both a higher minimum wage (Sahadi 2014; Edwards-Levy 2016; DeSilver 2017) and one that is indexed to the rate of inflation (Program for Public Consultation [PPC] 2017), and this support is overwhelming among moderate as well as liberal voters. Data from the American National Election Studies suggest that more than two-thirds of self-identified moderates support a minimum wage increase (Figure 1) and that almost two-thirds of self-identified Democrats who voted for Donald Trump do as well. Given that these are the likely swing voters going into the 2020 election, politicians would be unlikely to lose, and would in all likelihood gain, by raising the minimum wage.

A minimum wage increase would be costly, of course, but the costs would be borne by business rather than taxpayers. Leaked polls and documents suggest that 80 percent of businesses support an increase, with one well-known Republican pollster concluding that opponents of such proposals are "fighting an uphill battle, because most Americans, even most Republicans, are okay with raising the minimum wage" (DePillis 2016).

The 911-4w system would involve upfront and operating costs, to be sure, but they are not at all comparable to those involved in new entitlements. By way of illustration, consider the estimated deployment and operating costs of "Next Generation 911" service currently being considered by Congress, which would exploit the same skills and technologies as 911-4w. They are, under the most conservative scenarios, a rounding error in the federal budget (Mission Critical Partners 2018).

While the degree and nature of partisan support would thus vary with the details of the specific proposal, it should be easy to find a sweet spot that is both politically popular and productive—especially in the current economic environment. After all, the risk of inflation seems small. Most low-wage employment is found in nontradeable services that are invulnerable to offshoring. The current wage is more than a decade old. Rogue employers and greedy businesspeople are not popular (see, e.g., Rebovich and Kane 2002; Weakliem 2015).[6] And the new wage could be phased in over time, giving well-meaning employers the time they need to adjust.

FIGURE 1
Favor a Minimum Wage Increase by Partisan Ideology (percentage)

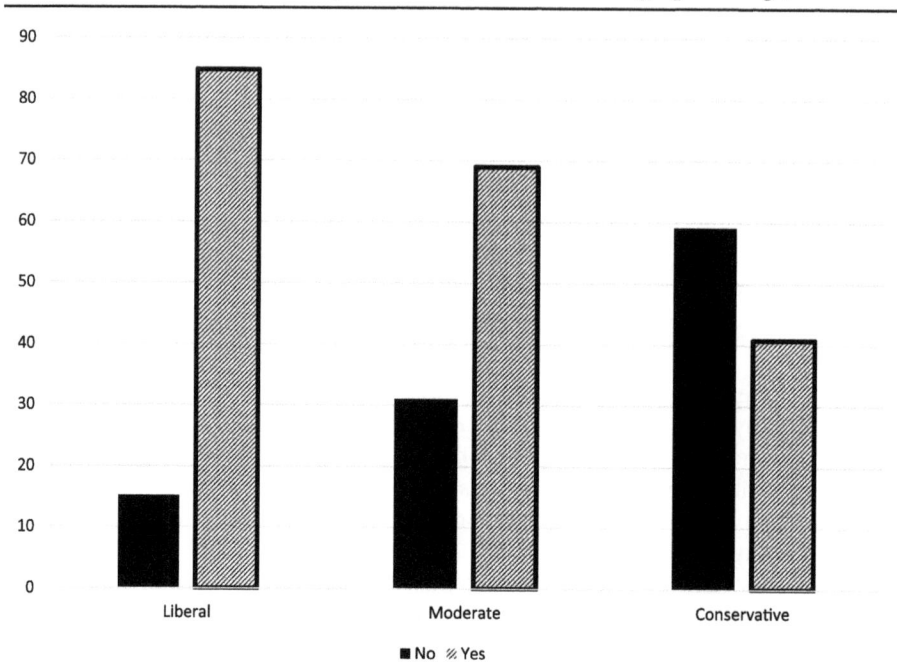

SOURCE: Author's calculation based on American National Election Studies, 2016. See www.electionstudies.org.

NOTE: $n = 3{,}033$; $\chi^2 = 469.6_{(df2)}$; $p < .001$. These materials are based on work supported by the National Science Foundation under grant numbers SES 1444721, 2014-2017, the University of Michigan, and Stanford University.

Conclusion

This article offers a straightforward—if by no means complete—solution to a vexing problem. The problem is the evaporation of worker voice in the contemporary United States and attendant increases in poverty, inequality, and exploitation. Workers have lost their voice not only due to "employers gone rogue" (Bernhardt, Spiller, and Theodore 2013), and their enablers in federal, state, and local governments, I argue, but also because of a deeper mismatch between labor market institutions established in the New Deal era and an economy that has passed them by.

New Deal labor market institutions presupposed the large-scale industrial employment of a largely homogeneous workforce on a long-term basis, allowing unions, regulators, and judges to exploit economies of scale and stability in their efforts to organize, oversee, and defend workers on an ongoing basis. Unions could organize an enormous number of blue-collar workers, and regulators and judges could ensure than their rights were protected, at relatively low cost. And unions could go on to reproduce and potentially strengthen the system over time through political action.

But large-scale industrial employment is largely a thing of the past, and today's workers would therefore be hard to organize, regulate, protect, and mobilize under the best of circumstances—for example, if the New Deal legal bargain were to be reestablished. While the "bricolage" (Fine 2011, 607) of organizations and strategies that make up alt-labor are beginning to fill the gap, in part by exploiting economies of scope that are better suited to a postindustrial economy, they are trapped in a vicious circle familiar to organizational pioneers throughout history: unless and until they achieve more shop floor or political victories, they are unlikely to grow and gain legitimacy; and unless and until they grow and gain legitimacy, they are unlikely to achieve enough victories to build a new system of labor and employment relations.

When confronted with similar transformations in the private sector, public policy-makers have stepped into the void in an effort to speed the transition. Most recently, for example, they accelerated the demise of the old economy and the rise of the new by entering trade and investment agreements that facilitated offshore manufacturing, encouraging research and development that facilitated automation, and bankrolling investments that fueled the growth of information technology—not to mention the Internet itself (Block and Keller 2011).

If public policy-makers can "pick winners" among employers, of course, and in so doing speed one transition, they can put a floor under workers, and in so doing ease another. After all, the proposal put forward here is not particularly controversial. It does not explicitly take sides in the debate between old and new labor, insofar as there is such a debate. It does not cost a lot of money, at least in relative terms. And it does not provoke much partisan hostility—since Americans favor raising the minimum wage by more than a two-to-one margin, and rogue employers are hardly popular. What it does do, however, is go some distance toward restoring the balance of power between workers and employers over the long run, a cause which is long overdue, by offering workers the support they need in the short run.

Notes

1. In contrast to economies of scale, which occur when an organization gains efficiencies by producing more—or a larger volume—of the same product, economies of scope occur when an organization gains efficiencies by producing a larger number or variety of products.

2. In rare exceptions, these state agencies were as large or larger than their federal counterparts. See, for example, the *New York Times* (1972) on the size of New York's occupational safety and health agency relative to OSHA.

3. Sebastián Etchemendy, personal communication, 2016.

4. We could go further by linking violators not only to sticks (e.g., the deprivation of subsidies or denial of contracts) but to carrots (e.g., compliance assistance in lieu of sanctions for first offenders). See Piore and Schrank (2018) for an example from Chile.

5. On average, moreover, an additional worker center is associated with a ten-cent increase in the minimum wage across the fifty states and D.C.; all differences are significantly different from zero at $p <$ .025. Full results are available from the author on request.

6. Political scientists and sociologists note that public opposition to inequality does not translate into support for redistribution, perhaps because Americans are more hostile to government and taxes than to

business and the elite (Weakliem 2015). Insofar as they exploit hostility to the better-off without transferring money to government, therefore, raising and enforcing the minimum wage may be ideal approaches to fostering redistribution.

References

Adler, Paul. 2003. Toward collaborative independence: A century of change in the organization of work. In *Industrial relations to human resources and beyond: The evolving process of employee relations management*, eds. Bruce Kaufman, Richard Beaumont, and Roy Helgoff, 353–400. Armonk, NY: M.E. Sharpe.

Avins, Jeremy, Megan Larcom, and Jenny Weissbourd. 2018. New forms of worker voice in the 21st century. Harvard Kennedy School-MIT Sloan Working Paper, Cambridge, MA.

Bernhardt, Annette, Michael Spiller, and Nik Theodore. 2013. Employers gone rogue: Explaining industry variation in the violation of workplace laws. *Industrial and Labor Relations Review* 66 (4): 8–32.

Block, Fred, and Matthew Keller, eds. 2011. *States of innovation: The U.S. government's role in technology development*. New York, NY: Paradigm.

Bobo, Kim, and Marien Casillas Pabellón. 2016. *The worker center handbook. A practical guide to starting and building the new labor movement*. Ithaca, NY: Cornell University Press.

Brandt, Philipp, Andrew Schrank, and Josh Whitford. 2018. Brokerage and boots on the ground: Complements or substitutes in the manufacturing extension partnerships. *Economic Development Quarterly* 32 (4): 289–99.

Burnham, David. 1996. *Above the law: Secret deals, political fixes, and other misadventures of the U.S. Department of Justice*. New York, NY: Scribner.

Card, David, and Alan Krueger. 1994. Minimum wages and employment: A case study of the fast-food industry in New Jersey and Pennsylvania. *American Economic Review* 84 (4): 772–93.

Carrillo, Arturo. 2017. Chicago's worker center movement: A structural analysis. PhD diss., University of Illinois at Chicago.

Colvin, Alexander. 2003. The dual transformation of workplace dispute resolution. *Industrial Relations* 42 (4): 712–35.

Compa, Lance. 2015. Careful what you wish for: A critical appraisal of proposals to rebuild the labor movement. *New Labor Forum* 24 (3): 11–16.

Compa, Lance. 2016. Lance Compa responds. *New Labor Forum* 25 (1): 23–25.

Cowie, Jefferson. 1999. *Capital moves: RCA's seventy-year quest for cheap labor*. Ithaca, NY: Cornell ILR Press.

Cowie, Jefferson. 2011. We can't go home again: Why the New Deal won't be renewed. *New Labor Forum* 20 (1): 10–14.

Cowie, Jefferson. 2016. Reframing the New Deal: The past and future of American labor and the law. *Theoretical Inquiries in Law* 17:13–38.

DeLong, J. Bradford. 30 September 2015. Must read. Blog post. Available from https://www.bradford-delong.com/2015/09/must-read-at-this-stage-neumark-salas-and-waschers-are-only-hurting-them-selves-and-hurting-confidence-not-just-in-t.html.

DePillis, Lydia. 4 April 2016. Leaked documents show strong business support for raising the minimum wage. *Washington Post*.

DeSilver, Drew. 4 January 2017. 5 facts about the minimum wage. Washington, DC: Pew Research Center.

Duff, Michael. 2014. Alt-labor, secondary boycotts, and toward a labor organization bargain. *Catholic University Law Review* 63 (4): 837–78.

Economic Policy Institute (EPI), AFL-CIO - America's Unions, Center for American Progress, National Employment Law Project, National Women's Law Center, and SEIU. 18 March 2019. The federal minimum wage should be a robust national wage floor, not adjusted region by region. Fact Sheet. Washington, DC: EPI.

Edwards-Levy, Ariel. 10 May 2016. Raising the minimum wage is a really, really popular idea. *HuffPost*.

Elk, Mike. 9 May 2018. Bernie Sanders introduces Senate bill protecting workers fired for union organizing *Guardian*.

Fine, Janice. 2006. *Worker centers: Organizing communities at the edge of the dream*. Ithaca, NY: Cornell University Press.

Fine, Janice. 2011. Worker centers: Entering a new stage of growth and development. *New Labor Forum* 20 (3): 45–53.

Fine, Janice, Tam Doan, and Jon Werberg. 2005. *Worker centers: Community-based and led worker organizing projects*. Washington, DC: Economic Policy Institute.

Freeman, Joshua. 2018. *Behemoth: A history of the factory and the making of the modern world*. New York, NY: W.W. Norton.

Galvin, Daniel. 2016. Deterring wage theft: Alt-labor, state politics, and the policy determinants of minimum wage compliance. *Perspectives on Politics* 14 (2): 324–49.

Garrick, Jessica. 2014. Repurposing American labor law: Immigrant workers, worker centers, and the National Labor Relations Act. *Politics & Society* 42 (4): 489–512.

General Accounting Office. 1988. *"Sweatshops" in the U.S.: Opinions on their extent and possible enforcement options*. Washington, DC: General Accounting Office.

Gill, Dee. 2018. Through the minimum wage looking glass: Economic consensus unrealized. *UCLA Anderson Review*. Available from https://www.anderson.ucla.edu/faculty-and-research/anderson-review/minimum-wage-primer-leamer.

Gottheil, Thomas. 2014. Not part of the bargain: Worker centers and labor law in sociohistorical context. *NYU Law Review* 89 (December): 2228–64.

Greer, Edward. 1976. Racism and U.S. steel. *Radical America* 10 (5): 45–68.

Gross, James. 2011. The NLRB: Then and now. *ABA Journal of Labor & Employment Law* 26 (2): 213–29.

Hacker, Jacob, and Paul Pierson. 2018. Policy feedback in an age of polarization: Crafting policy to rebalance American politics. Unpublished manuscript.

Henry, Kristine. 3 June 2002. Merged steel local forges new hope. *Baltimore Sun*.

Hirsch, Jeffrey, and Joseph Seiner. 2018. A modern union for the modern economy. *Fordham Law Review* 86 (4): 1727–83.

Hirschman, Albert. 1970. *Exit, voice, and loyalty: Responses to decline in firms, organizations, and states*. Cambridge, MA: Harvard University Press.

Jacobs, David. 2018. Rebuilding labor in the era of Trump. Paper presented to the Association for Evolutionary Economics.

Kaufman, Bruce. 2012. An institutional economic analysis of labor unions. *Industrial Relations* 51 (S1): 438–70.

Kochan, Thomas, Duanyi Yang, William T. Kimball, and Erin Kelly. 2019. Worker voice in America: Is there a gap between what workers expect and what they experience? *Industrial and Labor Relations Review* 72 (1): 3–38.

Krueger, Alan. 24 August 2018. Reflections on dwindling worker bargaining power and monetary policy. Paper presented at the Jackson Hole Economic Summit.

La Vigne, Nancy, Ellen Paddock, Yasemin Irvin-Erickson, KiDeuk Kim, Bryce Peterson, and Samuel Bieler. 2017. *A blueprint for interagency and cross-jurisdictional data sharing*. Washington, DC: Urban Institute.

Lee, Dayne. 2016. Bundling "alt-labor": How policy reform can facilitate political organization in emerging worker movements. *Harvard Civil Rights-Civil Liberties Law Review* 51:509–36.

Levine, Maryanne. 18 February 2018. Behind the minimum wage fight, a sweeping failure to enforce the law. *Politico*.

Lichtenstein, Nelson. 2011. Labor, liberalism, and the Democratic Party: A vexed alliance. *Industrial Relations* 66 (4): 512–34.

Milkman, Ruth, and Stephanie Luce. 2017. Labor unions and the Great Recession. *RSF: Russell Sage Foundation Journal of the Social Sciences*, April: 145–65.

Mishel, Lawrence, and Matthew Walters. 2003. How unions help all workers. Briefing Paper. Washington, DC: Economic Policy Institute.

Mission Critical Partners. October 2018. *Next generation 911 cost estimate: A Report to Congress*. Washington, DC: National Highway Traffic Safety Commission.

Neumark, David, and William Wascher. 2000. Minimum wages and employment: A case study of the fast-food industry in New Jersey and Pennsylvania: Comment. *American Economic Review* 90 (5): 1362–96.

New York Times. 30 December 1972. Judge bars job safety law extension.

Pager, Devah, and Bruce Western. 2012. Identifying discrimination at work: The use of field experiments. *Journal of Social Issues* 68 (2): 221–37.

Pierson, Paul. 2000. Increasing returns, path dependence, and the study of politics. *American Political Science Review* 94 (2): 251–67.

Piore, Michael. 1980. Economic fluctuation, job security, and labor-market duality in France, Italy, and the United States. *Politics & Society* 9 (4): 379–407.

Piore, Michael, and Andrew Schrank. 2018. *Root-cause regulation: Protecting work and workers in the twenty-first century*. Cambridge, MA: Harvard University Press.

Program for Public Consultation. 1 June 2017. Americans support greater federal efforts to reduce poverty. College Park, MD: Program for Public Consultation.

Quigley, Bill. 2016. Teacher, union leader, labor lawyer: Profile of Chris Williams, social justice advocate. *Counterpunch*.

Rebovich, Donald, and John Kane. 2002. An eye for an eye in the electronic age: Gauging public attitude toward white-collar crime and punishment. *Journal of Economic Crime Management* 1 (2): 1–19.

Reich, Michael, Ken Jacobs, and Annette Bernhardt. 2014. *Local minimum wage laws: Impacts on workers, families and businesses*. Berkeley, CA: IRLE.

Reutter, Mark. 2004. *Making steel: Sparrows Point and the rise and ruin of American industrial might*. New York, NY: Summit Books.

Sahadi, Jeanne. 9 June 2014. Strong support for raising the minimum wage. *CNN Money*.

Samuel, Howard. 2000. Troubled passage: The labor movement and the Fair Labor Standards Act. *Monthly Labor Review* 123 (12): 32–37.

Sauter, Michael. 10 October 2018. Faces of poverty: What racial social groups are more likely to experience it? *USA Today*.

Schlozman, Daniel. 2015. *When movements anchor parties: Electoral realignments in American history*. Princeton, NJ: Princeton University Press.

Schmitt, John. 2013. *Why does the minimum wage have no discernible effect on employment?* Washington, DC: Center for Economic Policy and Research.

Schrank, Andrew, and Josh Whitford. 2009. Industrial policy in the United States: A neo-Polanyian interpretation. *Politics & Society* 37 (4): 521–53.

Simmons, Melody. 24 May 2016. Sparrows Point developer plots 130-acre hotel, retail project. *Baltimore Business Journal*.

Steiner, Ina. 2017. Amazon to hire 120,000 workers to ship holiday orders. Available from www.ecommercebytes.com

Steinkopf-Frank, Hannah. 26 March 2019. Illinois manufacturing workers locked out and fired for one-hour strike. *In These Times*.

Sussman, Anna Louie. 11 January 2016. Q&A: Robert Reich on the "vicious circle of wealth and power." Available from https://gspp.berkeley.edu.

Theodore, Nik. 2016. Unions in the Obama era: Laboring under false pretenses? In *Urban policy in the time of Obama*, ed. James De Filippis, 149–63. Minneapolis, MN: University of Minnesota Press.

Thrush, Glenn. 13 September 2018. US recovery eludes many living below poverty level, census suggests. *New York Times*.

U.S. Department of Labor. 1 January 2019. Consolidated minimum wage table. Available from https://www.dol.gov/whd/minwage/mw-consolidated.htm.

Weakliem, David. 2015. Public opinion, the 1%, and income redistribution. In *Emerging trends in the social and behavioral sciences*, eds. Robert Scott and Stephen Kosslym, 1–13. Hoboken, NJ: John Wiley.

Weissbourd, Jenny. 23 May 2018. Comments in what is worker voice. Boston, MA: Federal Reserve Bank of Boston. Available from www.bostonfed.org.

Wood, Pamela. 21 August 2018a. Amazon offers sneak peek at massive high-tech fulfillment center opening soon at Sparrows Point. *Baltimore Sun*.

Wood, Pamela. 7 September 2018b. Tradepoint Atlantic hits a turning point, seeks government financing. *Baltimore Sun*.

Prescriptions: Criminal Justice

De-Policing America's Youth: Disrupting Criminal Justice Policy Feedbacks That Distort Power and Derail Prospects

By
VESLA M. WEAVER
and
AMANDA GELLER

The standard account of policy feedback holds that social policy can be self-reinforcing: policies provide resources that promote economic security and well-being, and they also encourage beneficiaries to engage with government. Criminal justice policies have typically had the opposite effect: they embolden those with interests in a punitive policy agenda, while disempowering those most affected by the policies. This is of particular concern for children and adolescents in race-class subjugated communities (RCS), whose first encounters with government beyond public schooling often come through police contact and carry adverse social and political consequences at a critical developmental stage. In this article, we reimagine youth engagement with the state, arguing for substantial reductions in police surveillance of young people and for the promotion of youth attachment to civic life. We call for an investment in institutions, both state-based and community-based, that reinforce political inclusion and civic belonging.

Keywords: policing; criminal justice; youth; civic engagement; policy feedbacks; community building; race-class subjugation

Policy feedback scholarship generally centers on redistributive policies that have self-reinforcing dynamics. A standard argument of this scholarship is that social provision not only has the effect of expanding human flourishing by

Vesla M. Weaver is Bloomberg Distinguished Associate Professor of Political Science and Sociology at Johns Hopkins University. She is coauthor of Arresting Citizenship: The Democratic Consequences of American Crime Control *(University of Chicago Press 2014) and* Creating a New Racial Order: How Immigration, Multiracialism, Genomics, and the Young Can Remake Race in America *(Princeton University Press 2012).*

Amanda Geller is a clinical associate professor of sociology at New York University. Her research examines the intersection of criminal justice and social inequality, with a focus on policing and incarceration. Her work has appeared in a variety of academic outlets, as well as in written reports and presentations to local, state, and federal policy-makers.

Correspondence: vesla@jhu.edu

DOI: 10.1177/0002716219871899

ensuring good health and economic security, but it also enhances political capacity, confidence in government, and a sense that individuals are rights-bearing citizens (Mettler 2002; Campbell 2003). Social provision often generates powerful groups that help to sustain the policies and mobilize when they are threatened (i.e., Social Security and the AARP). This feedback for citizens and the groups representing them are most evident when the policies and practices in question are visible to the public. But as social provision takes place through increasingly indirect expenditures, many progressive policies today submerge the role of government, encouraging Americans to see government as distant and inept, thereby undermining the potential development of strong progressive coalitions (Mettler 2011). The argument, therefore, is that visible provision and the feedbacks that ensue are desirable because progressive policies often further strong progressive coalitions and "create favorable political dynamics" (Hacker and Pierson, this volume).

Policy Feedback in the Criminal Justice Domain

Criminal justice policy has also been characterized by strong policy feedback, creating long-standing policy arrangements and institutions that endure over time (Weaver 2012; Gottschalk 2006; cf. Dagan and Teles 2016). It too is an area where policies can be thought of as producing citizens, affecting their positioning, civic habits, and identities. However, in marked contrast to the citizen-enhancing consequences of many social policies, contemporary policing practices and crime control policies have tended to deter engagement, cement inequality, and confer adverse legal and political socialization (Lerman and Weaver 2014; Western 2006). These policies give rise to pitched asymmetries of power, emboldening groups who do not bear the direct adverse effects of policing and punishment and diminishing the power of those who do. The criminal justice domain, then, is one with a tremendous need for the disruption of these powerful feedbacks, to move from adverse feedback dynamics (in which policies undermine citizen voice and give rise to negative political socialization) to constructive ones, where public policy and political arrangements activate race-class subjugated (RCS) communities and communicate that they are worthy of civic regard and incorporation.

In this article, we outline avenues to transform the "policing state" (Epp 2016), with a focus on youth. Our current politics, with its bipartisan disavowal of the status quo, is conducive to imagining alternatives to punitive responses to social problems. Before we outline our proposals—one focused on limiting contact between America's youth in RCS communities and surveillant state authorities and one focused on fostering their civic attachment—it is important to understand the four key ways in which the feedback dynamics of criminal justice policies differ from the feedbacks of progressive policy designs. We then return to the specific experiences and needs of youth in discussing opportunities for reform.

1. *Criminal justice policies have generated feedback that reinforces punitive policy approaches and institutional expansion and stimulates the power of police.*

Scholars often regard the 1960s and its aftermath as the era when a civil rights state was established and institutionalized, the heady days of rights expansions and protections (King and Lieberman 2017); recent work also demands that we understand this as the key period when the carceral state was institutionalized (Hinton 2016; Murakawa 2014; Gottschalk 2006; Schoenfeld 2018).

The policies put into place by cities, states, and the federal government over the last five decades built an incredibly dense set of institutions dedicated to the oversight of vulnerable Americans. Criminal justice policies created a new political constituency, strengthening police unions, correctional organizations, prosecutors, and companies attached to the business of managing and housing inmates and cementing their coordination with one another (Gottschalk 2016; Page 2011; Weaver 2012). Alongside a "punitive" political ideology that crossed party lines, these policies were easy to pass and incredibly difficult to undo. As many in the criminal justice field know, "When you build it, they will come."

The policies—from federal grants for state prison construction to sentencing policies that would keep those prisons filled—gave rise to a powerful criminal justice lobby and set of organizations with interests in solidifying their position at the same time as it diminished the power of opponents and displaced the influence of citizens groups (Gottschalk 2016). This feedback was not, as some journalistic accounts would have it, simply about the pecuniary benefits for private prison companies, the bail industry, or companies producing electronic monitoring ankle bracelets and Taser; indeed, state governments and the public sector were the primary beneficiaries (Pfaff 2017). In some states, as many as one in seven public sector employees works for the state department of corrections, and they receive $30 billion in salary and benefits.

The criminal justice policy environment therefore reflects the interest group terrain formed by policies that invested in punishment and surveillance. Federal crime bills, once a rare occurrence and with few groups showing up to testify, soon attracted hundreds of new criminal justice–related associations and agencies supporting further endowments (Weaver 2012). This, combined with institutional obstacles to passing progressive criminal justice policy, has meant that punitive politics has governed with little opposition until recently (Miller 2016).

This is particularly apparent in policies related to incarceration, by which the state capacity and physical structures to process, house, and release people created abundant spoils for new political interests, which in turn made later policies to further grow the carceral state more likely (Gottschalk 2006; Weaver 2012). But it is also true of policing, even if scholars have been slower to appreciate the policy feedbacks in the lower reaches of criminal justice.

Police have accrued a "considerable institutional presence" and political relevance over the past half century (Epp 2016). Dramatic changes in policing alongside new revenue streams to police agencies triggered an unbridled expansion in the capacity, scope, and authority of police over the past several decades. This created the context for police to assert themselves as a, if not *the*, primary institution able to reduce crime, and singular in its authority to deal with urban problems. The "new policing" consensus took hold amid other important political developments that would shape feedback dynamics, giving police a uniquely powerful status among other bureaucracies. Most importantly, the rise of police professionalization decoupled police from their prior role as in the service of partisan political machines, a development that ironically served to initiate them as active political forces in their own right (Schrader 2019). Police "were able to organize themselves as coherent and semiautonomous political actors with their own interests" (Schrader 2019, 602), upending the governing arrangement that long existed between police and elected officials, which inspired a new political logic. Instead of police being accountable to and working on behalf of the urban political machines, politicians became accountable to and instruments for police demands. Police organizations became key players in political life and anticrime policies, transforming their new "independence into self-interest" (Schrader 2019, 610).

At the same time, the massive federal program created by the 1968 Safe Streets and Crime Control Act created new spoils for police agencies (Weaver 2012). These outlays created an even more organizationally adept set of groups and stimulated demand for greater provision. Once adamantly opposed to federal intervention in crime, groups like the International Association of Chiefs of Police, the National Sheriffs' Association, and the National District Attorneys Association became key beneficiaries of newfound resources and, in turn, became key defenders of federal funding (Weaver 2012); and they lobbied, monitored policy proposals, and advocated their own model bills from their policy bank (Schrader, forthcoming; Epp 2016). As law enforcement capacity grew, so too did their political leverage and centrality in debates, so much so that they faced little opposition or counterdiscourse; by the 1990s, the stances of the International Association of Chiefs of Police (IACP) and federal policy-makers were "virtually indistinguishable" (Schrader 2019, 619). The $8.8 billion 1994 Clinton crime bill was directly responsive to police interests, creating for the first time a direct infusion of funds to pay for 100,000 new officers. The pattern of the federal government generously subsidizing police continued through the later Byrne and JAG grant programs, and by the end of the century, the federal government had lavished billions on local police forces, with few strings attached.

What this meant was that the dramatic expansion in spending on police and manpower occurred *without* an expansion in oversight or regulation. Police received more funds *and* more insulation from external review. RCS communities and civil rights advocates "repeatedly failed to gain adoption of a federal law bringing local police practices under federal oversight" (Epp 2016, 14). Coupled with a jurisprudence that was increasingly loathe to regulate police practices or limit their contact with citizens, gave police qualified immunity when they engaged in serious misconduct, and even "lent constitutional support to the proactive police enforcement practices" that developed under broken windows theory, the police enjoyed wide latitude characteristic of almost no other public entity (Epp 2016, 26; Lerman and Weaver 2014). Patrol discretion to stop virtually anyone for the thinnest of reasons became a vaunted legal norm. These two enduring features of the policing landscape meant that police enjoyed a radical expansion in the power to stop citizens and intervene in public space, and this power was rarely checked.[1] Police received augmented size *and* authority.

In due course, these "remarkable investments" in police authority and capacity were seen on the streets and in city budgets. City spending on police surged in both relative and absolute terms, from just $82 per city resident in 1951 (or 11.6 percent of city expenditures) to $286 per resident by 2012 (in constant dollars, or 16.1 percent of spending) (Epp 2016). Similarly, police departments across the nation saw dramatic expansions in personnel—from 1960 to 1980, police forces nationally doubled (Weaver 2012). Police agencies today receive a lion's share of municipal funds, displacing spending on welfare, housing, hospitals, and civic infrastructure (Epp 2016). Just as many aspects of social provision long relied on by the poor were being scaled back or going "underground" through the tax code and through private provision, police departments were receiving generous public expenditure. The structural context was thus set for the visible slide into a criminal justice approach to RCS communities. "By the 1990s," one scholar concludes, "a national complex of police-supportive institutions linked together the country's previously decentralized municipal police departments" (Epp 2016, 26).

Influence did not end at police-directed efforts to further endow police with more capacity. IACP, Sherriff's associations, the Police Foundation, and groups of law enforcement executives quickly became important actors in legislative debates, providing the coordination mechanism across the nation's eighteen thousand law enforcement agencies, securing favorable legislation at the national level, as well as abetting local policy entrepreneurs. They sought to protect their newfound fiscal capacity and autonomy from oversight and to defend police funding and authority against encroachment.

These feedbacks between revenues and police power and organizational influence were integrated into political learning. In 1960, it would have been unimaginable to think that the sprawling group of unprofessionalized and understaffed local law enforcement agencies would be called on to handle urban problems or the outcomes of collapsing labor markets for the unskilled. Today, however, police are positioned as the default institution to handle all manner of social problems in an era of austerity governance—discovering truant youth, targeting the urban poor who skip out on subway fares or jaywalk, making sure tenants and visitors in public housing are meant to be on the premise and not trespassing, aiding in eviction proceedings or removing homeless, dealing with those who are mentally ill, deputized as local immigration enforcement agents under "show me your papers" 287g policies, responding to and managing "surplus" populations who violate sprawling local civil codes (Beckett and Herbert 2009), and on and on. In short, the remit of policing expanded from not just policing crime but ensuring civility (Camp and Hetherton 2016). Police have become a central organizing feature of life in urban neighborhoods, and their role has migrated into activities once the province of social workers, school administrators, immigration agents, and other public servants. Poor communities too enlisted the police (Forman 2017). Historian Elizabeth Hinton describes the context poor people faced after the demise of many of the programs of the Great Society, "when law enforcement and criminal justice institutions became the last public agencies standing, the police were the service that could be summoned when help was needed" (2016, 9).

Thus, as policing established itself in new roles of monitoring and regulating public space, policing schools, participating in gentrification projects, carrying out the vast expansion of criminal law, and generating revenue for cash-strapped municipal budgets in a time of fiscal austerity, citizen exposure to police oversight was normalized and institutionalized, crowding out other imperatives and evolving a "policing state" that is historically unprecedented and breathtaking in its scope and limited accountability compared to other local bureaucracies. That this occurred even as police have been the primary target of two of the nation's largest social movements in the last century—the black freedom struggle in the 1960s and Black Lives Matter today—speaks to how established and autonomous police are as a political force.

2. *Contemporary policing policies tend to disempower race-class subjugated communities and create adverse policy feedbacks for citizen voice and the reproduction of social inequality.*

Criminal justice policy designs and their political effects diminish voice and political clout in several overlapping ways. At the broadest level, five decades of investment in the criminal justice arm of government has starved state budgets and soaked up the resources that could have remedied historical oppression and the collapse of the manufacturing sector. At a political level, the consistent investment in this surveillance and punishment-centered, one-size-fits-all approach to crime truncated the array of responses to crime on the political agenda when communities themselves demanded an "all-of-the-above" approach that would combine investment in jobs, education, and housing with greater police enforcement (Miller 2016; Forman 2017).

At a more immediate level, crime policy and practice also dilute the political and economic power of individuals and communities. First, unlike conventional social policy, criminal justice policies redistribute financial resources away from poor families and areas, through apportionment schemes that allocate funds and political seats/representatives to the political districts where justice-involved individuals are held and processed, rather than those in their communities of origin, giving a "hidden subsidy" to rural areas with inflated population counts where prisons are located (Walker et al. 2017; Walker and Thorpe 2018).

More directly, too, criminal justice policy extracts resources from justice-involved individuals through instruments known as "legal financial obligations" (i.e., court fees, victim restitution, etc.), and poor families who are the "safety net of last resort" of justice-involved people endure significant financial drain (Katzenstein and Waller 2015, 639; Friedman and Pattillo 2019; Harris 2016). Policing of minor infractions and civil code violations have similarly saddled low-income residents with fines and fees, a practice exposed by the Department of

Justice's Ferguson report, but a practice that exists in cities across the nation (Gordon and Hayward 2016). "Broken windows policing," one scholar rightly argues, "compels impoverished people to spend money on bail bonds, legal transcripts, appeals, attorneys' fees, and visits to prisons" (Lipsitz 2016, 124).

Second, the criminal justice system also directly imperils citizens' right to vote and participate in their government through outright disenfranchisement (Manza and Uggen 2008). The informal policy feedback of police and carceral institutions for individuals and communities has been a concern for social scientists over the past decade. Arrests, conviction, and incarceration result in decreased political participation and engenders mistrust in government among individuals and communities (Lerman and Weaver 2014; White 2019; Burch 2013); isolation from important civic, governing, and social institutions, called system avoidance (Brayne 2014); and isolation from social networks and civic life (Rios 2011; Stuart 2016; Burch 2013; Clear 2009). Furthermore, scholars have found that in high-incarceration neighborhood enclaves, the negative individual effects spilled over to communities, dampening the engagement of "the family, friends, and neighbors they leave behind" (Burch 2013, 92). Criminal justice policies have altered the civic practices, social capital, and political clout of citizens and communities in America, diverting citizens from having a say in their government.

As we discuss more in the pages to come, policing interventions also have corrosive effects on core democratic attitudes and legal socialization among youth. In a process she terms "legal estrangement," Monica Bell argues that people and communities facing aggressive policing who have limited options for remedying harms done are likely to disengage from civic participation more broadly; the voices of communities most affected by aggressive policing therefore do not get heard (Bell 2017).

In sum, criminal justice policies kept the civic power of the poor low and distorted the democratic norm of equal voice. By removing people from our political system—informally and formally—these policies undermined the most impacted communities' abilities to hold leaders and groups accountable. Together with its reproduction of inequality and the economic devastation wrought from incarceration and policing's material consequences, such political disempowerment continues to limit the capacity of RCS communities to resist punitive policy designs and the expansion of police surveillance. And because the negative feedbacks are concentrated on those with the least power and mostly invisible to those communities not interfacing with criminal justice routinely, coalitions that could yield transformation in this state of affairs are difficult to sustain, or even form.

3. *Criminal justice policy designs (and resulting institutional arrangements) inhibit reform and aid expansion by distorting who decides policy, who pays for prisons and policing, and who benefits.*

The political and electoral institutions of the United States are heavily implicated in punitive criminal justice policies, the lack of a poverty-reducing welfare state, and our responses to extreme rates of serious violence in cross-national perspective (Miller 2016; Gottschalk 2016; Lacey and Soskice 2013). We have an institutional context and political system that made partisan "punitive bidding wars" or a "law and order arms race" more likely and made blocking comprehensive social policy easily accomplished (Murakawa 2014, 24; Miller 2016; Lacey and Soskice 2013, 7). Specifically, in contrast to other democratic nations, the United States' "highly fragmented, racialized political system . . . [m]akes it easy to decouple crime and violence from other social conditions," giving rise to "policies aimed narrowly at punishing offenders rather than reducing the likelihood of victimization and other forms of risk" (Miller 2016, 9). These structural constraints and political features have meant that "cleaving" off the most punitive policies from other proposals to deal with social risk occurs again and again in our political system.

Who decides policy is also skewed. "Home voters" in suburbs decide the criminal justice policies that largely affect the cities (Stuntz 2010; Pfaff 2017; Lacey and Soskice 2013). In our federal system, groups that represent the communities most affected are not as well-heeled as groups representing those who stand to gain. Scholars have shown that policy debates about crime at the local level have a more even playing field, but a lot of the action happens at the state level where local groups have less access (Miller 2008). And even at the local level where community groups are more visible, police unions have exerted outsized influence in policies related to policing, opposing measures that stand in the way. They are active in elections, sought out for endorsements and donations, and lobby elected officials for favorable legislation or to impede reform of their practices. Although their influence on election or policy outcomes has been curiously understudied, and scholarly understanding of their clout is limited, police unions are important to understanding the consolidation of police power, the policy bias toward their interests, and the challenges encountered by those who wish to rethink police authority and its scope (Sieg and Wang 2019; Kupfer 2018; Douthat 2015; Bernd 2015).

For generations, intellectuals and activists of color have argued that those most failed by police practices must be a central part of the solution. Groups that represent those most affected are often missing from agenda setting at the federal and state levels and marginalized in the policymaking process. Their constituents are silenced through formal felon disenfranchisement (Manza and Uggen 2008). Even when they can legally vote, they are informally demobilized (Lerman and Weaver 2014). They receive little of the federal resources, and they have an entirely different perspective than the typical single-issue groups representing agencies tied to the criminal justice system, one that is more attentive to the social causes of crime, has a greater understanding of the multiple points of disadvantage that lead to differential offending, and frames the solution as not being reducible to punishment and enforcement (Miller 2008).[2] In the reform moment today, this dynamic is prominently on display. Subaltern activist groups often frame the necessary solutions quite differently—instead of better training, better technology, and other technocratic reforms, they proffer "freedom budgets" that redirect money spent on police and jails toward investment on communal infrastructure and jobs.

Who pays for the system is also skewed. Decentralization in the U.S. system has important implications for crime policies, generating a "pass the costs upstairs" dynamic (Lacey and Soskice 2013). When police make arrests, local prosecutors file the cases, but their local government often does not foot the bill for their decisions; the state does. What this means is that there is little financial reason not to file as many cases as possible. (It also means that it is cheaper to pursue a felony sentence than a misdemeanor one because, as John Pfaff points out, the latter means a county-funded jail stay while the former means a state-funded prison stay.) And while states pay the costs, they get weighty subsidies from the federal government. Given that cities do not finance incarceration, politically, local office seekers can pursue popular tough-on-crime policies that affect their communities without ever having to shoulder the direct costs (Lacey and Soskice 2013, 13). They get the benefits while not internalizing the costs. Thus, there is a built-in incentive to ramp up arrests. In the youth context, this dynamic is acute; for example, when states like Michigan considered how to reduce adolescent exposure to adult courts and prisons in a package of "raise the age" reforms, they faced the political dilemma of how to pay for it without making counties assume a significant new financial burden (the state pays for adult probation and prison, but the counties pay for juvenile justice) and ultimately the legislation failed. And the opposite is also true: there are few cost-based incentives to radically reduce crime control spending because of a "converse feedback blockage." As Nicola Lacey and David Soskice explain about the implications of decentralization for financial incentives, the "cost-savings produced by an effective crime prevention strategy at the local level will have to be massive before they register with policy-makers at the state level" (2013, 10). In other words, passing the cost savings upstairs is just as difficult as passing the costs upstairs is easily accomplished. But this same structural dilemma militates against local social provision. Local voters are less likely to support local policies that invest in goods provision that ameliorates high crime and the social risks underlying crime (Lacey and Soskice 2013).

Who pays for the system is also skewed in another key respect. As already mentioned and as documented by new work on the political economy of policing, the families and communities that are the most vulnerable to police surveillance and incarceration increasingly bear the financial burden of these very systems. From asset forfeiture to victim restitution to exorbitant municipal fines and fees imposed by police to court fees and money bail, arguably the communities least able to pay are the very ones being enlisted to shore up flagging municipal budgets (Katzenstein and Waller 2015; Harris 2016; Gordon and Hayward 2016). After Ferguson exposed the collusion between city managers and police to generate more revenue for the city, it became clear that many other cities had perfected the practice of directing the assets of poor residents into city coffers: "the top twenty-one 'collectors' [in St. Louis county] were municipalities that generated at least one-third of their revenue from court fines and fees, where, on average, 62 percent of the residents were Black and 22 percent lived below the poverty line" (Camp and Heatherton 2016, 30). Other costs, too, were foisted onto the justice-involved, like the $26 one pays if police deploy their Taser on you in the State of Missouri (Gottschalk 2016) or the many "pay-to-stay" jails across the country.

4. Progressive reforms of the criminal justice system often end up expanding it.

Carceral and police expansion has been a thoroughly bipartisan project. Liberal organizations and political leaders have aided the amplification of police power and state projects to criminalize mundane behavior (Hinton 2016; Gottschalk 2016; Murakawa 2014). From the pursuit of "law and order with justice" in the 1960s to the drug wars of the 1980s, the Left joined the effort to expand federal criminal justice authority. Liberal reformers often unwittingly enhanced carceral state power, bureaucratic administration, and institutional capacity; time and again, they grew the carceral state as they tried to regulate and improve it. Many of the progressive reforms in the 1960s were meant to professionalize the police, regulate abysmal prison conditions, or even fix the worst racial disparities, but ended up justifying expansion and new institutional capacity (Murakawa 2014; Schrader 2019; Schoenfeld 2018). Sometimes, this dynamic is the tragic outcome of a system that "selectively hears" (Hinton, Kohler-Hausmann, and Weaver 2016) and responds to the demands of RCS communities, as when black local policy-makers sought an urban Marshall Plan and greater policing; they got the latter in spades without the former (Forman 2017). CompStat, broken windows, "community policing," even the first major grant programs to aid state criminal justice reforms all trace their beginnings to liberal organizations and efforts to make the system more procedurally just, "efficient," or "evidence-based." School Resource Officers (SROs) and partnerships between school districts and local law enforcement agencies became common in the 1990s not only with the purpose of order and safety, but also to encourage positive interactions between youth and police and potentially improve police-community relationships (E. Owens 2017). But in so doing, liberals helped to construct one of the most incredible uses of state power in our time (Murakawa 2014), and the dynamic of liberal net-widening continues to be observed in the current reform moment.[3]

This point is not to harangue elite liberal politics; it is to recognize that problematic policy designs were generated in liberal circles because they often prioritized working *within* the existing system, adding to it rather than redefining the role of the state. The political and economic benefits of carceral expansion were also enjoyed across the political spectrum, and any effort to pull back the carceral state must grapple with this feature of partisan criminal justice politics. At the local level, progressives have relied heavily on the police to support redevelopment and defend gentrifying neighborhoods, segregate urban spaces and protect business interests, and increase property values (Stuart 2016). And nonelite whites and impoverished white communities almost certainly directly benefit from high, racially concentrated incarceration. The criminalization of black bodies, Paul Butler argues, "is something like an employment stimulus plan for working-class white people, who do not have to compete for jobs with all the black men who are locked up, or are underground because they have outstanding arrest warrants, or who have criminal records that make obtaining legal employment exceedingly difficult" (2017, 12). Towns in rural America that got a prison had a less sharp economic downturn than those that did not (Eason 2017). To dismantle carceral institutions, then, "white people lose—at least in the short term" (Butler 2017, 12), as the carceral expansion "links the economic stability of lower-class, rural whites to the continued penal confinement of poor, urban minorities" (Thorpe 2015, 618).

The Need for Reform

In calls for reform of our criminal justice system, many political observers have focused on its cost, its inability to enhance public safety, and its devastating economic consequences for individuals and families. For example, the bipartisan coalition that has supported reforms in recent years based on cost considerations promotes a "government is too large and spends too much" discourse that will threaten the kinds of investment needed to not only redact policing largesse but build real opportunity and power in places without it (Schoenfeld 2018).

Beyond these challenges, however, the criminal justice domain is unique in the extent to which its *policy feedbacks distort power, displacing those who are most affected by the system, keeping them from being able to change it.* Youth in particular cannot vote, and in many places, neither can some of the most impacted adults. Others may be able to vote but live around many neighbors who cannot (Burch 2013); when they do, they are selectively heard (Hinton, Kohler-Hausmann, and Weaver 2016); and when they organize against police violence, they are told they are violent. They live in unremedied structural violence, sometimes across generations (Sharkey 2013)—the lead-filled water, the schools that do not have heat in winter, and the jobs that do not pay. Because they do not enjoy policy agenda access and power at the levels making criminal justice policies, elite reform efforts have not recognized and may continue to ignore their lived experience and evade the deeper reforms needed.

Although the policy feedback challenges described here largely affect both youth and adults, we argue that young people have especially adverse experiences that require special attention but have been mostly ignored in public debate and reform efforts. The punitive consensus has started to give way; however, the *policing of youth consensus* has not, even as policing faces a legitimacy crisis among the next generation. In the many reform platforms being touted, one is hard-pressed to find any mention of youth exposure to police at all, despite the fact that it constitutes much of the exposure Americans have with police and acts as a force multiplier on social, economic, and political outcomes. It is even more striking that the more modest endeavor of enhancing civic capacity of disadvantaged youth in the near term alongside scaling back policing has not been proposed. De-policing without actually dealing with the community challenges faced by RCS youth or the chronic disinvestment of resources may reduce police power while "denying the structural features of the criminal justice system and the political economy that constrain opportunities in the first place" (Schoenfeld 2018, 228).

Therefore, an effective approach should combine reducing our reliance on punitive forms to deal with youth with building citizenship-enhancing civic infrastructure in working-class and poor communities. Such an approach demands that we first see the carceral state as linked to other aspects of state failure (Miller 2016)—the places that have endured state failure in schools, jobs, health, treatment, even water provision, often for generations, are the places enduring expansive surveillance and punishment. In the pages that follow, we describe the unique circumstances of RCS youth and their interactions with the police and other surveilling institutions. We then propose alternative ways in which young people might be engaged, efforts that both promote public safety and strengthen young people's ties to their communities and broader public life.

Policing as a Childhood Intervention

When we think of criminal justice interventions, we might imagine adults or those at the brink of adulthood. But this is not right. *Policing, in America at least, is a childhood intervention*. When we think of police stopping Americans, we should instead conjure up an image of a 14-, 12-, or even 10-year-old. Figure 1 documents the age distribution at onset of first police contact in a recent purposive sample of 11 highly policed neighborhoods.[4] Most were under 14. And the "dosage" of contact was strong and enduring: of those who were stopped before adulthood, 50.4 percent reported being stopped more than seven times. Similarly, a team of sociologists did a large survey of eighteen thousand students in Chicago; half had been stopped by police upon reaching ninth and tenth grade, and a quarter had been searched (Hagan, Shedd, and Payne 2005).

This is consistent with the findings of nationally representative studies. One in *Pediatrics* made headlines, finding that fully one-third of all Americans experienced an arrest by age 23 using the National Longitudinal Survey of Youth (Brame et al. 2012).[5] A study using the Fragile Families and Child Wellbeing Study year 15 interview of teens found that 19 percent of youngsters reported being stopped by police (Geller 2019). The average age of their first police encounter was between 12 and 13. These overall percentages grow more extreme once we look at black youth. For instance, in the study of Fragile Families, 39 percent of black boys reported being stopped by police by this young age (compared to 19 percent of white boys) (Geller 2019).[6] The findings of a black/white gulf among boys were "robust to controls for peer and family circumstances." In another, black youth *not engaged in offending* were more likely to be stopped and searched than white youth who *did* engage in crime (Human Impact Partners 2017). "Black boys are policed like no one else," one legal scholar argued recently, "not even black men" (Henning 2017, 58).

Explanations for these dramatically different experiences that are not reducible to differential offending are suggested by studies. Police do not *see* black kids as kids—studies show that police evaluate black boys as four years older on average than they actually are and as less innocent than white boys (Goff et al. 2014).

FIGURE 1
Age of Onset of Self-Reported Police Encounters

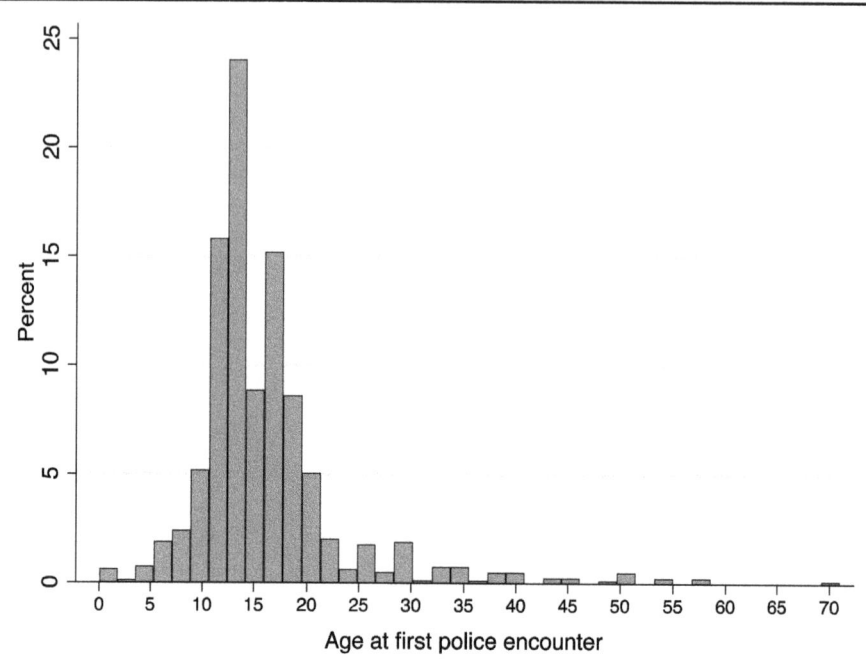

SOURCE: Portals Criminal Justice Dialogues Project.

Epstein, Blake, and Gonzalez (2017) suggest that similar dynamics may be at play for black girls (see also M. Morris 2016).

In the most extensive collection of firsthand, in-depth accounts of police in the United States ever amassed, Gwen Prowse, Vesla Weaver, and Tracey Meares (2019) recorded 850 conversations about policing across fourteen neighborhoods in six cities. They found that one of the most common expressions about police experience had to do with childhood experiences. As just one example—there are many—a man in Chicago recalled his first encounter:

> *Eight years old was my first time getting pulled over, nigga for, you know what I'm saying, like walking with a group of other little niggas. We was out in the hood, like, playing around with sticks and we all was wearing like the same colors and shit, you know what I'm saying, just to match each other because we was all friends type shit. But what they put that on? We gang banging, they just called us Vice Lords . . . we wasn't doing that shit.*

An 18-year-old woman in Milwaukee recounts,

> *When I was about 14 and 13, I always been a full figured girl. The police would stop me when I was walking outside with my friends at night, "Are you a prostitute?" Ask me questions like that. I'm a 13 year old girl at the time.*

Police stops are neither momentary nor neutral encounters with street-level bureaucrats, a quick check in to make sure adolescents are not up to illicit behavior. As we discuss in greater detail below, they are moments of humiliation, state force, and racial learning (Shedd 2015; Rios 2011; Brunson and Weitzer 2009; Brunson and Miller 2006; Butler 2017; Jones 2014). It would be difficult to capture the scope and intensity of political and racial learning that occurs in these youthful encounters, often occurring before youth have had positive or citizen-initiated interactions with governing authorities and representatives. Take one example from a man in Los Angeles:

> *I grew up with the police harassing me. The first time the police stopped me I was 11 years old and they stopped me 'cause I was playing water balloon fights, with my friends, during the summer. And, um, they handcuffed all of us, they paraded us in front of the community, they had the helicopter on us, and this was, this was a group of 11 year olds. Like, nobody was older than 13. And, like, they had guns on us, like they put guns on like. . . . They basically pointed a gun to my head, and they threatened our lives, and. . . . And they also like criminalized us, you know? Like, because afterwards, even though we were kids, like, the entire communities thought that we were up to something bad. So, like, it really changed the perspective of how like my neighbors looked at me. And how they reacted towards me. But it was like, you know, it wasn't, it wasn't a onetime thing, it was like the beginning of, basically. . . . Since then I've been getting stopped by the police a couple times every year. Uh, I thought it would stop, as I'd gotten older, but it hasn't. . . . Because, like, every time they stop me I feel like my life is on the line, and I feel like that could honestly be the last time I'll be breathing. 'Cause they feel threatened by me. I'm a big guy. I'm like 6'2" and I weigh about 260 pounds, so every time they like come around me they get really really nervous, and they always have their guns out, and it's just like a split second decision could end my life, basically, you know.*

Other qualitative accounts underscore that these early encounters give a lasting memory of the state's potential for violence against your person or community. Devon Carbado (2005) describes these moments as a "racial naturalization"; Paul Butler describes that young men experience frisks and searches as a moment of sexual terror (2017); Nikki Jones understands routine searches by police of adolescents as sending "the message that a Black, young, male body is state property" (2014, 45). Quantitative findings reveal that youth have extensive exposure to police across racial groups. But blacks experience qualitatively different treatment by police (Brunson and Weitzer 2009); according to an analysis by one of us (Geller 2019), fully 12 to 14 percent of black boys born in large cities between 1998 and 2000 had their bodies patted down or searched by police and placed in handcuffs, compared to a miniscule share of whites (see Figure 2). Hostile language and racial invectives were often used. Undertones of violence surrounded these encounters. For another example from the Criminal Justice Dialogues project (Prowse, Weaver, and Meares 2019), a 19-year-old man from Milwaukee recalls,

> *At a young age, like twelve years old, I, I experienced the police, they come in, into my house, they lookin' for one person but still they feel the need to put a gun to the head of a twelve-year-old, and I'm, that's my first time seeing a gun, and it's like, wow, this is what I'm exposed to, like just predetermined by who knows what, but not me being a young person. 'Cause, I just, I just hit nineteen, I just finished high school, and I'm, I'm tryin' my best to be a positive influence on my, my community and really do something big.*

FIGURE 2
Police Stop Experiences among Boys in the Fragile Families and Child Wellbeing Study

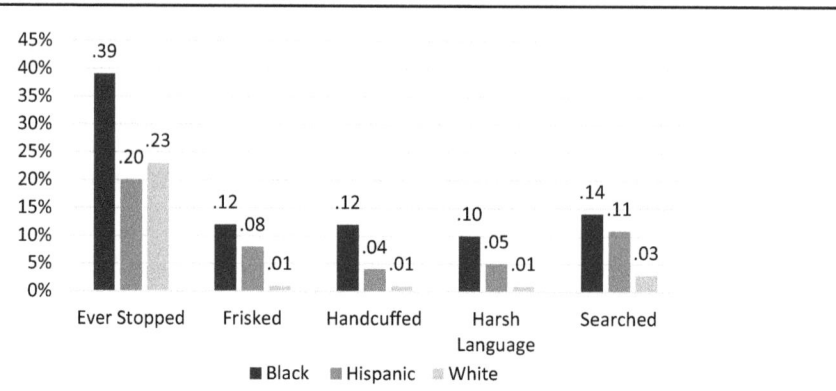

SOURCE: Authors' analysis of year 15 FFCWS data.
NOTE: While those identifying as multiracial also have more extreme stop experiences, the *N* is too low to represent their experiences.

The prominence of the police in the lives of young people is not simply an artifact of self-reports in retrospective surveys and qualitative interviews. Police-collected administrative data on officer stops from 2006 to 2016 in New York City, shown in Figure 3, document that police stopped more than 700,000 adolescents; to provide a sense of how large that is, it approximates the number of stops of adults in the 25- to 30-year-old group. Most minors approached by police were in the tail end of adolescence (15- to 17-year-old age range) but even in the youngest age range of 10 to 13 years old, police recorded 27,000 stops. If the data are presented instead as rates, black 15-year-old boys were stopped by police at a rate of more than 600 per 1,000 students in public schools (compared to under 200 for whites) and arrested at an alarming rate of 170 arrests per 1,000 students (compared to 50 per 1,000 for white boys) in the years 2004 to 2012 (Legewie and Fagan 2019). During these stops, black teens were exposed to more violence than whites *of all ages combined*, even after controls for their behavior were included (Kramer, Remster, and Charles 2017). Tamir Rice was not an outlier.

Research by policing expert Jeffrey Fagan (2010) has demonstrated that a large share of these stops are unconstitutional and a miniscule share generate an arrest or summons (indicating that the stop may have been reasonable but lacked an evidentiary basis for a formal charge). Many of those youth stopped by police were stopped for something that could have been handled without legal intervention.

Evidence from other cities abounds. Chicago police recently made news when it was revealed that they had placed thirty-three thousand children as young as 10 on a list of gang members. Cincinnati police are being investigated for using a Taser on an 11-year-old girl in a store. New York City is under legal scrutiny for routinely seizing and indefinitely storing the DNA of youth who are arrested but

FIGURE 3
Police Stops of Youth in New York City, 2006–2016

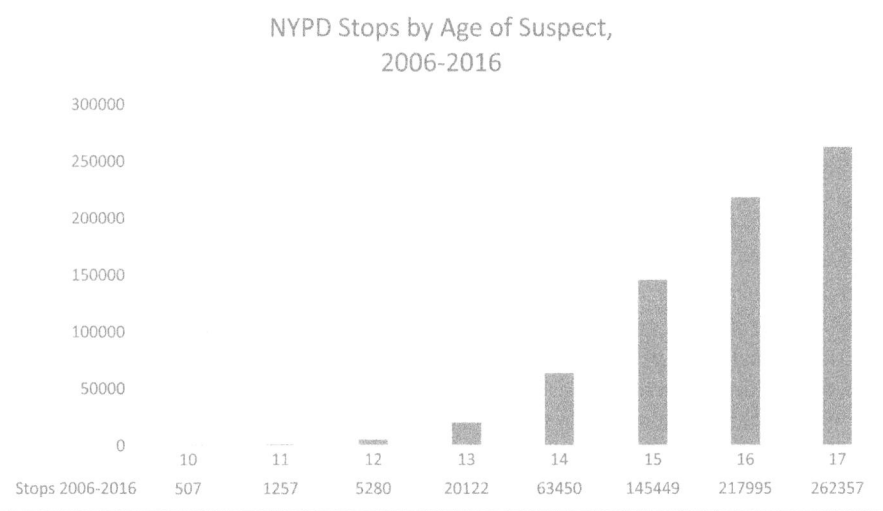

SOURCE: Authors' analysis of New York Policy Department (NYPD) data.

not convicted, retaining their genetic material in a growing city database (Joseph 2019). Police in Riverside County, California, were sweeping up "predelinquent" and "at-risk" youth into a probation program based on violating a noncriminal school code for not obeying "reasonable and proper orders or directions of school authorities"; if they did not adhere to strict requirements of the program, they would be referred to the district attorney (Townes 2018). And in many municipalities, police officers and routines have been increasingly inserted in social service agencies, community institutions, schools, and other spaces that do not serve a crime-reduction purpose but increasingly make ordinary spaces into places for surveillance and provide multiple "on ramps" for youth into the criminal justice system (Rios 2011; Stuart 2016).

Experts have known about the policing of youth for some time, but leaders have done little to counteract it. In his widely cited 1993 article, for example, Lawrence Sherman (1993) describes how young minority males were heavily exposed to "police disrespect and brutality, both vicariously and in person, *prior* to their peak years of first arrest and initial involvements in crime" (p. 464). We have known it dating back decades, since the National Longitudinal Survey of Youth started their interviews, finding that 36 percent of those in the 1979 cohort stopped by police were stopped at age 15 or younger, before the institutionalization of broken windows policing (Bureau of Labor Statistics 2014). And we have known it in virtually every national and local commission focused on policing since Kerner, which found that many of the cities that went up in flames revolted because of police violence *toward a black kid*. It was thus fitting that Childish Gambino's recent viral video "This Is America" featured police violence in the backdrop of black kids dancing in school uniforms.

What transpired to catalyze such high rates of youth surveillance? To develop a youth-appropriate policy response that can route the young toward civic-enhancing institutions requires understanding the political forces that amplified youth surveillance in the first place.

The policing of children

The policing of children was designed by policy, supported by legal institutions, grounded in theoretical justification, and encouraged by new policing practices. Over time, several important shifts led to an expansion in the surveillance of youth.

In the aftermath of one of our nation's biggest challenges to police power during the resistance of the 1960s, a few pages by two academics in an American literary magazine would utterly transform the logic of policing in our nation and more importantly warrant a vast expansion of state authority into RCS communities. Under the broken windows theory, policing pivoted sharply toward minor violations of order, targeting not serious threats to public safety but rather "seeking out the possibility of crime" by enforcing codes against RCS communities (Camp and Heatherton 2016; Wilson and Kelling 1982; Soss and Weaver 2017, 573). Most major cities across the nation rolled out "quality of life," zero-tolerance, or order-maintenance policing, shifts affecting adults and youth alike. As a result, high-volume stops and petty arrests and profligate citations for misdemeanors "were weakly correlated with crime but showed a strong connection to race, poverty, and place" (Soss and Weaver 2017, 571).

Policing also had a friend in our nation's highest court landmark policing cases, which have effectively deregulated policing and have encouraged police stops of citizens based on the thinnest of reasons. It was also bolstered by the hundreds of civil ordinances that "invite police to make contact with Americans for virtually any or no reason at all," based on the criminalization of ordinary behaviors (Prowse, Weaver, Meares 2019).

It was also around this time that several prominent policy experts trained their eyes on young people, constructing a new discourse around black young "superpredators" who were "not merely unrecognizable but alien" (Dilulio 1996). They predicted a coming crisis, with young predators terrorizing the streets, uniquely brutal and "without remorse," and resistant to rehabilitation. Such sensational public claims never materialized—indeed, violent offending by youth has declined sharply since the mid-1990s—but they did ensure a swift increase in attention to youthful offending and gave justification for policies and practices that targeted youth and children for routine behaviors that had previously not elicited police attention. Soon, status offenses became invitation for police rather than school administrators or counselors or parents.

The structural context also helped to ensure that the superpredator discourse could be implemented as policy. The policies and institutional arrangements discussed in the beginning of this article were important foundations for police capacity; so when Dilulio and others advanced the superpredator idea, police were institutionally able to focus on kids.

As the "new policing" was taking shape on the streets in poor and historically oppressed neighborhoods, school environments also embraced a more punitive, surveillant logic. "Zero-tolerance" school discipline policies became de rigueur along with the adoption of SROs. It used to be that security guards were positioned at schools to keep the children within safe from external forces; now, SROs were enlisted to police the schoolchildren themselves. With substantial funding flowing from the Community Oriented Policing Services (COPS) program, more than six thousand new SRO positions were created from 1999 to 2004 (E. Owens 2017). Today, just over a quarter of all schools employ SROs within their buildings, and studies with representative samples of urban youth find that more attend schools with a police officer in their school than a security guard.[7] Indeed, a new report tells of a shocking development: 1.6 million students attended schools without a single school resource counselor that also had a law enforcement officer patrolling onsite (Blad 2016). (Many more attended schools with both.)

Given what we know about the racial targeting of school discipline and suspension, the children who encountered such environments of stripped-down services but muscular surveillance were black and brown. A number of studies have established that while the role of law enforcement in school has increased across the board, 85 percent of black students attend schools with harsh disciplinary environments where police surveillance, monitoring, and control is extensive and normative (Shedd 2015; Bruch and Soss 2018b). Black and brown kids are much more likely to be arrested in school through the NYPD's "School Safety Division." In 2012, black kids made up under a quarter of the student population in New York City but were the subject of 63 percent of arrests and summonses in school (Vitale 2017, 168). Discipline follows, not leads, the use of armed school police. For example, schools with an SRO on staff saw "a 402.3 percent increase in this [disorderly conduct] arrest rate per one hundred students. This percent increase remains large even after controlling for poverty" (Theriot 2009, 285). In Los Angeles, which boasts one of the largest police systems in its unified school district, youth received more than ten thousand misdemeanor tickets in a recent year for schoolyard fights and other youthful conduct, and almost half were meted out to kids under 15 (Adams 2013).

Many school environments today are policed, criminalized spaces. In addition to the ten thousand police officers in schools, schools are increasingly initiating juvenile court referrals; students pass through metal detectors on their way to government or art or band; and sweeps of lockers by drug-sniffing dogs are routine. Instead of upholding the Deweyan ideal that schools be "called upon to produce a more competent, engaged citizenry, underwrite a more egalitarian political order, and function as local sites of democratic public engagement," they have become places that organize more authoritarian than democratic relations, giving students instead experiences of criminal authorities (Bruch and Soss 2018b, 36–37).

The new policing and criminalization of youth in schools began to be reflected in amplified arrest rates among youth net of criminal offending. We examined different cohorts of youth in a national longitudinal survey and found that exposure to police arrest grew substantially. In 1980, 11 percent reported being arrested; but among the cohort coming of age two decades later, after a period of substantial crime declines, almost a quarter had been arrested. This shift reflects policy changes in policing. Even more important, though, is that the relationship to offending transformed. Arrest exposure is conditioned less on patterns of behavior than in prior generations (Weaver, Papachristos, and Zanger-Tishler 2019). Our system slipped from one where police involvement was a relatively good proxy for offending to one where a bigger share of young Americans experienced arrest even though they reported no illegal acts. This transformation in the relationship between crime and criminal justice contact changed dramatically in one generation. Figure 4 shows reported arrest proportions for those who did and did not engage in criminal offending and illegal drug use for two generational cohorts on either side of the rise of broken windows policing. It reveals a sharp generational shift between those who came of age before and just after the major shifts in police capacity and practices. Committing few to no crimes in 1980, one has close to a zero probability of arrest; by 2002, 18 percent of those who had not broken the law had been arrested. This relationship also became racially inflected over time—"blacks had a much higher probability of arrest than both blacks of generations prior and whites of the same generation" (Weaver, Papachristos, and Zanger-Tishler 2019, 89).

Possibilities and Concrete Prescriptions

Much of the conversation related to criminal justice reform has centered on decarceration. The policy space is full of viable and ambitious ideas for overhauling the system at all levels to reduce our reliance on prisons. Most progressive reform efforts are focused on the tail end of criminal justice: incarceration or imprisonment or sentencing. Look to the front end, however—policing, misdemeanor justice, encounters that occur before conviction—and you see the disappearance of conservative reformers from the coalition, and the conversation quickly moves to improvements in technology (i.e., body cameras) and away from institutional failures or investing in the social roots of crime. But the front end, we argue, is even more important, not only because it creates the "sample" for the back end but because it contains a lot more discretion, a lot more innocence, and a lot more kids. Because of this, reform is more plausible, potentially impactful, and more disruptive to the adverse feedbacks that we have described here.

Make contact with the criminal justice system a last resort for minors

> Exposure [of] young adults to these policing tactics is woven into the developmental landscape of children and adolescents, potentially skewing their socialization to law, legal actors, and underlying social norms. (Geller and Fagan 2019, 28)

Before we discuss how a transformation in the policing of children might take place, we first describe the uniformly negative outcomes of youthful police contact based on a substantial evidence base across law, sociology, economics, health,

FIGURE 4
Probabilities of Arrest among Two Generational Cohorts, before and after Broken
Windows Policing

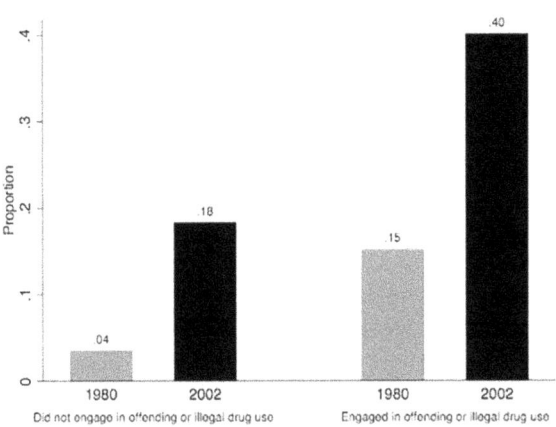

SOURCE: Created using data from Weaver, Papachristos, and Zanger-Tishler (2019).

and political science. Police encounters have widespread effects, but they are "particularly consequential for youth" (Legewie and Fagan 2019, 4). Rather than making them safer, police practices and policies encouraging greater surveillance put youth at risk of state violence and adverse outcomes.

Being confronted by armed state authorities does substantial—sometimes irreversible—harm to children in their most "impressionable years." It interrupts normal adolescent development. Ample research has now shown that exposure to police encounters (even those not leading to arrest) affect the health (McFarland, Geller, and McFarland 2019), mental well-being (Geller 2018; Geller, Tyler, and Link 2014), educational achievement (Legewie and Fagan 2019), and economic prospects of the young, not only after the encounter itself, but potentially well beyond their adolescence.

Police encounters affect child development. For example, researchers have observed post-traumatic stress disorder (PTSD) symptoms among teens who have had a police encounter that are robust to controls for the factors that select the teens into contact with the police (Geller 2018). Teens reporting police contact also report greater levels of anxiety and depression symptoms than their counterparts with no contact (Geller 2018; see also Sugie and Turney [2017] on how criminal justice interventions act as a stressor that leads to worse mental health).

Police contact has disastrous effects for educational outcomes. Children who experience an arrest are two times as likely to later drop out of school (some schools can use an arrest to expel students) and obtain 1 to 1.5 fewer years of education (Kirk and Sampson 2012). Children who lived in a high-policing zone saw their test scores drop (Legewie and Fagan 2019). That study used variation in the timing of the rollout of a police surge that encouraged officers to "conduct high volumes of investigative stops" and sent fifteen hundred more police officers to these areas, many of whom were fresh out of the academy (Operation Impact). In these impact zones, stops of pedestrians by police increased by 34 percent for blacks and 15 percent for Latinos. Arrests for minor violations also surged. Black male students showed a substantial decline in math and reading scores after the implementation of the saturation policing program (Legewie and Fagan 2019).

Among those who do complete schooling, an arrest record imperils access to higher education or jobs, acting as a strong negative credential. Adolescents and young adults who experience being charged with an offense have 20 percent reduced earnings as adults (Human Impact Partners 2017). For all the attention to "adverse childhood experiences" (ACES) in public health, police encounters do not make the list; but they should. And this is to say nothing of the effects of incarceration on children, pulled into focus by Kalief Browder's suicide after waiting for three years on Riker's Island to go to trial—he was 16.

Police involvement channels kids into more surveillance and system embeddedness. The criminal stigma of arrest tends to attach to youth and follow them. Police contact with preteens and teens makes them more likely to be sought out for police intrusion and oversight later through what sociologists refer to as a labelling mechanism—they are tagged as troublemakers and thus more likely to draw police gaze (Liberman, Kirk, and Kim 2014). Once a kid experiences an initial arrest, they are 7.5 times more likely to be re-arrested; this effect occurs independent of being currently engaged in crime, giving rise to a "secondary sanctioning" process (Liberman, Kirk, and Kim 2014). In other words, the later arrests occur due to the independent effect of being initially labelled by police; those with similar levels of delinquency but no prior arrest were less likely to get caught up. Other studies have found a parallel trajectory among youth who experience arrest in their early teens—they are 20 percent more likely to be incarcerated and 10 to 12 percent more likely to be arrested in adulthood (Human Impact Partners 2017).

Thus, policing of youth not only reflects inequality, it reproduces it. If the effects remained there, we might design methods of interrupting the vicious cycle of system involvement, giving rise to more system involvement. But police contact also has more pernicious effects. It converts existing disadvantage into political marginalization and racial injustice. Many people who have contact with police are formally cut off from the democratic process; for example, as a result of being under correctional supervision or disenfranchised, only one in five young blacks who did not finish high school cast a vote in the 2008 election (Pettit 2012).

Beyond formal disenfranchisement, though, police contact restructures the citizen-state relationship (Epp, Maynard-Moody, and Haider-Markel 2014). Police stops are dramatic "occasions for political learning," where people incorporate negative lessons about how public institutions operate and position them, lessons that cultivate deep distrust and racialized alienation from the state and erode civic skills (Bruch and Soss 2018, 37). In one of the first empirical studies on the topic, Lerman and Weaver (2014) argued that police encounters helped to transform the lived experience of citizenship by exposing people to antidemocratic institutions. They empirically demonstrated that contact with criminal justice results in lowered levels of trust in political actors and institutions, a diminished sense of standing and equality of chances, a reduced faith that the state will respond to one's needs, and lessened engagement in civic and political life. Even minor contacts with police and arrests are associated with political withdrawal, as well as short jail spells from misdemeanors (White 2019). In a similar vein, Justice and Meares (2014) argued that the criminal justice system "educates" its subjects in "anticitizenry" and endows people with a "hidden curriculum" of how government works. Other studies, too, have documented political withdrawal and "system avoidance," the idea that residents who have been singled out by police recoil from institutions beyond the police, including medical, labor market, and financial institutions, and develop habits of "ducking and dodging" and going underground (Goffman 2015; Brayne 2014).

Criminal justice institutions are also a key site of racial socialization, "where what it means to be black is conveyed and learned, mostly involuntarily" (Lerman and Weaver 2014, 158). Even after accounting for a range of relevant respondent characteristics, blacks who undergo adversarial contact with law enforcement and criminal justice were much more pessimistic about racial equality in America, more likely to perceive widespread discrimination against themselves and their group, and more likely to believe the prospects for their group were severely limited (Lerman and Weaver 2014). Carla Shedd's (2015) book-length study illuminated the feelings of powerlessness and heightened perceptions of racial injustice that surveilled youth developed.

For example, let us look briefly at dispositions toward government in a study of youth and young adults aged 15 to 25 (see Figure 5). In these data, 64 percent of respondents reported having been stopped by police and 24 percent reported being arrested. We found that youth who had been stopped by police were less likely to believe in equality of opportunity and more likely to believe that government cared very little about people like them and that government treated immigrants better than black citizens.

The early experiences with police can continue to shape ideas about government and civic aspirations into adulthood. Bruch and Soss (2018b) documented that experiencing punitiveness early on through school disciplinary practices negatively affects later odds of voting and trusting government and that "young adults may carry their school-based evaluations of authority with them into young adulthood, and generalize them to government as a whole" (p. 48).

Ethnographic accounts of highly policed neighborhoods, though they do not focus on political alienation per se, show that young men learn lessons about state dominance and arbitrariness, inhabit a criminalized identity, diminish future expectations, incentivize habits in toxic masculinity and avoidance of people and places, decimate social networks, and constrict mobility through the neighborhood (Rios 2011; Shedd 2015; Stuart 2016; Goffman 2015). Police stops of youth communicate to these kids that they are not seen as children but instead as potential offenders and should be singled out for surveillance; they confirm expectations that they will end up in the system, that they are regarded by state authorities as suspicious, deserving of oversight and scorn, and marked as citizen pariahs. In response, these kids take up elaborate strategies to minimize their

FIGURE 5
Perceptions of Government and Equal Opportunity

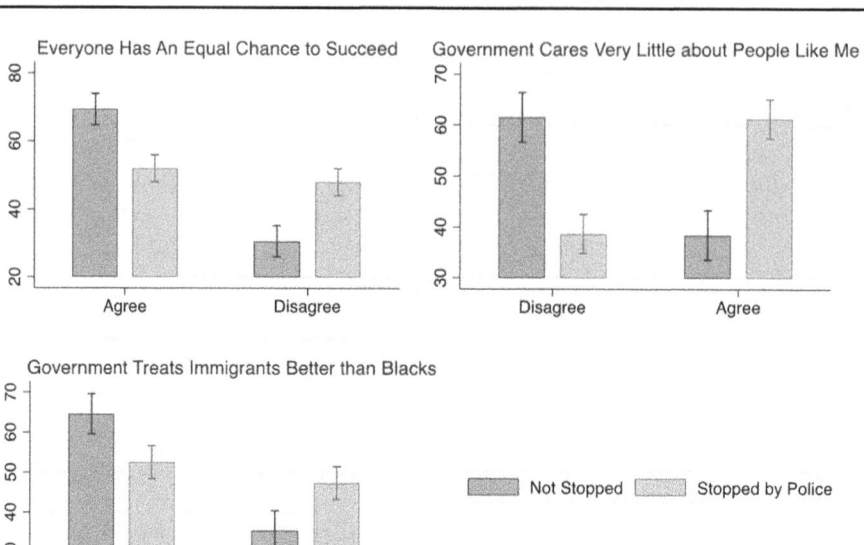

SOURCE: Authors' analysis of Black Youth Culture Survey. Black and Latino respondents only.
NOTE: $N = 1,029$.

encounters with state authorities, habits that trouble the extent of their freedom of association, movement, and right to privacy.

Closely related to political socialization is legal socialization. Legal scholars have documented how police interventions give rise to lower reserves of trust in the law and that aggressive encounters that are perceived as unfair lead people to have less faith in the legitimacy of law enforcement. Scholars have found that intrusive stops by police have a corrosive effect on police legitimacy among youth, and lead to legal cynicism and legal estrangement; a relationship that is not explained by youthful offending (Geller and Fagan 2019; Tyler, Fagan, and Geller 2014; Bell 2017; Kirk and Matsuda 2011). In other words, youth are less likely to have respect for the law or believe in the moral authority and fairness of law. For example, among those who reported being stopped by police in the Fragile Families year 15 data, 59 percent believed "the police create more problems than they solve" compared to about one-third of those who had not been stopped.[8]

In sum, we are hard-pressed to find another policy domain within or beyond criminal justice where the clear and detrimental effects of our approach are so mismatched with the lack of any benefit for the public. Aggressive order maintenance policing, for example, showed no significant crime reductions (Braga, Welsh, and Schnell 2015), while virtually ensuring that policed teens have worse future prospects. Youth surveillance is a policy failure.

Policing should not be the unofficial childhood policy of the United States: Engage other institutions and practices

Police contact in RCS communities may be considered the unofficial childhood policy in the United States, rivaling contact with other institutions especially as other social protections and civic infrastructure for kids contract. Yet this has largely not been a focus among researchers or criminal justice policy experts (with the exception of work cited here). Policies recognizing the prevalence of police contact with youth have sought to limit the damage of such encounters, not radically scale them back. For example, states such as Texas and New Jersey adopted bills that require all kindergarten through twelfth-grade schools to give formal instruction on how to interact with law enforcement, recognizing the reality that a large share of their student population will have this early interaction with police and that it is imperative to give them formal curriculum on how to survive the encounter. Many states and localities have developed programs to divert youth prearrest or to develop graduated responses to juvenile offenders. These efforts, while laudable, do not pose a challenge to the underlying phenomenon of high levels of police contact with kids in the first place, like the exceptionally high rate of police stops of kids that may not generate an official arrest or sanction (Fagan 2010).

There is scant evidence that police stops and arrests of youth are protective or deterrent or better their outcomes or neighborhoods. Like incarceration, police contact often makes a poor situation worse. There is no compelling public safety logic to encouraging police to have such frequent contact with children or to commandeer oversight normally entrusted to parents. Police encounters with kids do not separate the bad from the good; they distinguish the kids growing up without resources and in areas of high surveillance from the rest. In studies of police stops, many, if not most, youth were (unconstitutionally) stopped for being out of place, being too boisterous, being in a group, or to inquire about where they were going. And we are beginning to find out that stops themselves are criminogenic, facilitating later delinquency, not the reverse: boys who were stopped and had not broken the law were much more likely to later commit a crime (del Toro et al. 2019; Wiley and Esbensen 2016). Police stops—instead of targeting crime-prone youth—create their own self-fulfilling prophecy. Thus, one way to disrupt the current criminal justice system and its deleterious feedbacks is to *focus on eliminating police contact with children and simultaneously promote contact with citizenship-building institutions*.

Most experts recognize that police are not the appropriate authority to deal with youthful problems and traumatic childhoods. Yet this recognition has not translated into practice. While there is growing attention to children among criminal justice scholars, it tends to be a focus on children of incarcerated parents or kids at the more extreme end of criminal justice (i.e., life without parole, juvenile prison conditions, kids shackled while in court). In the policy realm, there are many prearrest and postarrest diversion practices but very few models to limit contact in the first place. Indeed, diversion practices and policies actually perversely incentivize police making a stop or an arrest because courts, not police, will be reimbursed for diversion. There is substantial attention to maximizing diversion once youth are in the system *but little emphasis on minimizing entrance into the system.*

To date, only a few local jurisdictions have attempted to draw down police interventions with the young, mostly after successful litigation. In Denver, Colorado, the public schools and police department brokered a deal to reign in police writing tickets of school-aged kids engaged in minor conduct like cursing and required police in that city to be trained in youth psychology (Henning 2017). The Philadelphia police chief issued a directive to officers to end the practice of youthful arrests for minor possession of marijuana and other minor violations, after recognizing that they constituted a majority of arrests of kids in school in that city (Henning 2017). And in Boston, the Massachusetts Bay Transportation Authority (MBTA), in response to a youth-led lawsuit, developed a program to train officers in how to deal with youth; after efforts to improve youth-police contacts, MBTA arrests of youth dropped from 680 in 2001 to 84 (Human Impact Partners 2017). Texas Appleseed has initiated a number of policy reforms that have reduced the number of police/youth interactions, especially in schools.[9] In addition, some locales have designed programs to put more distance between youth and police. For example, the Effective Police Interactions with Youth training curriculum out of Connecticut aims to reduce negative outcomes of police/youth interaction (though not necessarily reduce the number of stops altogether) and has demonstrated a change among youth in their attitudes toward the police.[10] The Think About It First! Cards by Strategies for Youth is also a good example; it has been used in nine states so far.[11] While the primary purpose is to educate youth on the consequences of entering the juvenile justice system, it also alerts officers to the consequences of their decision to arrest a minor. The Inner Harbor Project has useful models, notably the Youth Engagement Training that is designed and taught by Baltimore teens to those police officers assigned to the harbor area.[12] Since launching in 2012, youth arrests have decreased 65 percent in the inner harbor. They also have a successful peer mediation program to address disputes between youth "who have been referred . . . by the Baltimore City School Police Force" to avoid escalation and law enforcement involvement.[13] Although these examples are few and far between, there is a broader model to emulate.

De-policing of youth has a natural predecessor: the deinstitutionalization of youth. Similar efforts to eliminate criminal justice interventions in childhood have succeeded, with minimal opposition. Incarceration experts Bruce Western and Vincent Shiraldi have argued that the criminal justice system was not developmentally appropriate for those in early adulthood; because their brains are still developing into their 20s, they have reduced ability for impulse control, self-regulation, and future orientation. Youth and young adults are more likely to take risks, are more susceptible to negative peer influence and have reduced capacity for decision-making in highly charged situations. Indeed, these youngsters may actually be more psychosocially akin to children than adults (Schiraldi, Western, and Bradner 2015). Incarceration, they argued, should therefore be used "sparingly" (Schiraldi, Western, and Bradner 2015, 16). In a little noticed but radical victory, juvenile correctional institutions have been shuttered in almost every single state, with little to no fanfare or negative fallout. By 2012, there were 970 fewer juvenile prisons than a decade earlier, and youth incarceration rates were cut in half overall and by two-thirds in the five largest jurisdictions (McCarthy, Schiraldi, and Shark 2016).[14] Closing these institutions was relatively politically easy, and advocates used developmental psychology to justify the move to community supervision. In the many commentaries on criminal justice reform, the abolition of youth prisons was barely noticed despite the fact that it cut youth incarceration rates almost overnight (Schiraldi 2017).

These experts also started using this developmental age logic to argue for raising the age for adjudicating youth as adults. The age when youth brains had fully developed capacity was more akin to the age at which people are able to first rent a car or the age at which they are no longer covered by a parent's health insurance than the arbitrary age of 18, a holdover from the late-nineteenth-century family court. This too is beginning to be successful. Several states have debated, and some have passed, legislation raising the age of juvenile jurisdiction, including California, Connecticut, Massachusetts, Michigan, and Vermont; and nineteen states have undertaken reforms to reduce youth involvement in the adult justice system.

This developmental age argument has a strong basis here in the United States and internationally, where countries such as Sweden and Germany try people up to the age of 21 or 25 as juveniles. Indeed, many protections that exist for justice-involved youth and juvenile courts have survived from their inception in the early twentieth century and are designed to be clearly distinct from adult adjudication, from the more rehabilitative focus of youth confinement, to strict limits on exposing their records, to lessened sentences. Later, the United States clearly set out important legal norms surrounding youth based on developmental immaturity: kids could not be killed by the state (death penalty) or confined in perpetuity (life without parole sentences). As the authors of a National Institute of Justice initiative argued, "Our jurisprudence fully accepts that adolescents are entitled to a separate system of justice, with separate facilities, confidentiality protections, and more individualized treatment in a more robust network of rehabilitative programming" (Shiraldi, Western, and Bradner 2015, 8).

Yet this legal and practical consensus around the "diminished capacity" of youth and the specific youth protections in the later stages of the criminal justice system that it yielded *has not carried into the earlier stages of criminal justice*, moments that are just as critical if not more so given their greater prevalence in young lives and their harmful effects. Police approach children and minors as they would adults. There are no youth-specific limits to touch, force, and speech acts. There are no special constraints on police conduct given the smaller bodies and emerging cognitive and emotional development of kids. Police in most jurisdictions have no training on how to deal with youth. Criminal records of youth are sealed, but arrest records are not. If your son or daughter is stopped by police, he or she may very well be treated the same way an adult would be. But if convicted and confined, he or she will be treated as a kid. The conspicuous absence of youthful protections in police contact is arbitrary and demands reconsideration.

Ending police-kid contact will not be easy. Police are so thoroughly entrenched in the lives of youth and the institutional fabric of poor neighborhoods, walling them off from surveillance will be difficult. Youthful spaces have become punitive spaces, in symbolic and literal ways. Children are escorted home by police in some Chicago neighborhoods; they might play on jail-themed playgrounds in New York;[15] and in many neighborhoods, police substations are the most physically present public infrastructure outside of schools. While most child development experts would agree that other entities and outlets should oversee youth, police are still often positioned as a first, not last, resort. If designing a system that roped as many adolescents into having arrest profiles and police encounters as possible were the goal, it would be difficult to imagine a system more efficient than our current one.

How to Minimize the Footprint of Police in the Lives of Youth

The political and policy shift toward de-policing of youth that we are suggesting could happen a few different ways. Local courts are often reimbursed for the number of kids who are diverted from confinement; policies could be designed to reward police agencies that reduce their contact with youth in similar fashion. Policies could instruct separate procedures for police-kid contact, providing agencies with a nonpolice youth caseworker or street outreach workers so that when contact is made, there is an authority present who is specifically trained in working with kids and in de-escalation and alternatives to arrest. We could pursue policies and practices that limit the reach of police into spaces that deal with youth, like community centers, clinics, and schools, a quarter of which employ uniformed police; and hospitals, which lead people to forgo emergency healthcare (Lara-Millán 2014). Local practices could be developed to position other institutions in the community as the first site of contact for "at-risk" youth before police are called; turning to other institutions that understand trauma and adolescent development and are better poised to meet needs would obviate the need for police. More broadly, we might develop a "best practice" that police should only approach youth under certain concrete circumstances where grave harm is imminent (i.e., not for standing on a corner) and always as a last resort when other methods have been used first. If the American Association of Pediatrics can set standards against private discipline (i.e., parents spanking a child) given adverse outcomes for the brain, why can't the United States pursue a similar set of standards regarding public discipline of kids?

Of course, even among minors, some police contact is still necessary. Police should make contact with youth who "pose clear and demonstrable risks to public safety" (McCarthy, Schiraldi, and Shark 2016, 18). When police contact does happen, we should design ways to mitigate the harms to mental and physical well-being and ensure that arrest records of youth do not throw up insurmountable obstacles to jobs and college. Youth who do offend often have serious mental health and substance abuse problems, and justice-involved youth have already witnessed a range of traumatic life events. We should recognize that police are ill-suited to provide the necessary interventions to deal with these problems.

We can do this with few negative consequences for public safety. We can reduce youth contact with police *and* have less youth crime. After a court ordered New York City to stop its unconstitutional stop-and-frisk practices, that city showed a dramatic decline in police stopping youth (see Figure 6). Crime complaints remained static. A more striking example is that after closures of youth prisons swept the states—from Virginia to Connecticut to New York and California—youth crime actually went down. For example, as the number of incarcerated youth dropped from more than ten thousand to fewer than one thousand in California due to closures, violent and property crime and arrests of youth also declined (McCarthy, Schiraldi, and Shark 2016).

There are several positive political consequences to an approach to youth that minimizes police surveillance. Early police contact is a gateway to system involvement later; if policy constrains it to a last resort, a key input of the system is starved. If lowered police contact minimizes arrest records, which it most certainly will, later incarceration is less likely given that prior records figure prominently in sentencing decisions in the United States. But a large share of these kids will avoid involvement with the criminal justice system altogether given that people "age out" of offending and given the findings that stops themselves amplify deviance, not the reverse. This shift in policy and practice will most positively affect black kids who are more likely to have contact even if they are law-abiding; black kids who experience arrest are less likely to be diverted from court adjudication than white kids (Stevens and Morash 2015), so limiting first contact will likely affect racial disparities later in the pipeline.

Above all, this reform priority is a key step in advancing new relations between citizens in race-class subjugated communities and government (Soss and Weaver 2017). It interrupts a key moment when distrust in government and political alienation are formed. Aggressive policing and school discipline are "formative political experiences" that depress trust and engagement in political life (Bruch and Soss 2018b). Through policing, these young Americans "receive a crash course in how state power operates and what citizenship entails for those at the lower reaches of the social order" (Bruch and Soss 2018a). In the long term, such an approach will ensure this youngest generation learns that the state authorities see them as rights-bearing, not potential assailants deserving of oversight.

Reorient our nation's approach to youth

Undermining police contact with youth is a backstop. It is a critical first step in preventing youth from a distinctly poor parallel trajectory identified in studies of police involvement. However, to achieve more just outcomes for youth and create feedback loops away from justice involvement, *we need to promote attachment to institutions reinforcing citizenship and civic health*. We must reorient our broader approach to youth. It requires not just *reducing* contact with authoritarian and surveillant institutions but *replacing* it with greater contact with

FIGURE 6

The Dramatic Post–*Floyd*[a] Decline in Stops of Youth by the NYPD

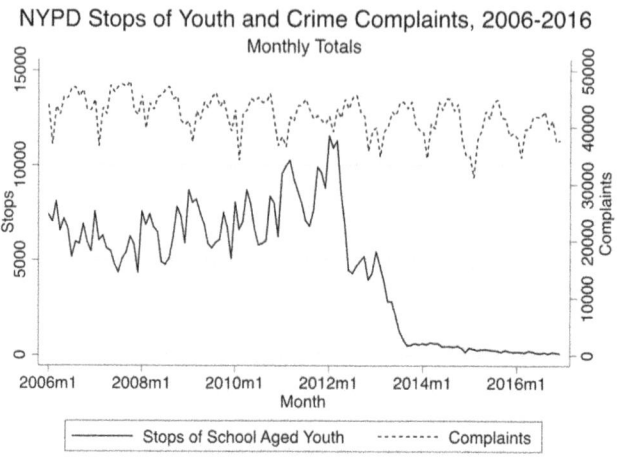

SOURCE: Authors' analysis of NYPD data.

a. *Floyd et al. v. City of New York et al.* (959 F. Supp. 2d 540).

institutions that promote civic attachment and youth empowerment. Adolescence is a period when paths are not yet hardened into deep grooves, where small decisions might have large consequences for later trajectories. What if we conceived of these young years as a crucial moment for civic incorporation and growth? What if instead of future wards going through processes of civic ostracism and criminalized identity development, we positioned youth as civic anchors and active democratic citizens with civic significance?

One way of disrupting negative political socialization from youthful police encounters is to focus on moving youth toward civic-enhancing institutional interactions. Youthful police contact is a bureaucratic encounter that is designed to limit voice and carry few mechanisms for electoral accountability (Lerman and Weaver 2014). These encounters with governing authorities are about control, submission, and compliance; and, often, convey lack of dignity, respect, and agency; they do not provide lessons in the state seeing you as rights-bearing, deserving of positive intervention, or as a principal. Instead of modeling equality, regard, citizen voice, or deliberation, they model submission, docility, group stigma, and racial hierarchy. Thus, we need to divert kids to institutions with a more democratic character, institutions that enhance civic skills, habits, and positive socialization and affirm worth. Kids should have more opportunities for exposure to institutions that model pro-civic behaviors and political agency, not stigmatizing relations with government. What does healthy adolescent political development entail?

We must recognize that youth coming into contact with police have experienced other institutional failures even at a tender age—they attend "cruddy" schools that prioritize discipline over school counselors; they live in areas beset by disinvestment and intergenerational poverty and segregation; their public institutions have failed to protect them from lead-filled buildings and environmental harms; they live in areas of concentrated violence and negative forms of social capital like gangs and where the drug economy has offered more opportunities than the traditional labor market.

Currently, there is a dearth of viable opportunities for young people in communities to become civically engaged (Flanagan and Levine 2010). Over the last two decades, we have seen a sharp decline in institutions focused on civic incorporation of youth (i.e., community centers, after school programs, youth empowerment programs). Thus, the rising penetration of police in public and civic spaces like neighborhood corners and schools has occurred alongside the decline of vital civic infrastructure. To put it crudely, we invested heavily in one kind of public good and infrastructure—policing—while other pro-civic institutions were allowed to languish. One organization calls such communities "civic deserts"—places characterized by a severe lack of civic/religious organizations, cultural institutions, and nonprofits and where "there are no physical places where they could address local issues" together (Levine 2018). In such places, opportunities for learning about political life and opportunities for meaningful civic engagement and political agency are few. Many scholarly experts from a range of fields argue that civic deserts contribute to political alienation, distrust, decline in collective efficacy, frayed community cohesion, and even violence (Putnam 2001; Sampson 2011; Sharkey 2018; Klinenberg 2018). At a broader level, political theorist Bonnie Honig (2017) argues that democracy is in dire need of "public things," places that promote the daily practice of "agonistic democratic citizenship" (p. 36); otherwise, democratic routines get reduced to "procedures, polling and policing" (p. 4).

Thriving civic spaces foster the opposite. For example, in his magisterial study of Chicago, Robert Sampson (2011) found that neighborhoods with higher collective efficacy ("the willingness of local residents to intervene for the common good") was a key indicator of communal public safety, net of race and economic status. It is the processes that activate informal social control in neighborhoods that create the foundation for public safety. His student, Patrick Sharkey, found that flourishing community groups and nonprofit density played a major role in the "great crime decline" of the past decades (Sharkey 2018). In *Palaces for the People*, Eric Klinenberg (2018) identified physical structures that promote the development of social cohesion and civic renewal. In studying the devastation of the Chicago heat wave, he found that even in similarly situated neighborhoods, the places that witnessed fewer deaths were those that had public gathering hubs such as libraries and community organizations. J. Phillip Thompson (2005) calls this "deep pluralism"—the recognition and civic incorporation of all group statuses within a polity.

Youth civic engagement and social networks are major factors in later success and economic mobility (Chetty et al. 2014). Youth who work together on local problems are more likely to develop civic skills and less likely to drop out of school. Conversely, urban youth who confront few opportunities for engagement in organizations seek alternative forms of collective collaboration that are dangerous and provide negative social capital (i.e., gangs). According to one study: "Youth living in a Civic Desert are generally less experienced in civic and political life and largely disengage from politics; have few, if any, opinions about current affairs; and are less likely to believe that civic engagement like voting and civic institutions—from Congress to local nonprofits—can benefit the community. They were also less likely to help others in informal ways, like helping neighbors and standing up for someone who is being treated unfairly" (Kawashima-Ginsberg and Sullivan 2017).

Instead of providing an education in marginality and subjectivity, we should be investing in expanding kids' opportunities to take action together, make claims on their governing institutions, and expand youth voice. We should be developing youth as active and engaged citizens, not subjects of surveillance, normalized to the routines of a police pat-down or "kissing the pavement." And given that civic opportunity gaps are raced and classed, we need to think about how to democratize access to such goods. Several programs to provide meaningful civic opportunities and leadership of community projects to address local problems to youth in RCS communities have taken shape: YouthBuild USA, Opportunity Nation, and the Black Youth Project. These opportunities are not only intrinsic goods for youth prospects. They are critical to expanding our nation's wider democratic knowledge and pointing toward democratic threats in our time. This is nowhere more plain than in the "Black Spring" that activated youth to reimagine policing in the aftermath of police killings of youth in Ferguson, Baltimore, Chicago, and elsewhere. Activist groups led by youth ignited renewed political discourse and enhanced local civic capacity and youth mobilization toward the goal of strengthening black and brown liberation, including We Charge Genocide; Black Lives Matter; Million Hoodies for Justice; Dream Defenders; Malcolm X Grassroots Movement; BYP100; and LetUsBreathe Collective. These groups not only heightened attention to policing and expanded the political imagination with newly resonant political frames but led to several youth-mobilized electoral victories, such as the ousting of prominent prosecutors in major cities, the undoing of predatory municipal codes, and the passing of criminal justice reforms. Other less-well-known local initiatives to engage youth, amplify their voice, and communicate their civic worth should be seen as models. The Invisible Project conducted conversations with Chicago youth, giving them center stage in telling their narrative.[16] Yes Loitering is a youth-led program that reimagines public spaces to be more youth-friendly, to provide an enriching and safe environment where teens are welcome and can, therefore, avoid police interactions over infractions like loitering and trespassing.[17] Greater organization and activism of youth can also lend itself to more accountable public institutions like the police. Neighborhoods with strong community-based organizations were able to counteract the demobilizing effects of criminal justice (M. Owens and Walker 2018).

Today, the nation is beginning to shift course in the decades-long prison expansion. Many have celebrated the dawn of a new era, as our system has been roundly judged unfair, ineffective, and, mostly, too expensive. Less often remarked upon, it is also a system that targets and destroys youth. Changing police tactics must be accompanied by a broader consideration of how government orients itself toward young people. Once we begin to reestablish youth engagement with citizen-building organizations and reorient government's relationship to young people, we can turn vicious cycles of feedback into virtuous ones.

Notes

1. The Department of Justice can now initiate oversight of local agencies engaged in a "pattern and practice" of unconstitutional policing. In practice, this oversight occurs only in the most egregious violations.

2. Analyzing a large sample of hearings related to crime and punishment over time—at local, state, and federal levels—Miller (2008) finds that in national hearings, agencies and individuals representing those connected to criminal justice with an interest in extending punishment become the dominant voice in congressional debates over violence and sentencing policy (i.e., prosecutors, police, prison guards, gun lobby). Conversely, victims, community groups, and those serving the communities who directly experience criminogenic neighborhoods and the consequences of returning ex-offenders are largely absent from the creation of national-level policy. This asymmetry in representation not only results in a different way of framing the crime problem, but it also narrows the range of policy options.

3. Liberal reformers often couch their proposals to reduce sentences for less serious crimes on the rationale that it will free up resources for longer confinements of the "real bad guys," a dynamic scholars call bifurcation (Beckett 2018; Schoenfeld 2018). And they sometimes package progressive and draconian reforms together; a quarter of justice reinvestment laws—seen as a progressive reform to incentivize diverting commitments to prison—were enacted in the same legislative session as those that expanded sentences for life without parole (Schoenfeld 2018). Or they design "alternatives to incarceration" that ironically widen the net of who comes into contact with criminal justice or for how long; for example, states may pursue sentencing reforms that divert offenders from prison but put them on probation for 10 years.

4. Based on a sample from communities undergoing moderate to high levels of police surveillance. Portals Criminal Justice Dialogues project, Principal Investigators Tracey Meares and Vesla Weaver; www.portalspolicingproject.com.

5. A more conservative estimate was produced by the police-citizen contact survey conducted by the Bureau of Justice Statistics; just over a quarter of youth and young adults aged 16 to 25 had experienced police (though not all of these were police-initiated involuntary encounters), a higher share than older adults (Hyland, Langton, and Davis 2015).

6. Based on a representative sample of American children born in twenty U.S. cities in the late 1990s and followed to their 15th birthday.

7. Authors' calculation based on the Fragile Families and Child Wellbeing Study, Year 15 adolescent survey.

8. Analysis by authors.

9. https://www.texasappleseed.org.

10. https://portal.ct.gov/OPM/CJ-JJYD/Just-Start/Just-START-Training-curriculum.

11. https://strategiesforyouth.org/sfysite/for-police/how-to/how-to-think-about-it/.

12. http://www.theinnerharborproject.org/what-we-do.

13. https://static1.squarespace.com/static/5764668ae3df2833602df1bf/t/59a78a1fe3df28057d0544d5/1504152099505/Peer+Mediation+Curriculum+%281%29.pdf.

14. One negative outcome, however, was that confinement of white minors dropped faster than it did for black youth, exacerbating already large racial disparities. In 2015, 44 percent of youth detained in juvenile centers, jails, and prisons were black, compared to being 16 percent of the nation's population. See https://www.sentencingproject.org/publications/black-disparities-youth-incarceration/.

15. https://cityroom.blogs.nytimes.com/2010/03/26/the-strange-case-of-the-playground-jail/.

16. https://invisible.institute/ypp.

17. https://www.theyesloiteringproject.com.

References

Adams, Jane Meredith. 4 October 2013. State law encourages alternatives to school-based police while federal grants increase their presence. *EdSource*. Available from https://edsource.org/2013/school-police-under-greater-focus/39952.

Beckett, Katherine. 2018. The politics, promise and peril of criminal justice reform in the context of mass incarceration. *Annual Review of Criminology* 1:235–39.

Beckett, Katherine, and Steve Herbert. 2009. *Banished: The new social control in urban America*. New York, NY: Oxford University Press.

Bell, Monica C. 2017. Police reform and the dismantling of legal estrangement. *Yale Law Journal* 126:2054–2150.

Bernd, Candice. 2015. Is campaign cash from police unions watering down Democrats' reform efforts? *Truthout*. Available from https://truthout.org/articles/is-campaign-cash-from-police-unions-watering-down-democrats-reform-efforts.

Blad, Evie. 9 December 2016. Schools with police but no school counselors: A closer look. *Education Week*. Available from https://blogs.edweek.org.

Braga, Anthony A., Brandon C. Welsh, and Cory Schnell. 2015. Can policing disorder reduce crime? A systematic review and meta-analysis. *Journal of Research in Crime and Delinquency* 52 (4): 576–88.

Brame, Robert, Michael G. Turner, Raymond Paternoster, and Shawn D. Bushway. 2012. Cumulative prevalence of arrest from ages 8 to 23 in a national sample. *Pediatrics* 129 (1): 21–27.

Brayne, Sarah. 2014. Surveillance and system avoidance: Criminal justice contact and institutional attachment. *American Sociological Review* 79 (3): 367–91.

Burch, Traci. 2013. *Trading democracy for justice: Criminal convictions and the decline of neighborhood political participation*. Chicago, IL: University of Chicago Press.

Bureau of Labor Statistics, U.S. Department of Labor. 2014. National Longitudinal Survey of Youth, 1979 cohort, 1979–2012 (rounds 1–25). Columbus, OH: Center for Human Resource Research, Ohio State University.

Bruch, Sarah K., and Joe Soss. 2018a. The lessons students learn. *Jacobin*. Available from https://www.jacobinmag.com/2018/03/school-authority-punishment-police-citizenship.

Bruch, Sarah K., and Joe Soss. 2018b. Schooling as a formative political experience: Authority relations and the education of citizens. *Perspectives on Politics* 16 (1): 36–57.

Brunson, Rod K., and Jody Miller. 2006. Gender, race, and urban policing: The experience of African American youths. *Gender & Society* 20 (4): 531–52.

Brunson, Rod K., and Ronald Weitzer. 2009. Police relations with black and white youths in different urban neighborhoods. *Urban Affairs Review* 44 (6): 858–85.

Butler, Paul. 2017. *Chokehold: Policing black men*. New York, NY: The New Press.

Camp, Jordan T., and Christina Heatherton, eds. 2016. *Policing the planet: Why the policing crisis led to Black Lives Matter*. New York, NY: Verso Books.

Campbell, Andrea Louise. 2003. *How policies make citizens: Senior political activism and the American welfare state*. Princeton, NJ: Princeton University Press.

Carbado, Devon W. 2005. Racial naturalization. *American Quarterly* 57 (3): 633–58.

Chetty, Raj, Nathaniel Hendren, Patrick Kline, and Emmanuel Saez. 2014. Where is the land of opportunity? The geography of intergenerational mobility in the United States. *Quarterly Journal of Economics* 129 (4): 1553–1623.

Clear, Todd R. 2009. *Imprisoning communities: How mass incarceration makes disadvantaged neighborhoods worse*. New York, NY: Oxford University Press.

Dagan, David, and Steven Michael Teles. 2016. *Prison break: Why conservatives turned against mass incarceration*. New York, NY: Oxford University Press.

Del Toro, Juan, Tracey Lloyd, Kim S. Buchanana, Summer Joi Robins, Lucy Zhang Bencharit, Meredith Gamson Smiedt, Kavita S. Reddy, Enrique Rodriguez Pouget, Erin M. Kerrison, and Phillip Atiba Goff. 2019. The criminogenic and psychological effects of police stops on adolescent black and Latino boys. *Proceedings of the National Academy of Sciences* 116 (17): 8261-8268.

Dilulio, John J., Jr. 1996. My black crime problem, and ours. *City Journal* 6 (2): 14–28.

Douthat, Ross. 3 May 2015. Our police union problem. *New York Times*.

Eason, John M. 2017. *Big house on the prairie: Rise of the rural ghetto and prison proliferation*. Chicago, IL: University of Chicago Press.

Epp, Chuck. 2016. Building the policing state. Paper presented at the Conference on Police Actions and Citizen Mobilization in Democratic Societies, Yale University, April 22, New Haven, CT.

Epp, Charles R., Steven Maynard-Moody, and Donald P. Haider-Markel. 2014. *Pulled over: How police stops define race and citizenship*. Chicago, IL: University of Chicago Press.

Epstein, Rebecca, Jamila J. Blake, and Thalia Gonzalez. 2017. *Girlhood interrupted: The erasure of black girls' childhood*. Washington, DC: Georgetown Law School Center on Poverty and Inequality. Available from http://www.law.georgetown.edu/academics/centers-institutes/poverty-inequality/upload/girlhood-interrupted.pdf.

Fagan, Jeffrey. 2010. Expert Testimony. *Floyd et al. v. City of New York et al.* 08 CIV 1034 (SAS).

Flanagan, Constance, and Peter Levine. 2010. Civic engagement and the transition to adulthood. *The Future of Children* 20:159–79.

Forman, James, Jr. 2017. *Locking up our own: Crime and punishment in black America*. New York, NY: Farrar, Straus and Giroux.

Friedman, Brittany, and Mary Pattillo. 2019. Statutory inequality: The logics of monetary sanctions in state law. *RSF: The Russell Sage Foundation Journal of the Social Sciences* 5 (1): 174–96.

Geller, Amanda. 18 August 2018. The mental health consequences of police contact. Paper presented to the American Sociological Association.

Geller, Amanda. 2019. Policing America's children: Police contact among urban teens. Unpublished manuscript.

Geller, Amanda and Jeffrey Fagan. 2019. Police contact and the legal socialization of urban teens. *RSF: The Russell Sage Foundation Journal of The Social Sciences* 5 (1): 26–49.

Geller, Amanda, Jeffrey Fagan, Tom Tyler, and Bruce G. Link. 2014. Aggressive policing and the mental health of young urban men. *American Journal of Public Health* 104 (12): 2321–27.

Goff, Phillip Atiba, Matthew Christian Jackson, Di Leone, Brooke Allison Lewis, Carmen Marie Culotta, and Natalie Ann DiTomasso. 2014. The essence of innocence: Consequences of dehumanizing black children. *Journal of Personality and Social Psychology* 106 (4): 526–45.

Goffman, Alice. 2015. *On the run: Fugitive life in an American city*. New York, NY: Picador.

Gordon, Colin, and Clarissa Rile Hayward. 9 August 2016. The murder of Michael Brown. *Jacobin*.

Gottschalk, Marie. 2006. *The prison and the gallows: The politics of mass incarceration in America*. New York, NY: Cambridge University Press.

Gottschalk, Marie. 2016. *Caught: The prison state and the lockdown of American politics*. Princeton, NJ: Princeton University Press.

Hacker, Jacob S., and Paul Pierson. 2019. Policy feedback in an age of polarization. *The ANNALS of the American Academy of Political and Social Science* (this volume).

Hagan, John, Carla Shedd, and Monique R. Payne. 2005. Race, ethnicity, and youth perceptions of criminal injustice. *American Sociological Review* 70 (3): 381–407.

Harris, Alexes. 2016. *A pound of flesh: Monetary sanctions as punishment for the poor*. New York, NY: Russell Sage Foundation.

Henning, Kristin. 2017. The role of policing in the socialization of black boys. In *Policing the black man: Arrest, prosecution, and imprisonment*, ed. Angela J. Davis, 57–94. New York, NY: Pantheon Books.

Hinton, Elizabeth. 2016. *From the war on poverty to the war on crime*. Cambridge, MA: Harvard University Press.

Hinton, Elizabeth, Julilly Kohler-Hausmann, and Vesla Weaver. 2016. Did blacks really endorse the 1994 crime bill? *New York Times*.

Honig, Bonnie. 2017. *Public things: Democracy in disrepair*. New York, NY: Oxford University Press.

Human Impact Partners. June 2017. *Reducing youth arrests keeps kids healthy and successful: A health analysis of youth arrest in Michigan*. Oakland, CA: Human Impact Partners.

Hyland, Shelley, Lynn Langton, and Elizabeth Davis. 2015. *Police use of nonfatal force, 2002–11*. Washington, DC: US Department of Justice, Office of Justice Programs, Bureau of Justice Statistics. Available from http://www.bjs.gov/index.cfm?ty=pbdetail&iid=5456.

Jones, Nikki. 2014. "The regular routine": Proactive policing and adolescent development among young, poor black men. *New Directions for Child and Adolescent Development* 143:33–54.

Joseph, George. 10 January 2019. Judge attacks NYPD practice of seizing teens' DNA without parental consent. *The Appeal*. Available from https://theappeal.org.

Justice, Benjamin, and Tracey L. Meares. 2014. How the criminal justice system educates citizens. *The ANNALS of the American Academy of Political and Social Science* 651 (1): 159–77.

Katzenstein, Mary Fainsod, and Maureen R. Waller. 2015. Taxing the poor: Incarceration, poverty governance, and the seizure of family resources. *Perspectives on Politics* 13 (3): 638–56.

Kawashima-Ginsberg, Kei, and Sullivan, Felicia. 26 March 2017. Study: 60 percent of rural millennials lack access to a political life. *The Conversation*. Available from https://theconversation.com.

King, Desmond, and Robert C. Lieberman. 2017. The civil rights state. In *The many hands of the state: Theorizing political authority and social control*, eds. Kimberly J. Morgan and Ann Shola Orloff, 178–202. Cambridge: Cambridge University Press.

Kirk, David S., and Mauri Matsuda. 2011. Legal cynicism, collective efficacy, and the ecology of arrest. *Criminology* 49 (2): 443–72.

Kirk, David S., and Robert J. Sampson. 2013. Juvenile arrest and collateral educational damage in the transition to adulthood. *Sociology of Education* 86 (1): 36–62.

Klinenberg, Eric. 2018. *Palaces for the people: How social infrastructure can help fight inequality, polarization, and the decline of civic life*. New York, NY: Crown.

Kramer, Rory, Brianna Remster, and Camille Z. Charles. 2017. Black lives and police tactics matter. *Contexts* 16 (3): 20–25.

Kupfer, Theodore. 2 February 2018. Law-enforcement unions have too much power. *National Review*. Available from https://www.nationalreview.com.

Lacey, Nicola, and David Soskice. 2013. Why are the truly disadvantaged American, when the UK is bad enough? A political economy analysis of local autonomy in criminal justice, education, residential zoning. LSE Legal Studies Working Paper No. 11/2013, London School of Economics.

Lara-Millán, Armando. 2014. Public emergency room overcrowding in the era of mass imprisonment. *American Sociological Review* 79 (5): 866–87.

Legewie, Joscha, and Jeffrey Fagan. 2019. Aggressive policing and the educational performance of minority youth. *American Sociological Review* 84 (2): 220–47.

Lerman, Amy E., and Vesla M. Weaver. 2014. *Arresting citizenship: The democratic consequences of American crime control*. Chicago, IL: University of Chicago Press.

Levine, Peter. 2018. What does youth civic engagement have to do with inequality? Available from http://wtgrantfoundation.org/youth-civic-engagement-inequality.

Liberman, Akiva M., David S. Kirk, and Kideuk Kim. 2014. Labeling effects of first juvenile arrests: Secondary deviance and secondary sanctioning. *Criminology* 52 (3): 345–70.

Lipsitz, G. 2016. Policing place and taxing time on Skid Row. In *Policing the planet: Why the policing crisis led to Black Lives Matter*, eds. Jordan T. Camp and Christina Heatherton, 123–40. New York, NY: Verso Books.

Manza, Jeff, and Christopher Uggen. 2008. *Locked out: Felon disenfranchisement and American democracy*. New York, NY: Oxford University Press.

McCarthy, Patrick, Vincent Schiraldi, and Miriam Shark. 2016. *The future of youth justice: A community-based alternative to the youth prison model*. Washington, DC: U.S. Department of Justice, National Institute of Justice.

McFarland, Michael, Amanda Geller, and Cheryl McFarland. 2019. Police contact and health among urban adolescents: The role of perceived injustice. *Social Science and Medicine* 238. https://doi.org/10.1016/j.socscimed.2019.112487

Mettler, Suzanne. 2002. Bringing the state back in to civic engagement: Policy feedback effects of the GI Bill for World War II veterans. *American Political Science Review* 96 (2): 351–65.

Mettler, Suzanne. 2011. *The submerged state: How invisible government policies undermine American democracy*. Chicago, IL: University of Chicago Press.

Miller, Lisa L. 2008. *The perils of federalism: Race, poverty, and the politics of crime control*. New York, NY: Oxford University Press.

Miller, Lisa Lynn. 2016. *The myth of mob rule: Violent crime and democratic politics*. New York, NY: Oxford University Press.

Morris, Monique. 2016. *Pushout: The criminalization of black girls in schools*. New York, NY: New Press.

Murakawa, Naomi. 2014. *The first civil right: How liberals built prison America*. New York, NY: Oxford University Press.

Owens, Emily G. 2017. Testing the school-to-prison pipeline. *Journal of Policy Analysis and Management* 36 (1): 11–37.

Owens, Michael Leo, and Hannah L. Walker. 2018. The civic voluntarism of "custodial citizens": Involuntary criminal justice contact, associational life, and political participation. *Perspectives on Politics* 16 (4): 990–1013.

Page, Joshua. 2011. *The toughest beat: Politics, punishment, and the prison officers union in California*. New York, NY: Oxford University Press.

Pettit, Becky. 2012. *Invisible men: Mass incarceration and the myth of black progress*. New York, NY: Russell Sage Foundation.

Pfaff, John. 2017. *Locked in: The true causes of mass incarceration—And how to achieve real reform*. New York, NY: Basic Books.

Prowse, Gwen, Vesla M. Weaver, and Tracey L. Meares. 2019. The state from below: Distorted responsiveness in policed communities. *Urban Affairs Review*. https://doi.org/10.1177/1078087419844831.

Putnam, Robert D. 2001. *Bowling alone: The collapse and revival of American community*. New York, NY: Simon and Schuster.

Rios, Victor M. 2011. *Punished: Policing the lives of black and Latino boys*. New York, NY: NYU Press.

Sampson, Robert J. 2011. *Great American city: Chicago and the enduring neighborhood effect*. Chicago, IL: University of Chicago Press.

Schiraldi, Vincent. 26 September 2017. Juvenile prisons: It's time to close "factories of failure". *The Crime Report*. Available from https://thecrimereport.org.

Schiraldi, Vincent, Bruce Western, and Kendra Bradner. 2015. *Community-based responses to justice-involved young adults*. Washington, DC: U.S. Department of Justice, National Institute of Justice.

Schoenfeld, Heather. 2018. *Building the prison state: Race and the politics of mass incarceration*. Chicago, IL: University of Chicago Press.

Schrader, Stuart. 2019. To protect and serve themselves: Police in U.S. politics since the 1960s. *Public Culture* 31 (3): 601–23.

Sharkey, Patrick. 2013. *Stuck in place: Urban neighborhoods and the end of progress toward racial equality*. Chicago, IL: University of Chicago Press.

Sharkey, Patrick. 2018. *Uneasy peace: The great crime decline, the renewal of city life, and the next war on violence*. New York, NY: WW Norton & Company.

Shedd, Carla. 2015. *Unequal city: Race, schools, and perceptions of injustice*. New York, NY: Russell Sage Foundation.

Sherman, Lawrence W. 1993. Defiance, deterrence, and irrelevance: A theory of the criminal sanction. *Journal of Research in Crime and Delinquency* 30 (4): 445–73.

Sieg, Holger, and Yu Wang. 2019. The impact of unions on municipal elections and urban fiscal policies. Available from https://www.sas.upenn.edu/~holgers/papers/sw_jme_f.pdf.

Soss, Joe, and Vesla M. Weaver. 2017. Police are our government: Politics, political science, and the policing of race–class subjugated communities. *Annual Review of Political Science* 20:565–91.

Stevens, Tia, and Merry Morash. 2015. Racial/ethnic disparities in boys' probability of arrest and court actions in 1980 and 2000: The disproportionate impact of "getting tough" on crime. *Youth Violence and Juvenile Justice* 13 (1): 77–95.

Stuart, Forrest. 2016. *Down, out, and under arrest: Policing and everyday life in Skid Row*. Chicago, IL: University of Chicago Press.

Stuntz, William J. 2011. *The collapse of American criminal justice*. Cambridge, MA: Harvard University Press.

Sugie, Naomi F., and Kristin Turney. 2017. Beyond incarceration: criminal justice contact and mental health. *American Sociological Review* 82 (4): 719–43.

Theriot, Matthew T. 2009. School resource officers and the criminalization of student behavior. *Journal of Criminal Justice* 37 (3): 280–87.

Thompson, J. Phillip, III. 2005. *Double trouble: Black mayors, black communities, and the call for a deep democracy*. New York, NY: Oxford University Press.

Thorpe, Rebecca U. 2015. Perverse politics: The persistence of mass imprisonment in the twenty-first century. *Perspectives on Politics* 13 (3): 618–37.

Townes, Carimah. 10 July 2018. California county law enforcement puts kids on probation for bad grades. *The Appeal*. Available from https://theappeal.org/california-county-law-enforcement-puts-kids-on-probation-for-bad-grades.

Tyler, Tom R., Jeffrey Fagan, and Amanda Geller. 2014. Street stops and police legitimacy: Teachable moments in young urban men's legal socialization. *Journal of Empirical Legal Studies* 11 (4): 751–85.

Vitale, Alex S. 2017. *The end of policing*. New York, NY: Verso Books.

Walker, Hannah, and Rebecca Thorpe. 15 February 2018. How changes to how the Census counts people has implications for democracy and inequality. *USApp - American Politics and Policy Blog*.

Walker, Hannah L., Rebecca U. Thorpe, Emily K. Christensen, and J. Anderson. 2017. The hidden subsidies of rural prisons: Race, space and the politics of cumulative disadvantage. *Punishment & Society* 19 (4): 393–416.

Weaver, Vesla. 2012. The significance of policy failures in political development: The Law Enforcement Assistance Administration and the growth of the carceral state. In *Living legislation: Durability, change, and the politics of American lawmaking*, eds. Jeffery A. Jenkins and Eric M. Patashnik, 221–54. Chicago, IL: University of Chicago Press.

Weaver, Vesla M., Andrew Papachristos, and Michael Zanger-Tishler. 2019. The great decoupling: The disconnection between criminal offending and experience of arrest across two cohorts. *RSF: The Russell Sage Foundation Journal of the Social Sciences* 5 (1): 89–123.

Western, Bruce. 2006. *Punishment and inequality in America*. New York, NY: Russell Sage Foundation.

White, Ariel. 2019. Misdemeanor disenfranchisement? The demobilizing effects of brief jail spells on potential voters. *American Political Science Review* 113 (2): 311–24.

Wiley, Stephanie A., and Finn-Aage Esbensen. 2016. The effect of police contact: Does official intervention result in deviance amplification? *Crime & Delinquency* 62 (3): 283–307.

Wilson, James Q., and George L. Kelling. 1982. Broken windows. *Atlantic Monthly*.

Feedback Effects and the Criminal Justice Bureaucracy: Officer Attitudes and the Future of Correctional Reform

By
AMY E. LERMAN
and
JESSIE HARNEY

Although political scientists have documented the effects of incarceration on those serving time in prison and jail, there has been much less discussion about feedback effects on the attitudes of those who work in correctional institutions. This is a considerable oversight, given the enormous growth of the correctional workforce and its importance in the implementation of crime policy. In this article, we present original survey data from a large sample of California correctional officers. Our analyses suggest that characteristics of the institutions where correctional officers work—the levels of violence to which they are exposed, the proportion of inmates involved in high-quality rehabilitation programs, as well as the quality of management—help to shape officers' attitudes toward rehabilitation. These dynamics have important implications for how public policies can create political constituencies among criminal justice officers. The attitudes of these officers should therefore be a concern for scholars, advocates, and practitioners who are interested in political strategies for long-term, meaningful reform to the correctional system.

Keywords: correctional officer; mass incarceration; prison; policy feedback; criminal justice; rehabilitation

For the first time in more than 50 years, the United States has seen a nearly 5 percent decline in the size of its inmate population, with some states experiencing decreases of between 14 and 25 percent (Sentencing Project 2017). These declines are the result of political

Amy E. Lerman is a professor of public policy and political science at the University of California, Berkeley, and associate dean of the Goldman School of Public Policy. Her research is focused on issues of race, public opinion, and political behavior, especially as they relate to punishment and social inequality in America.

Jessie Harney is a graduate student researcher and PhD student at the Goldman School of Public Policy. Her research interests are in criminal justice system reform with a specific focus on mental health.

Correspondence: alerman@berkeley.edu

DOI: 10.1177/0002716219869907

ANNALS, AAPSS, 685, September 2019   227 reform efforts at every level of government. Many local police departments are rethinking their approach to low-level crimes; several states have instituted policy changes aimed at reducing criminal penalties for low-level and nonviolent offenses; and a federal, bipartisan coalition has been working on a substantial legislative package for sentencing reform (Scott 2014; American Bar Association 2019). These are important signs that the growth of mass incarceration might finally be slowing, or even beginning a reversal of course.

These changes are the culmination of decades-long efforts by civil and human rights advocates, who have shed light on the myriad harms inflicted on low-income and minority communities by the nation's aggressive approach to crime control that began with Nixon's declaration of a "War on Drugs" in 1971. These harms have been well documented and rightfully demand our attention. In this article, however, we argue that policy reformers today might usefully broaden their scope to consider also the health and safety of correctional workers.

Previous studies have shown that individual demographics such as race and partisanship predict officers' attitudes toward criminal justice, just as they do in the public as a whole (Unnever 2014; Lerman and Page 2012, 2015). However, we show in this study that characteristics of the institutions where correctional officers work—the levels of violence to which they are exposed, the proportion of inmates involved in high-quality rehabilitation programs, as well as the quality of training and management—also predict officers' attitudes toward rehabilitation, inmates, and the purpose of corrections. Our results are unique in that we employ original survey data from a large sample of California correctional officers, including questions related to both workplace experiences and attitudes toward rehabilitation. Additionally, responses were collected from officers working in thirty-three different state prisons, allowing us to measure the influence of institutional factors on a range of attitudinal outcomes, as well as allowing us to leverage institutional variation in the likelihood of exposure to violence.

The dynamics we uncover have important implications for our understanding of how public policies can create political constituencies in the criminal justice domain. Although political scientists have documented the effects of mass incarceration on those who serve time in prison and jail (e.g., Manza and Uggen 2008; Lerman and Weaver 2014), there has been much less discussion about feedback effects on the attitudes of those who work in correctional institutions. This is a considerable oversight, given the enormous growth of the correctional workforce. By 2000, almost 13 percent of state and local public employment (and a larger percentage in at least fifteen states) was in the criminal justice domain (Hughes 2006). According to the most recent available data, approximately 468,600 correctional officers and bailiffs were employed in the United States in 2016, more than by General Motors and Ford combined (Bureau of Labor Statistics 2019; General Motors 2016; Ford Motor Company 2017).

The policy attitudes of law enforcement personnel matter to criminal justice politics and policy reform in several distinct ways. As Michael Campbell notes in his account of the punitive politics of Texas criminal justice, "Law enforcement actors and the occupational organizations that represent them occupy an important and somewhat ambiguous theoretical terrain: They are simultaneously interest groups and state functionaries" (2011, 635). As a large group of citizens with a personal stake in the outcomes of criminal justice policy debates, law enforcement personnel represent an "issue public"—a group of citizens who are highly attuned to a specific political issue. Individuals within these issue publics "are likely to think frequently about those attitudes, to perceive competing candidates as being relatively polarized on the issue, and to form presidential candidate preferences on the basis of those attitudes. Also, policy attitudes that citizens consider personally important are highly resistant to change and are therefore especially stable over long periods of time" (Krosnick 1990, 59).

Law enforcement personnel are also frequently well organized; many officers belong to public-sector unions, as well as benevolent and fraternal associations, that represent their attitudes and interests in public debates. These law enforcement organizations can have an outsize influence on crime policy (Gottschalk 2006; Miller 2008; Page 2011). In California, for example, the California Correctional Peace Officers Association (CCPOA)—the public-sector union representing roughly thirty thousand correctional officers, parole officers, and other public safety personnel in the state—plays a central role in state policy debates over criminal justice reform, as well as in electoral campaigns across California. Upwards of 95 percent of eligible employees belong to the union, and this provides the organization with both a large membership base and ample resources to expend representing their interests. In the early 1990s, the union was California's second largest political action committee, and between 2000 and 2009, it ranked among California's top twenty largest special interest groups in political spending. In some political campaigns, it has been among the state's largest organizational donors (Page 2011).

The attitudes of law enforcement officers are important because they represent a sizable population with a clear self-interest in the future of American crime policy. But they are also critical because officers' attitudes influence how they conduct themselves at work (e.g., Crewe, Liebling, and Hulley 2011; Garland 1990; Kauffman 1988; Liebling 2000, 2008; Liebling, Price, and Shefer 2010; Lin 2000; Vuolo and Kruttschnitt 2008). Officers play a central role in the implementation of criminal justice policy. Their attitudes should therefore be of primary concern to scholars, advocates, and practitioners seeking political strategies that can enable long-term, meaningful reform to the correctional system.

As seminal studies on the "street-level bureaucrat" emphasize, the attitudes of public-sector workers influence how they carry out their professional obligations (e.g., Lipsky 2010) Indeed, correctional officers enjoy a great deal of discretion in how they perform their duties and responsibilities in the workplace (Liebling, Price, and Shefer 2010). Most critically, their attitudes inform the quality of their interactions with inmates and, thereby, shape the way prisons are experienced by prisoners (e.g., Crewe, Liebling, and Hulley 2011; Liebling 2008); through their actions, officers can either heighten or mitigate the "pains of imprisonment" (Sykes 1958/2007). As Alison Liebling writes, "Staff attitudes translate into regime qualities that can make the difference between a survivable experience of imprisonment and an unbearable one" (2008, 118).

More broadly, officers' actions are crucial to defining the culture of correctional institutions (e.g., Crewe, Liebling, and Hulley 2011; Liebling 2000; Liebling, Price, and Shefer 2010). Correctional officers and other front-line personnel are "primary actors in the penal system and the individuals who are directly responsible for implementing new penal policies" (Vuolo and Kruttschnitt 2008, 309) and as such are the "agents who do the most to transform cultural conceptions into penal actions" (Garland 1990, 210). Because of this, understanding officers' experiences and attitudes is crucial to understanding why prison reforms ultimately succeed or fail. As one early scholar of prison staff noted, "Failure to understand officers—their characters and motivations, problems and perspectives—has inevitably undermined efforts to reform prisons and has contributed to the everyday misery of those who live and work behind the walls" (Kauffman 1988, 3). Without securing the buy-in of correctional officers and other staff, changes in policy are unlikely to translate into meaningful differences on the ground (Lin 2000).

The Factors That Shape Officer Attitudes

Economists and sociologists have raised calls of alarm about the many harms associated with mass incarceration in America, showing that a wide range of individual, familial, and community outcomes are negatively affected by imprisonment (for a review, see Mauer and Chesney-Lind 2002). It is only more recently, however, that political scientists lent their voices to these concerns; we now have numerous studies showing that contact with the criminal justice system can have profound effects on citizens' political attitudes and behaviors (e.g., Manza and Uggen 2008; Lerman and Weaver 2014; but see also Gerber et al. 2017). For instance, Weaver and Lerman (2010; see also Lerman and Weaver 2014) find that having been stopped by police, arrested, convicted of a crime, or sentenced to imprisonment is associated with substantially lower levels of trust in government, feelings of "second-class" citizenship, and lower rates of voter registration and turnout.

We know much less about the attitudes and behaviors of other actors affected by criminal justice agencies, including the officers and front-line supervisors employed by state and local corrections. Correctional officers are among the "invisible ghosts of penality" (Liebling 2000, 337) whose attitudes and experiences have rarely been the subject of serious inquiry (Liebling, Price, and Shefer 2010, 6–13). In particular, we do not have a great deal of information about how officers' attitudes are shaped by their experiences on the job. As a result, we do not know much about the sorts of reforms that might build political capital among correctional personnel. Reformers aimed at rolling back the harms of mass incarceration are generally silent on the role of correctional officers and other staff and do little to account for how changes in institutional culture and practice will shape prison workers' attitudes and experience.

It is certainly possible that officers, as a rule, do not adapt in significant ways to the particular environments in which they work. Continuity theory (Atchley

1989), importation theory (Irwin and Cressey 1962), and representative bureaucracy theory (Mosher 1968) would all lead us to expect that officers' values, self-
perceptions, and attitudes are already well established by the time they enter
corrections. As a result, their experiences in the workplace do not substantially
change their basic orientations toward punishment and related ideas. Instead,
officers' attitudes toward rehabilitation and other criminal justice issues are predicted by demographics and earlier life experiences. Factors such as race and
gender, age and level of education, as well as partisan identification, have all been
shown to predict officers' orientations toward correctional work (e.g., Jurik 1985;
Cullen et al. 1989; Crewe, Liebling, and Hulley 2011; Lerman 2013; Lerman and
Page 2012, 2015).

Alternatively (or in addition), it might be that officers do adapt in some ways
to their occupational role, but they do so in line with their shared position within
the correctional system (e.g., Jacobs and Retsky 1980; Liebling 2008; Lin 2000;
Sykes 1958/2007). Specifically, officers are assigned a unique job within the
prison context—the maintenance of order and security—and their perspectives
might reflect this fundamental responsibility, irrespective of differences they
encounter in their particular workplace (Liebling 2000, 338). As Jacobs and
Retsky point out, "Prevention of escape and riot is the primary task around which
the role of the guard is organized. Closely related is maintenance of a modicum
of internal order and security" (1980, 56). As a result, officers generally perceive
inmate rehabilitation to be outside their immediate sphere of influence (Crewe,
Liebling, and Hulley 2011; Lin 2000). For some, this results in cynicism about
whether rehabilitation programs and other prison interventions can successfully
divert adult offenders from criminality (Jacobs and Retsky 1980, 71). When officers do support rehabilitation programs for inmates, it often reflects their belief
that programs can help to maintain order within the prison by reducing boredom
and unstructured time (DiIulio 1991; Lin 2000).

However, we suspect that the specific policy context in which officers work can
also matter for how they come to see the purpose and nature of corrections. As
work by Lerman and Page (2015) suggests, "formal and informal training, daily
interactions, subcultural norms and values, and institutionalized relationships
shape employee orientations more than demographic or other individual-level
factors" (p. 579; see also Crawley 2004; James and Retsky 1980). Some of the
factors that most immediately impact an officer's work-life are related to the
individuals who are incarcerated within a particular prison. This includes the type
of people with whom an officer has the most direct daily contact (e.g., the security level of an institution) and how the staff-inmate relationship is structured and
experienced (e.g., levels of violence). In addition, the policy environment matters
by communicating the "indirectly expressed organizational goals" (Liebling 2008,
108) of the specific institution in which officers work (e.g., the extent and quality
of existing rehabilitation programs).

Other policies and practices of the prison that might be salient for how officers
come to view criminal justice policy are those that are directed at officers themselves. For instance, officers' orientations toward rehabilitation might be affected
by how they perceive their supervisors and management, whether they have

access to the resources they need to keep themselves safe, and whether they receive the training they require to support their own health and well-being. We expect that these features of the prison context, both inmate-oriented and officer-directed, will help to determine how officers come to see the nature of corrections and criminal justice policy.

New Evidence on Officer Attitudes

To examine how both demographic and institutional factors shape the policy attitudes of public-sector criminal justice workers, we use data from two waves of the California Correctional Officer Survey (CCOS). The CCOS is an original, large-scale survey designed to measure the experiences and attitudes of law enforcement officers in the State of California. We distributed the first wave in 2006, yielding a sample of 5,670 participants—a response rate of 33 percent. We fielded the subsequent wave in 2017, resulting in a final sample of 8,436, for a response rate of 42 percent.[1] Table 1 details the demographic profile of our participants, as well as officer population demographics from 2006 and 2015 (the most recent year available). Both the proportion of female correctional officers and the racial composition of our sample are quite similar across years and to the population.

To measure policy-related attitudes, we asked four questions in both CCOS surveys: the extent to which officers agree that "Rehabilitation should be a central goal of incarceration" and "The job of a prison is to keep the public safe, not to help inmates"; and whether "The purpose of a prison is rehabilitation, punishment, or both" and "Most people who end up in prison are there because of personal failure, or because they did not have advantages like strong families, good education, and job opportunities." We created a summary additive index from these four survey questions, reverse-coded when necessary and rescaled to range from zero to one.[2] We then constructed a second index to assess officer support for providing inmates with access to specific rehabilitation programs, including academic training up to and including General Education Development (GED) preparation; vocational training; and alcohol and drug treatment. Similar to the first index, we summed the Likert-scale questions and then scaled the index from zero to one, allowing for interpretation as percent difference.[3]

We take three distinct analytical approaches to assessing the relationship between public-sector work experience and our outcomes of interest. First, we use multilevel models with random intercepts at the prison level to predict policy attitudes using data from 2017. This lets us look at the relationship between prison context and officer attitudes, all else equal. We then present results from change-over-time models, utilizing average outcomes aggregated by prison. This second analysis allows us to assess whether changes in institutional context are associated with changes in officers' attitudes toward rehabilitation. Finally, we restrict our sample to only correctional officers at the beginning of their careers. Among these new officers, assignment to different

TABLE 1
Demographic Profile of CCOS (2006/2017) and Officer Population (2006)

	Sample	Population	Sample	Population
		2006	2017	2015
Gender				
Female	914 (16.3%)	3,760 (18.0%)	1,087 (17.6%)	—
Male	4,702 (83.7%)	17,419 (82.0%)	5,088 (82.4%)	—
Race/ethnicity				
Black	481 (8.8%)	2,612 (12.3%)	581 (9.6%)	2,951 (11.4%)
White	3,235 (59.3%)	9,814 (46.2%)	2,794 (46.3%)	9.859 (38.2%)
Hispanic	1,490 (27.3%)	7,307 (34.4%)	2,103 (34.9%)	10,621 (41.2%)
Asian	163 (2.9%)	382 (1.8%)	276 (4.6%)	773 (3.0%)
Other	409 (7.2%)	1,125 (5.3%)	620 (10.3%)	1,606 (6.2%)

NOTE: Population data are drawn from a report by the Department of Corrections and Rehabilitation Office of Personnel Services on October 12, 2006, and from Bargaining Unit data as of January 1, 2015. Gender data on the officer population from 2015 were not available. Sample race sums to more than 100 percent due to some respondents identifying as more than one racial category. Proportions of nonmissing values are reported.

prison institutions is quasi-random, allowing us to more plausibly estimate the causal effect of prison context.

Results

We find substantial variation in attitudes toward rehabilitation within our sample as a whole, though attitudes skew somewhat in the direction of punitiveness (see Figure 1). For example, in 2017, roughly three in five respondents indicated the belief that most (39.8 percent) or all (21.8 percent) of the reason individuals end up in prison is due to personal failure, rather than a lack of advantages. About a quarter (27.4 percent) suggested that both personal failure and lack of advantages were equal contributors. A slightly smaller proportion of officers indicated that the purpose of prison was either mostly (39.7 percent) or totally punishment (8.4 percent), rather than rehabilitation. In response to this question, roughly one-third (35.8 percent) indicated that the purpose of prison was equally punishment and rehabilitation.

In comparison, a large majority reported agreeing that those who want access to rehabilitation programs while incarcerated should be able to receive them. Specifically, 84.8 percent of officers indicated that inmates should have access to GED preparation, and 80 percent supported giving inmates access to vocational training. Likewise, 87.9 percent agreed that inmates should be given access to alcohol and drug treatment if they want it.

FIGURE 1
Purpose of Prison and the Reason People End Up in Prison

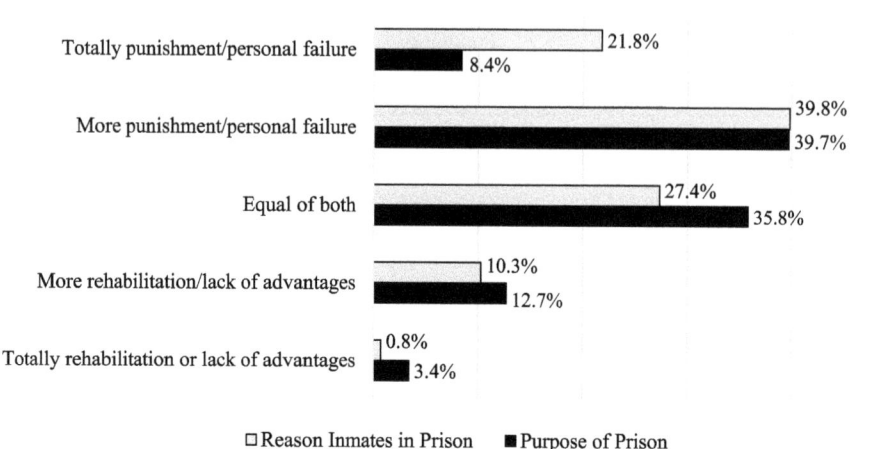

Table 2 presents results from multilevel models estimating the effects of demographics, exposure to violence, and institutional factors on officers' policy-related attitudes in the 2017 survey.[4] Higher scores on the outcome variable indicate increased support for a punitive purpose of corrections (first and second columns) or lower support for rehabilitation programs (third and fourth columns). As the table shows, a variety of demographic factors appear clearly associated with these attitudes. In particular, black correctional officers were more likely to indicate being supportive of a rehabilitative purpose of corrections compared to whites, and being a Democrat or Independent (versus identifying as a Republican) is associated with a less punitive set of beliefs. Those with more education voiced greater support for a rehabilitative purpose of corrections and rehabilitation programs. Conversely, age was negatively correlated with these outcomes.

Notably, institutional factors were also significant contributors to support for rehabilitation, controlling for other factors. For instance, the lower the perceived level of support from and competency of supervisors, the less likely an officer was to support rehabilitation as an ideology. Similarly, the better the perceived resources available to officers, the more support they voiced for providing inmates with access to rehabilitation programs. Personal experience with rehabilitation was also a correlate of officers' support for rehabilitation. Specifically, the larger the percentage of inmates currently participating in a high-quality rehabilitation program at the prison where they work, the less likely officers were to support a punitive purpose of prison and the more support they expressed for programs.

The most notable difference between the two models is in the relationship to violence. When it comes to whether officers hold a more punitive ideology of corrections, our models indicate that greater exposure to violence was associated

TABLE 2
Predicting Rehabilitation Attitudes

	More Punitive Ideology		Opposition to Rehabilitation Programs	
	Demographics and Violence	Demographics, Violence, and Institutional Factors	Demographics and Violence	Demographics, Violence, and Institutional Factors
	b (SE)	b (SE)	b (SE)	b (SE)
Demographics				
Male	.02° (.01)	.03°° (.01)	.01 (.01)	.02° (.01)
Race/ethnicity				
Asian	.02 (.01)	.02 (.01)	.03° (.01)	.03° (.01)
Black	−.07°°° (.01)	−.06°°° (.01)	−.04°°° (.01)	−.03° (.01)
Latino	−.01 (.01)	−.01 (.01)	.03°°° (.01)	.03°°° (.01)
Native Hawaiian/PI	−.02 (.02)	−.02 (.02)	.03 (.02)	.02 (.02)
Other race	−.00 (.01)	−.00 (.01)	.01 (.01)	.01 (.01)
Partisanship				
Democrat	−.07°°° (.01)	−.07°°° (.01)	−.03°° (.01)	−.02° (.01)
Independent	−.04°°° (.01)	−.04°°° (.01)	−.02°° (.01)	−.02° (.01)
No preference	−.03°°° (.01)	−.04°°° (.01)	−.01 (.01)	.00 (.01)
Education				
Some college	−.02 (.01)	−.02° (.01)	−.02° (.01)	−.02° (.01)
Associates	−.04°°° (.01)	−.04°°° (.01)	−.04°°° (.01)	−.04°°° (.01)
College plus	−.04°° (.01)	−.04°°° (.01)	−.05°°° (.01)	−.05°°° (.01)
Age	−.00°°° (.00)	−.00°°° (.00)	−.00°°° (.00)	−.00°°° (.00)
Violence				
Security level				
II	.03 (.01)	.02 (.02)	.01 (.02)	−.01 (.02)
III	.04°° (.01)	.02 (.02)	.02 (.02)	.00 (.02)
IV	.04°° (.01)	.01 (.02)	.02 (.02)	−.01 (.02)
Violence				
Inside	.04°°° (.01)	.00 (.01)	−.01 (.01)	−.03°°° (.01)
Outside	.01 (.02)	.01 (.02)	.00 (.02)	.00 (.02)
Before	.04°°° (.01)	.03°° (.01)	−.01 (.01)	−.01 (.01)
Safety				
Inmates very dangerous		.01°°° (.00)		.02°°° (.00)
Inmates not dangerous		−.00 (.00)		−.01 (.00)
Equipment index		−.03 (.02)		−.05°° (.02)
Response to violence index		−.06°°° (.01)		−.06°°° (.01)

(continued)

TABLE 2 (continued)

	More Punitive Ideology		Opposition to Rehabilitation Programs	
	Demographics and Violence	Demographics, Violence, and Institutional Factors	Demographics and Violence	Demographics, Violence, and Institutional Factors
	b (SE)	b (SE)	b (SE)	b (SE)
Institutional Factors				
Management				
Supervision index		.08°° (.02)		−.02 (.02)
Resources index		−.01 (.02)		−.08°°° (.02)
Quality of stress management training		.02 (.00)		.01°° (.00)
Inmate rehabilitation				
Proportion inmates in high-quality programs		−.02°°° (.00)		−.01°°° (.00)
Has received rehabilitation training		−.01° (.00)		−.01°° (.00)

NOTE: Marital status (married, divorced, never married, separated, widowed) and veteran status (served in military, has not served in the military) are also included as independent variables in all models but were not significantly associated with outcomes and are not shown. °$p < .05$. °°$p < .01$. °°°$p < .001$.

with lower support for rehabilitation, on average. Likewise, the higher the proportion of inmates that officers perceived as very dangerous, the more they tended to support a punitive purpose of incarceration.[5] In contrast, the greater an officer's exposure to violence inside prison, the *greater* his or her predicted support for providing inmates with rehabilitation programs. This makes sense, given the perceived role of programs in helping to maintain order and safety in the prison (DiIulio 1991; Lin 2000). Similarly, we see that the better the quality and availability of safety equipment and the stronger the organizational response to violence when it occurs, the higher officers' support for providing inmates with access to rehabilitation programs.

Change over time and causal inference

In addition to looking at predictors in 2017, the CCOS allows us to estimate how changes over time in institutional characteristics (measured by officers' perceptions of change) predict changes in policy-related views (see Table 3). Here again we find a role for experiences with violence; prisons where officers report

TABLE 3

Predicting Change in Orientations towards Rehabilitation (2006 to 2017)

Parameter	Estimate	SE	t	p
Intercept	66.40	28.82	2.30	.0334
Baseline proportion supporting a rehabilitative purpose of corrections	−0.89	0.43	−2.04	.0559
Change in exposure to violence	0.08	0.02	4.53	.0003

NOTE: Higher scores on the purpose of corrections index indicate greater support for a puni-tive purpose of corrections. Control variables included in the model but not shown: change in the proportion of female officers; change in the proportion of officers identifying as Republicans; change in the proportion of officers identifying as Democrats; change in the proportion of officers identifying as Latino/Hispanic; change in the proportion of officers iden-tifying as black/African American; change in the average age of officers; change in the propor-tion of officers indicating that when a violent incident occurred, the institution's response was adequate; change in the proportion of officers who indicated they had been harassed by a supervisor or management in the last six months; change in the proportion of officers who had problems with poor performance feedback or lack of recognition in the last six months; and change in the proportion of officers who had issues with scheduling or pay in the last six months.

a larger change in exposure to violence also show modest, but greater, change in support for a rehabilitative purpose of corrections. In contrast, we do not find evidence that changes in violence or other institutional factors have implications for officers' attitudes toward the provision of specific rehabilitation programs.

In sum, the evidence thus far suggests that institutional factors play a role in predicting officers' support for rehabilitation. However, this does not yet allow us to say anything about whether these factors are *causing* the development of rehabilitation-oriented attitudes. Instead, we are limited to interpreting our results as an association between features of the prison environment and the attitudes expressed by officers who work within it. This leaves open the possibility that self-selection explains our results: officers with particularly punitive (or rehabilitation-oriented) attitudes might systematically choose to work in prisons that have different institutional characteristics.

To address this concern, we conduct one final analysis in which we narrow our focus to only early tenure correctional officers in California. Among this sub-group, job assignment to prisons with varying security levels is quasi-random. It is only as officers complete a mandatory apprenticeship period and accrue greater seniority that they can begin to sort into the prison institution that matches their preferences (Lerman 2013). This allows us to more plausibly esti-mate the causal effect of different work environments on support for rehabilita-tion among correctional officers at the beginning of their career.

Table 4 details mean differences in support for rehabilitation between appren-tice officers who have been assigned to lower- versus higher-security settings. As

TABLE 4
Effects of Low versus High Security on Policy Attitudes and Behavior

	Low Security (I and II)	High Security (III and IV)	Difference (High – Low)	Effect Size
Support for rehabilitation index	0.55	0.62	0.08°	.42
Rehabilitation as central goal of prison	3.46	4.04	0.59°	.36
Keeping the public safe	3.41	2.79	−0.62°	−.39
Purpose of prison	3.07	3.45	0.37°	.41
Reason for imprisonment	3.64	3.74	0.10	.11
Inmate access to programs index	0.35	0.38	0.03	.18
GED preparation	4.79	4.45	−0.34	−.25
Vocational training	4.09	4.02	−0.07	−.04
Alcohol/drug treatment	4.85	4.62	−0.23	−.17

NOTE: °Indicates a significant difference from both a t-test and nonparametric Mann-Whitney at $\alpha = .05$.

the table shows, we see significantly different average scores on our ideological measures across security levels, with individuals assigned to higher-security institutions expressing substantially more punitive attitudes. In contrast, we do not find significant differences across security level in how officers think about the provision of rehabilitation programs, including GED, vocational, or drug and alcohol treatment.

We interpret these results to suggest that new officers assigned to work in higher-security prisons quickly develop different orientations toward rehabilitation. We do not know if these differences persist or strengthen over time, as officers accrue greater tenure. However, we do see evidence that attitudes toward the purpose of corrections are relatively stable across levels of tenure. When we divide officers' work tenure into quartiles, we find no substantial differences in attitudes toward a rehabilitative ideology.[6] By comparison, we do find substantial differences across these tenure cohorts when it comes to the provision of rehabilitation programs, with early career officers evidencing somewhat lower levels of support.

Questions for Future Inquiry

In line with previous work, we find that demographics are predictive of officers' attitudes. At the same time, our results indicate the potential for important feedback effects for correctional officers from experiences in the workplace. First, we find that exposure to violence is a significant predictor of support for rehabilitation. At the same time, though, the better the quality of supervision and management, and the better the availability of equipment and access to resources, the greater the degree of expressed support for rehabilitation. We also find that experience with rehabilitation programs makes a difference. Officers who work at institutions where a larger proportion of inmates are involved in high-quality rehabilitation programs are more likely to express support for rehabilitation in both theory and practice.

Our analysis has several limitations that should be mentioned. First, our data come from surveys of officers and, thus, reflect officers' *perceptions* of their institutional context. One important question is whether these self-reported measures reflect objective differences across prisons. In future work, it might be feasible to gather administrative data on institutional and officer characteristics that parallel the subjective measures that we have reported here.

We would also hope to establish more conclusively the role of institutional factors in causing changes to officer attitudes. Though we have tried to address this issue in our analysis, much of our evidence is descriptive in nature. In future work, experimental evidence on the role of institutional context would help to further this line of inquiry. For instance, we might imagine randomly assigning some officers to participate in rehabilitation or officer wellness training, or to engage in programs aimed at improving relationships between supervisors and staff. We could then assess the causal effects of these interventions on officers' attitudes.

Despite these caveats, the results that we have presented here make an important contribution to policy feedback research and suggest a broad agenda for future scholarship. Our focus here has been on officers' ideological orientations toward rehabilitation, but other politically relevant attitudes might similarly be shaped by the policy environment in which correctional workers are embedded. For instance, preferences over specific legislative reforms—both within criminal justice as well as in related domains like education and mental health—could plausibly be affected by the learning that occurs among officers while they are interacting with inmates, other officers, and supervisors in the prison context. Scholars might also pursue questions related to the generalizability of our results. California's prison system represents a particularly compelling case, given its relative size and its prominence in national discussions of correctional reform. However, correctional systems vary widely in size, composition, and punitiveness, and this might influence the extent to which the work environment impacts officers' political attitudes (e.g., Lerman and Page 2015).

We might also examine officers' engagement with their union and other forms of political and civic participation. In places like California, officers are members of a powerful interest group, CCPOA, whose resources and advocacy help to shape the direction of criminal justice reform and state politics more broadly. Understanding how personal experience with public policies and political institutions shapes not just individual attitudes, but also the likelihood of engaging in collective action, is an important but understudied feature of policy feedback. Organizations like CCPOA help to aggregate and mobilize individual attitudes into politically consequential behavior.

Relatedly, we might look at feedbacks among other prison workers. For instance, there are roughly forty thousand counselors, educators, medical personnel, and other nonsworn staff (e.g., technical, support, or other administrative staff) working inside correctional institutions. Likewise, we might explore whether our results generalize to the approximately 175,000 officers and supervisors working in local jails and the more than 700,000 sworn officers working in police departments, sheriff's offices, highway patrol, and other general-purpose law enforcement agencies (Hyland 2018). Like officers in state prisons, these workers are represented by public-sector unions that are active in political debates over the future of crime control policy at both the state and local levels.

Considering Officers in Efforts to Reform

Our results offer clear implications for policy-makers, practitioners, and others seeking ways to reform the nation's broken criminal justice system. Namely, our findings highlight the importance of considering officers' experiences on the job when developing, implementing, and enforcing criminal justice reform. Understanding the attitudes of correctional workers and other law enforcement personnel matters for at least two distinct reasons: because they constitute a large group of citizens with a personal interest in the politics of imprisonment and because they are public-sector workers who play a key role in the implementation of criminal justice policy. Officers represent an important constituency, and reformers would be well advised to consider the likely effects of policy change on how officers perceive (and, thus, carry out) their work.

To the extent that officers' attitudes toward rehabilitation are driven by demographics, the best way to influence debates over criminal justice is by seeking changes to the composition of the officer workforce. Indeed, increasing organizational diversity has become an explicit goal for many law enforcement agencies, both to address historical inequities and in the hope of improving effectiveness (U.S. Department of Justice and U.S. Equal Employment Opportunity Commission 2015). A recent report from the Center for Quality Policing provides three recommendations for helping law enforcement agencies to increase the diversity of their personnel: (1) appointing a leader within the department who sets goals and manages outreach initiatives, (2) making diversity a key element of the organization's culture, and (3) incorporating accountability mechanisms within the organization (e.g., using organizational data to assess whether promotion practices are equitable across racial/ethnic groups, gender, and so on) (Haddad et al. 2012).

However, there is mixed evidence about whether increasing the diversity of law enforcement personnel translates into differences in officer behavior. For instance, one study of a 10-year reform of England and Wales police departments found that for a one standard deviation increase in the proportion of minority officers in the department, there was an associated 20 to 39 percent decrease in the proportion of minorities searched by the police (Hong 2017). Another study, using data from the 2005 Police-Public Contact Survey, found that minority officers tended to be perceived more objectively and positively by minority citizens (Cochran and Warren 2012). Other evidence, however, suggests that minority officers can actually be *more* punitive than their white counterparts. In a study of the Cincinnati Police Division, white officers were, on average, more likely to make arrests than black officers. However, black officers were more likely to arrest black suspects, compared to white officers (Brown and Frank 2006). Another study using survey data and interviews from two police departments, one in Indiana and another in Florida, indicated that although black officers tended to be more responsive in resolving conflict, they were also more likely to engage in coercive action (Sun and Payne 2004).

In addition to focusing on the demographics of law enforcement personnel, it is therefore important to consider the experiences officers have in the workplace. In particular, personal experience with prison violence can shape perceptions of the purpose of imprisonment and related concerns. In our data, we find high levels of exposure to violence among officers. Specifically, 76 percent of correctional officers reported that they had seen or handled a dead body, 85 percent had seen someone seriously injured or killed, and almost 30 percent had been seriously injured themselves. Other data bear this out: correctional officers experience the second highest rate of workplace violence, surpassed only by police officers (Finn 2000). We find that violence of this kind is associated with significantly more punitive attitudes toward corrections.

Certainly, the desire to reduce prison violence has long been at the forefront of correctional administration, and efforts to reduce prison violence can be broadly categorized into initiatives that focus on inmates, on staff, and on management (Byrne and Hummer 2007). In terms of inmate-focused interventions, programs that implement cognitive-behavioral training, or where prisoners build skills that foster healthier relationships, may be especially promising (Auty, Cope, and Liebling 2017; Specter 2006). More broadly, empirical evidence supports the link between prison violence and a variety of institutional factors, including the quality and experience of staff; the extent and quality of programming for inmates; the quality of management practices; and other contextual factors, such as inmates' level of autonomy (Byrne and Hummer 2007). Our data suggest that reforms like these that are aimed at increasing prison safety might have the added effect of helping to build support for rehabilitation among officers.

It is important to note these sorts of institutional improvements are likely to be politically feasible. This is because, when it comes to institutional violence, the incentives of correctional officers and inmate advocates are well aligned, and violence reduction strategies are thus a political win-win. By reducing prison violence, advocates can achieve practical policy benefits, while also building support for rehabilitation among correctional staff. There is evidence of this in California, where union leadership has increasingly recognized their shared interests with other criminal justice stakeholders around issues of prison safety. As one commenter writes,

> Even Lance Corcoran, a longtime union leader known as a hardliner, now comes off like a bleeding heart. "I'm not saying I'm sympathetic to people who go to prison," he says,

a little cautiously. "But I'm empathetic. I don't want them to suffer unnecessarily." Corcoran says the union has been talking with prison-reform organizations, and the two sides have found some common ground that would have seemed impossible a few years ago. As he explains, "Safer places for their loved ones to live in mean safer places for our members to work." (Abramsky 2008, para. 11.1)

Other institutional factors that predict officers' support for rehabilitation may appear less directly impactful for inmates, but they are likely to be good for the health and well-being of officers—and thus ultimately good for prisoners in the long term. These include policies that make prisons not just safer, but also better, places to work. Increasingly, researchers are recognizing the enormous stress associated with correctional work. This manifests in extraordinarily high rates of mental and physical health conditions, including elevated risks of stress-related disease (i.e., ulcers, heart disease, and hypertension) (Cheek and Miller 1983); post-traumatic stress disorder rates that rival those of combat veterans, prisoners of war, and disaster survivors (Spinaris, Denhof, and Kellaway 2012; Stadnyk 2003); and a life expectancy roughly 16 years lower than the population as a whole (Cheek and Howard 1984). Attention to the causes and correlates of these and other work-related stresses will therefore have profound importance for this group of Americans, as well as their families and communities. Yet as a recent Department of Justice report points out, "Health and wellness among those who work in correctional agencies is an issue that has always existed, but is just starting to get the increasing attention that it deserves" (Brower 2013, 1).

Research suggests that work-related stress among correctional officers is exacerbated by a lack of support or conflict with supervision and management, a lack of control over the institutional happenings that affect their day-to-day jobs, and role ambiguity (e.g., Lambert, Hogan, and Allen 2006). Targeting institutional efforts to build better relationships between correctional staff and management, and providing programs that help officers to manage stress, thus appear promising for reducing officer stress and burnout. Interventions aimed at improving the well-being of correctional staff might hold less appeal for reformers whose primary sympathies lie with the prisoner population. However, our results suggest that supporting efforts to improve officer wellness is likely to be effective as part of a broader political strategy aimed at improving correctional programs and policies for prisoners.

In sum, while more research is needed to understand the causal impact of institutional factors on officers' support for rehabilitation, it is clear that officers' attitudes are shaped by the experiences they have on the job. Taken together, our results suggest that strengthening the relationship between officers and management, ensuring officers have the equipment and training they need to keep themselves safe, and providing officers with the resources they need to resolve work-related problems will likely help to build support for prisoner rehabilitation among correctional staff. These factors will also be consequential for the future of policies aimed at scaling back the nation's decades-long trend toward mass incarceration. By improving the quality of prison work, we can increase policy feedback effects that make rehabilitation-oriented reforms more likely to succeed. In the end, a commitment to officer health and safety will be good not only for individual officers but for the well-being of inmates and the prison system as a whole.

Notes

1. This includes 8,334 correctional officers and 102 parole officers or other sworn personnel.

2. Cronbach's alpha of the four purpose-of-corrections variables was .66. Additional details on scale construction is provided in the appendix.

3. The first of our indices measures support for rehabilitation as an ideology, while the second captures the more practical or programmatic aspect of support for rehabilitation. These are related, but distinct, dimensions of officer attitudes (Lerman and Page 2015).

4. Some questions used as controls varied from the 2006 to 2017 data given changes to the survey; all questions used for the analysis and any changes from 2006 to 2017 are detailed in the appendix.

5. Dangerousness variables are coded as quartiles of the proportion of officers that felt inmates are dangerous or very dangerous.

6. For the rehabilitation as the central goal of prison variable, we do find significant mean differences between the second tenure quartile (4 to 10 years) and the third tenure quartile (11 to 17 years).

References

Abramsky, Sasha. 2008. When prison guards go soft. *Mother Jones*. Available from https://www.mother-jones.com/politics/2008/07/when-prison-guards-go-soft/.

American Bar Association. 2019. *Federal sentencing reform*. Available from https://www.americanbar.org.

Atchley, Robert C. 1989. A continuity theory of normal aging. *The Gerontologist* 29 (2): 183–90.

Auty, Katherine M., Aiden Cope, and Alison Liebling. 2017. Psychoeducational programs for reducing prison violence: A systematic review. *Aggression and Violent Behavior* 33:126–43.

Brower, Jaime. 2013. *Correctional officer wellness and safety literature review*. Washington, DC: U.S Department of Justice.

Brown, Robert A., and James Frank. 2006. Race and officer decision making: Examining differences in arrest outcomes between black and white officers. *Justice Quarterly* 23 (1): 96–126.

Bureau of Labor Statistics, U.S. Department of Labor. 2019. Correctional officers and bailiffs. In *Occupational outlook handbook*. Available from https://www.bls.gov/ooh/protective-service/correctional-officers.htm.

Byrne, James M., and Don Hummer. 2007. Myths and realities of prison violence: A review of the evidence. *Victims and Offenders* 2 (1): 77–90.

Campbell, Michael C. 2011. Politics, prisons, and law enforcement: An examination of the emergence of "law and order" politics in Texas. *Law & Society Review* 45 (3): 631–65.

Cheek, Francis, and Roberta Howard. 1984. *Stress management for correctional officers and their families*, vol. 106. College Park, MD: American Correctional Association.

Cheek, Francis E., and Marie DiStefano Miller. 1983. The experience of stress for correction officers: A double-bind theory of correctional stress. *Journal of Criminal Justice* 11 (2): 105–20.

Cochran, Joshua C., and Patricia Y. Warren. 2012. Racial, ethnic, and gender differences in perceptions of the police: The salience of officer race within the context of racial profiling. *Journal of Contemporary Criminal Justice* 28 (2): 206–27.

Crawley, Elaine. 2004. *Doing prison work: The public and private lives of prison officers*. Cullompton: Willan Publishing.

Crewe, Ben, Alison Liebling, and Susie Hulley. 2011. Staff culture, use of authority and prisoner quality of life in public and private sector prisons. *Australian & New Zealand Journal of Criminology* 44 (1): 94–115.

Cullen, Francis T., Faith E. Lutz, Bruce G. Link, and Nancy Travis Wolfe. 1989. The correctional orientation of prison guards: Do officers support rehabilitation? *Federal Probation* 53:33–42.

DiIulio, John J. 1991. *No escape: The future of American corrections*. New York, NY: Basic Books.

Finn, Peter. 2000. *Addressing correctional officer stress: Programs and strategies*. Washington, DC: U.S. Department of Justice, Office of Justice Programs, National Institute of Justice.

Ford Motor Company. 2017. Form 10-K 2017. Available from http://www.sec.gov/edgar.shtml.

Garland, David. 1990. *Punishment and modern society: A study in social theory*. Chicago, IL: University of Chicago Press.

General Motors. 2016. Form 10-K 2016. Available from http://www.sec.gov/edgar.shtml.

Gerber, Alan S., Gregory A. Huber, Marc Meredith, Daniel R. Biggers, and David J. Hendry. 2017. Does incarceration reduce voting? Evidence about the political consequences of spending time in prison. *Journal of Politics* 79 (4): 1130–46.

Gottschalk, Marie. 2006. *The prison and the gallows: The politics of mass incarceration in America*. New York, NY: Cambridge University Press.

Haddad, Abigail, Katheryn Giglio, Kirsten M. Keller, and Nelson Lim. 2012. Increasing organizational diversity in 21st-century policing. RAND Occasional Paper, Washington, DC.

Hong, Sounman. 2017. Black in blue: Racial profiling and representative bureaucracy in policing revisited. *Journal of Public Administration Research and Theory* 27 (4): 547–61.

Hughes, Kristen A. 2006. *Justice expenditure and employment in the United States, 2003*. Washington, DC: U.S. Department of Justice.

Hyland, Shelley. 2018. *Full-time employees in law enforcement agencies, 1997–2016*. Washington, DC: Bureau of Justice Statistics. Available from https://www.bjs.gov/content/pub/pdf/ftelea9716.pdf.

Irwin, John, and Donald R. Cressey. 1962. Thieves, convicts and the inmate culture. *Social Problems* 10:142–55.

Jacobs, James, and Harold Retsky. 1980. Prison guard. In *The keepers: Prison guards and contemporary corrections*, ed. B. Crouch, 1–71. Springfield, IL: Charles C. Thomas.

Jurik, Nancy. 1985. Individual and organizational determinants of correctional officer attitudes toward inmates. *Criminology* 23 (3): 523–40.

Kauffman, Kelsey. 1988. *Prison officers and their world*. Cambridge, MA: Harvard University Press.

Krosnick, Jon A. 1990. Government policy and citizen passion: A study of issue publics in contemporary America. *Political Behavior* 12 (1): 59–92.

Lambert, Eric G., Nancy Lynne Hogan, and Reva I. Allen. 2006. Correlates of correctional officer job stress: The impact of organizational structure. *American Journal of Criminal Justice* 30 (2): 227–46.

Lerman, Amy E. 2013. *The modern prison paradox: Politics, punishment, and social community*. New York, NY: Cambridge University Press.

Lerman, Amy E., and Joshua Page. 2012. The state of the job: An embedded work role perspective on prison officer attitudes. *Punishment & Society* 14 (5): 503–29.

Lerman, Amy E., and Joshua Page. 2015. Does the front line reflect the party line? The politicization of punishment and prison officers' perspectives towards incarceration. *British Journal of Criminology* 56 (3): 578–601.

Lerman, Amy E., and Vesla M. Weaver. 2014. *Arresting citizenship: The democratic consequences of American crime control*. Chicago, IL: University of Chicago Press.

Liebling, Alison. 2000. Prison officers, policing and the use of discretion. *Theoretical Criminology* 4 (3): 333–57.

Liebling, Alison. 2008. Why prison staff culture matters. In *The culture of prison violence*, eds. J. Byre, F. Taxman, and D. Hummer, 105–22. Boston, MA: Pearson.

Liebling, Alison, David Price, and Guy Shefer. 2010. *The prison officer*. London: Willan.

Lin, Ann Chih. 2000. *Reform in the making: The implementation of social policy in prison*. Princeton, NJ: Princeton University Press.

Lipsky, Michael. 2010. *Street-level bureaucracy: Dilemmas of the individual in public service*. New York, NY: Russell Sage Foundation.

Manza, Jeff, and Christopher Uggen. 2008. *Locked out: Felon disenfranchisement and American democracy*. New York, NY: Oxford University Press.

Mauer, Marc, and Meda Chesney-Lind, eds. 2002. *Invisible punishment: The collateral consequences of mass imprisonment*. New York, NY: The New Press.

Miller, Lisa L. 2008. *The perils of federalism: Race, poverty, and the politics of crime control*. New York, NY: Oxford University Press.

Mosher, Frederick C. 1968. *Democracy and the public service*. New York, NY: Oxford University Press.

Page, Joshua. 2011. *The toughest beat: Politics, punishment, and the prison officers union in California*. New York, NY: Oxford University Press.

Scott, Bobby. 2014. *Democratic views on criminal justice reforms raised before the Over-Criminalization Task Force & the Subcommittee on Crime, Terrorism, Homeland Security, and Investigations*. Charleston, SC: CreateSpace Independent Publishing. Available from https://bobbyscott.house.gov/sites/bobbyscott.house.gov/files/OTF FULL REPORT FINAL.pdf.

The Sentencing Project. 24 May 2017. *U.S. prison population trends 1999–2015: Modest reductions with significant variation*. Available from www.sentencingproject.org/publications/u-s-prison-population-trends-1999-2015-modest-reductions-significant-variation/.

Specter, Donald. 2006. Making prisons safe: Strategies for reducing violence. *Washington U Journal of Law & Policy* 22:125–34.

Spinaris, Caterina G., Michael D. Denhof, and Juie A. Kellaway 2012. Posttraumatic stress disorder in United States corrections professionals: Prevalence and impact on health and functioning. *Desert Waters Correctional Outreach*, 1–32.

Stadnyk, B. L. 2003. *PTSD in corrections employees in Saskatchewan*. Saskatchewan: Registered Psychiatric Nurses Association. Available from http://www.rpnas.com/wp-content/uploads/PTSDInCorrections.pdf.

Sun, Ivan Y., and Brian K. Payne. 2004. Racial differences in resolving conflicts: A comparison between black and white police officers. *Crime & Delinquency* 50 (4): 516–41.

Sykes, Gresham M. 1958/2007. *The society of captives: A study of a maximum security prison*. Princeton, NJ: Princeton University Press.

Unnever, James D. 2014. Race, crime and public opinion. In *The Oxford handbook of ethnicity, crime, and immigration*. New York, NY: Oxford University Press.

U.S. Department of Justice and U.S. Equal Employment Opportunity Commission. 2015. *Diversity in law enforcement: A literature review*. Washington, DC: U.S. Department of Justice. Available from https://cops.usdoj.gov/pdf/taskforce/Diversity_in_Law_Enforcement_Literature_Review.pdf.

Vuolo, Mike, and Candace Kruttschnitt. 2008. Prisoners' adjustment, correctional officers, and context: The foreground and background of punishment in late modernity. *Law & Society Review* 42 (2): 307–36.

Weaver, Vesla M., and Amy E. Lerman. 2010. Political consequences of the carceral state. *American Political Science Review* 104 (4): 817–33.

Appendix

Our primary outcome of interest is the extent to which officers express support for rehabilitation in criminal justice. To measure policy-related attitudes, we asked four questions in both the 2006 and 2017 CCOS. These variables include the following:

- *Rehabilitation as central goal:* Participants were asked how strongly they agreed or disagreed with the statement, "Rehabilitation should be a central goal of incarceration." The 2006 CCOS did not include a neutral response (6-point Likert), while the 2017 CCOS did (7-point Likert).
- *Keeping the public safe:* Participants were asked how strongly they agreed or disagreed with the statement, "The job of a prison is to keep the public safe, not to help inmates." The 2006 CCOS did not include a neutral response (6-point Likert), while the 2017 CCOS did (7-point Likert).

- *Purpose of prison:* Participants were asked, "Do you feel that the purpose of a prison is rehabilitation, punishment, or both?" Response options included (1) Totally rehabilitation; (2) More rehabilitation, but still punishment; (3) Equally rehabilitation and punishment; (4) More punishment, but still rehabilitation; and (5) Totally punishment.
- *Reason for imprisonment:* Participants were asked, "Do you think that most people who end up in prison are there because of personal failure, or because they did not have advantages like strong families, good education, and job opportunities?" Response options included (1) Totally lack of advantages; (2) Mostly lack of advantages, but still personal failure; (3) Equally lack of advantages and personal failure; (4) More personal failure, but still lack of advantages; and (5) Totally personal failure.

For most analyses, we created an index from these four survey questions. The indices sum the above four Likert-scale questions, reverse-coded when necessary, and scaled from zero to one. These zero-to-one scaled additive indices can be interpreted in terms of percent difference.

Our control variables used for modeling include those listed below, categorized into three groups: (1) demographics; (2) violence; and (3) institutional factors. The text used for the survey items and possible responses for each item are included below, along with details on recategorization, where relevant.

Demographics

- Gender: Participants were asked, "What is your gender?" with possible responses of female or male.
- Race/Ethnicity: Participants were asked, "Which category best describes your race or ethnicity? Please mark all that apply." Possible responses included Asian or Asian-American, Black or African American, Hispanic/Latino, White/Caucasian, Native Hawaiian or Pacific Islander, or Other.
- Partisanship: Participants were asked, "Do you consider yourself a..." to address partisanship, with possible responses of Republican, Independent, Democrat, Other Party, or No Party.
- Education: Participants were asked, "What is the highest level of education you have attained so far?" and possible responses included GED or High School degree; Some college (no degree); Associate's degree; Bachelor's degree; Master's degree; Ph.D. or professional degree (J.D., M.D.).
- Age: Participants were asked, "In what year were you born?" with an open-text, write-in response.

Violence

- Security level: Participants were asked, "With what security-level inmates have you worked most often during the past 6 months?" with possible responses of Levels I, II, III, and IV.
- Questions on exposure to violence (inside prison, outside prison, before starting at the California Department of Corrections and Rehabilitation

(CDCR) were used to create the various violence and trauma indices. Questions 8, 9, 11, and 12 asked if officers had experienced a particular type of violent incident, and possible responses to these questions are yes or no. Questions 8-A, 9-A, 11-A, and 12-A are all follow-up questions that were only presented to participants if they said they *had* experienced the particular type of violent incident posed in questions 8, 9, 11, and 12, respectively. The follow-up questions address the time and place of each incident, with possible responses including: Before I started working for CDCR; After I started working for CDCR, while working inside the prison; and After I started working for CDCR, but outside the prison while I was not working. Question text for 8, 9, 11, and 12 and the follow-up questions include the following:

- 8: "At any time in your life, have you ever been in a situation in which you were seriously injured?"
  - 8-A: "When you were in a situation in which you were seriously injured? Please mark all that apply."
- 9: "At any time in your life, have you ever been in a situation in which you feared you might be killed or seriously injured?"
  - 9-A: "When you were in a situation in which you feared you might be killed or seriously injured? Please mark all the apply."
- 11: "At any time in your life, have you ever seen dead bodies (other than at a funeral) or had to handle dead bodies for any reason?"
  - 11-A: "When did you see dead bodies (other than at a funeral) or have you had to handle dead bodies for any reason? Please mark all that apply."
- 12: "At any time in your life, have you ever seen someone seriously injured or killed?"
  - 12-A: "When did you see someone seriously injured or killed? Please mark all that apply."

- Inmate perceived dangerousness: Quartiles of the percent of inmates perceived as very dangerous, dangerous, and not dangerous were created from the following survey question: "In your opinion, what percentage of the inmates at the prison where you work do you think are. . ." Responses were open-text, write-in (with additional clarification that all items should sum to 100 percent).
- Equipment index: The equipment index was constructed from the following questions, each including responses from a 7-point Likert scale ranging from *very dissatisfied* to *very satisfied*: "How satisfied or dissatisfied are you with the availability of safety equipment at work?" and "How satisfied or dissatisfied are you with the quality of safety equipment at work?"
- Response to violence: The index for organizational response to violence was constructed from the following questions: "When a staff member has been assaulted at the prison where you work, how often has any action been taken by the institution to discipline the inmate or inmates involved?" and "When action was taken in response to an instance of inmate-on-staff violence, how often do you feel that the action taken was adequate?" Possible responses

for both questions included: never, rarely, now and then, often, very often, always, and don't know.

Institutional Factors

- Supervision index: The survey asked respondents the extent to which they agreed or disagreed with the statements: "My direct supervisor is competent in doing his or her job"; "My direct supervisor shows very little interest in the feelings of subordinates"; "There is a level of commitment to professionalism at all levels of this organization"; and "Our top management does not try to make this organization a good place to work." Agreement was measured with a 7-point Likert scale from *strongly disagree* to *strongly agree*, with a neutral option of neither agree nor disagree.
- Resources index: The index was constructed from questions concerning the availability and use of resources for work-related problem-solving, including the following:
  - "To what extent do you agree or disagree with the following statement: When I have a problem at work, there is someone I can talk to who will really help me solve it." Agreement was measured with a 7-point Likert scale from *strongly disagree* to *strongly agree*, with a neutral option of neither agree nor disagree
  - "When you have a problem at work, who do you feel you can talk to who will really help you solve it? Please mark all that apply." The variable includes the sum of all endorsed responses (i.e., different individuals that would help the participant solve their problems at work).
  - "If you were to have a work-related problem in the future, would you consider contacting someone at CCPOA to resolve it?" Possible responses include yes, no, and not sure.
  - "If you were to have concerns specifically about your personal health and well-being, who might you consider talking to in order to get help? Please mark all that apply." The variable includes the sum of all endorsed responses (i.e., different individuals that the participant would consider talking to get help with personal health and well-being).
  - 45: "Have you ever used any of the following resources to address work-related stress, anxiety, depression, or other issues related to health and well-being? Please mark all that apply." The variable includes the sum of all endorsed responses (i.e., different types of resources the participant reports having used to address work-related stress, anxiety, depression, or other issues).
  - "What concerns do you have, if any, about using resources like the Employee Assistance Program (EAP) or Peer Support Volunteer program? Please mark all that apply." The variable includes the sum of all endorsed responses (i.e., different types of concerns about utilizing resources).

- ○ Quality of Stress Management Training: The question used for the presence and quality of stress management training was taken from the following matrix response question: "Please evaluate the quality of training you have received on each of the following topics. Has this training been excellent, good, fair, or poor, or have you not received any training on that topic?" Specifically, the subitem utilized was 23-J: "Stress management for law enforcement officers." Possible responses included: excellent, good, fair, poor, and have not received this training.

- Inmates in high-quality rehabilitation programs: The variable includes the quartile of the response to the question, "What percentage of inmates at the prison where you work would you say are actively involved in at least one high-quality rehabilitation program?"

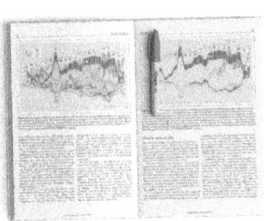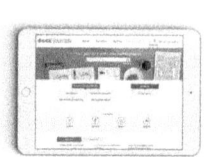

⑤SAGE research**methods**

The essential online tool for researchers from the world's leading methods publisher

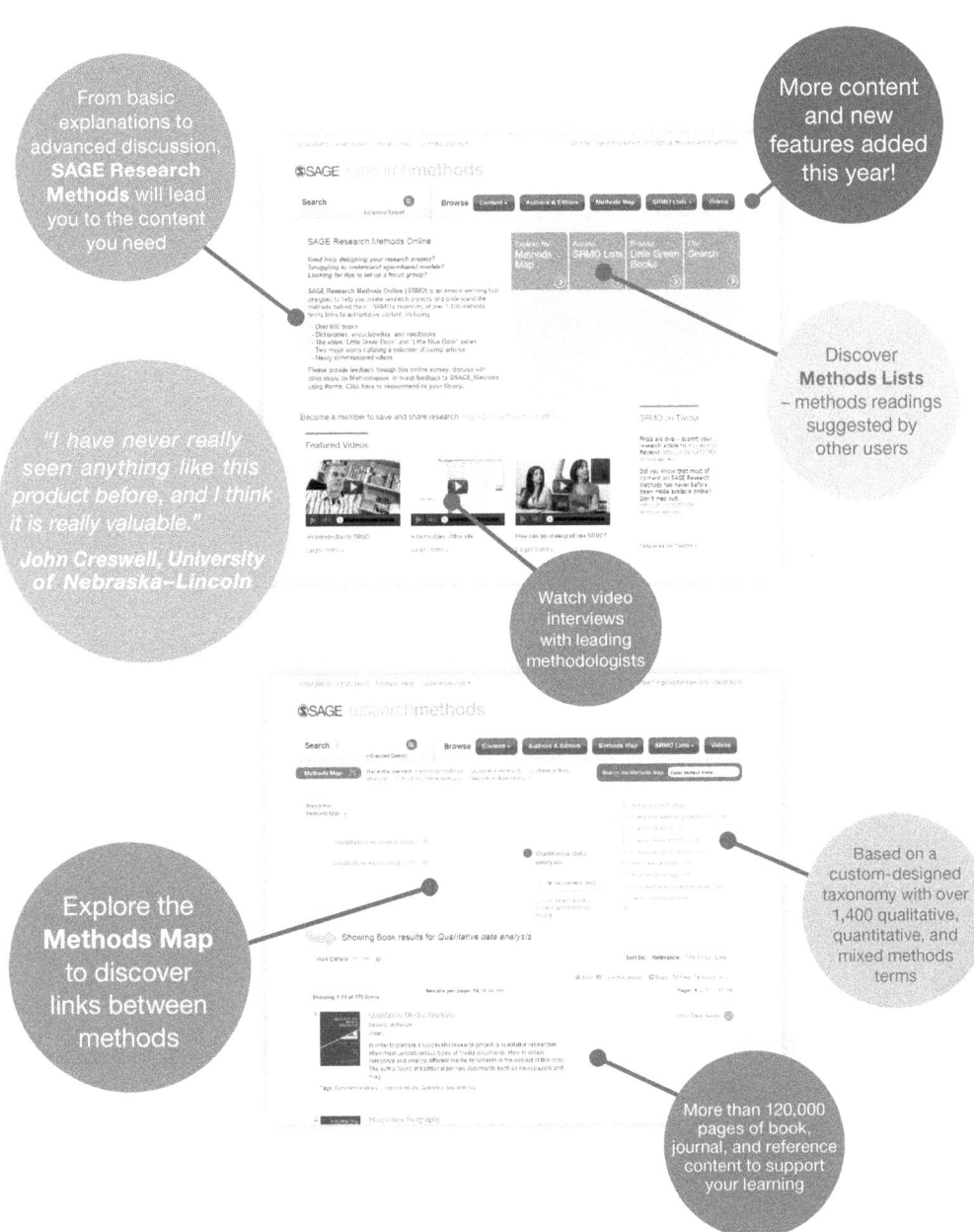

From basic explanations to advanced discussion, **SAGE Research Methods** will lead you to the content you need

More content and new features added this year!

Discover **Methods Lists** – methods readings suggested by other users

"I have never really seen anything like this product before, and I think it is really valuable."

John Creswell, University of Nebraska–Lincoln

Watch video interviews with leading methodologists

Explore the **Methods Map** to discover links between methods

Based on a custom-designed taxonomy with over 1,400 qualitative, quantitative, and mixed methods terms

More than 120,000 pages of book, journal, and reference content to support your learning

find out more at
www.sageresearchmethods.com

How do you get more people to read and cite your research?

EXPLAIN
it in plain language

SHARE
it via web, email
and social media

GET STARTED
www.growkudos.com

✓ Free service
✓ Quick and simple to use
✓ Proven to increase readership
✓ Keeps track of outreach wherever you do it
✓ Across all publications with a CrossRef DOI

KUDOS
Greater Research Impact

SAGE
Publishing

⑨SAGE research**methods**

The essential online tool for researchers from the world's leading methods publisher

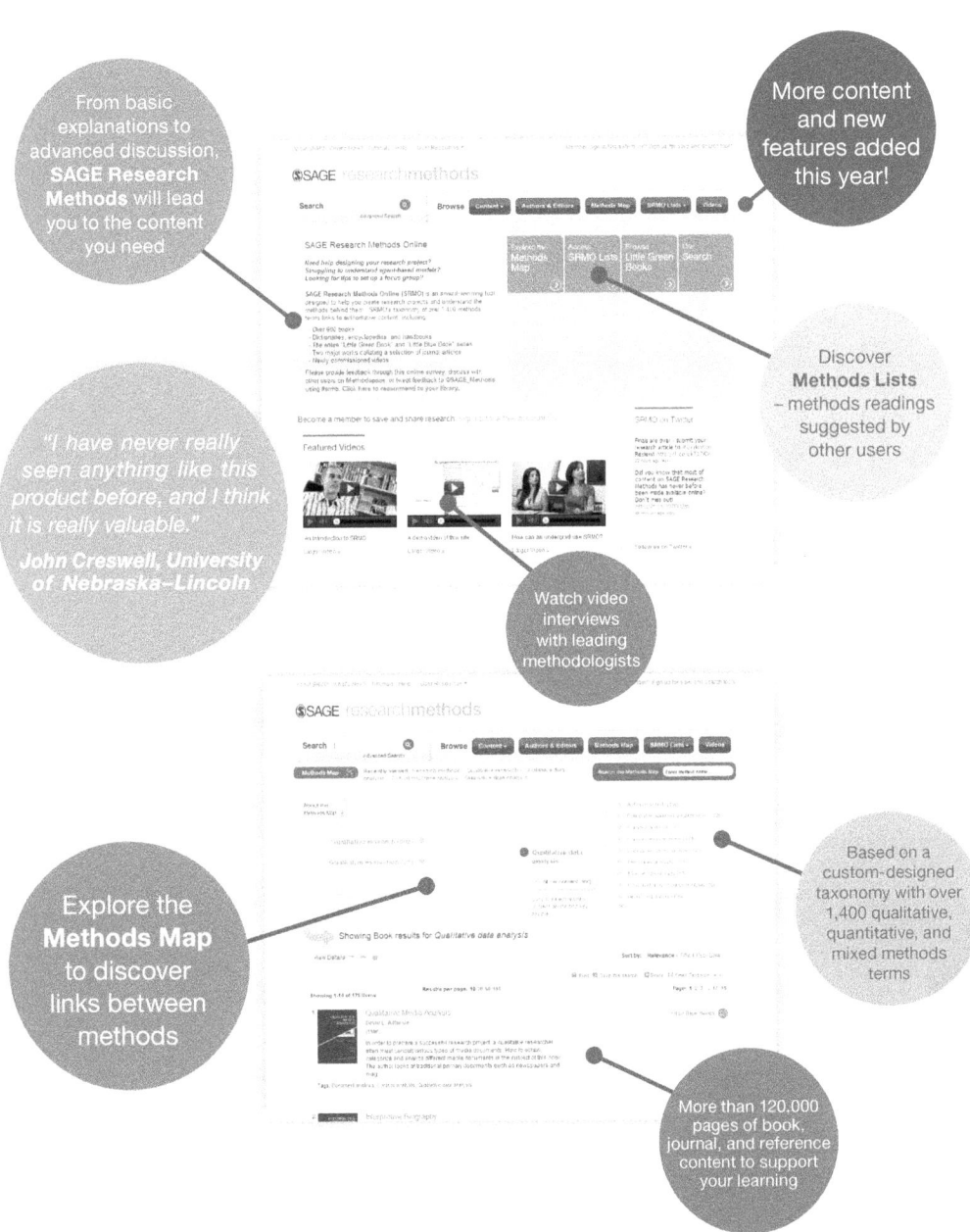

From basic explanations to advanced discussion, **SAGE Research Methods** will lead you to the content you need

More content and new features added this year!

Discover **Methods Lists** – methods readings suggested by other users

"I have never really seen anything like this product before, and I think it is really valuable."

John Creswell, University of Nebraska–Lincoln

Watch video interviews with leading methodologists

Explore the **Methods Map** to discover links between methods

Based on a custom-designed taxonomy with over 1,400 qualitative, quantitative, and mixed methods terms

More than 120,000 pages of book, journal, and reference content to support your learning

find out more at
www.sageresearchmethods.com

How do you get more people to read and cite your research?

EXPLAIN
it in plain language

SHARE
it via web, email and social media

GET STARTED
www.growkudos.com

✓ Free **service**

✓ Quick **and simple to use**

✓ Proven **to increase readership**

✓ Keeps track **of outreach wherever you do it**

✓ Across all publications **with a CrossRef DOI**

KUDOS
Greater Research Impact

www.ingramcontent.com/pod-product-compliance
Ingram Content Group UK Ltd.
Pitfield, Milton Keynes, MK11 3LW, UK
UKHW022220170526
471099UK00001B/111